A Biblical Approach to Mission in Context

Sr. Prof. Teresa Okure, SHCJ

A Biblical Approach to Mission in Context

A Festschrift in Honor of Sr. Prof. Teresa Okure, SHCJ

EDITED BY MICHAEL UFOK UDOEKPO

Forewords by John Onaiyekan and Camillus R. Umoh

WIPF & STOCK · Eugene, Oregon

A BIBLICAL APPROACH TO MISSION IN CONTEXT
A Festschrift in Honor of Sr. Prof. Teresa Okure, SHCJ

Copyright © 2022 Michael Ufok Udoekpo. All rights reserved. Except for brief quotations in critical publications or reviews, no part of this book may be reproduced in any manner without prior written permission from the publisher. Write: Permissions, Wipf and Stock Publishers, 199 W. 8th Ave., Suite 3, Eugene, OR 97401.

Wipf & Stock
An Imprint of Wipf and Stock Publishers
199 W. 8th Ave., Suite 3
Eugene, OR 97401

www.wipfandstock.com

PAPERBACK ISBN: 978-1-6667-4703-4
HARDCOVER ISBN: 978-1-6667-4704-1
EBOOK ISBN: 978-1-6667-4705-8

11/17/22

Contents

Contributors   vii
Acknowledgments   xi
Foreword I by John Onaiyekan   xiii
Foreword II by Camillus R. Umoh   xv
Introduction: Biblical Approach to Mission In Context   xvii

Chapter 1 | The Mission of Israel as a Nation of Priests (Exod 19:5–6; Isa 61:6)   1
    James C. Okoye, CSSP

Chapter 2 | Miriam at Kadesh and Cana? Making Numbers 20:1–13 and John 2:1–11 Dialogue on the Servants' Mission   13
    Paul Béré, SJ

Chapter 3 | Another Look at Mission through the Witness of the Israelite Servant Girl (2 Kgs 5:1–19)   26
    Emmanuel O. Nwaoru

Chapter 4 | The Missionary Spirit of Psalm 67   36
    Mary Jerome Obiorah, IHM

Chapter 5 | Amos' Polemical Mission against Religious Hypocrisy (Amos 5:21–27) in African Context   50
    Pilani Michael Paul

Chapter 6 | The Prophetic Mission of Obadiah in the Context of African Christianity   69
    Michael Ufok Udoekpo

Chapter 7 | An Unsung Faith Heroine and an Unrecognized Evangelizer: Another Look at the Encounter between Jesus and the Samaritan Woman in John 4:1–42   86
    Bernard O. Ukwuegbu

Chapter 8 | The Request of the Mother of James and John in Matthew 20:20–28: Its Missionary and Masculinity Implications   106
    Gesila N. Uzukwu, DMMM

Chapter 9 | The Samaritan Woman's Witness to Jesus in John 4:39 as an
Evangelizing Model 117
ANTHONY IFFEN UMOREN, MSP

Chapter 10 | Christology, Pneumatology, and Missiology in Luke 4:16–21 131
ROWLAND ONYENALI, CMF

Chapter 11 | The Commisioning of the Apostles in John 20:19–23 and
Its Relevance to Christians in Africa 144
PAUL DANBAKI JATAU

Chapter 12 | Identity and Mission in John 6 158
MARY SYLVIA NWACHUKWU, DDL

Chapter 13 | Women and Religious Tolerance in Children in Nigeria in Light
of John 13:33–35 167
OYERONKE OLADEMO

Chapter 14 | Receiving and Sharing Johannine Jesus' Abundant Life in the
African Context (John 10:10) 176
AGNES SOLOMON, SHCJ

Chapter 15 | Exploring the Scope of Jesus' Mission in Matthew 10:5–8 in the
Context of the Nigerian Church 185
PETER C. ONWUKA

Chapter 16 | Human Import as Instrument of Divine Mission in the Prophecy of
Ezekiel 36:22–23 200
GERALD EMEM UMOREN

Chapter 17 | Sr. Teresa Okure, SHCJ: A Narrative of Personal Encounter
Rooted in John 10:10 214
BERNADETTE EYEWAN OKURE, SHCJ

Chapter 18 | Living the New Life in Christ (Col 3:1–4) and Its Implications
for Nigerian Christians 220
VIRGINIA SHUAIBU, OFL

Chapter 19 | Mission on the Margins: Reading Matthew 10:5–7 in
Contemporary Nigeria 233
CAROLINE N. MBONU, HHCJ

Chapter 20 | The Mission of Jesus as Purposed by God in 1 Peter 1:18–20 and
Its Resonance among African Christians 245
CHRISTOPHER NASERI

Chapter 21 | Knowing the True God in the Liberation Account of Exodus 1–14
and Its Missionary Significance 256
LUKE EMEHIELE IJEZIE

Chapter 22 | The Bible, Migration, and Mission — 270
    GRANT LeMARQUAND

Epilogue I | A Well-Deserved Honor — 283
    BISHOP MARTIN D. A. OLORUNMOLU

Epilogue II | Sister Teresa Okure, SHCJ: A Great and Unassuming Leader from Behind at the Service of the Church — 285
    ANIEDI OKURE, OP

Contributors

Paul Béré, SJ, is a professor of Old Testament exegesis and biblical hermeneutics at the Pontifical Biblical Institute (Rome). He has been a member of the Pontifical Biblical Commission since 2020.

Luke E. Ijezie is a professor of Old Testament theology at the Catholic Institute of West Africa (CIWA), Port Harcourt, and currently the Dean of Theology of the same institution.

Paul Danbaki Jatau is a priest of the Catholic Diocese of Kafanchan as well as a New Testament lecturer at the Catholic Institute of West Africa, Port Harcourt, Nigeria.

Grant LeMagraund is professor of New Testament, Trinity School for Ministry, and retired Anglican Bishop of the Horn of Africa as well as an active member of PACE/APECA.

Sister Caroline Mbonu, HHCJ, a Handmaid of the Holy Child Jesus, is a professor of New Testament at the University of Port Harcourt. Her research interest includes a contextual reading of the sacred text and gender hermeneutics; she is co-editor of *Under the Palaver Tree: Doing African Ecclesiology in the Spirit of Vatican II The Contribution of Elochukwu E. Uzukwu*, forthcoming.

Christopher Naseri, as Priest of Calabar Archdioces, teaches at the Department of Religious and Cultural Studies, University of Calabar.

Mary Sylvia Nwachukwu, DDL, is a member of the Daughters of Divine Love. She is professor of biblical theology and deputy vice chancellor of Godfrey Okoye University, Enugu.

Emmanuel O. Nwaoru is a priest of the Catholic Diocese of Ahiara. He is a professor of the Old Testament and lectures in Old Testament exegesis and theology and biblical languages at the Catholic Institute of West Africa, Port Harcourt, Nigeria.

CONTRIBUTORS

Mary Jerome Obiorah, IHM, is a member of the Religious Institute of the Sisters of the Immaculate Heart of Mary, Mother of Christ. She specializes in sacred Scripture and is a lecturer at Blessed Iwene Tansi Major Seminary, Onitsha, and University of Nigeria, Nsukka.

James Chukwuma Okoye, CSSP, is director of the Center for Spiritan Studies, Duquesne University, Pittsburgh. He held the Carroll Stuhlmueller Chair of Old Testament Studies. His most recent publications are *Genesis 1—11: A Narrative Theological Commentary* (2018) and *Genesis 12—50: A Narrative Theological Commentary* (2020).

Aniedi Okure, OP, is a General Promoter of Justice and Peace Permanent Delegate to the United Nations, Order of Preachers.

Bernadette Eyewan Okure, SHCJ, is a member of the Society of the Holy Child Jesus and fulltime faculty, Cornelian Centre, Lagos. Within and outside her congregation nationally, continentally, and internationally, she serves as Process Consultant, Spiritual/Retreat Director, and in addition serves as the current National Coordinator, Africa Faith and Justice Network—Nigeria (AFJN-N) and visiting Faculty/Immediate Past Executive Director, Centre For Renewal—CFR Jos.

Oyeronke Olademo is a professor of comparative religious studies in Nigeria. She has published nationally and internationally in the fields of religious studies, African cultures and religion, and women studies.

Bishop Martin D. A. Olorunmolu is the Catholic Bishop of Lokoja, in Nigeria.

Peter Chidolue Onwuka is head of the Biblical Theology Department, Catholic Institute of West Africa, Port Harcourt.

Rowland Onyenali, CMF, is a Claretian missionary and a lecturer of biblical theology at the Spiritan International School of Theology, Attakwu. He is currently the priest in charge of spirituality and community life, as well as the head of the biblical apostolate and communications department of the Claretian missionaries, East Nigeria, province.

Pilani Michael Paul is a Catholic priest from the Catholic Diocese of Bauchi, Nigeria. He is an Old Testament scholar and currently lectures at Veritas University, Abuja.

Virginia Shuaibu, OLF, is a Perpetual Professed Member Congregation of Our Lady of Fatima, Jos, Nigeria. She is currently the principal of St. Theresa Girls' College, Jos, and Vicar General of her congregation. Sr. Shuaibu has a passion for teaching and moderating workshops, seminars, and retreats and spiritual direction.

Agnes Solomon, SHCJ, is a member of the Society of the Holy Child Jesus. She lectures at the University of Calabar in the Department of Religious and Cultural Studies, Faculty of Arts. She holds a PhD from the Catholic Institute of West Africa in Port Harcourt, Nigeria.

Michael Ufok Udoekpo is a priest of the Catholic Diocese of Ikot Ekpene and a professor of biblical theology and Old Testament exegesis at Veritas University Abuja (the Catholic University of Nigeria), where he currently serves as the dean of the Faculty of Humanities. Udoekpo, a member of many professional associations, is widely published in books and journals and has lectured both within and outside of Nigeria.

Bernard Onyebuchi Ukwuegbu is a priest of the Catholic Diocese of Orlu, Nigeria, and a chief lecturer and the director of academic planning at Imo State Polytechnic Omuma. He is the author of the *Emergence of Christian Identity in Paul's Letter to the Galatians* (2003) and *Words of Encouragement, Years A, B and C* (2013, 2017, and 2020), and a regular contributor to national and international peer-reviewed journals and collections on the Bible and biblical interpretation.

Anthony Iffen Umoren, MSP, is a Catholic priest of the Missionary Society of St. Paul of Nigeria, and currently professor of New Testament at the Catholic Institute of West Africa (CIWA), Port Harcourt, Nigeria. He is the author of many works including *Paul and Power Christology: Exegesis and Theology of Romans 1:3–4 in Relation to Popular Power Christology in an African Context* (2008), and *Mary in the Bible: Biblical Answers to Some Questions* (2020).

Gerald Emem Umoren, a priest of the Catholic Diocese of Ikot Ekpene, is a Senior Lecturer of Biblical Studies in the Department of Religious and Cultural Studies, University of Uyo, Nigeria. He lectures also in St. Joseph Major Seminary, Ikot Ekpene, and in Seat of Wisdom Major Seminary, Ariam, Umuahia, Nigeria. In the academia, Umoren is very well published nationally and internationally.

Gesila Nneka Uzukwu, DMMM, is a New Testament scholar, presently a lecturer in the Department of Philosophy and Religious Studies, Faculty of Arts, Nasarawa State University, Keffi, Nigeria. Uzukwu studied at Katholieke Universiteit Leuven, Belgium, where she obtained her BA Theology, MA and Licentiate in Theology and Religious Studies, and PhD in New Testament Studies. She has written several articles in both national and international journals. She is the author of *The Unity of Male and Female in Jesus Christ: An Exegetical Study of Galatians 3:28c in Light of Paul's Theology of Promise*.

Acknowledgments

The idea for this erudite collection of essays in honor of Sr. Professor Teresa Okure, SHCJ, was proposed, discussed, and unanimously adapted by members at the November 2021 virtual Conference of the Catholic Biblical Association of Nigeria (CABAN), where Okure has served as a pioneer president. Fr. Prof. Michael Ufok Udoekpo was asked by the association to lead this praiseworthy project. Udoekpo co-opted two other scholarly co-editors: Sr. Dr. Mary Jerome Obiorah, IHM, and Fr. Prof. Luke E. Ijezie. The three editors brainstormed and arrived at the central theme to this Festschrift.

We are profoundly indebted to those who responded overwhelmingly and contributed meticulously and in a timely manner to this monumental volume. Their eager willingness to participate in this project and to engage in editing, proofreading, and advancing the theological discussion is matched only by the extraordinary patience exhibited from the time the actual invitation were sent out to contributors, peer reviewed, and to the time the articles were submitted to the actual publication by WIPF Publications, to whom we are equally thankful.

We are also grateful to the supporting and encouraging roles Teresa's family and siblings, particularly Aniedi and Bernadette, have contributed toward this volume. They truly love their sibling (Teresa).

May we also acknowledge with great gratitude His Eminence John Cardinal Onaiyekan, Bishop Camillus Raymond Umoh, and Bishop Martin D.A. Olorunmolu, who not only wrote the forewords and epilogues but supported financially the long and difficult process that finally gave birth to this publication. We are convinced that the breadth and diversity of positive interest and contributions found in this *vade mecum* reflects the selfless missionary spirit, intellectual vitality, and passion that Teresa Okure, SHCJ, herself brought to the discipline of biblical studies. To God be all glory!

Foreword I

First, I commend all those behind this laudable project of a Festschrift in honor of our dear and highly respected biblical scholar, Rev. Sr. Prof. Teresa Okure, SHCJ.

The theme of the publication is "Biblical Approach to Mission." All the contributions relate somehow to the theme of the publication. This is a theme that has been for a long time close and dear to the heart of Sr. Teresa, who has acquired in Nigerian biblical circles the noble title of "Auntie Tessy."

This interest in a biblical approach to mission already preceded her seminal doctorate thesis, published in 1988 as volume 2 of the prestigious *Wissenschaftliche Untersuchungen zum Neuen Testament* (*WUNT*). Since then, she has been returning to the same theme in many forms—in scientific publications, articles in learned journals, and academic conferences and lectures, right down to popular articles and talks to members of Christ's faithful at the lowest level of diocesan and parish gatherings.

Auntie Tessy first entered the arena of biblical missiology in the 1970s and 1980s, at the apex of theological ferment and interest on missiological matters soon after the Second Vatican Council and its decree *Ad Gentes*.

Then, toward the new millennium until now, it would appear that there has been a lull in concern for the missions, not only in terms of theological reflection but also more significantly in terms of practical commitment to missionary engagement. We only need to look at the drastic decline in missionary institutions and fall in number of personnel in those regions of post-Vatican II vibrant missionary endeavors.

The call of Pope John Paul II for a "New Era of Evangelization" since the 1980s to Pope Benedict XVI's creation of a dicastery for the "New Evangelization," different from and maybe parallel to *Propaganda Fide*, can all be seen as efforts to fan into flame the fire of missions that seemed to be quenching.

This special publication, in the form of a Festschrift in honor of our Auntie Tessy, will hopefully be a significant contribution toward rekindling the missiological flame in our ecclesial environment. We must congratulate and thank Auntie Tessy for offering us the valuable opportunity and forum to achieve this.

In line with the efforts of the church to rekindle the flame of evangelization, both old and new, we are witnessing in these days a drastic reorganization of the Roman Curia as promulgated on March 19, 2022, by Pope Francis in his apostolic constitution *Praedicate Evangelium,* to take effect on June 2, 2022. In this new arrangement, it is significant that Pope Francis has effectively placed evangelization as top priority of the concerns of the church. He has created a new Dicastery of Evangelization that is not only first in the list of the offices of the curia after the Secretariat of State, but has the pope himself as head of the dicastery. The former two prefects of Propaganda Fide and the dicastery for the New Evangelization have become "Pro-Prefects" under the pope, heading their previous offices that have now been merged into the one new Dicastery of Evangelization. The move certainly seems logical. But we shall be watching to see what the Holy Spirit will do with this new reorganization.

There is no doubt that the divine mandate and command to "go preach the gospel to all nations" still has a long way to go beyond administrative restructuring. It may well continue "until the end of time," as Jesus himself seemed to have already hinted Matthew 28:20.

Congratulations and *ad multos annos* to our dear Rev. Sister Professor Teresa Okure, SHCJ.

+John Cardinal Onaiyekan (CON)
Archbishop Emeritus of Abuja.

Foreword II

Let me begin by commending the editors of this laudable project *Biblical Approach to Mission in Context: A Festschrift in Honor of Sr. Prof. Teresa Okure, SHCJ*, my one time teacher. May I also thank the editor, Fr. Prof. Michael Ufok Udoekpo, for inviting me to write this foreword.

In the Gospel of John 10:10, Jesus announces his mission that "he came that they may have life" (*egō ēlthon hina zōēn echōsin*). This Scripture passage, which I later embraced as my episcopal motto, has a profound impact on Okure and many of her students. The passage expresses the mission of the universal church—namely, proclaiming eternal life, which originates from God the Father and through Jesus Christ as empowered by the Holy Spirit.

This evangelizing mission is ever continued and renewed in the teachings of the Second Vatican Council as truly highlighted in the Decree on the Church's Missionary Activity (*Ad Gentes*). The councils defines evangelization as the implanting of the church among peoples in which she has not yet taken root. It urges even the young churches all over the world, including Africa, to engage in evangelization as soon as possible and stresses the importance of adequate training of missionaries.

This invitation by the Second Vatican Council must have given birth to two possible outcomes. First, the training of the young Teresa Okure, the first African sister of the Society of the Holy Child Jesus in Sacred Scripture, the soul of theology (DV 24, VD 31). Second is her well-argued and highly acclaimed Fordham University Doctoral Thesis: *Johannine Approach to Mission: A Contextual Studies of John 4:1–42*, later published in 1988 as volume 2 of *Wissenschftliche Untersuchungen zum Neuen Testament* (*WUNT*).

Over the years and since the completion of her post-graduate studies, this missionary-biblical spirit, in context, has continued to shape her engagements in many ways: in teaching, editing, counseling, directing retreats, publishing, moderating conferences and papers, mentoring students, and leading professional associations, both within and outside Africa.

As evident in this praiseworthy volume of rich and diverse contributions, Sr. Prof. Teresa Okure, SHCJ, an New Testament exegete and contextual hermeneuticist, will always remain one of the greatest mission-oriented biblical scholars of our time. We are very grateful for the services this dedicated and faithful religious woman and missionary has rendered to the church and society.

+Most Rev. Camillus Raymond Umoh
Bishop of Ikot Ekpene Diocese

Introduction
Biblical Approach to Mission In Context

Mission from the perspective of the Bible is the subject matter of this Festschrift in honor of Sister Professor Teresa Okure, SHCJ. Its Latin derivation, *missio*, means "sending." This may have led some to relate mission to the Hebrew Bible root *šalāḥ* ("to send"), or narrowly to the notion of a mandate or commission for preaching to outsiders for the purpose of conversion, say to the God of Israel.[1] Sending terminology or motifs, heard especially in the Fourth Gospel, includes "*apostellō*," "*pempō*," and "*erchomai*."[2] Another sense of the word "mission" roughly equates "mission" with "ministry," perhaps in an attempt to invoke a person's sense of calling, vocation, or purpose. Different biblical authors, as enfolded in this volume, may vary in their approach and mission terminology and theology. Some may also liken the concept of mission to the term "discipleship."[3] Of course, in the past, numerous studies on this same concept have been theologically done as it relates to different biblical passages.[4] In all these, Lucien Legrand believes that, "like Christian life itself, mission is *koinonia*, the communion of a plurality and variety of gifts in the Spirit."[5]

In this context, therefore, mission could broadly be seen as specific actions that bear witness to the good news of what God has done for his people the world over. Israel, Jesus Christ, and the church, as illustrated in both the Old Testament and the New Testament, all, in their different ways and contexts and settings, bear witness to the saving acts of God in history. God chose Israel to be his own people and bring the good news of his salvation to the world. God's mission through Israel is fulfilled in the mission of his servant and continues through the mission of the church.

---

1. Okoye, *Israel and the Nations*, 10.
2. See the 1986 study of Prescott-Ezickson, "The Sending Motifs in the Gospel of John."
3. See Köstenberger, *The Missions of Jesus*, 1.
4. Some of these past studies include: Arias and Alan Johnson, *The Great Commission*, 1992; Bosch, *Transforming Mission*, 1991; Zato, *Die Völkermission im Markusevangelium*, 1986; Ketelge, ed., *Mission im Neuen Testament*, 1982; Uro, *Sheep Among the Wolves*, 1987; Wilson, *The Gentiles and the Gentile Mission in Luke-Acts*, 1973.
5. Legrand, *Unity and Plurality*, 7.

The chosen Israel remains from one generation to another a conduit of divine promises and blessings to all nations, including Africans, through Abraham (Gen 12:2–3; 18:18; 22:18; 26:4; 28:13–14; cf. Acts 3:25; Gal 3:8). She is called to be a nation of priests (Exod 19:5–6; Isa 61:6) and to bear witness to other nations(Gen 41:6; Exod 7:16–17; 1 Kgs 19:9; 2 Kgs 5:3; Dan 2:44–47; 3:16–18; Isa 66:19; Matt 23:15).[6]

As promised to Abraham and his descendants, God's mission in Israel is fulfilled in the Messiah (Isa 11:10; 42:1–6; 49:6; 52:15; Ps 72:17; Rom 15:12; Gal 3:16). In the Jewish texts and imagination, shaped especially by the prophetic tradition, the Messiah was to be an eschatological anointed one of God, the sociopolitical hoped-for offspring of David who would bring God's salvation, renew the religious life of the people, and establish a new order of peace, justice, and righteousness.[7] In the New Testament passage Mark 7:28–29, familiar to Okure, the Messiah is used "as a Christological confession of Jesus' identity."[8]

Jesus Christ came to reveal God, to announce the coming of God's kingdom, and to redeem a fallen humanity through his death on the cross. This truth is articulated in many forms in many ecclesiastical documents, including John Paul II's 1990 encyclical letter *Mission of the Redeemer, Celebrating the Twenty-Fifth anniversary of the Vatican II's Decree on the Church's Missionary Activities, Ad Gentes Divinitus.* Paragraph one of *Redemptories Missio* fittingly says:

> The mission of Christ the Redeemer, which is entrusted to the Church, is still very far from completion. As the second millennium after Christ's coming draws to an end, an overall view of the human race shows that this mission is still only beginning and that we must commit ourselves wholeheartedly to its service. It is the Spirit who impels us to proclaim the great work of God, "for if I preach the Gospel, which gives me no ground of boasting. For necessity is laid upon me. Woe to me if I do not preach the Gospel" (1 Cor 9:16).[9]

Echoes of this significant missionary document, *Redemptoris Missio,* are further heard in Pope Francis's Apostolic Constitution *Praedicated Evangelium* (Mark 16:15; Matt 10:7–8) as the task that the Lord Jesus entrusted to his disciples.[10] Though he came first to the Jews, the scope of Christ's mission described in these documents includes the whole of the human race and continues through the Spirit-empowered witnesses of the church. Christian mission of every context, Africa in particular, is empowered by the Holy Spirit.

---

6. Useful biblical and scholarly divergent ideas, models, and hermeneutics of mission are well captured in Okoye, *Israel and the Nations,* 1–23.

7. For a detailed concept of the messiah in Judaism and Christianity, see Charlesworth, "From Messianology to Christology," 3–35; Lucass, *The Concept of the Messiah,* 2011; Perkins, " Mark," in *The New Interpreter's Bible Commentary,* esp., 7:470–71.

8. Perkings, "Mark," 470.

9. John Paul II, *Redemtoris Missio,* no.1.

10. Pope Francis, *Praedicate Evangelium,* March 19, 2022.

In sum, God chose Israel to be his own people and bring the good news of salvation to the world. God's mission through Israel's judges, kings, prophets, and priests is fulfilled in the mission of his Son and servant, Jesus Christ, and continues in the church today through the Holy Spirit and missionary agents of our time and culture par excellence, such as Sr. Professor Teresa Okure, SHCJ, a Johannine scholar and the current president of the Catholic Biblical Association of Nigeria (CABAN), who not long ago celebrated her eightieth birthday.

This mission volume, which is composed of carefully selected biblical and theological essays on mission by outstanding scholars, represent a token of honor to our great, passionate, and consecrated sister; a church woman, excellent teacher and communicator; a respectable colleague, a contextual theologian, global missionary icon, erudite biblical scholar, author, and exegete of no mean repute.

It is worth reiterating that the choice of the theme that hosts these essays was inspired by her well-argued Fordham University Doctoral Thesis *Johannine Approach to Mission: A Contextual Studies of John 4:1–42*, later published in 1988 as volume 2 of *Wissenschftliche Untersuchungen zum Neuen Testament (WUNT)*.

Commenting on Okure's monograph a few decades ago, in 1988, Andreas J. Köstenbeger thought the work, in spite of its minor weaknesses, represented at that time the most important treatment of mission in the Fourth Gospel. Focusing on John 4:1–42, Okure rhetorically, literarily, and contextually analyzed this passage as a paradigmatic function for the Johannine concept on mission.[11]

Unique to this creative volume in honor of Professor Okure is its sensitivity to the fact that it comes after the publication of Pope Francis's *Praedicate Evangelium*, which emphasizes the missionary conversion of the church. Also, with the blooming of missiology into a full-fledged academic discipline, perhaps African biblical scholars may have yielded too much of mutual dialogue to missiologists. In other words, this project opens a renewed line of communication and dialogue between missiologists, pastoral theologians, and biblical scholars who are sensitive to the relationship between text and context, as recommended in relevant biblical and church documents. It challenges all to rethink a biblical theology of mission in the context of Africa and beyond.

The twenty-two essays in this volume, along with forewords and epilogues, represent colleagues, students, and fellow commentators from Africa, Europe, and North and South America. Some of the authors have done detailed exegetical studies. Others are concerned with theological methods and contextual approaches from a variety of standpoints. Still others seek to relate biblical exegesis, theology, and inculturation—faith—hermeneutics to current interest in social-contextual methods of interpretation that reflect African values. The breadth of interests reflects something of the bursting of intellectual vitality and passion which Sr. Professor Teresa Okure, SHCJ, brought to the discipline.

---

11. See Köstenbeger, *Mission*, 14; Okure, *Johannine Approach*, 56, where she calls John 4:1–42 "a miniature of the whole Gospel."

INTRODUCTION

The brief narrative written by Bernadette Okure, forewords by John Cardinal Onaiyekan and Bishop Camillus Raymond Umoh, as well as epilogues by Bishop Martin D.A. Olorunmolu and Fr. Aniedi Okure, OP, provide additional insight into the historical and socio-cultural contexts within which Okure's formation and contributions unfolded.

In chapter 1, "The Mission of Israel as a Nation of Priests (Exod 19:5–6; Isa 61:6)," James Chukwuma Okoye acknowledges that the mission in the Old Testament receives diverse responses from scholars, as do Exodus 19:5–6 and Isaiah 61:6. After his general exposition of Exodus 19:5–6 in context, Okoye outlines three different hermeneutical lines of exegesis and their foundations in the text. These include:(a) an argument that the text focuses on Israel's election and special relationship with YHWH; (b) that the text is a pivotal evangelistic text portraying Israel's missionary or mediatorial role on behalf of the nations; and (c), his favorite, that the text portrays Israel's role as ontological—her very life or mission is meant to reveal the knowledge and holiness of YHWH.

In chapter 2, "Miriam at Kadesh and Cana? Making Numbers 20:1–13 and John 2:1–11 Dialogue on the Servants' Mission," Paul Béré argues that although many Johannine studies have discerned Old Testament parallels to the Cana story in John 2:1–11, Numbers 20:1–13 does not appear. Yet it offers a narrative framework with characters in Kadesh, comparable to the event at Cana. An intertextual study shows that the narratives shed light on each other. No claim is made as to an intended redactional relationship. Instead, in both, the place of Miriam in the mission of the servants is highlighted: Miriam, Moses' sister in Kadesh, could not play any role because she was dead, whereas Miriam, Jesus' mother in Cana, plays an essential role through her intervention. In Béré's view, the Evangelist makes us understand not only what is at stake in the presence of Miriam, sister or mother, in the mission of the servants, but also offers readers a key to understanding the story of Numbers, as well as the importance of the mother's initiative at Cana.

Emmanuel O. Nwaoru, in chapter 3, "Another Look at Mission through the Witness of the Israelite Servant Girl (2 Kgs 5:1–19), notices that when the young Israelite girl was taken captive to Syria and served Naaman's wife (2 Kgs 5:2), it never came to mind that God was preparing her for another kind of mission in Syria. She saw her enslaved condition as an opportunity to propagate her faith and to bear witness to the healing/salvific power possessed by YHWH's representative, the prophet in Samaria. Her witnessing defiled all due process of a "normal" missionary activity and yet accomplished the ultimate goal of every missionary endeavor—namely, conversion: profession of faith and renunciation of sins. In this thought-provoking and creative essay, Nwaoru reads the text of 2 Kings 5:1–19a very closely and critically examines the character and missionary venture of this servant girl, a minor character in the narrative, to uncover why her witnessing opened doors for the process of Naaman's healing and subsequent conversion, even when there was no outright preaching of any doctrine. That God's purpose can be accomplished not only through powerful missionary agents, but also through the simple utterance of ordinary or "inconsequential" persons like the servant girl, calls for us to rethink what sets the parameter for missionary activity today.

In "The missionary Spirit of Psalm 67," chapter 4, Mary Jerome Obiorah studies with commendable expertise Psalm 67 as one of those Old Testament texts which communicates the ardent longing to share the true knowledge of God outside the confines of Israel. Obiorah insists the author of Psalm 67 articulates and elucidates this in the strict refrain inserted in strategic points in his song. Usually, refrains in Hebrew poems, among other functions, emphasize the theme intrinsic to the text. When the psalmist exclaims "Let the peoples praise you, O God; let all the peoples praise you," the yearning to make God known among other peoples becomes evident. Employing a literary method with emphasis on the poetic techniques in Psalm 67, Obiorah invites all toward an understanding the message of this ancient poem and its relevance for us today. As Christians, we share in the mission of Christ and of the church and his great desire to make the Father known, loved, and praised among all his creatures. Like the psalmist, we should desire this, sing it constantly in our hearts, and be ready to translate it into action.

In chapter 5, "Amos' Polemical Mission against Religious Hypocrisy (Amos 5:21–27): In African Context," Pilani Michael Paul observes that the religious structures and traditions that are at variance with ethical standards of living in the day-to-day life of the people constitute one of the central themes in the prophetic mission of Amos. Pilani sees the text of Amos 5:21–27 as a typical polemic against any form of unethical worship and religion beyond the northern kingdom of Israel. He critically and historically evaluates the theological material of the text and considers it a timeless critique and challenge for all forms of religious worship in Africa and beyond that is inclined to promote injustice, corruption, violence, and other inhuman conditions. Pilani's article recommends worship with missionary ethics to all forms of religions in Africa, Nigeria in particular.

In chapter 6, "The Prophetic Mission of Obadiah in the Context of African Christianity," Michael Ufok Udoekpo observes that even though Obadiah's prophecy is the shortest book in the Hebrew Bible, composed of only twenty-one verses, its missionary-oriented review of the ancient familial conflict between Esau and Jacob is relevant for all. He exegetically and contextually explores the sacredness of global family and the tragic consequences of tensions and indifferent attitudes among family members and neighbors inherent in Obadiah, one of the Twelve Minor Prophets elected and sent by God. Udoekpo theologically argues that Obadiah's voice—speaking of divine judgment (vv. 1–4), the taunting of Edom (vv. 5–8), divine indictment (vv. 12–14), the Day of the Lord (vv. 15–18), and Israel's restoration (vv. 19–21)—deserves a second reading and hearing (v. 1c) in the context of African Christianity and the church-family in Africa, where echoes of conflict and violence are still being perceived and heard today.

Bernard Ukwuegbu, in his "An Unsung Faith Heroine and an Unrecognized Evangelizer: Another Look at the Encounter between Jesus and the Samaritan Woman in John 4:1–42," chapter 7, argues that Jesus' encounter with the Samaritan woman (John 4:1–42) articulates a point of view about how one should respond to Jesus and the fruits of such a response (cf. John 2:13–3:36). With the "word" of Jesus as the criterion, the story of Jesus' presence among the Samaritans progresses from a situation of no faith (vv. 1–15) to the partial faith of the Samaritan woman (vv. 16–30) to the authentic Johannine belief of the Samaritan villagers (vv. 39–42) in the world beyond the boundaries of Judaism. As the narrative develops (4:27–30), the woman goes into the town to bring her people to Jesus, the Messiah, in a manner consistent with the pattern established in other Johannine discipleship stories (cf. 1:40–49). Ukwuegbu maintains that the conscious effort by the narrator to posit the "logos" of Jesus rather than the *laila* of the woman (cf. 4:39–41) as the basis for the coming to faith of the Samaritan community shows how much this passage has been used to undermine the role of the Samaritan woman as a heroine of faith and as an evangelizer of the word, a fate still suffered by many such heroes and heroines of faith and evangelizers from the margins of the society.

In chapter 8, "The Request of the Mother of James and John in Matthew 20:20–28: Its Missionary and Masculinity Implications," Gesila Nneka Uzukwu explores the question put forth by the mother of James and John in Matthew 20:20–28 as a missiological request that functions within Matthew's Gospel to project the purpose of the mission of Christ—namely, salvation in the afterlife. She considers insufficient past redactional-critical approaches to Matthew 20:20–28 and Mark 10:35–40 to highlight Markan priority over Matthew or of the role of the mother of the sons of Zebedee to accentuate one of the Gospel themes of Matthew. For this reason, Uzukwu addresses the place of the "request-type scene" in Matthew 20:20–28 in relation to other mother request-type scenes to highlight the missionary element in the text under debate and to show how the "mission-theme" of Matthew 20:20–28 provides a basis for understanding the apocalyptic mission discourse in Revelation 5.

In chapter 9, "The Samaritan Woman's Witness to Jesus in John 4:39 as an Evangelizing Model," Anthony Iffen Umoren, from his perspective, argues that in John 4:39, the Greek verb *martureō* ("to bear witness," "testify," or "give testimony") is used to describe the activity of the Samaritan woman who, having had an encounter with Jesus at Jacob's well, came to know, accept, and bear witness to him as the Messiah, such that other Samaritans from her city also came to believe in Jesus. This is not withstanding that this favorite Johannine verb appears thirty-four times in John's Gospel and is primarily used to refer to the witness which Jesus gives of the Father or of himself. It is also used in reference to the witness which the Scriptures, the works of Jesus, the Spirit, and John the Baptist bear to Jesus as the one sent by God. In this context of celebrating Teresa Okure, a woman who has been bearing witness to Jesus as a biblical scholar, Umoren submits that John must have consciously painted this unique picture in the text so that it would be noticed that, despite her androcentric culture, a woman—a Samaritan woman at that—indeed successfully and in an exemplary manner evangelized others by bearing witness to Jesus.

In chapter 10, "Christology, Pneumatology, and Missiology in Luke 4:16–21," Rowland Onyenali discusses the inaugural preaching of Jesus in Luke 4:16–21. Using a narrative-critical approach within the overall context of the Gospel of Luke, Onyenali's essay identifies the key issue in the passage as the central role of the Spirit of God in the fulfillment of the mission of Jesus and stresses in the paper the interest of pneumatology and Christology as it pertains to the mission of Jesus.

In chapter 11, "The Commissioning of the Apostles in John 20:19–23 and Its Relevance to Christians in Africa," Paul Danbaki Jatau historically and contextually studies John 20:19–23 from the point of view of mission and the Holy Spirit as the principal agent of evangelization. Jatau's goal is to draw out the implication of this Johannine text for Christians in Africa, who are daily engaged in the missionary work of proclaiming the good news in this challenging time of persecution, wars terrorism, banditry and kidnappings.

In chapter 12, "Identity and Mission in John 6," Mary Sylvia Nwachukwu studies John 6, which communicates Jesus' consciousness of the unity of his identity and mission. She does this in light of the current phenomenon of some ministers and religious people who experience complications which arise from polarization of interests in ministry, and which is the result of conflict between the sacred ideals of the call and the secular demands. Nwachukwu argues that John 6 not only shows why it is important for ministers to understand themselves in relation to the specific mission, but also presents the figure of Jesus as a minister who, in spite of the growing pressure raised by the crowd, who wanted to distract him from the objectives of his ministry, remained exemplarily faithful and devoted to his service.

Oyeronke Oladkemo, in chapter 13, "Women and Religious Tolerance in Children's Socialization in Nigeria in Light of John 13:33–35," insists that primary socialization—that is, the process of learning the attitudes and values appropriate to individuals as members of a particular society—is necessary for every human society. Drawing examples from John 13, Oladkemo argues that children must be guided by their mothers through the proper processes of socialization, including religious tolerance and love of ones' neighbor.

In chapter 14, "Receiving and Sharing Johannine Jesus' Abundant Life in the African Context (John 10:10)," Agnes Solomon analyzes John 10:10 in the overall context of the Fourth Gospel in order to bring out its meaning and share in the life that flows freely from the source for those who come to believe in the person of Jesus. Solomon submits that a deeper understanding of this text will help one discover what Jesus means when he talks about abundant life.

In "Exploring the Scope of Jesus' Mission in Matthew 10:5–8 in the Context of the Nigerian Church," chapter 15, Peter Onwuka examines Matthew 10:5–8 with the intention of explaining the nature and scope of the mission of Jesus as enunciated in it and its implication for the Nigeria church. He maintains that Matthew 10:5–8 indicates a very important aspect in the ministry of Jesus Christ: the commissioning of the Twelve to participate in the very ministry of Jesus Christ. It specifies where they should go and what they should do. The mission instruction or mandate has remained a very important guide not only for the Twelve but for the church as a body and Christians individually in participating in the mission of Jesus Christ. Varied understanding of this instruction has given rise to varied emphases in sharing in this very important mission.

In chapter 16, "Human Import as Instrument of Divine Mission in the Prophecy of Ezekiel 36:22–23," Gerald Emem Umoren descriptively and analytically discusses the human instrumentality in divine mission as found in the prophecy of Ezekiel 36:22–23.

In chapter 17, "Sr. Teresa Okure, SHCJ: A Narrative of Personal Encounter Rooted in John 10:10," Bernadette Eyewan Okure reflects on aspects of her personal experiences with her mentor, who mentored her during her academic and life's journeys. She articulates her elder sister's rootedness in Scripture with particular reference to John 10:10, brought to bear in that encounter and experiences.

In chapter 18, "Living the New Life in Christ (Col 3:1–4) and Its Implications for Nigerian Christians," Virginia Shuaibu analytically and contextually discusses Colossians 3:1–4 in the context of Nigerian Christianity, where the pluralism of churches has not been translated to a deeper imitation of Christ's life, as stated in the text of Colossians under investigation.

In chapter 19, "Mission on the Margins: Reading Matthew 10:5–7 in Contemporary Nigeria," Caroline Mbonu engages in a narrative critical reading of Matthew's missionary discourse, part of the sending of the Twelve, with instructions about missioning to those in the margins in all nations (Matt 10:5–7). She argues that such a reading is much needed today in Nigeria, where much of the pluralism of preaching and ministries unfortunately remains what she calls "an inversion of the gospel in favor of material wellbeing."

In "The Mission of Jesus as Purposed by God in 1 Peter 1:18–20, and Its Resonance among African Christians," chapter 20, Christopher Naseri argues that such mission consisted in liberating the Petrine Christians from the emptiness and hopelessness that surrounded the way of life of their ancestors. African readers of 1 Peter 1:18–20, he says, must appropriate the air of redemption inaugurated by Christ and feel liberated from superstitious practices and beliefs that impede their progress and enslave them.

Luke E. Ijezie's contribution in chapter 21, "Knowing the True God in the Liberation Account of the Exodus 1–14 and Its Missionary Significance," occupies a chiastic position with chapter 1 of this volume. It examines how the theme of knowing YHWH as the true God helps us to understand the structure of the narrative and the type of missionary function it performs.

In chapter 22, "The Bible, Migration, and Mission," Grant LeMarquand, in honor of Okure, recognizes that the global problem of refugees and migrants is a vast and multidimensional issue. Grant "deliciously" advances the claim that, among many other things, the Bible is a book about migrants and refugees as well as outlines the refugee experience in the place where he was formerly the Anglican bishop—in western Ethiopia near the border with South Sudan.

This is finally followed by two enlightening epilogues by Bishop Martin D. A. Olorunmolu and Teresa's sibling Fr. Aniedi Okure, OP. In all, we hope this comprehensive "biblical mission volume" will serve, among other purposes, as a timely contribution and *vade mecum* toward a biblical theology of mission, which provides the basis for the mission and contextual practice of the contemporary church in Africa and beyond.

Michael Ufok Udoekpo
Veritas University, Abuja
Chief Editor
September 12, 2022

Chapter 1

The Mission of Israel as a Nation of Priests
(Exod 19:5–6; Isa 61:6)

James C. Okoye, CSSP

INTRODUCTION

Elohim who appeared to Moses at the mountain of God, Horeb (Exod 3:1), told him, "When you have brought the people out of Egypt, you will serve God at this mountain" (3:12). In the third month after the liberation from Egypt, Moses and the Israelites encamped in front of the mountain, here called Sinai (Exod 19:2). Moses went up, and YHWH gave him his message for "the house of Jacob, the children of Israel." The name YHWH—the confessional name of Israel's God—is appropriate for a text that begins to outline the identity of Israel in relation to her God.

Exodus 19–24 is a closely interwoven unit.[1] The divine promise of a covenant at the beginning is ratified in Exodus 24. The people's willing response, "Everything the Lord has said, we will do," (19:8),[2] is repeated as a framing *inclusio* at 24:7. Since at 19:8 YHWH had not yet given stipulations, Exodus 19:3b–8 can be understood as "an anticipatory summary and interpretation of the Sinai pericope as a whole."[3] It is editorial guidance to the reader as to its inner meaning. Exodus 19:5–6 spells out this inner meaning: the goal of the liberation from Egypt.

---

1. It is a great pleasure to offer this entry on mission in the Old Testament in honor of Sr. Professor Teresa Okure, SHCJ.

2. The biblical text is cited following the New American Bible Revised Edition (NABRE), unless the contrary is indicated.

3. Wells and Allen Scult, *God's Holy People*, 35.

EXPOSITION

YHWH begins by recalling Israel's experience ("you have seen") of divine redemption. The rescue is painted in the image of an eagle soaring aloft with Israel on its wings—it was swift and sure. "And brought you to myself (*ēlāi*)" introduces a leit-motif. "To myself" can mean "to my domain," "into my possession"; the prohibition of coming near to or touching the mountain imbues it with the holiness of YHWH. It can also signify proximity to God's self, fellowship.[4] Elohim already called them "*my* people, the children of Israel" (Exod 3:10, emphasis mine). The ritual of belonging and possession will now follow. Having proven his goodwill and trustworthiness, YHWH now gives Israel an exegesis of what "you will serve God at this mountain" means. "The Hebrews who 'served' Pharaoh (in slave labour), are to come away in order to 'serve' (worship and obey) YHWH"[5] as uniquely beloved. "And now" (*we-'attâ*) recalls Fretheim's fourfold structure of covenant: God elects, God saves, human beings respond in worship and faith, and only then does God establish covenant.[6] The relationship is predicated on freedom, the people's free choice ("if"). Addressed in the second person plural, each person answers for themselves and for the whole people. "If listening, you listen to my voice and keep my covenant" (my translation). This agrees with Deuteronomy that the people heard YHWH give the Decalogue directly (contrasts with Exod 20:19, where the people say to Moses, "You speak to us and we will listen," which portrays Moses as covenant mediator).[7] Covenant (*bᵉrît*)[8] has appeared in this narrative in Genesis 9 (covenant with Noah), Genesis 15, and Genesis 17 (with Abraham). The first was divine self-obligation for the stability of creation; Genesis 15 was a self-obligation on God's part on behalf of Abraham; and Genesis 17 concerned circumcision. Covenant here assumes the ratification of the covenant in 24:3–8;[9] hence, it is best read as "the covenant I intend to make with you."[10] "You shall be *to me* a personal possession (*sᵉgullâ*) from (*mikkol*) all peoples, for *to me* is all the earth" (my translation, emphasis mine). *Sᵉgullâ* is used six times in the Old Testament of the people as a whole in relation to YHWH (three of which, *'am sᵉgullâ*, people of [God's] possession, occur in Deut 7:6; 14:2; 26:18) and twice for a prized treasure (1 Chr 29:3; Eccl 2:8), usually gold or silver.[11] It may, as such, express the depth or exclusiveness of a relationship or the inherent value of what/who it so designates. *Mikkol* suggests that the one item

---

4. Davies, *A Royal Priesthood*, 40. "Bringing to myself" focuses on relationship rather than location.
5. Okoye, *Israel and the Nations*, 59.
6. Fretheim, *The Pentateuch*, 48.
7. Childs, *The Book of Exodus*, 360.
8. Although *berît* appears in Hosea 8:1, the majority of scholars now think that the term "covenant" for describing YHWH's relation with Israel did not predate the seventh century and the book of Deuteronomy.
9. Childs, *Exodus*, 360.
10. Cassuto, *A Commentary on the Book of Exodus*, 227, following Rashi.
11. Lipiński, *Segullâ*, TDOT, X, 144–48, here 144.

setting Israel apart from all nations is that she is YHWH's *sᵉgullâ*.¹² I read with the Hebrew text and put a full stop after "all the earth," corresponding with the *soph pasuq*. The paradox is that "for to me is all the earth" hardly justifies "you shall be to me a personal possession from all peoples."

The interpretations to follow propose diverse solutions. "And you (*we-attem*) will be to me a kingdom of priests (*mamleket kōhānîm*) and a holy nation." The absolute noun, *mamlakâ* ("kingdom"), may refer to a territory or the people in it. It may also refer to sovereignty, the office or exercise of kingship, and in this sense be understood collectively as royal house or dynasty.¹³ Most of the ancient versions¹⁴ read three designations here—kings, priests, and holy nation¹⁵ (a reading taken up in Rev 1:6; 5:10; 20:6)—but it is unclear whether the three apply to all collectively or are parts of a whole. Ephrem's take was, "Some shall be kings, some shall be priests, and all shall be holy."¹⁶ The paradox is that though the priesthood was instituted at Exodus 28–29, priests are already mentioned at the theophany at Exodus 19:22 (they must not approach without sanctifying themselves), and Aaron seems then already to function as priest. But how should one understand kingship and priesthood applied collectively to Israel? Davies outlines these possible meanings:¹⁷

- A kingdom composed of priests (who individually have access to God);
- A kingdom possessing a legitimate priesthood;
- A kingdom with a collective priestly responsibility on behalf of all peoples;
- A kingdom ruled by priests; and
- A kingdom set apart and possessing collectively, alone among all peoples, the right to approach the altar of YHWH.

Some, like Moran, interpret "kingdom of priests" as priest-kings who rule "a holy nation"—the two together making up the whole.¹⁸ "Holy nation" occurs only here in the Hebrew Bible, but "a holy people" (*'am qādôš*) is frequent in Deuteronomy (e.g., Deut 7:6; 14:2; 26:19). YHWH promised Abraham he would become a great nation (*gôy gādôl*). "Holy nation" reapplies this promise to Abraham. Holiness is the essence

---

12. Hamilton, *Exodus: An Exegetical Commentary*, 303.

13. Davis, *A Royal Priesthood*, 70, 73.

14. Usefully outlined in Davies, *A Royal Priesthood*, 64–66 and Kugel, *Traditions of the Bible*, 672–73.

15. The Targums: kings, priests, and a holy nation (Onk; Neof; FragT); kings adorned with the crown, ministering priests, and a holy people (Ps-Jon); Pesh: a kingdom and priests and a holy people. Philo, *On Abraham* 56: "that race, which species is called 'royal' and 'priesthood' and 'holy nation'"; LXX: *basileion hierateuma kai ethnos hagion* can read as "a palace/kingship, a priesthood, and a holy nation," or "a royal priesthood and a holy nation."

16. Ephrem, *Commentary on Exodus*, 19:1.

17. Davies, *A Royal Priesthood*, 216.

18. Moran, "A Kingdom of Priests," 7–20, here 11–12.

of YHWH; Israel is brought near to the presence of YHWH to participate in this holiness, and this is her distinctive mark.[19] It should be noted that while Exodus–Leviticus challenge Israel to become holy, Deuteronomy posits Israel as already a holy people, though focusing on separation from other nations and their ways.[20] The New Testament portrays the same when it calls believers "saints" (holy) yet exhorts them to be holy. I now give three takes on the above passage.

A. The Text Focuses on Israel's Election as Special Relationship to YHWH

Ancient Jewish tradition reads this text as a classic text on Israel's election, although the technical term, *bāḥar* ("to choose, elect") is lacking. Kaminsky forewarns about the Christian tendency to reduce Israel's election to its service to the larger world, the instrumental aspect of Israel's election. "Yet, within the Bible, God never discloses the total meaning of his unique relationship to Israel."[21] Several texts ground it in the mystery of God's special love for the patriarchs and their descendants (Deut 7:7–8).

> Thus you will say to the house of Jacob and tell the sons of Israel" (my translation). House of Jacob refers to the women, sons of Israel the men. Tell them the details of the precepts, for they are able to understand. Why command the women first? Because they are prompt in the fulfillment of the commandments. Another explanation: so that they introduce their children to the study of the Torah. Still another: In Eden I commanded Adam first and Eve came and transgressed and upset the world. If I do not now call the women first, they will nullify the Torah (ExodR. 28:2).

It continues:

> "I bore you on eagles' wings." Mekilta[22] gives two interpretations. It refers to the speed with which they were gathered and brought to Rameses. Another interpretation: "All the other birds carry their young between their feet, being afraid of other birds flying higher above them. The eagle, however, is afraid only of men who might shoot at him. He, therefore, prefers that the arrows lodge in him rather than in his children." "And I brought you to myself," that is, before Mount Sinai. Another interpretation: to the Temple.[23] Targum Onkelos: and brought you near to my service (followed by Rashi); Ps-Jon/Neof: and brought you nigh to the instruction of the Law. "If ye will hearken"—take it upon yourselves now. All beginnings are difficult, but if you begin to hearken, you will continue to hearken. "And keep my covenant." R. Eliezer: this

---

19. See Okoye, *Israel and the Nations*, 61.
20. See Hamilton, *Exodus*, 305.
21. Kaminsky, "The theology of Genesis," 635–56 here 646–47.
22. *Mekilta de-Rabbi Ishmael*, 202–3.
23. *Mekilta*, 203

refers to the covenant of the Sabbath. R. Akiba: this refers to the covenant of circumcision and to the covenant against idolatry.[24] Rashi[25]: this refers to the covenant I shall make with you regarding the observance of the Torah. "Then you shall be mine": You shall be turned to me and be occupied with the words of the Torah and not with other matters.[26] "Own treasure": just as a man's treasure is precious to him, so you will be precious to me.[27]

Rashi: *segullâ*, a cherished treasure, the same as Eccl 2:8, "and treasures of kings"—costly vessels and precious stones which kings store up. In the same manner shall ye be unto me a cherished treasure more than other peoples . . . all the earth is mine, but in my eyes and before me they are as naught. Ibn Ezra: even though all the earth and all nations are mine, yet I can separate one nation to be an especially beloved treasure. In other words, because all the earth is mine, to deal with as I choose, I can decide upon whom I wish especially to bestow my love. "And ye shall be unto me a kingdom of *kōhănîm*." Rashi: that is, princes, just as you say (2 Sam 8:18), "and the sons of David were princes" (*kōhănîm*), which cannot denote priests since his sons were of the tribe of Judah and not of Levi, the priestly tribe. As already mentioned (see note 15), the Targums understand *mamleket kōhănîm* as kings, priests (and a holy nation). Mekilta: "and ye shall be unto me": I shall not appoint nor delegate anyone else . . . to rule over you, but I myself will rule over you. "A kingdom": I will allow only one of your own to be king over you . . . But king might mean one who goes around making conquests? It says, however, "and priests." But "priests" might mean non-functioning priests, as when it says, "and David's sons were *kōhănîm*, priests (2 Sam 8:18)?"

Therefore, Scripture says, "and a holy nation." Hence the Sages said, the Israelites, before they made the golden calf, were eligible to eat of the holy things. But after they made the golden calf, these holy things were taken from them and given to the priests exclusively.[28] That is, "kings,'"priests," and "holy nation" are to be read together as applying to Israel collectively, each term interpreting the other. Hence, Ps-Jon: "And you will be before me kings adorned with the crown, ministering priests, and a holy people." Hamilton rightly points out that whereas Latin for "priest," *pontifex* (bridge-builder), seems to point to a mediatorial role toward others, Hebrew *kōhēn* has no such bridge-building nuances.[29] Some modern Jews, however, read "priesthood" here as mediatorial, for example, Cassuto: "a people comprised wholly of priests, a people that will occupy among humanity the place filled by the priests within each nation."[30]

24. Mekilta, 204.
25. *Pentateuch with Targum Onkelos, Haphtaroth and Rashi's Commentary: Exodus*, 98.
26. Mekilta, 204.
27. Mekilta, 204.
28. Mekilta, 205.
29. Hamilton, *Exodus*, 304.
30. Cassuto, *Exodus*, 227.

Isaiah 61:5–6 fits in here: "Strangers shall stand ready to pasture your flock, foreigners shall be your farmers and vinedressers. You yourselves shall be called, 'priests of the Lord.' 'Ministers of our God' you shall be called." *Mᵉšartîm*, ministers, serve in the courts of kings. Serving in YHWH's royal court, Israelites will be royal courtiers, leaving all the agricultural labour to foreigners.

B. The Text Is Pivotal Evangelistic Text

Scholars who go this route usually make Genesis 12:1–3 an intertext. That text promises to make Abraham a blessing for all families of the earth. Wright writes of Exodus 19:5–6:

> This is a key missiological text . . . It is as pivotal in the book of Exodus as Genesis 12:1–3 is in Genesis . . . The universal perspective, for which we enlist it here, is explicit in the double phrase *all nations* and *the whole earth*. Although the action is taking place between YHWH and Israel alone at Mount Sinai, God has not forgotten his wider mission of blessing the rest of the nations of the earth through this particular people whom he has redeemed.[31]

Another tendency is a type of canonical criticism that insists on the unity of faith in both Testaments. Kaiser writes:

> The "people of God" in all ages have been one. Together they have all been called to the same privilege of service and ministry on behalf of the coming Man of Promise. All were to be agents of God's blessing to all on earth. Nothing could be clearer from the missionary and ministry call issued in Exodus 19:4–6.[32]

Wright translates Exodus 19:5–6 as follows: "You will be for me a special personal possession among all the peoples; for indeed to me belongs the whole earth but you, you will be for me a priestly kingdom and a holy nation."[33]

The single Hebrew word *kî* ("for," "because")[34] is rendered twice ("for indeed"), combining the causal and asseverative senses. The break in the sentence (Hebrew *soph pasuq*) is moved forward from "all the earth" to "all the peoples." The *waw* ("and") of *we-'attem* ("and you") is read as adversative ("but you," "you"). The *min* of *mikkol* is read inclusively as *min* of comparison ("from among," "to a greater extent than"), not as *min* of separation. The idea of inclusion is suggested by adding "special" to "personal possession" to translate *sᵉggulâ*. This way, the translation of *sᵉggulâ* takes account

---

31. Wright, *The Mission of God*, 224.
32. Kaiser Jr., *Mission in the Old Testament*, 22.
33. Wright, *The Mission of God*, 255.
34. It is not clear how the phrase "all the earth is mine" fits into the unit. Many scholars consider it parenthetic or an insertion that upsets the logical flow of the piece. Wright tries to make the best sense of it within the piece.

of "to me belongs the whole earth," as if to say, "The whole earth is my personal possession, but you are my *special* personal possession."

Another trend is to include the concept of mission in the meaning and function of *sᵉggulâ*. The word may mean Israel's election, her unique relationship with YHWH, but it is taken for granted *a priori* that election invariably functions for mission to others. Wright writes:

> Just as the call of Abraham is explicitly for the benefit of the nations, so the choice of Israel for a special relationship with God is likewise made with the rest of the world clearly in view . . . in other words, *the particularity of Israel here is intended to serve the universality of God's interest in the world. Israel's election serves God's mission.* This is an utterly crucial point to grasp.[35]

Alternatively, and as Kaiser writes, the election of Israel, far from meaning the rejection of the other nations of the world, was the very means of salvation of the nations. Election was not a call to privilege, but a choosing for service. As such, the priestly character of the nation of Israel came into view almost from the beginning of her existence as a nation. The people were to be God's ministers, his preachers, his prophets to their own nation as well as to the other nations.[36]

The translation of *mamleket kōhānîm* as "priestly kingdom,"[37] heightened by the parallel "a holy nation," allows for Israel to assume a priestly character among and on behalf of the nations: "Her role as a nation was a mediatorial role as they related to the nations and people groups around them."[38]

Lest it might appear that all evangelicals go this route, Schrock cautions that "Deuteronomy says nothing about Israel being set apart for the nations. Rather, Israel is set apart from the nations."[39] Also,

> [We interpret] Exodus 19:6 less as an evangelistic commission and more as a restoration of covenant blessing to God's people . . . from a canonical reading it seems unlikely that Exodus 19:6 gives Israel a mission to the nations. This confuses the nature of the Old Covenant and the New; it imports, anachronistically, the calling of Jesus' disciples to the nations of Israel.[40]

Davies notes that divine grant is preeminently one of relationship with him. The other nations are not in view as objects of Israel's attention. The expression "all the earth is mine" (v. 5) will not serve this role of marking the nations as the beneficiaries of Israel's service. It is simply the backdrop for the divine election of Israel. The nearest reference to the nations in relation to Israel as an active agent in the wider context is at

35. Wright, *Mission of God*, 256–57.
36. Kaiser, *Mission in the Old Testament*, 22.
37. It can also be rendered "a kingdom of priests."
38. Kaiser, *Mission in the Old Testament*, 22.
39. Schrock, "Restoring the Image of God," 25–60, here 47.
40. Schrock, "Restoring the Image of God," 52.

Exodus 17:14–16, which concerns the obliteration of the memory of the Amalekites! The Sinai pericope simply contains no direct reference to Israel's responsibilities toward the nations.[41]

C. The Text Portrays Israel's Community in Mission

Israel's very life is meant to manifest the knowledge and holiness of YHWH. Okoye traces four faces of mission in the Old Testament.[42] The first is that of the universality of salvation and universality of righteousness before YHWH—all can be righteous or evil before him. The second is "community in mission": Israel's very life was meant as a divine pattern for individual and social life that draws humanity to YHWH. The third is "centripetal mission," in which the nations stream to Zion to be instructed in God's ways; a few become God-fearers and proselytes. The final face is "centrifugal mission," in which active effort is made to reach outsiders and incorporate them in the covenant. Exodus 19:5–6 registers as community in mission. I translate it as follows.

> And now, if you obey my voice and keep my covenant, you shall be to me a personal possession out of all the peoples, for to me is all the earth. And you shall be to me a kingdom of priests and a holy nation.[43]

The absolute noun *mamlakâ* ("kingdom") may refer to a territory or the people in it. It may also refer to sovereignty, the office or exercise of kingship, and in this sense be understood collectively as royal house or dynasty.[44] The translation of *mamleket kōhānîm* as "a kingdom of priests" (not "royal priesthood"[45]) retains the parallel to "a holy nation" (to be explained soon). It designates "a people comprised wholly of priests."[46] The "intention is to characterize Israel's special position in the family of kingdoms and nations with respect to its priestly status as a sacral theocracy."[47]

The focus of the unit is on the leit-motif *lî* ("to myself"), what Israel will be to YHWH if she consents to the proposal. Having proven his goodwill and trustworthiness,[48] YHWH now gives Israel an exegesis of what "you will serve God at this mountain" means. "The Hebrews who 'served' Pharaoh (in slave labour) are to come away in order to 'serve' (worship and obey) YHWH"[49] as uniquely beloved. Talk

---

41. Davies, *A Royal Priesthood*, 97.
42. Okoye, *Israel and the Nations*, 10–12.
43. I followed the Hebrew scansion and also kept the same translation for *lî* ("to me").
44. Davis, *Royal Priesthood*, 70, 73.
45. Those who translate as "royal priesthood" will have to show what "royal" contributes to "priesthood" in this passage.
46. Cassuto, *Exodus*, 227.
47. K. Seybold, *Melek*, TDOT, VIII, 360.
48. Fretheim, *The Pentateuch*, 48 talks of the fourfold structure of covenant: God elects, God saves, human beings respond in worship and faith, and only then does God establish covenant.
49. Okoye, *Israel and the Nations*, 59.

of covenant here is proleptic, as is the people's response, "everything the Lord has said, we will do." Both refer to the covenant ratified in Exodus 24.

From all the nations, YHWH is choosing Israel for a special relationship with him. He may do so as he wishes, "for to me is all the earth." One notices a matching of terms: "You shall be *to me* a personal possession out of all the peoples for *to me* is all the earth."

The choice of Israel is not because Israel belongs to YHWH as Moab belongs to Chemosh. In fact, such a view is found in Deuteronomy 32:8: when the Most High gave the nations each their heritage, when he partitioned out the human race, he assigned the boundaries of the nations according to the number of the children of God, but Yahweh's portion was his people; Jacob was to be the measure of his inheritance. Rather, YHWH is exercising sovereign freedom as Lord of all in bestowing his special love upon a select nation. *Sᵉgullâ* ("personal possession") is a personal possession of a king, as distinguished from what accrues to him from the state. For example, Zion is David's personal possession (Latin *peculium*, from which derives the English word "particular") because he conquered it on his own. The word imports election, Israel's unique relationship with YHWH. YHWH proposes to have Israel particularly close to him. What follows, "and you shall be to me a priestly kingdom and a holy nation," teases out what is involved in being YHWH's personal possession. "Kingdom of priests" is parallel to "holy nation," each interpreting the other. Christian scholars tend to fill the term "priest" with their conceptions of priesthood, as outlined by Davies.[50] He correctly insists that "Israel does not participate in any active mission . . . rather they [nations] will recognize the holiness of God because they see Israel's holiness." He cites Ezekiel 36:23, "But I will show the holiness of my great name, desecrated among the nations, in whose midst you desecrated it. Then the nations shall know that I am the Lord—oracle of the Lord God—when through you I show my holiness before their very eyes."

He concludes that, as a nation, Israel is assured of the privilege of royal status, a royalty characterized by the essence of priesthood—namely, access to the divine presence. Israel's corporate priesthood is preeminently that which is exercised toward God, not other nations.[51]

The holy is that with which God's presence abides. "Holy" corresponds to priestly as "nation" corresponds to kingdom. "Holy" (*qādôš*) expresses the goal of Israel's calling—a religious dimension, in the manner of priest: "Israel must live for God . . . Israel

---

50. Davies, *A Royal Priesthood*, 95: Israel will serve the nations as the Levitical priests would serve Israel (Cassuto, *Exodus*, 227; Childs, *Exodus*, 367); Israel will mediate blessing or redemption to the nations (Kaiser, *Mission in the Old Testament*); Israel will intercede for the nations (Merrill, *Kingdom of Priests*, 80); Israel will teach the will of God to the nations (McNeile, *Exodus*, 111); Israel will have a liturgical mission to the nations (Kleinig, "On Eagles' Wing," 16–27, here 19); what Israelite priests are for Israel, Israel as a whole will become for the other peoples of the world (Auzou Georges, *De la servitude au service: "etude du livre de l'exode*, 251).

51. Davies, *A Royal Priesthood*, 102.

must relate to others. Holy does not infer a separation in terms of isolation . . . Indeed, we may suggest it even demands a relationship with others, for if Israel is invested with God's presence, then it may represent it and mediate it to others."[52] One may conclude by saying that "God's holiness will become evident to all especially through the holiness of Israel . . . Holiness has a missionary intention!"[53] Exodus 19:5–6 helps us perceive that the life of a people is the vehicle for mission.[54] The effort to be true to the character of God as the Holy One of Israel also manifests God to the world. Such an effort to conform to God is integral and is not merely "spiritual," hence it affects all levels of the life of a people.[55]

CONCLUSION

It is shown that each of the three interpretations has basis in the text. Israel heard and lived the word of God for centuries before the advent of Christianity. Christians stand to gain by dialoguing with that experience and with Israel's interpretation of it.

> Christians can and ought to admit that the Jewish reading of the Bible is a possible, in continuity with the Jewish Sacred Scriptures from the Second Temple period, a reading analogous to the Christian reading which developed in parallel fashion.[56]

A certain type of canonical criticism of the Old Testament tends to subsume the Old in the New, instead of letting the Old unveil itself in the New[57] and respecting the eras of revelation. In this respect, this author pursued a two-stage approach in his commentary on Genesis[58] in which Jewish and Christian traditions flowing from the text are identified and the underlying hermeneutical moves analyzed.

As already indicated, the book of Revelation read Exodus 19:6 as referring to "a kingdom and priests" (*basileian kai hiereis*, Rev 5:10, see 1:6). Persecuted Christians, now serving as priests at the heavenly altar, will reign with Christ for a thousand years (Rev 20:4–5). First Peter 2:9 follows the LXX in reading *mamleket kōhānîm* ("a kingdom of priests") as *basileion hierateuma* ("a royal priesthood"). The author transfers to the Christian community the prerogatives of Israel—chosen race (election), people of God (*laos theou*), God's personal possession (recalls the Hebrew $s^e gull\hat{a}$). In Christ, and "like living stones, let yourselves be built into a spiritual house to be a

---

52. Wells and Scult, *God's Holy People*, 56–57.
53. Wells and Scult, *God's Holy People*, 240.
54. Legrand, *Unity and Plurality*, 35.
55. Okoye, *Israel and the Nations*, 66.
56. Pontifical Biblical Commission, *The Jewish People and their Sacred Scriptures*, no. 22.
57. I hint at Augustine's "*Novum in Vetere latet, Vetus in Novo patet*" (The New Testament lies hidden in the Old, the Old Testament is unveiled in the New).
58. Okoye, *Genesis 1–11*, 2018; *Genesis 12–50: A Narrative Theological Commentary*, 2020.

holy priesthood (*eis hierateuma hagion*) to offer spiritual sacrifices acceptable to God through Jesus Christ" (1 Pet 2:5). Their function as priests is to "announce the praises of him who called you out of darkness into his own wonderful light." The Christian community is the place of the dwelling and manifestation of God; in worship and behavior Christians glorify and reveal God.[59]

The preface of Sunday 1 of Ordinary Time brings all this to a close:

> For through his Paschal Mystery, he accomplished the marvellous deed, by which he has freed us from the yoke of sin and death, summoning us to the glory of being now called a chosen race, a royal priesthood, a holy nation, a people for your own possession, to proclaim everywhere your mighty works, for you have called us out of darkness into your own wonderful light.

BIBLIOGRAPHY

Georges, Auzou. *De la servitude au service:"etude du livre de l'exode*. Orante, 1964.

Cassuto, Umberto Moshe David. *A Commentary on the Book of Exodus*. Skokie, IL.: Varda Books, 2005.

Childs, Brevard S. *The Book of Exodus: A Critical Theological Commentary*. Philadelphia: Westminster Press, 1974.

Davies, John A. *A Royal Priesthood: Literary and intertextual Perspective on an Image of Israel in Exodus*. New York: Bloomsbury, 2004.

Ephrem, Saint. *Selected Prose Works: Commentary on Genesis, Commentary on Exodus, Homily on Our Lord, Letter to Publius*. The Fathers of the Church 91. Translated by Edward G. Matthews Jr. and Joseph P. Amar. Washington, DC: Catholic University of America, 2010.

Fretheim, Terence. *The Pentateuch*. Nashville: Abingdon Press, 1996.

Hamilton, Victor P. *Exodus: An Exegetical Commentary*. Grand Rapids: Baker, 2011.

Kaiser, Walter C., Jr. *Mission in the Old Testament: Israel as a Light to the Nations*. Grand Rapids: Baker, 2000.

Kaminsky, Joel S. "The Theology of Genesis." In *The Book of Genesis. Composition, Reception, and Interpretation*. Edited by Craig A. Evans, Jeol N. Lohr, and David L. Petersen. Atlanta: Society of Biblical Literature Press, 2012.

Kleinig, John W. "On Eagles' Wing: An Exegetical Study of Exod 19:2–8." *Lutheran Theological Journal* 21, no. 1 (1987) 16–27.

Kugel, James L. *Traditions of the Bible: A Guide to the Bible as It Was at the Start of the Common Era*. Massachusetts: Harvard University Press, 1998.

Legrand, Lucien. *Unity and Plurality: Mission in the Bible*. Maryknoll: Orbis, 1990.

Lipiński, E. *S^{e}gullâ, TDOT*, X. Grand Rapids: Eerdmans, 1999.

McNeile, Alan Hugh. *The Book of Exodus, with Introduction and Notes*. London: Methuen, 1911.

Merrill, Eugene H. *Kingdom of Priests: A History of Old Testament Israel*. Grand Rapids: Baker Academic, 2008.

---

59. The reader may consult Okoye, *Israel and the Nations*, 64–66, for a more detailed development of the theme here.

Mekilta de-Rabbi Ishmael. Vol. 2. Translated by Jacob Z. Lauterbach. Philadelphia: Jewish Publication Society of America, 1961.

Moran, W. L. "A Kingdom of Priests." In *The Bible in Current Catholic Thought*, 7–20. Edited by J. L. McKenzie. New York: Herder, 1962.

Okoye, James Chukwuma. *Israel and the Nations: A Mission Theology of the Old Testament*. Maryknoll: Orbis, 2006.

———. *Genesis 1–11: A Narrative Theological Commentary*. Eugene, OR: Cascade Books, 2018.

———. *Genesis 12—50: A Narrative Theological Commentary*. Eugene, OR: Cascade Books, 2020.

Pentateuch with Targum Onkelos, Haphtaroth and Rashi's Commentary: Exodus. New York: Hebrew Publishing Company, 1972.

Philo. *Volume VI: On Abraham, On Joseph, On Moses*. Translated by F. H. Colson. Loeb Classical Library 289. Cambridge, MA: Harvard University Press, 1935.

Pontifical Biblical Commission. *The Jewish People and their Sacred Scriptures in the Christian Bible*. Vatican City, 2002.

Schrock, David. "Restoring the Image of God: A Corporate-Filial Approach to the 'Royal Priesthood' in Exodus 19:5–6." *SBJT* 22, no. 2 (2018) 25–60.

Seybold, K. *Melek, TDOT*, VIII, 1997, 346–74.

Wells, Jo Bailey, and Allen Scult. *God's Holy People: A Theme in Biblical Theology*. London: Bloomsbury, 2000.

Wright, Christopher J. H. *The Mission of God: Unlocking the Bible's Grand Narrative*. Downers Grove: IVP Academic, 2006.

Chapter 2

Miriam at Kadesh and Cana?
Making Numbers 20:1–13 and John 2:1–11 Dialogue on the Servants' Mission

Paul Béré, SJ

INTRODUCTION

Engelbert Mveng, a Cameroonian Jesuit and artist, painted a "Eucharistic" fresco of biblical scenes in a triptych in the chapel of Hekima University College.[1] The sign of Cana in John 2:1–11 is recognizable. The viewer is surprised by the representation of the servants who fill the water jars or distribute the bread. The artist depicts them as female figures. On the bread side, the disciples are not all adults; there are children carrying baskets on their heads. On the water side, a woman is accompanied by children carrying water on their heads. One of the children is probably a boy, judging by his clothing. This artistic interpretation of the story in African cultural language means that the figure of the woman, or even the mother with her children or the sister with her brothers and sisters, is associated with food. Thus, next to Jesus, the Master, we have a servant woman. Man and woman cannot be separated from the sphere of life.[2]

In Numbers 20:1–13 and John 2:1–11, we find the reference to the woman in these two stories where water and wine are mentioned. This woman is, on the one hand, "sister," and on the other, "mother," but in both accounts, she has the same name: Miriam.[3] Both are present in the mission of the servants. The honoree of

---

1. Hekima University College is a Jesuit higher learning institution based in Nairobi (Kenya).
2. This fresco reflects the author's understanding of African anthropology. It is worth an in-depth study.
3. In John's Gospel, the name of the "mother of Jesus" never appears. We know her as Miriam or

these studies has taught us to link femininity and mission.[4] In this study, therefore, I propose to understand what these two narratives bring to each other in terms of mutual enlightenment.[5] To try to determine whether the story of Numbers is the source of John 2 would, it seems to me, be impoverishing.[6] The Christian canon invites us to understand the latter in the light of the former, as hinted at in Luke 24, so as to keep the New Testament on the horizon of the Old Testament. This connection also reminds us that events in the course of human history, beyond the Johannine community's experience, offer new keys to understanding the "Scriptures." They become a lamp that illuminates the questions that each era and each context poses to the text. The role of Miriam—woman and mother—in these stories may have arisen from the questioning that the "invisible presence" or the "suppressed voice"[7] of women poses to our contemporary society.

We will look for the role played by Miriam in the two narratives in relation to the mission of the servants: Moses and Aaron in the narrative of Numbers, and the anonymous servants in the narrative of John. The latter, we believe, serve as models for the disciples of Jesus, who witness the interaction between the servants and their master. We shall see that in order for it to be effective, the absence or presence of the woman is not indifferent in the life and mission of the servants who must put the word of God into action. For their obedience becomes deficient or efficient and total depending on whether the woman is present or absent, even if, in the end, the manifestation of the holiness or glory of God depends on none but God himself. This will be shown by first highlighting the essential elements that call for an intertextual approach to these two stories (I). Then, I will point out what is at stake in their respective narrative frameworks (II). Finally, I will investigate the potential meanings that one can glean through this intertextual exercise around the servants' mission in both narratives (III).

Mary based on the Synoptic Gospels. "We would not know his [Jesus'] mother's name if other traditions did not mention it. She is only present here and at the cross (19:25–27): her maternal function is emphasised each time," writes Simoens, *Selon Jean. 2. Interprétation*, 135.

4. Okure, *Johannine Approach to Mission*, 1988.

5. The comparison of NT texts with those of the OT has been the subject of various studies ranging from the search for NT source texts in the OT to echoes, quotations, and allusions. From a theoretical point of view, Julia Kristeva is the author of the concept of "intertextuality."

6. See Aichele and Phillips, "Introduction: Exegesis, Eisegesis, Intergesis," 11. For decades, studies of the Old Testament "echoes" or sources of John 2:1–11 have been growing. See, for example, Schulz, "Das Wunder zu Kana im Lichte des Alten Testaments," 93–96, which highlights the role of Mary; Lütgehetmann, *Die Hochzeit von Kana*, 272, where the author remarks that in the OT there is no account of the changing of water into wine. He nevertheless references the accounts on water from the rock in "Exod 15:23–25 (see also Num 20:1–13)." This is the only reference to the Kadesh story. Little, *Echoes of the Old Testament*, 37–41, describes the OT patterns recognizable in the Cana story.

7. See Masenya, "African Womanist Hermeneutics," 149–55.

I. THE PARALLEL BETWEEN THE KADESH AND CANA STORIES

A careful reading of Numbers 20:1–13 in parallel with John 2:1–11 reveals some salient points that can improve our understanding of these two texts.[8] As a preamble, it should be kept in mind that in John's Gospel, the mother of Jesus is never presented by her name. The focus is not on her individuality, only her relationality to the Son. However, we know from the Synoptic Gospels that her name was Miriam/Mariam (depending on whether one chooses the Hebrew or Greek name). For the audience of the Gospel story, the mother of Jesus is Moses' sister's namesake. And Jesus himself is often compared to Moses. In this study, therefore, I will look at the two Miriams in search of the unique contribution of their status as women in the servants' mission.

Both stories seem to describe a transitional situation: in Kadesh, the people complete their desert journey (Num 20:1, 13ff) and contemplate the promised land (see the report of the explorers in Num 13–14), and in Numbers 20:14, Moses sends emissaries to Edom. They will continue their journey without Miriam, his sister. In Cana, Jesus initiates his public ministry, a threshold in his life and mission. After the first sign at the wedding, he moves to Capernaum with his disciples, his brothers, and his mother, the other Miriam (John 2:12). In both cases, the background is a covenant: a symbolic structure of the relationship between YHWH and his people, on the one hand, and, on the other, the wedding where the mother (Miriam) and the son (Jesus) are present.

As will be shown in the table below, we can identify five common elements that correlate the two stories:

1. Miriam is present in the narrative in the modality of an absence because, on the one hand, she is dead (Num 1:1), and on the other, she is unnamed (John 2:1). The two forms of absence are not identical. In the case of the sister of Moses and Aaron, she cannot intervene, since she is dead. In Cana, the name is replaced by a term of relationship: the "mother of Jesus." It is therefore expected that she will act in this capacity. The narrator also makes it clear that Jesus and his disciples were invited.

2. In Kadesh there is no water to quench the thirst of the people. They turn to Moses and Aaron, who turn to YHWH (Num 20:2–6). At Cana, the wedding feast lacks wine. Jesus' mother turns to Jesus with a request (John 2:3–4). The situation is not dramatic in the second case as it is in the first, but it is no less critical.

3. In Kadesh, YHWH answers Moses and instructs him to speak to the rock in the eyes of the congregation. Water will come out of it for the congregation to drink (Num 20:7–8). At Cana, Jesus' mother addresses the servants and invites them to show him total obedience (John 2:5). Jesus in turn instructs the servants to

---

8. Zumstein, *L'évangile selon saint Jean (1–12)*, 94, proposes the following structure: exposition (vv. 1–2); preparation for the miracle (vv. 3–5); indirect description of the event (vv. 6–8); confirmation of the miracle as a conclusion (vv. 9–10); commentary by the narrator (v. 11), the protagonist's change of location (v. 12).

fill up the six stone water jars (John 2:7a; cf. 2:6). The fact that the jars are made out of stone should not be considered insignificant. Water will indeed flow from the rock (stone) when Moses strikes it, and water in the (stone) jars will become wine when the servants fill them up.

4. In Kadesh, the execution of Moses and Aaron proves imperfect. This imperfect obedience is often understood in relation to the instrument used to bring the water out of the stone. For some, it is because Moses uses the rod rather than "speaking to the rock" as instructed by YHWH. He and Aaron are punished with exclusion from the land (Num 20:9–12).[9] When, at Cana, the servants are invited to "fill" the jars with water (John 2:7a), the narrator specifies that "they filled them up to the brim" (John 2:7b).

5. Both events share a strikingly similar ending: the people are led to experience the manifestation of the holiness of YHWH (Num 20:13) in Kadesh, and the glory of Jesus (John 2:11) in Cana.

The following chart aims to sum up the ongoing observations:[10]

	Num 20:1–13	**John 2:1–11**
1	v.1 [Context of Sinai Covenant] "Miriam is absent"; Moses and Aaron are present.	v.1–2 Context of Nuptial Covenant; "Miriam is present"; Jesus and his disciples are present.
2	v.2–6 Lack of water; People to turn to Moses and Aaron; Moses and Aaron to turn to YHWH.	v.3 Lack of wine; "Miriam" turns to Jesus.
3	v.7–8 Yhwh speaks to Moses; There is a rock.	v.4–7a Jesus speaks to "Miriam"; "Miriam" speaks to the servants; There are stone jars; Jesus speaks to the servants.

---

9. See Gray, *A critical and exegetical commentary on Numbers*, 256ff.

10. For the sake of the exercise in intertextuality, I will designate the 'mother of Jesus' by her name 'Miriam'.

4	v.9–11 Moses and Aaron exhibit imperfect obedience; YHWH speaks to Moses and Aaron (punishment).	v.7b–10 Servants exhibit perfect execution of the command; Jesus speaks to servants.
5	v.12–13 YHWH reproaches Moses and Aaron for not having manifested his holiness before the people; YHWH manifested his holiness.	v.11 Jesus manifested his glory, and the disciples believed.

These parallels reveal the often-unnoticed importance of the place of the woman, either sister or mother. The fact that the evangelist did not use Mary/Miriam's name but rather her title of mother emphasizes her relationship with Jesus, her son. Moreover, it stresses the fact that she is a woman. As a matter of fact, Jesus' response to her request highlights her gender: "τί ἐμοὶ καὶ σοί, γύναι;" ("What concern is that to you and to me, *Woman*?" [John 2:4]).[11] One may legitimately ask whether, in Kadesh, the absence of Miriam did not prejudice the quality of the obedience of her brothers.

MUTUAL ENLIGHTENMENT

After the outline of the parallel elements, we can try and deepen the questions raised by each pericope in the light of the other. There is no doubt that the account of Kadesh precedes chronologically that of Cana. Therefore, the question of the author's relationship to the account of Numbers is not the objective of our investigation. The redactional problem of the Fourth Gospel has been extensively investigated.[12] As mentioned earlier, no intertextual study of the two narratives has so far been offered, as far as I know. It proves fruitful when we realize that one story sheds light on the other, especially in trying to grasp the relation between the female characters with the servants' mission.

The Obituary of Miriam: To What End?

In the Kadesh narrative, the obituary of Miriam seems to be an added note with no specific function in the narrative. *Prima facie*, no link to the thirst of the people can be discerned, although the resolution of the Meribah incident resulted in Moses and

---

11. This verse has been extensively discussed. My point here is the gender issue which will come back again at the end of Jesus' life and ministry (John 19).

12. See Lütgehetmann, *Die Hochzeit von Kana (Joh 2, 1–11)*, 20; Zumstein, *L'évangile selon saint Jean (1–12)*, 2014; Zumstein, *La mémoire revisitée: études johanniques*, 2017.

Aaron being denied access to the promised land. Some interpreters believe that the mention is simply related to the fact that Miriam died in Kadesh. Others, however, note that "her status as a prophet and leader in the community is affirmed by this notice."[13] There is, however, more than an appendix in this reference. Miriam's death occurs before the miracle of Meribah. She is thus absent from an event that barred the way to her brothers, Moses and Aaron, as the people journeyed to the promised land.

Now, for the aural audience of the Cana story in the Fourth Gospel, the underlying text, or say "hypotext," to which the miracle of the wine would echo would be the one in which the other Miriam, Moses' sister, is mentioned. Unlike her two brothers, Miriam does not die because she disobeyed YHWH.[14] She is no longer there when her brothers do not do exactly what YHWH asks of them. The role that Miriam, the mother of Jesus, will play at Cana offers a key to interpreting the Kadesh story, in a flashback mode. In other words, Miriam's absence is no longer merely marginal information; it has an explanatory link to the ensuing story of the people's thirst and the inaccurate response of Moses and Aaron. If I may paraphrase the second Miriam, I would say that Moses and Aaron could have heard from their sister the following invitation: "Do whatever YHWH tells you."

The Intervention of Jesus' Mother: What Does She Have to Do With It?

The story of Cana is perplexing to the uninformed audience. Without a story like Meribah as background, one wonders: "Invited like Jesus, why would the mother of Jesus be concerned by the lack of wine?" There seems to be no reason for her to interfere in the logistics of the feast. This initiative was understood in many ways.[15] In the light of the Kadesh story, however, Miriam, the mother of Jesus, mediates between those who are thirsty and the one who can act on their behalf. Unlike Miriam, the sister of Moses and Aaron, who is absent, the mother of Jesus will mediate and allow the servants to obey the Lord and act in accord with his command. Even though it may sound speculative, I guess Miriam, the sister, could have contributed to avoiding the exclusion of Moses and Aaron from the land since the reason given for barring them from entering the land is the incident of Meribah, and not the verdict of Numbers 14. There, YHWH says:

13. Launderville, "Number," 327.

14. The fate of Aaron and Moses is narrated in Num 20:22–29 and Num 27:12–23, respectively. Both accounts share the same pattern: (1) announcement of the coming death [Aaron: 20:24a–26b; Moses: 27:13]; (2) reason for the verdict being the disobedience at the waters of Meribah [Aaron: 20:24b; Moses: 27:14]; (3) appointment of the successor [Aaron/Eleazar: 20:25–26a.; Moses/Joshua: 27:15–18]; (4) investiture of the successor (Eleazar: 20:27–28; Joshua: 27:19–23); (5) effectiveness of the death [Aaron: 20:29]. This pattern calls for two observations: first, Miriam's death occurs before her brothers' disobedience at Meribah; second, unlike her brothers Moses and Aaron, Miriam does not have a successor.

15. Brown hypothesized that Jesus' mother was the groom's aunt, but that was qualified as a legend by E. Haenchen, R.W. Funk, and U. Busse, *John*, 175.

none of the people who have seen my glory and the signs that I did in Egypt and in the wilderness, and yet have tested me these ten times and have not obeyed my voice, shall see the land that I swore to give to their ancestors; none of those who despised me shall see it. But my servant Caleb, because he has a different spirit and has followed me wholeheartedly, I will bring into the land into which he went, and his descendants shall possess it. (Num 14:22–24)

As stated in YHWH'S pronouncement, Caleb is set apart because he showed a different spirit. Moses and Aaron could have been redeemed as well.

The Punishment of Moses and Aaron

Miriam, the mother of Jesus,[16] approaches her son and, subsequently, the servants, whom she invites to total obedience, in a way that can draw attention to the absence of Miriam, the sister. Jesus' mother mediates between "those who have no wine" and Jesus, the wine giver (John 2:3), on the one hand, and between the servants, mission executors, and Jesus, the mission giver (John 2:5), on the other. She takes up a leadership role. At Kadesh, Moses and Aaron mediate between the thirsty people and YHWH, the giver of water (Num 20:2f). Does this mean that Miriam could have influenced the course of the events narrated in Meribah? From the perspective of intratextuality, based on Numbers 12:1f, where Miriam takes the initiative to reproach Moses about his Kushite wife,[17] her character as a leader stands out. From the perspective of intertextuality, the initiative taken by Miriam, the mother, might suggest such a possibility in Numbers.[18] In effect, when she invites the servants to "do whatever he tells you" (John 2:5), they do listen to her voice, as remarked by the narrator's comment: "They filled them to the brim" (John 2:7b: ἐγέμισαν αὐτὰς ἕως ἄνω). Jesus had in fact asked them to simply fill the jars with water (John 2:7a: γεμίσατε τὰς ὑδρίας ὕδατος). But the servants did not simply fill the jars in accordance with the command, for the narrator specifies "ἕως ἄνω." This is indeed what seems to have been missing from Aaron and Moses' experience: a voice that would have invited them to stick to what YHWH commanded them.

YHWH'S command to Moses is that he take his staff and, together with Aaron his brother, gather the congregation. Then, he was to *speak* to the rock before the people (וְדִבַּרְתֶּם אֶל־הַסֶּלַע לְעֵינֵיהֶם) so that the rock would give water. Had he spoken

---

16. In John 19:26–27, the two terms "mother" and "son" are used to refer to the "mother of Jesus" and the "disciple whom he loved," respectively.

17. We will not discuss the leadership issues about Miriam, Aaron, and Moses.

18. Almost no commentary highlights the fact that Miriam died before the incident of the water at Meribah that will become the reason for the exclusion of Moses and Aaron from the land. Milgrom does note that the story of Meribah "constitutes the climax of a series of rebellions: first, by the people (chap. 14); then, by the Levites and chieftains (chap. 16); and, finally, by the leaders, Moses and Aaron. The punishment for all of them is the same: They will not inherit the land but, instead, will die in the wilderness." Milgrom, *Numbers*, 163.

to the rock, Moses would have appeared as YHWH'S spokesman. Now, Moses did remove the staff from before YHWH, then, together with Aaron, summoned the assembly to face the rock (Num 20:10) as YHWH had ordered (Num 20:9). But instead of speaking, he used the staff to perform the miracle by striking the rock twice (Num 20:11).[19] As a consequence of Moses' disobedience, YHWH decided that Moses and Aaron will not enter the land because לֹא־הֶאֱמַנְתֶּם בִּי לְהַקְדִּישֵׁנִי לְעֵינֵי בְּנֵי יִשְׂרָאֵל ("they did not believe in him so as to manifest his holiness in the eyes of the people," Num 20:12).

The Glory of Jesus Manifested and the Holiness of YHWH Revealed

The water from the rock and the wine from the stone jars revealed the *holiness* of YHWH at Kadesh (Num 20:13) and the *glory* of Jesus at Cana (John 2:11) by their extraordinary character. For an aural audience, familiar with the first story, the Gospel account is a new, almost parabolic, version of it, in order to reveal the divine identity of Jesus, albeit possibly before his appointed time.[20] In terms of the required attitude vis-à-vis God's mission, the failure of Moses and Aaron, and the perfect obedience of the servants, who did whatever Jesus asked them to do, set the example for the disciples and for all of us in their footsteps.

WHAT IS AT STAKE IN THE TWO STORIES FOR THE MISSION OF THE SERVANTS

At the end of this short intertextual look at the two narratives, it seems to be useful to reexamine them afresh around the mission of the servants, entrusted by God, and in which the woman holds an important role of leadership.[21] Gender hermeneutics constantly tries to remind us of this, but sometimes women become "transparent" to (male) interpreters. In the following paragraphs, I will pay attention to the presence of women, the obedience of the servants, and the manifestation of the divinity in covenant relationship with humanity.

---

19. The literature on the reason for YHWH'S punishment is immense. Some emphasize the difference between the word and the rod, as we do; others insist on striking the rock "twice" as signifying doubt or lack of faith in YHWH; still others think that Moses' words in Num 20:10 indicate that Moses had put himself in the center instead of YHWH; see Launderville, "Numbers," 327; Milgrom, *Numbers*, 163ff.

20. Is the hour of Jesus, often associated with his death on the cross (John 17:1; 19:27), not the hour of the unveiling of his divinity (John 2:4b)?

21. See Brown, "Roles of Women in the Fourth Gospel," 688–99.

The Presence of the Woman

The presence of the two women at the threshold of the two narratives signals, it seems to me, their role in the fulfillment of the "sign" from which the divinity of YHWH and Jesus is revealed. Miriam, the sister of Moses and Aaron, is the female prominent presence in the leadership of the migrating Israel. Although her role is silenced, with a few exceptions (Exod 15:20–21; Num 12), tradition remembers her as part of the trio of leaders as attested to in Micah: "For I brought you up from the land of Egypt, and redeemed you from the house of slavery; and I sent before you Moses, Aaron, and Miriam" (Mic 6:4). Irudayaraj did not fail to note this when he writes that:

> In the exodus context, the mentioning of Moses and Aaron seems natural, but Miriam makes a rare yet striking appearance. Given her status as a prophetess (Exod 15:20) and the solidarity that her person commended from her fellow Israelites when she was struck with leprosy (Num 12:15), the Micah inclusion of Miriam is an explicit acknowledgment of her importance.[22]

As we can see, the important place of women in the management of the community has been lost with the eclipse of the figure of Miriam. However, the fact that she was removed from the Meribah incident of disobedience and that her two brothers failed to do so suggests that she had a discreet and effective action on them. Despite the leadership failure, YHWH manifested his holiness by bringing water from the rock.

In the Cana story, we note that the narrator has emphasised the exemplary obedience of the servants who fill the jars "to the brim." The fact that those for whom Miriam, the mother of Jesus, intervened did not know the origin of the wine says a lot about the effective discretion of that woman. Those who did know, however, were the disciples of Jesus: they witnessed the manifestation of Jesus' glory and believed in Jesus. By her gesture, Miriam, the mother, offered to the disciples present and to all the disciples listening to this story an example of servanthood or discipleship in fulfilling the word of Jesus. The servants in the story thus serve as models for the disciples of Jesus and for us today.

The Obedience of the Servants

Moses and Aaron are anti-models of servants because they did not carry out the word entrusted to them by YHWH. It could be argued that they knew, with reference to Exodus 17:1–7, that their action would bring forth water for the people to drink. But the fact that the two brothers called the thirsty people "rebels" shows that they felt insecure in front of their audience. They doubted. They lacked assertiveness. Could it not be the absence of their sister (the woman) which deprived them of strength in

---

22. Irudayaraj, "Micah," 1090. It is astonishing that Deuteronomy, which organizes the social life of Israel, only mentions Miriam's leprosy (Deut 24:9).

front of the people? It is customary to attribute the lack of assertiveness to the woman. The story of Cana seems to contradict this cliché.

Miriam, the mother, found herself between Jesus' question ("What is there between me and you, woman?") and the servants. The way this "woman" spoke to the servants suggests that they witnessed the conversation between Jesus and his mother. They witnessed Jesus' refusal on account of the hour not yet arrived. Yet she does not give in, and tells the servants: "Whatever he tells you, do it!" (John 2:5). The indeterminacy of the subject ("he") reinforces the idea that the servants were present. Jesus' disciples are spectators as well. Miriam, the mother, shows her tenacity, her assertiveness, because she knows Jesus, her son.[23]

What was he going to do? The servants did not know. It might look strange though that a guest should give them orders. They have no questions to ask. They have no doubts. They don't know why they have to fill the jars. And yet, they carry out Jesus' word because the woman told them to obey. This seems to have happened in a small circle, far from the general public. The master of ceremonies, as a matter of fact, did not know where the good wine came from, but the servants did (John 2:9). The actual target of this first sign, we learn at the end of the narrative, is the disciples of Jesus, for it is for them that the glory of Jesus is made manifest since when they saw it, they believed (John 2:11).[24] It is perhaps not insignificant to note that at the foot of the cross, through Jesus' mediation, the beloved disciple and the mother of Jesus become "son" and "mother" (John 19:26–27).[25] Here again, Jesus addresses his mother by calling her "woman" (John 19:26: γύναι, ἴδε ὁ υἱός σου). Since it was through her mediation that the glory of Jesus was manifested, the disciples/servants, then and now, learn that it is by allowing the woman to take her place in the management of the community that their mission will manifest God's glory.[26]

The Manifestation of Divinity in the Context of the Covenant

Both narratives are told against a covenantal background. In the Numbers account, Moses, Aaron, and Miriam are committed to serving the people of the covenant that has just been made at Sinai. YHWH is responsible for his people. The servants he has chosen are supposed to reassure his people. Therefore, the trial at Meribah, like all the trials in the desert, is intended to demonstrate the holiness of YHWH. The servants are the first to show the path to the people. The fact that, despite their imperfect

23. Brown, "Roles of Women," 698, shows that Jesus is careful not to treat Mary as *his* mother but the mother of the "Beloved Disciple" because what matters for him is the discipleship.

24. Brown, *Gospel of John*, 105, noticed an evolution on the theme of the disciples' faith: it began in John 1:37, then gets affirmed in 1:50, and fulfilled in 2:11.

25. See Moloney, *Gospel of John*, 65–74.

26. Brown, "Roles of Women," 699, calls women in the Fourth Gospel "first-class" disciples based on the fact that Jesus loved Martha and Mary, he treated Mary Magdalene as his "own" in calling by her "name," and women were the first to see him when he rose from the dead.

obedience, YHWH manifests his holiness to his people by showing them that he is capable of saving them attests that his promise to his people does not depend on mediatory figures. The manifestation of his holiness assures the Israelites that their God will not fail to protect them. Thus, the miracle of the water that gushes from the rock, something humanly unthinkable, becomes the sign that he is present among his people.

In the Cana story, the initiative of Jesus' mother takes place in a nuptial context.[27] This human covenant symbolizes the covenant between God and humanity. The manifestation of Jesus' glory is affirmed in John 2:11 as the beginning of the signs (ἀρχὴν τῶν σημείων).[28] As stated above, the sign points to something beyond human capacity. And thus, it reveals God's presence in the midst of humanity. As long noticed by Brown, John 2–4 describes the "replacement of Jewish institutions and religious views." So, God's presence here surpasses that of Kadesh because Jesus' glory reveals his divinity. Jesus, the mother's son, becomes the visible face of the invisible God. God's presence becomes proximity, and his mediation becomes immediacy. It is the result of Miriam's tenacious faith.

Returning to the role of Miriam, the audience of John's account also becomes aware of the quality of the bond between the "sister" or "mother." The fact that Jesus constantly calls his mother "woman," and that she is found at crucial moments in the Johannine Gospel (beginning in John 2 and ending in John 19), invites us to deepen our understanding of the role of the woman in the life and mission of Jesus and the disciples. What the disciples of Jesus contemplated was the whole scene of the miracle of Cana: the water changed into wine, of course, but also the role played by the mother or the woman, the obedience of the servants to the word not only of Jesus but also of Miriam, the mother of Jesus. For, in the end, it is she or her word that instigated the first sign.

CONCLUSION

The Old Testament stories are not always at the background of the Gospels' aural audience since Jesus' time. This brief intertextual study of John 2 and Numbers 20 has served to show the importance of keeping both Testaments related as we listen to stories from one or the other, for they are constantly in dialogue with each other. Better still, the enigmas of each narrative are illuminated in the light of the other. Thus, the sister of Moses, named Miriam, becomes the hollow figure of the mother of Jesus, unnamed in the Fourth Gospel. This name gap is filled by the Synoptics, however, from which we know that Jesus' mother was called Mary or Miriam. Thus, the Cana story in John 2 is open to its many echoes in the Old Testament through the great symbols

---

27. Moloney, *Gospel of John*, 66, highlights the "initiative" of the mother of Jesus (John 2:3–5) and parallels it to the "initiative" of Jesus (John 2:6–10).

28. Zumstein, *L'évangile selon saint Jean*, 99.

of the wedding feast and the wine, in an explicit way. The link between Miriam, the sister (Num 20), and Miriam, the mother (John 2), deserves to be explained in order to enrich our understanding of the Scriptures.

This study invites us, in an oblique way, to take the Christian canon in the totality of its reading. The fathers of the church postulated that the New is hidden in the Old and that the Old becomes manifest in the New. However, we realise that the New does not only make the Old explicit. It also receives insights from it, provided the aural audience is familiar with the Old, which it presupposes. Thus, we have seen a woman in the trio leadership of Israel in the desert: Moses, Aaron, and Miriam. The absence of women in our Christian communities' leadership is not primarily a problem of social justice. It reminds us that the church as a body grows when the charisms are allowed to operate (1 Cor 12; cf. Rom 12).[29] As we have seen, the role that Miriam, sister or mother, plays in the stories I examined helped the other servants see human needs, listen, and obey in all things the voice of God (YHWH and Jesus Christ). Decades ago, M. Masenya pointed out, "Teresa Okure argues that African women are aware that the Bible is basically a community book. Its message is addressed to both women and men who together form the community of God's people and who together must form the community of its interpretation."[30]

BIBLIOGRAPHY

Aichele, George, and Gary A. Philips. "Introduction: Exegesis, Eisegesis, Intergesis." *Semeia* 69–70 (1995) 7–18.

Brown, Raymond, E. "Roles of Women in the Fourth Gospel." *Theological Studies* 36, no. 4 (1975) 688–99

———. *The Gospel According to John (I–XII)*. AYB 29. Garden City, NY: Doubleday 1966.

Gray, George B. *A Critical and Exegetical Commentary on Numbers*. International Critical Commentary. New York: C. Scribner's Sons, 1903.

Haenchen, Ernst, Robert Walter Funck, and Ulrich Bussse. *John: A Commentary on the Gospel of John*. Hermeneia. Philadelphia: Fortress, 1984.

Irudayaraj, Dominic. "Micah." In *Jerome Biblical Commentary for the Twenty-First Century*, 1083–92. Edited by J. J. Collins, Gina Hens-Piazza, Barbara Reid OP, and Donald Senior CP. 3rd fully revised edition. London: T&T Clark, 2022.

Lauderville, D. "Numbers." In In *Jerome Biblical Commentary for the Twenty-First Century*, 310–35. Edited by J. J. Collins, Gina Hens-Piazza, Barbara Reid OP, and Donald Senior CP. 3rd fully revised edition. London: T&T Clark, 2022.

Little, Edmund. *Echoes of the Old Testament*. Paris: Gabalda, 1998.

---

29. The newly promulgated Constitution *Predicate Evangelium* (2022) opens the way to that new understanding of what it means to be a community of Christ's disciples in line with Paul's teaching to the Galatians (Gal 3:28).

30. Masenya, "African Womanist Hermeneutics," 149–55 (quotation on 153–54); Okure, "Feminist Interpretations in Africa," 78.

Lutgehetmann, Walter. *Die Hochzeit von Kana (Joh 2, 1-11): Zu Ursprung und Deutung einer Wundererzählung im Rahmen johanneischer Redaktionsgeschichte.* Biblische Untersuchungen 20. Regensburg: Friedrich Pustet, 1990.

Masenya, Madipoane J. "African Womanist Hermeneutics: A Suppressed Voice from South Africa Speaks." *Journal of Feminist Studies in Religion* 11, no. 1 (1995) 149-55.

Milgrom, Jacob. *Numbers. The JPS Torah Commentary.* Philadelphia: Jewish Publication Society, 1990.

Moloney, Francis. *The Gospel of John.* Sacra Pagina. Collegeville, MN: Liturgical Press 1998.

Okure, Teresa. *Johannine Approach to Mission: Contextual Study of John 4:1-42.* WUNT 2/31. Tübingen: Mohr Siebeck, 1988.

———. "Jesus and the Samaritan Woman (Jn 4:1-42) in Africa." *Theological Studies* 70 (2009) 401-18.

———. "Das Neue Testament und die Barmherzigkeit." *Concilium* 53, no. 4 (2017) 385-93.

Schulz, Alfons. "Das Wunder zu Kana im Lichte des Alten Testaments." *Biblische Zeitschrift* 16 (1922-1924) 93-96.

Tull, Patricia K. "Intertextuality and the Hebrew Scriptures." *Current Research in Biblical Studies* 8 (2000) 59-90.

Von Wahlde, Urban C. "John." In *Jerome Biblical Commentary for the Twenty-First Century*, 1378-1444. Edited by J. J. Collins, Gina Hens-Piazza, Barbara Reid OP, and Donald Senior CP. 3rd fully revised edition. London: T&T Clark, 2022.

Zumstein, Jean. *L'évangile selon saint Jean (1-12).* Commentaire du Nouveau Testament Iva. Genève: Labor & Fides, 2014.

———. *La mémoire revisitée : études johanniques.* Genève : Labor et Fides, 2017.

CHAPTER 3

Another Look at Mission through the Witness of the Israelite Servant Girl

(2 Kgs 5:1–19)

EMMANUEL O. NWAORU

1. INTRODUCTION

The miraculous narratives of the Elisha-Cycle are dotted with the activities of secondary minor characters, frequently identified as servants. Their appearances in the narrative are abrupt and short-lived; but their roles, especially their counsels, are essentially strategic and often lead to a successful result when they are adhered to. More importantly is that they cause the beneficiary to encounter the prophet Elisha or his activity in order to obtain the hoped-for miracle/relief. Prominent among these minor characters is the unnamed young captive Israelite girl that serves the wife of Naaman, the high-ranking army chief of Syria.[1] She is further distinguished from other minor characters by her characterization. She is female (*naʿărāh*), young/little (*qěṭannāh*), and captive (2 Kgs 5:2). Although her gender, rank, and status may be regarded as inconsequential, she is introduced alongside Naaman at the beginning of 2 Kings 5, a subunit in the Elisha story known as the "Story of Naaman." Her role is remarkable and her witnessing effective (2 Kgs 5:3–5).

Nobody had an inkling of what missionary dimension the witnessing of this captive maid would be until it opened doors for the process of Naaman's healing and subsequent conversion. There was no outright preaching of any doctrine, but her courage

---

1. Apart from being a Syrian army general, a man of great authority, position, popularity, and prestige, he is also a man of valor and conquest, a national military hero through whose hands Syria recorded military success upon success, including over Israel.

to bear witness to the healing/salvific power possessed by YHWH's representative, "the prophet who is in Samaria" (v. 3), performed the miracle of Naaman's healing and conversion. After all, the goal of every genuine missionary endeavour is conversion, a conversion perceived not just as a change of membership from one denomination or religious body to the other, but as a radical turnaround from one's (religious) beliefs and practices. Two elements are always prominent in every conversion: profession of faith and renunciation of sins. Those two elements are evidently realized in Naaman when he followed the advice/witness of the Israelite servant girl. One notices that Naaman, the Syrian leprous army general, moved by his healing experience, professed faith in YHWH, the God of Israel, and confessed his sins (2 Kgs 5:14–15, 18).

It is because the witnessing of this servant girl meets the ultimate goal of mission that her role in the narrative becomes a missionary endeavour of a sort. This has necessitated naming the narrative variously such as "Proselyte Narrative,"[2] "Conversion Story,"[3] etc. It is within such a background that this essay will be piecing together through close reading what is missionary about the role of this servant girl, a minor character in the narrative. There is no doubt too that a thoughtful analysis of this text with diverse structures and elements will help us to understand better the essence of good interaction between master/mistress and servant/maid. It is hoped that the exposition of the pivotal role the Israelite servant girl played in the conversion of Naaman will lead to a rethinking of what sets the parameter for missionary activity in our context.

2. MISSION AS CONCEPT

In common parlance, the word "mission" is understood as witnessing. It means giving testimony by word or deed to one's religious faith. In mission one attests to the reality of one's religious experience. In a classical sense, however, mission as its Latin root (*mittere, missio*) suggests has to do with "sending." Hence a "normal" missionary activity involves due process—that is, a competent authority sending/employing designated candidates for mission with a well-defined and proper method. In other words, official sending (John 20:21–23) and commissioning (Matt 10:5–15; 28:16–20) are characteristic of a typical mission. As Hellwig puts it, mission "refers to the official designation of individuals or congregations to carry the Good News and saving presence of Christ in his Church beyond the boundaries of present membership."[4] Any such designated candidate is expected to be an expert witness—one who has knowledge of the subject matter, not normally possessed by an average person. The fact that the Old and New Testaments occasionally narrate expansionist religious missionary activities which took place without any formal sending out, or formal planning and

---

2. This designation is precisely limited to vv. 17–19a. Cf. Jones, *1 and 2 Kings*, II, 412.
3. See the title Cogan and H. Tadmor gave to 2 Kgs 5 in *II Kings*, 64.
4. Hellwig, *The Modern Catholic Encyclopedia*, 575.

strategy,⁵ seems to justify Coffele's view that "mission" in its technical sense is not the primary concern of the Old Testament and in Judaism.⁶

It is perhaps within the context of informal and unofficial missionary endeavour that our text makes sense to the reader. For almost everything about the narrative stands in reversal to a *typical* mission story. There is no outright exposition of any doctrine by the servant girl; and there is also no thought-out plan to expand Israelite faith beyond its boundaries. It was just enough to witness to the fact that there was God's saving power in Israel and the miracle of Naaman's healing and conversion took place. Thus, the witnessing of the servant girl can be said to have defiled all due processes and yet accomplished the ultimate goal of mission. Her mission is a counter-voice to the orthodox and traditional view on mission and missionary activity.

3. THE SERVANT GIRL IN NAAMAN'S NARRATIVE (2 KGS 5:1-19)

The role—nay, the missionary activity—of the little Israelite girl in this essay cannot be fully appreciated unless one understands her background and portrayals in the narrative. And this is well-articulated in two verses (2 Kgs 5:2-3) that state who she is and what she said, respectively. Thus, verse 2 in form of an exposition states: "The Arameans had gone out in bands, and had taken captive a little girl from the land of Israel; and she served Naaman's wife." The fact that v. 1 introduces Naaman as a Syrian army chief and v. 2a talks of military raid and v. 2b of taking captive situates the background of the narrative within the conflict between Syria/Aram and Israel, with the Arameans raiding and ravaging the land and people of Israel (cf. 2 Kgs 6:23-31). In other words, the little Israelite girl is a victim of conflict and aggression she knows very little about. She is a symbol of an innocent sufferer and national misery. Beyond being a captive, she is characterized as little/small⁷ and identified as a girl, indeed the *only* female among the other minor characters. From all viewpoints, she is disadvantaged not only because she is *little* in terms of stature and perhaps age, but also because *qĕṭannāh* occasionally evokes the idea of weakness and inconsequentiality (cf. 1 Kgs 2:20; 1 Sam 9:21; 15:17; also Isa 11:6; 60:22). No wonder hers is seen as the role of a minor secondary character in the narrative!

But in reality, she is a protagonist in the narrative and, indeed, the main character of this essay, the first to speak in the narrative. Her words to her mistress, "If only my lord were with the prophet who is in Samaria! He would cure him of his leprosy" (v. 3), set other events in motion, determining also their end. Although this servant girl shares two life conditions (suffering and servanthood) with Naaman the army

---

5. Cf. Num 11:26-29; Mark 9:38-40; Luke 9:49-50; Acts 8:4-8; 11:19-22.
6. Cf. Coffele, "Mission," 712.
7. This is the only instance where the designation *nacă[set caron over a]rāh qĕṭannāh* ("little girl") is used in OT.

commander,[8] she certainly refused to be cowed by her enslaved condition or remain embittered by fear and resentment. On the contrary, she is sensitive to the suffering of her master (a fellow sufferer) and his need for help. Moreover, she sees her problems of life as opportunities to bear witness to her faith. Granted that she is captive and small, the Israelite girl proves herself highly knowledgeable and wise. She knows not only about Elisha and his whereabouts, "the prophet who is in Samaria," but also with certainty[9] his approachability and healing capabilities. It is from this insight that Naaman was able to locate Elisha for healing (vv. 8–14) and for conversion (vv. 15–19).

4. HER WITNESSING AND ITS MISSIOLOGICAL VALUE

There is no better paradigm in the Old Testament with which to assess the efficacy and missiological value of witnessing than in the role of the Israelite captive girl in relation to the healing and conversion of Naaman, the leprous Syrian army chief. Surprisingly, her role has scarcely been mentioned in commentaries as instrumental to the conversion of Naaman and, so, has not been given the missiological value it deserves. Yet the words of this little servant girl are characteristically testimonial and prophetic in a foreign land. For if she had not spoken up, Naaman would never have been directed to Elisha, the man of God, for healing and consequent conversion. Without being named a missionary or prophetess in the classical sense of the words, the young girl carried out a function proper to missionaries and prophets. She spread by word of mouth—or rather proclaimed—the "mighty acts of God," which would resound normally through the instrumentality of God's prophet. This unnamed captive maid has by her singular act implicitly spread Jewish faith and the message of God's saving power in Israel, thus fulfilling the purpose and mission for which God had chosen Israel *ab initio* to be the source for making his name known among all the nations.

The efficacy and power of her witnessing can only be measured by the urgency with which her superiors, her mistress and her master Naaman, and even the king of Syria accepted and executed her judicious suggestion (vv. 4–5). A letter was written by the king, and Naaman at the end submitted himself to the God of Israel. Their prompt acceptance and execution of the advice in their respective ways shows that the little girl's words are not only generative but also predictive. They brought about lasting changes in Naaman's perception. First and foremost, Israel was no longer seen as the land of the enemy but rather a land from which he could seek healing, offer gifts, and fulfill diplomatic propriety.[10] A geographical movement that would have been almost

8. Naaman suffers from leprosy and is designated as servant of the king of Aram (v. 1); likewise, the Israelite servant girl suffers from servitude and captivity (v. 2) and is the maidservant of Naaman's wife (v. 2)

9. This is implied in the interjection 'aḥălê ("if only") in v. 3.

10. Moreover, Naaman has to visit the king of Israel under whose authority he and the king of Syria imagined the prophet was. See Walter, "The Major Import of Minor Characters in the Elisha-Story Cycle," 87–88.

impossible to imagine becomes a necessity at the recommendation of a maidservant. Secondly, there is a visible transformation of Naaman's character and attitude toward life. Naaman learns to be humble, obedient, patient, and even grateful, following the course the Israelite servant girl charted for him: "If only my lord were in the presence of the prophet who is in Samaria! He would cure him of his leprosy" (2 Kgs 5:3).

It is remarkable that Naaman experiences not only a profound outer but also inner transformation. It is such an intrinsic transformation, engendered by efficacious witnessing, that results in Naaman's reversal of fortune. He was truly set free[11] from his leprosy, and his leprous flesh "returned" (*šûḇ*)[12] like the flesh of a small boy (*naʿar qāṭōn*), and he was clean (v. 14). Above all, his concept of the deity changed completely, as he confessed, "Now I know that there is no God in all the earth except in Israel" (v. 15).[13] Naaman, who was angered by Elisha's seeming indifference and lack of propriety on his arrival (vv. 9–11), robbed himself of all dignity to name himself the prophet's servant (v. 15).[14] He was at last contented to go back to Aram conquered by Israel's religion and converted to YHWH at the testimony of a servant girl.

Naaman's quick conversion may not only be attributed to his leprous state, a crisis condition that demanded his seeking prompt solution,[15] but also to the fact that faith comes from hearing. As McKnight rightly observed, "Conversion does not take place on passive humans, rather, it leads to a widespread change in perception."[16] Naaman only truly became himself when he learned in humility to give himself to another[17] and to acknowledge and follow the one who interpreted the will of God for him, not minding whether they were of rank or not. Naaman's first reaction as he receives his faith is of great importance. It is the reaction of one who is led out of

---

11. We recall here the initial request made by the king of Syria on Naaman's behalf, asking the king of Israel "to remove, take away" (*'sph*) Naaman's leprosy (vv. 3, 5–6)—in other words, to set Naaman free (cf. Gen 30:23; Ps 85:4; contrast Jer 16:5).

12. It is remarkable that the verb *šûḇ* is frequently used for repentance/conversion in the Bible, especially in the prophetic tradition as in Hos 3:5; 6:1; 7:10; 11:5; 14:2; Isa 6:10; 10:22; Jer 3:7, 12, 14, 22; 4:1; 5:3; 1 Kgs 8:33, 48; etc. See *BDB* 997; esp. #6, c–d. One has to appreciate this word even more in this context where it occurs as the end result of the act of removing (*'sph*) Naaman's leprosy as requested by the king of Syria (vv. 3, 5–6). Thus, the healing process of Naaman has a unique theological dimension. It combines the idea of setting free (salvation?) as implied by *'sph* and conversion expressed by *šûḇ*. J. Nissen is right to remark that healing is concerned with the restoration of the fullness of human life in those who have lost it. Cf. "Matthew, Mission and Method," 77.

13. For a similar change in perspectives, see also Gen 26:28; Exod 18:8–11; Num 22–24; Josh 2:9–11; 2 Kgs 10:18–24; Jdt 5:5–21.

14. The expression *cmd liphnê* ("to stand before") used earlier in the verse may also signify "to serve"; cf. 1 Sam 16:21; Jer 15:1.

15. According to McKnight, in his, "Missions and Conversion Theory," 118–139; 124. "Conversion doesn't take place without a crisis." The crisis which prompts a person to seek resolution may be massive or small.

16. McKnight, "Missions and Conversion Theory," 125.

17. McKnight, "Missions and Conversion Theory," 133, presupposes this in his quoting the passage, "I became my own only when I gave myself to Another" from *The Letters of C. S. Lewis*, W. Lewis and W. Hooper, 432.

ignorance. His words "Now I know that (*hinnēh-nā' yāda‘tî kî*) . . ." (v.15) are in accord with expressions often used when, as it were, scales fell off the eyes of a foreigner in recognition of the truth about Israel's God, Israel's religion and prophet (cf. Exod 18:11; Josh 2:9; 1 Kgs 17:24; also Isa 45:3).[18] The use of this formula is understable in the case of Naaman, who could have probably sought cure from Aramean prophets and physicians[19] and offered prayers for healing through priests in the temple of Rimmon, where he had customarily accompanied his master (5:18) to no avail, and now realised that his cure came about "according to the word of the man of God" (v.14) and testimony of an Israelite captive girl. In other words, conversion is a process of leading one out of ignorance.

Beyond Naaman's profession of faith in YHWH is his public renunciation of any act that might militate against his worship of the true God. Also of great value is his asking for pardon of sins (v. 18) and making a firm resolution never again to "offer burnt offering or sacrifice to any god except the Lord" (v. 17b). This singular act marks out Naaman's profession of faith from any other. It is a unique instance where a foreigner prays for forgiveness for the worship of foreign gods.[20] In all this, Naaman meets for all time the concerns of the Deuteronomic law, which proscribes all forms of worship that are not in consonance with the worship of YHWH.[21]

Except for her nurtured faith, it is doubtful that this little captive girl may have intended to provoke such a quick response from all who heard her testimony. But missionary activities are never short of surprises and ironies. Here the master/superior of the house receives and obeys the advice of a servant girl of the house. This seeming irony has an important missiological implication—namely, that every credible witnessing, like that of this maidservant, exposes God's kind desire to save and grant healing/salvation to all, as it is evident in Naaman's case.

5. ISSUES AND CHALLENGES IN CURRENT APPROACH TO MISSION

The basics of mission demand, more than anything else, a mediary of God's creative word. For that reason, "mission" should not be conceived as something classified for those up there, or tied to organized missionary endeavors through congregations, crusaders, etc. Rather, it can always be accomplished by person(s) taken by God to carry out his purpose, notwithstanding their gender, rank, and status. In other words, the role of those who are thought not to be in the mainstream, especially those at the margin, like the servant girl of this essay, must not be underestimated as collaborators

---

18. Mitchell, *Together in the Land,* 162; also, Frank Anthony Spina, "Rahab," 1125.

19. Cf. Davis, in http://www.intouch.org/myintouch/mighty/naaman Accessed 22/12/2021

20. Here is the only instance in which the verb *slḥ* is used in reference to the performance of a foreign religious rite.

21. See, Noth, *The Deuteronomistic History*, 137.

and missioners in their own right. From below they give the solidarity that faith requires to blossom to fruition and without which conversion would be impossible. This is particularly true of the mission of this servant girl through her incisive and persuasive advice (v. 3). She showed absolute confidence that the power of her own witness would bear fruit and accomplish its purpose (vv. 3, 14–19).

To be successful, mission demands absolute collaboration. This is evident in the processes through which the witness of the servant girl passed to yield its final result. In fact, a chain of collaborative actions was involved, starting from her mistress and her husband, Naaman (v. 4), to the king of Syria (v. 5) and the king of Israel (vv. 6–7), to the prophet Elijah (vv. 8–9) and his messenger (v. 10), and to Naaman's servants (vv. 11–13). Unfortunately, the contacts from the echelon of society did not pay off much. For instance, the king of Syria thought he would facilitate the healing of Naaman through a high-level contact with the king of Israel. But the letter he wrote to the king of Israel in favor of Naaman nearly back-clashed and hindered the healing process and the conversion of Naaman (2 Kgs 5:5–7). This is because of the unfriendly relations of Syria and Israel. Thanks to the timely intervention of Elisha, which saved the dangerous situation. Rather, the overwhelming success recorded on Naaman's healing and conversion came from the marginal actors, the collaborating servants. This, indeed, is a subtle critique against the attitude of those who think they matter in the episode—the kings—and those who may reason like them today.

Obviously, the fruits of mission may come not without great challenges. Such challenges are experienced in the course of Naaman's conversion, especially in his refusal to cooperate with the prophet (vv. 11–12). This was provoked by Elisha's refusal to address this man of honor, position, and popularity in person but by proxy, through a messenger (vv. 9–10a). Thanks again to the timely intervention of Naaman's servants, which prepared the soil for the word of the little Israelite servant girl and that of the man of God to bear fruit (v. 14). Hence, mission requires patience, persuasion, and thoughtful logic on the part of the missioner in dealing with the prospective convert and not coercion. In fact, only a few missionaries would imagine today that their activities would be successful without their physical presence. But our text debunks this understanding and challenges us on what actually makes mission successful. It demonstrates that neither the healing nor the consequent conversion of Naaman depended on the physical presence of the prophet or the little girl whose witness initiated the process, but on God's power and his grace to win people, even foreigners, to himself.

6. LESSONS FOR OUR CONTEXT

There are certain elements in the narrative and, especially in the role of this little Israelite girl, that will compel one to look again at the mechanics of mission today. Granted that her witnessing is unique and indispensable, it could not in isolation result in Naaman's healing and conversion. As we have earlier remarked, there are chains of actions leading to conversion, demonstrating that mission demands lateral thinking. The process does no longer need to be rigid, conservative, and opinionated. Likewise, the entire process, as in the case of Naaman's conversion, exposes that conversion is not always automatic and hitch-free; it may take time to mature and often gradually within the community of believers in their cultural context. Moreover, it shows that conversion is not just a matter of one single religious experience but an enduring relationship of the convert with God. Any meaningful missionary activity has to ensure that the convert experiences such a lasting relationship beyond his/her "initial encounter."[22]

In doing so, the missioner must keep in view God's liberty to choose whatever means he wants in bringing healing or/and salvation to whomever he wishes. For the means and object of God's salvation are beyond human comprehension.[23] They are oftentimes very unfamiliar, even as God continually remains at work to lead people to salvation, no matter their life situation. We have noticed the "exhibition" of divine liberty in making the witness of a servant girl result in the phenomenal conversion and admission of Naaman, a foreigner, into the community of YHWH worshipers. The admission was without preconditions (cf. Ruth 1–4; Mal 1:11), and Naaman was not required to perform any set down rite of conversion, such as circumcision, as would be demanded in the postexilic period. No set of laws of any kind was imposed upon him. Instead, Elisha sent him back to his own heathen environment and placed him and his faith under the guidance of YHWH, in whose service he had pledged himself to continue to be (vv. 15–19).

Elisha's response to Naaman's request (v. 17) is considered today a paradigm for profound missionary insight and concern.[24] The response challenges those on mission and, indeed, the church to be ready to give urgent and honest answers to matters of genuine concern to the missioned. In this regard, individual missionaries are to be trained in inculturational principles to enable them to address thorny issues relating to divine worship and the culture of the people. For instance, must neophytes/converts in mission land continue to separate themselves from their cultural practices and beliefs in order to be "born again" into "Western" Christianity rather than in Christ? It is remarkable that Naaman's conversion story is one of those instances in the Old Testament where the worship of the gods on the part of non-Israelites is presented without being judgemental (v. 18; contrast 2 Kgs 19:37; Ps 66:4). This is not an admission of polytheism; on the contrary, it is the opposite. It is an affirmation that there is only one God, no matter who the other nations claim to worship.[25]

22. Cf. Kraft, *Christianity in Culture,* 330; also Chew, "I am Kneeling On the Outside, but I am Standing On the inside: Another Look at the Story of Naaman through the Lenses of Kraft," 69.
23. See, Nwaoru, *Divine Plan versus Human Ignorance,* 2003.
24. Cf. von Rad, *Old Testament Theology* II, 32.
25. See Bratcher, "Naaman, Dirt, and Territorial Gods: The Canonical Functions of 2 Kings

Today, missioners have incorporated healing as an essential missionary activity. The narrative indicates that the power of Elisha to heal (2 Kgs 5:8) is integrated into the process of mission. But to Naaman's dismay, Elisha did not in any way behave like an exorcist (v. 11). There was neither gesture over the affected area nor any expressed ritual of some sort, yet Naaman's leprosy was cured because it was the man of God who provided the prescription for it.[26] Elisha's method of healing contrasts greatly with the excesses and exuberances of the missionary miracle workers of today. Many create the impression that the power of healing lies in the volume of shouting and quaking generated in their prayer houses and "healing crusades/arenas." The narrative projects the contrary for our caution. It underscores the fact that a missionary is not coterminous with the word or mighty acts of God which he/she proclaims. That is why the healing power of God's word remains effectual, not minding that it is delivered through Elisha's messenger.

There is need for the present-day missionary agents to curb their ego and self-glory. It is instructive that the little Israelite girl is neither celebrated nor even mentioned again in the narrative after the success story that follows her witnessing. Instead, her role, like that of the prophet Elisha, is played down in order to highlight the role of God as the perfecter and finisher of every process of healing and conversion. All attention is turned to God through his prophet as the central and ultimate agent who brings all missionary endeavour to a successful end. It would be "another kind of mission" in our time if, after a successful mission, the agent adopted the attitude of the psalmist and said: "Not to us, O Lord, not to us, but to your name give glory" (Ps 115:1a).

7. CONCLUSION

After a hard look at the story built on the witnessing of the little Israelite servant girl and its aftermath, one can say it is a tale of another kind of mission. The witnessing of the little servant girl is a unique act of mediation of salvation (healing) and conversion and, therefore, a missionary endeavour. It is a kind of mission that requires no classified agents—those up there, or tied only to organized missionary endeavors. Rather it shows that mission can always be accomplished by person(s) taken by God to carry out his purpose, notwithstanding their gender, rank, and status. What counts supreme is that the purpose of mission is reached—namely, conversion to the true God and a frantic effort to reform one's life.

It is also a tale of a mission that inspires a new approach. As the interjection "if only" at the beginning of the servant girl's counsel suggests (v. 3), her witnessing has more an air of conviction and advocacy than of aggressive and militant "campaign" that often characterizes mission today. What the servant girl deposits in her witness

---

5:17–19 at http://www.cresourcei.org/naaman Accessed 21/12/2021

26. Cf. Avalos, *Illness and Health Care in the Ancient Near East*, 264.

led Naaman to discover the true God and freely profess his faith in God and reconcile with his environment. It is hoped that the present-day missioners would conceive mission from the perspective of her witnessing—namely, that mission is a process that revolves around people moving gradually from ignorance and misconceptions to genuine knowledge of God. Such an understanding will be a credible way to check not only the militant and hasty approach to mission but also the danger double allegiance poses to many religious adherents today.

BIBLIOGRAPHY

Avalos, H. *Illness and Health Care in the Ancient Near East: The Role of the Temple in Greece, Mesopotamia and Israel*. Atlanta: Scholars Press, 1995.

Begg, C. T. "2 Kings." In *The New Jerome Biblical Commentary*, 10:46. Edited by R. E. Brown, et al. London: Geoffrey Chapman, 1993.

Botterweck, G. J., and H. Ringgren, eds. *Theologisches Wörterbuch zum Alten Testament* (*TWAT*) VII. Stuttgart: W. Kohlhammer Verlag, 1993.

Brown, F., S. R. Driver, and C.A. Briggs. *The New Brown, Driver, and Briggs Hebrew and English Lexicon of the Old Testament* (*BDB*). London: Oxford University Press, 1907.

Coffele, G., "Mission." In *Dictionary of Fundamental Theology*, 712. Edited by R. Latourelle and R. Fisichella. New York: Crossroad, 1994.

Cogan, M., and H. Tadmor. *II Kings. A New Translation with Introduction and Commentary*. AB 11. New York: Doubleday, 1988.

Eichrodt, W., and Trans J. A. Baker. *Theology of the Old Testament* II. Philadelphia: Westminster Press, 1967.

Farmer, W. R., et al., eds. *The International Bible Commentary*. Collegeville, MN: The Liturgical Press, 1998.

Gesenius, H. F. W., E. Kautzsch, and A. E. Cowley, eds., *Gesenius' Hebrew Grammar*. Oxford: Oxford University Press, 1910.

Gray, J. *I & II Kings, A Commentary*. Philadelphia: Westminster, 1963.

Hellwig, M. K. *The Modern Catholic Encyclopedia*. Collegeville, MN: Liturgical Press, 1994.

Jones, G. H. *1 and 2 Kings II*. NCBC Grand Rapids: Eerdmans, 1984.

McKnight, S. "Missions and Conversion Theory." *Mission Studies* XX-2, 40 (2003) 118–39.

Mitchell, G. *Together in the Land: A Reading of the Book of Joshua*. JSOTSup 134. Sheffield: JSOT Press, 1993.

Nissen, J. "Matthew, Mission and Method." *IRM* XCI, 360 (2002) 73–86.

———. "Testament in Mission: The Use of the New Methodological and Hermeneutical Reflections." *Mission Studies* 21, no. 2 (2004) 167–99.

Noth, M. *The Deuteronomistic History*. JSOTSup 15. Sheffield: JSOT Press, 1991.

Nwaoru, E. O. *Divine Plan versus Human Ignorance: A Biblical Perspective*. Nimo: Rex Charles & Patrick, 2003.

Rad, G. von. *Old Testament Theology II*. London: SCM Press, 1965.

Robinson, J. *The Second Book of Kings*. Cambridge: Cambridge Press, 1976.

Spina, F.A. "Rahab." In *New International Dictionary of Old Testament Theology and Exegesis* 4: 1121–26. Edited by W. A. VanGemeren. Carlisle: Paternoster, 1997.

CHAPTER 4

The Missionary Spirit of Psalm 67

MARY JEROME OBIORAH, IHM

INTRODUCTION

In a religious setting, the meaning of the term "mission" (from Latin *mission,* "a sending off, sending away, a letting go," and the verb *mittere* "to send, to let go, to dispatch") is primarily to send persons to communicate content of received faith to those who are yet to know it and make it their own. Its tripartite dimension consists of the sender, the person sent, and the message. The objective is invariably to transmit the faith so that another will come to know and adhere to its content and tenets. Among Christians, "The ultimate purpose of mission is none other than to make men share in the communion between the Father and the Son in their Spirit of love."[1] In the Old Testament, Israel as the chosen people of God believe they have a mission in the world: to proclaim the knowledge of the true God so that all nations of the earth will know and fear him. "Israel is to be, before the nations, the 'witness' to the one God."[2] To fear God in this context is "adoring reverence for the transcendent and glorious mystery of God."[3]

These two dimensions (to know and fear God) of mission's objective are found in Psalm 67, chosen for this study. "It is a brief but compelling text, which opens out on an immense horizon, to embrace in spirit the peoples of the earth."[4] The choice

---

1. *The Catechism of the Catholic Church* no.850.
2. The Pontifical Biblical Commission, *The Jewish People and their Sacred Scriptures,* no. 33.
3. John Paul II, *Psalms and Canticles,* 185.
4. John Paul II, *Psalms and Canticles,* 184.

for Psalm 67 is largely informed by its openness to other nations and the inherent desire that these nations will come to praise God. This is articulated in a refrain occurring twice in a text of only seven verses in its English version. Usually, a refrain encapsulates the message of the poem where it is found. The refrain in Psalm 67, *yôdûkā 'ammîm ĕlōhîm yôdûkā 'ammîm kullām* ("let the peoples praise you, O God; let all the peoples praise you"), bears its meaning. "The extant text communicates the strong conviction that God is worthy of every nation's praise."[5] Therefore, all nations and peoples should know and fear him. This stresses an aspect of missionary activity which is a prayer that non-believers may come to believe.

Psalm 67 is an ancient poem with characteristic features of Hebrew poems. The literary method adopted in its study here takes into cognisance its poetic devices which the psalmist used to communicate its message. These devices and their functions are highlighted in the study, which is divided into three major parts: an investigation into the meaning of Psalm 67, a review of the place of this psalm in the life and mission of the church, and a brief reflection on its message in the context of Christian missionary mandate.

INSIGHT INTO PSALM 67

A study of an ancient poem like Psalm 67 takes into consideration the chronological gap between the composer and the first recipients and those of us who read this text today. This gap has generated many conjectures to specify the *Sitz im Leben* (life situation that gave rise to the composition of the text) and its literary genre. Some of these are mentioned here to elucidate the missionary orientation inherent in this poem.

So Much in Literary Techniques of Psalm 67

The English translation of Psalm 67 has seven verses because in the Hebrew version the superscription of the psalm is the first verse. The versification used in this study is according to the Hebrew text. One of the difficulties often encountered in the translation of Psalm 67, which invariably affects its interpretation, is choosing appropriate tenses for the finite verbs of its Hebrew text.[6] The translation in the *New Revised Standard Version* adopted mainly in this study is as follows:[7]

> [1] To the leader: with stringed instruments. A Psalm. A Song.
> [2] May God be gracious to us and bless us and make his face to shine upon us,
> Selah

---

5. Gerstenberger, *Psalms Part 2 and Lamentations*, 33.
6. Luurtsema, "Psalm 67."
7. The versification is according to the Hebrew text.

> ³ that your way may be known upon earth, your saving power among all nations.
> ⁴ Let the peoples praise you, O God; let all the peoples praise you.
> ⁵ Let the nations be glad and sing for joy, for you judge the peoples with equity and guide the nations upon earth. Selah
> ⁶ Let the peoples praise you, O God; let all the peoples praise you.
> ⁷ The earth has yielded its increase; God, our God, has blessed us.
> ⁸ May God continue to bless us; let all the ends of the earth revere him.

Discernable literary/poetic techniques employed by the author in conveying the theme of blessing are conspicuous at the beginning (v. 2) and at end (vv. 7–8). This forms an inclusio or envelope figure in the text. An inclusio is "the repetition of the same phrase or sentence at the beginning and end of a stanza or a poem."[8] It is only in these three verses that the psalmist addresses God in the third person. In the rest of the poem, the verbs and pronouns predicated of God are in the second person.[9] Furthermore, reading closely through this psalm, the "us" sentences are found only in these three verses, and the rest of the verses are the "they" sentences. This "they" refers to other nations and peoples other than the people of Israel; they are called in the text *gôyim*, "nations" (v. 3), *'ammîm*, "peoples" (2x in vv. 4, 6, and 1x in v. 5), and *lᵉ'ummîm*, "peoples" (2x in v. 5). The psalmist speaks about his nation with the theme of blessing at the two ends of the poem.

Psalm 67 is an example of a Hebrew poem where a refrain[10] plays an essential role in the structure of the text. It has a strict type of refrain in vv. 4 and 6 because there is no variation in the repeated words. The refrain in the text is stated in a staircase parallelism. This means that a sentence is started, interrupted by an epithet, then resumed and concluded without the epithet. In Hebrew the refrain reads: *yôdûkā 'ammîm ĕlōhîm yôdûkā 'ammîm kullām*. The sentence begins with *yôdûkā 'ammîm* ("let the peoples praise you"); before it is concluded, an epithet *ĕlōhîm* ("O God") is inserted. The sentence is resumed as at the beginning with *yôdûkā 'ammîm*; then a new word *kullām* ("all") is added to conclude it. Schematically, we have

> *yôdûkā 'ammîm* Let the peoples praise you,
> *ĕlōhîm* O God;
> *yôdûkā 'ammîm kullām* Let all the peoples praise you.

---

8. Watson, *Classical Hebrew Poetry*, 282–83.

9. The mixture of second and third persons is frequent in the psalms (e.g., Pss 9:6–13; 48; 66:1–12; 68; 78; 77:14; 89; 92; 97; 99).

10. This is "a block of verse which recurs more than once within a poem"; see Watson, *Classical Hebrew Poetry*, 295.

With this refrain occurring twice,[11] the psalm is often divided into three parts: vv. 2–4, 5–6, and 7–8.[12] The first verse is the superscription. However, having discovered that v. 2 has affinity with vv. 7–8, these verses will be explained as a unit, while vv. 3–6, which are also linked by "they" sentences and comprise the only part that refers to nations outside the people of Israel, will be considered separately.

The literary technique in vv. 7–8 is conspicuous. In the Hebrew text, the second part of v.v7 is *yᵉbārᵉkēnû ʾĕlōhîm ʾĕlōhênû* ("God, our God has blessed us"); v. 8 begins with the same phrase but without the word *ʾĕlōhênû* ("our God"). This device is called *anadiplosis*,[13] which is reduplication, the beginning of a sentence, line, or clause with the concluding, or any prominent, word of the one preceding. It is also called *terrace pattern*, which is a form of repetition where the last part of a line is repeated as the beginning of the next line. The function, just like many other types of repetition, is to emphasize the point being made. In the text, the emphasis is on the blessing received from God. There is also in these two verses the figure of duplication (*epizeuxis*), "when the words do not immediately succeed each other but are separated by one or more intervening words."[14] The intervening word between *yᵉbārᵉkēnû ʾĕlōhîm* repeated in vv. 7–8 is *ʾĕlōhênû* ("our God"), and it is the yoke that joins the repeated words.

Most verses of Psalm 67 are distich strophes; the only exception is v. 5, which is tristich. Verses 2, 3, and 7 have synonymous parallelism. The second and third stiches of v. 5 form a similar synonymous relationship. The import of this literary device will be explained in the close reading of this psalm in subsequent paragraphs. The second part of v. 8—that is, the last sentence of this psalm—contains a "they" sentence that resembles what we have in vv. 3–6, and an address to God in the third person. In Hebrew it is *wᵉyîrᵉʾû ʾōtô kol-ʾapsê-ʾāreṣ* ("let all the ends of the earth revere him"). This has the features of vv. 2, 7–8 in addressing God in the third person; it also aligns with vv. 3–6 in the use of "they" sentences. In addition to this, *kol-ʾapsê-ʾāreṣ* ("all the ends of the earth") calls to mind the words for other nations and peoples in vv. 3–6. This final sentence of Psalm 67 seems a well calculated conclusion because it relates to its two parts. Explanation of the two identified parts of this poem will elicit its message, the desire for mission, seen in its universalistic language. These two parts are vv. 2,7–8a and vv. 3–6, 8b.[15]

---

11. In the Catholic Liturgical Books, this refrain occurs again at the end of the psalm.

12. See, however, Amzallag, "Psalm 67 and the Cosmopolite Musical Worship of YHWH," 171–15, for a more sophisticated structural analysis of this psalm.

13. It is very common and a characteristic of Psalms of Ascents (Pss 120–134). Further examples are found in Isa 38:11; 1 Chr 12:33; Ps 96:12b–13. The function of this literary device is to link the components of a strophe or stanza. It serves to create tension, to denote duration in time, to express inevitability, and to help the poet improvise verse (see Watson, *Classical Hebrew Poetry*, 208–9).

14. Bullinger, *Figures of Speech Used in the Bible*, 189, 193.

15. Tate, *Psalms 51–100*, 156–57, has similar structure of Ps 67; he calls v. 2 initial supplication; vv. 3–6 hymnic core; vv. 7–8 concluding supplication.

Israel's Communal Prayer for Blessing (vv. 2, 7–8a)

The key word in these verses is the verb "to bless," which occurs three times, once in each of the verses. Grammatically, they all have the same form, *yᵉbārᵉkēnû*, and the subject is God called with the generic name *ʾĕlōhîm*, perhaps in view of the universalistic orientation of this psalm. It is the only divine name used in the text. Though *yᵉbārᵉkēnû* has the form of Hebrew imperfect conjugation expressing a future action or habitual, it can also have the connotation of a jussive employed in prayerful wishes.[16] This explains the translation "may God bless us" in v. 2b, and it harmonizes with the first verb (*yᵉḥānnēnû*, "may he [God] be gracious to us") of v. 2a. In v. 7 *yᵉbārᵉkēnû* does not have jussive meaning because of the verb (*nātᵉnāh*, "it [the earth] has given") that comes immediately after it. Thus, *yᵉbārᵉkēnû* bears the same tense "he [God] has blessed us." In v. 8a it has jussive meaning, "may God bless us." The NRSV adds an adverb, "continually," to it in order to clarify the meaning because God has already blessed them through the earth that yielded its fruit.

"May God be gracious to us and bless us" is the first prayer for blessing in Psalm 67. The first verb *yᵉḥānnēnû*, "may he [God] be gracious to us," is from *ḥānan*, which means to be gracious, to show favor. It is a special attribute of God to be gracious.[17] The adjective *ḥānnûn*, "graciousness," is almost exclusively predicated of YHWH in the Old Testament.[18] In his covenant with the people of Israel, the Lord introduced himself as a God of grace (cf. Exod 34:6). He grants favor, and he is also a demanding God who punishes offenders (Exod 34:7). The author of Psalm 67 asks for divine favor and blessing for his people. At the time of Israel's patriarchs, blessing was linked with the gifts of descendants, land, and properties (cf. Gen 12:1–4; 15:1–6; 17). Other things that are considered as blessing include rain (Pss 29:10–11; 65:11), green fertile land, and its produce (Job 42:12–15). With this, one can understand the import of Psalm 67:7: *ʾereṣ nātᵉnāh yᵉbûlāh yᵉbārᵉkēnû ʾĕlōhîm ʾĕlōhênû* ("The earth has yielded its increase; God, our God has blessed us"). It is a blessing when the earth yields its increase. The prayer for blessing in v. 2 also includes this. Based on this, some believe that the life situation that gave rise to the composition of Psalm 67 was harvest or the new year festival.[19] Gunkel explains it as a communal thanksgiving song after a

---

16. Psalm 67:2 is one of the instances where the subject comes before a jussive because jussive of optative sentences, as we have here, are mostly found before the subject. A similar example is seen in an ancient Arad inscription 18:2 (cf. Paul Joüon and T. Muraoka, *A Grammar of Biblical Hebrew*, 2006] no.155l. When word order varies in Hebrew, there is usually an emphasis on the word that comes first; in v. 2 *ʾĕlōhîm* can be said to be in an emphatic position.

17. Coniglio, "'Gracious and Merciful is YHWH . . .' (Psalm 145:8)," 40, argues that this divine attribute is a unifying factor in the Psalter.

18. Freedman, "ḥānan," *TDOT* 5, 30.

19. Tate, *Psalms 51–100*, 155. This author explains that Ps 67 was probably recited at the end of a worship occasion before the people left for their homes.

bountiful harvest;[20] he calls it a full thanksgiving song like Psalms 66:8–12; 124; 129, and Isaiah 12:3–6. For some others, it is a prayer for rain.[21]

The second part of v. 2 stands in a synonymous parallelism with the first stich. In this second half, the psalmist prays *yāʾēr pānâw ʾittānû* ("make [he] his face to shine upon us"). The blessing being asked is the light of the face of God, a recurrent prayer in the Psalms (e.g., Pss 4:7; 27:8; 31:17; 44:4; 80:4, 8, 20; 89:16; 119:135). The prayer that God's face may shine on the petitioners is a metaphor for God's goodwill and blessings.[22] It is also an example of anthropomorphism; the psalmist attributes human form to God. When God makes his face to shine on his people, he blesses them and grants their prayers. Light is a symbol of divinity in many cultures.[23] This prayer for blessings is reminiscent of the Priestly Prayer in Numbers 6:24–26.

> [24] The Lord bless you and keep you;
> [25] the LORD make his face to shine upon you, and be gracious to you;
> [26] the Lord lift up his countenance upon you, and give you peace.

The psalmist believes that God has blessed his people. It is instructive that it is not a personal prayer but communal. The people share in the blessing of Abraham their patriarch (Gen 12:1–4), and this blessing has a universalistic tag at the end: "And in you all the families of the earth shall be blessed" (Gen 12:3). In Psalm 67 and many other parts of the Old Testament there is a desire that God be known and praised by other peoples and nations. Israel wishes that the graciousness of God which they experience as a nation be extended to others. The "they" section (vv. 3–6; 8b) of Psalm 67 articulates this in various ways.

Prayer as an Aspect of Missionary Activity (vv. 3–6, 8b)

The prayer for divine blessings on Israel in v. 2 is extended to other nations in the "they" section of Psalm 67, beginning from v. 3. The psalmist prays that God's way (*derek*) may be known upon the earth and God's saving power among all nations. In v. 3 this prayer is stated in a distich strophe with synonymous parallelism where, on the one hand, God's way (*darkekā* "your [God's] way") corresponds to his saving power (*yᵉšûʿāt̲ekā*), and on the other hand, *bāʾāreṣ* is synonymous to *bᵉkol-gôyim* ("among all the nations"). The verb governing all these is *lādaʿat* ("to know"). From the parallelism, God's way means salvation. It is also a synonym of Torah (Law, God's self-manifestation); knowledge of this and adherence to its contents bring salvation. Israel is the privileged witness and apostle of God's love for humanity.[24] In v. 3 the

---

20. Gunkel and Joachim Begrich, *Introduction to Psalms*, 43, 45, 240.
21. Watson, *Classical Hebrew Poetry*, 302.
22. Tate, *Psalms 51–100*, 157.
23. Schökel, *A Manual of Hebrew Poetics*, 138.
24. Ravasi, *Il Libro dei Salmi*, 355.

psalmist announces this prophetically to the whole world. Others will come to know God when they follow his way. This is the desire and the prayer of the petitioner, that all may come to know God's way that leads to salvation. "The purpose of the demand is the conversion of peoples of all lands, so that the ways of Elohim may be known on the earth."[25] In the Old Testament, other peoples designated here as *gôyim*[26] are often presented as a political threat to Israel and its anointed king (Pss 2:1, 8; 46:7) and Israel should have nothing to do with them because they do not follow the way of the Lord. In the missionary spirit of Psalm 67, the psalmist prays for their salvation.

With this insight, the sense of the strict type of refrain in vv. 4 and 6 is clearer. Other nations who accept God's way will express their adherence in cultic celebration. "Often a repeated refrain drives home the main point of a psalm. In this case the main point is the hope or expectation that all the peoples of the earth will join in the praise of Israel's God."[27] In this refrain, another word for people is used, and it is *'am*, a very recurrent (1,868x) word in the Old Testament, and it means "people."[28] The verb (*ydh*) used here and repeated twice in each of the refrain is a typical one for the solemn celebration of the *tôd̲āh* ("thanksgiving") sacrifice (cf. Pss 33:2–3; 100:4; 105:1; 106:1; 107:1; 118:1; 136:1). The object and cause of this thanksgiving is Israel's divine blessing, inherited from the Abrahamic blessing (Gen 12:1–3) and shared by other nations (Gen 12:3). It is the desire and prayer of the psalmist that other nations join in this thanksgiving and praise of God, whose special attribute is graciousness and who alone is God (cf. 1 Kgs 8:59–60). "Blessing and the spread of life-giving knowledge of Yahweh to the people of the earth"[29] are highlighted in Psalm 67, particularly in its "they" section. Verse 5 makes this more explicit from another perspective.

We have already noted above that v. 5 is the only verse that is tristich. It also contains another word (*lᵉ'umîm*; the singular is *lᵉ'ōm*) for "people," not as frequent as *'am* and *gôy*. Furthermore, this verse introduces two other actions of the nations/peoples in relation to the psalmist's desire for making God known among them. Having prayed in v. 3 for divine knowledge for the peoples and wished that they join in praising God (vv. 4, 6), in v. 5 the psalmist desires that the peoples join in the universal joy in the Lord. The two verbs (*yiśmᵉḥû*, "let them be glad"; *wîrannᵉnû*, "and sing for joy") employed respectively express internal and external joy. In other words, they refer to the holistic joy of those who have come to the knowledge of God. In the remaining parts of v. 5, the reasons for this call for joy are established by the particle *kî*

---

25. Terrien, *The Psalms*, 484.

26. This is a very frequent (circa 550x) word in the OT; the singular is *gôy*, and unlike *'am*, another word for "people" in the OT, it is never used with suffixes referring to any deity; see Clemens, "*gôy*," *TDOT* II, 427.

27. Wilson, *The NIV Application Commentary: Psalms 1*, 927.

28. Hulst, "'am, gôy," 898–99.

29. Tate, *Psalms 51–100*, 159.

("because, for") and provide the content for the song of praise.[30] The psalmist states two reasons for this summon for joy: God judges with equity and he leads the peoples. In the missionary spirit of this psalm, it is not said that the divine judgment is in favor of the people of Israel; it is for all the peoples. "The assembled community prays for the blessing of the God of Israel, but especially for an extension of this blessing to universal proportions."[31]

The last part of the "they" section of Psalm 67 is its final stich in v. 8b: *w^{e}yîr^e'û ōṯô kol-'apsê-'āreṣ* ("let all the ends of the earth revere him"). The phrase "ends of the earth," which occurs in other parts of the Psalter (cf. Pss 2:8; 22:27; 59:13; 72:8; 98:3) means cessation, discontinuation of existence; it is that point beyond which no habitable land exits.[32] Together with the terms for other nations and peoples (*gôyim, 'am, l^e'umîm*), it further emphasises the universalistic view in Psalm 67.[33] There is an impression that Israel lives in the center of the earth while other nations are at the edges. The final stich of Psalm 67, "Let all the ends of the earth revere him," is an invitation to all the habitable parts of the earth to experience the saving power of God, for "the election of Israel does not imply the rejection of the other nations."[34] We recall that the "they" section of our psalm begins in v. 3 with a petition for knowledge of God, and in v. 8b it ends with fear of God. Knowledge of God and fear of God are two essential aspects of human attitude as *homo religiosus*.[35] These are the focus of the psalmist's prayer for other nations.

The life situation of Psalm 67 might be the new year festival according to some scholars, a thanksgiving celebration for a bountiful harvest, as it can be elicited in v. 8a,[36] a general hymn of praise for blessings received from God, or a prayer imploring divine blessings. In all these Israel prays that its national blessings and experience of God's saving power be extended to all peoples. This missionary impulse of making the true God known and venerated by all nations is included in King Solomon's prayer for the dedication of the temple where he opens the horizon with a prayer that all peoples of the earth may know that the Lord is God:[37] "So that all the peoples of the earth may know that the Lord is God; there is no other" (1 Kgs 8:59–60). One finds a similar opening of horizon in Psalm 67. In fact, every mission has a content and objective; in Psalm 67, the content is the experience of God's graciousness and saving power manifested in his blessings; the objective is that this will be known by all nations so

---

30. Gunkel and Begrich, *Introduction to Psalms*, 29.
31. Kraus, *Psalms 60–150*, 40.
32. Keel, *The Symbolism of the Biblical World*, 42.
33. Schökel and C. Carniti, *I Salmi 1*, 982
34. The Pontifical Biblical Commission, *The Jewish People and their Sacred Scriptures*, no. 33.
35. Ravasi, *Il Libro dei Salmi*, 357.
36. Hossfeld and Zenge, *Psalms 2*, 2005.
37. O'Brien and Campell, "1–2 Kings," 672.

that they will come to venerate and share in this blessing promised to Abraham: "In you all the families of the earth shall be blessed" (Gen 12:3).

Psalm 67 in the Life and Mission of the Church

In the "us" section (vv. 2, 7–8a) of Psalm 67, the community behind the text was aware of its special relationship with the true God. Its prayer for divine favor, blessings, and experience of the face of God manifests a group that knew its privileged position on earth. God "has chosen this people for himself, setting them apart for a special relationship with him and for a mission in the world."[38] Israel knew and experienced God and thus prayed that this be extended to all nations. Their prayer is that all may come to the knowledge of God and consequently praise and revere him. Experience of the divine and motivation to share are central to every missionary activity. It is believed that in his letter to the Ephesians 3:5–6 Paul alludes to Psalm 67 in his teaching on universal salvation:[39] "In former generations this mystery was not made known to humankind, as it has now been revealed to his holy apostles and prophets by the Spirit: that is, the Gentiles have become fellow heirs, members of the same body, and sharers in the promise in Christ Jesus through the gospel." After his conversion, Paul became a great missionary of the Gentiles.

Intrinsic to the nature of the church is her universality, closely linked to her missionary mandate. By their baptism and adherence to the teaching of Christ, her members have experienced the graciousness of God and his saving power not just for themselves but to be shared by the whole world. By her missionary mandate, she has been commissioned to be true to her universalistic nature. "Missionary activity flows immediately from the very nature of the Church. Missionary activity extends the saving faith of the Church, it expands and perfects its catholic unity."[40] This is Jesus' parting instruction to his followers: "Go into all the world and proclaim the good news to the whole creation" (Mark 16:15; cf. Matt 28:18–20; Acts 1:8; 24:47–48, Col 1:23). Just like in Psalm 67, early Christians believed that Jerusalem was destined to receive the good news; it was the center from which it spread to other places: "But you will receive power when the Holy Spirit has come upon you; and you will be my witnesses in Jerusalem, in all Judea and Samaria, and to the ends of the earth" (Acts 1:8).

Christian reading and interpretation of Psalm 67 are seen in how this text is used in liturgical celebrations. Psalm 67, for instance, is one of the invitatory psalms at the church's daily morning prayers. Expressing the universal stance of the psalmist, she invokes all nations and peoples to join in praising God as she does in other

---

38. The Pontifical Biblical Commission, *The Jewish People and their Sacred Scriptures in the Christian Bible*, no. 33. "The idea of election is fundamental for an understanding of the Old Testament and indeed for the whole Bible."

39. Ravasi, *Il Libro dei Salmi*, 358.

40. Vatican II, *Decree on the Church's Missionary activity* (*Ad Gentes Divinitus*), no. 6.

invitatory psalms (Pss 23; 95; 100). On Wednesday of the Fourth Week of Easter, the church responds with Psalm 67 to the reading of Acts 12:24–13:5a, which narrates how Barnabas and Saul (Paul) were prepared to bring the good news to the Gentiles. Again, her understanding of the universal dimension of Psalm 67 is evident in the use of this psalm as a response after the reading of Acts 15:1–2, 22–29 on the Sixth Sunday of Easter (Year C), which narrates the challenge of the nascent church in accommodating non-Jews. Guided by the Holy Spirit, the early Christians were able to make some decisions in favor of the catholicity of the church, thereby proclaiming that Christ's message of salvation is not limited to Jews but to all nations. The author of Psalm 67 predicted this in his prayerful desire for all nations to know, praise, and revere God. Similarly, on the Twentieth Sunday in Ordinary Time (Year A), Psalm 67, specifically its refrain, is the response to a reading from Isaiah 56:1, 6–7. In this reading the Lord proclaims universal salvation for all who sincerely honor him; foreigners are particularly mentioned in this text. The church considers Psalm 67 as a fitting response to God's word of invitation to non-Jews. "The spiritual and social dangers inherent in a closed society are far greater than those of an open society, particularly in the community of faith."[41] A closed society is not missionary; its message of hope can become extinct out of lack of openness to others. On the contrary, the sustainability of its values is assured when it is accepted by others effectively prepared for it. Aware of its mission in the world, the church reminds her members of the need for mission. She does this through prayerful reading of relevant sacred texts like Psalm 67 and in the context that makes its message understandable.

Divine blessings celebrated as petitions in Psalm 67 (cf. vv. 2, 7–8a) and desired for other nations of the earth (vv. 3–6) are also highlighted in the church's liturgy. A reading from the instructions in Leviticus 25 on how to observe Jubilee Year is followed by singing Psalm 67 on Saturday of the Seventh Week in Ordinary Time (Year 1). In the text, "The permissibility of eating freely from the produce that grows that year is repeated for emphasis."[42] It reminds one of the first stich of Psalm 67:7: *ereṣ nāteˁnāh yebûlāh* ("the earth has yielded its increase"), a blessing that would stir humanity into songs of praise and recognition of the graciousness of God. The church recalls this again in her liturgy of every first January with a reading from the Priestly Blessing in Numbers 6:24–25, which has a close affinity with Psalm 67. No other psalm can be a more appropriate response to this reading than Psalm 67. In this liturgy of the first day of the year, the church agrees with those scholars who believe that the life situation that gave rise to the composition of Psalm 67 was the new year festival. God is praised for his blessings as we read in Psalm 67 and Numbers 6:24–25.

Apart from these salient instances of the use of Psalm 67 in the life and mission of the church, this psalm appears regularly in the morning and evening prayers in some days of the week. This shows its importance in the liturgy and in the church's

---

41. Watts, *Isaiah 34–66*, 251.
42. Hartley, *Leviticus*, 434.

understanding of her mission in the world. It also accentuates the place of the word of God in liturgy, "for the liturgy is the privileged setting in which God speaks to us in the midst of our lives; he speaks today to his people, who hears and responds."[43]

Learning from Psalm 67

Faith in God is a gift that everyone who has received it strives to pass on to others. This missionary motivation is intrinsic to the gift. The author of Psalm 67 seems to be aware of this in his words repeated as refrain: "Let the peoples praise you, O God; let all the peoples praise you." Okure explains evangelization or missionary endeavour in this way: "Evangelization (the proclamation of the Good News), then is the passing on to others the good news received so that they too can believe or receive God's good news as living, active and ever current power that can enrich and transform their lives and their world. The activity is not a past but an ever present, alive and active."[44] Indeed, missionary activity should be ever-present in our time. Every true Christian is a missionary because the missionary mandate entrusted to the church is for everyone according to each person's capacity. "The mission *ad gentes* is incumbent upon the entire People of God."[45]

In Psalm 67 the content of the desired mission is the knowledge of the true God; this knowledge gives life, natural and spiritual blessings. The prospective recipients are peoples and nations who do not know God. Christians should be solicitous about evangelization—about making God known to persons who are still far from the knowledge of God. The speaker in Psalm 67 might not be a priest or a minister in Israel's cultic celebrations, but he believed to have received the faith and wished that all nations of the earth share in this. The work of evangelization is not reserved only to those called to ministerial priesthood and consecrated life who have mission in their charisms. It is a mandate for all Christians. Each one can help in various ways.

Fervent daily prayer for the conversion of non-Christians is a good way to make the missionary spirit of Psalm 67 present, alive, and active today. One can make it a point of duty to pray for this intention in fulfillment of Christian missionary mandate.[46] In the missionary prayer of the author of Psalm 67, one can read the promise made to Abraham, "In you all the families of the earth shall be blessed" (Gen 12:3),[47] and other blessings in Genesis 12:2–3. "The promises of blessing to the patriarchs are thus a reassertion of God's original intentions for man."[48] Knowledge of God and of

---

43. Benedict XVI, *Verbum Domini*, no. 52.
44. Okure, "President's Welcome Address," xx.
45. John Paul II, *Redemptoris Missio*, no. 71.
46. John Paul II, *Redemptoris Missio*, no. 78.
47. This is the last of the seven blessings bestowed on Abraham in Gen 12:2–3 (cf. Clifford, "Genesis," 20), and this final blessing is the basis for many missionary statements, like Ps 67, in the OT.
48. Wenham, *Genesis 1–15*, 275.

his way, which in Psalm 67 is expressed as *darkekā* ("your way"), is the purpose of human life on earth. It is also the purpose of missionary motivation, as in Psalm 67, that all may know God and follow his way. A thanksgiving celebration at the basis of this psalm becomes a prayer for all nations to know and fear God.[49]

While some are out there in the field toiling to bring the good news of salvation to all nations, they need the prayers and support of others. Contributions for missions can take various dimensions. Some can pray for sustainability of missionary courage and zeal; others can make material contributions; still others can encourage prospective missionaries through financial support in their formation. In this way, all Christians share in carrying out the mission mandate entrusted to the church. This is necessary because "mission defines our core identity as disciples, even as it defines that of Jesus, the Messiah."[50]

Many Christians have contributed immensely to the conversion of non-Christians through authentic witnessing to the Christian faith. They live according to the tenets of their faith. Therefore, foremost in the missionary endeavors is the life we live as followers of Christ. In the early church, many became Christians because they saw the difference between their lives and that of the early Christians. We can become missionaries wherever we find ourselves, bearing in mind that "the reason for missionary activity lies in the will of God, 'who wishes all men to be saved and to come to the knowledge of the truth' (1 Tim 2:4)."[51]

CONCLUSION

Noticeable in Psalm 67 and a clue to the understanding of its meaning is the strict refrain repeated twice in it. This refrain points at the orientation of the poet and elucidates the other contents of this psalm. In the Old Testament, the people of Israel are aware of their privileged divine election, which goes with the responsibility of making the true God known and revered in all ends of the earth. Psalm 67 highlights this in its use of various terms for other nations and peoples, and with a more encompassing variant, *kol-ʾapsê-ʾāreṣ* ("all the ends of the earth"). The poet turns his thanksgiving song into a prayer that all nations may know and fear God. These two prayer intentions are the hinges of human religious attitude. The aspect of mission that is found in the text is a prayerful wish for other nations to know the true God. Psalm 67 agrees with other texts of the Old Testament where the people of Israel express desire for mission.

The church understands this central message of Psalm 67 in her life and mission. Her perception of the meaning of this text is manifested in her interpretation lived in her liturgical celebrations. She is the new Israel and the heir of the promises of Abraham in Genesis 12:1–3. Just as Israel sees itself as being in the center of the

---

49. Girard, *Les Psaumes redécouverts*, 208.
50. Okure, "Gospel and Faith in the Parable of the Prodigal Son (Luke 15)," 189.
51. Vatican II, *Ad Gentes Divinitus*, no. 7.

world and is a source of blessings for other peoples, the church in her liturgy is aware of her mission mandate to be Christ's witness to the ends of the earth (Acts 1:8). She is intrinsically missionary, and all her members participate in this common vocation according to each person's state of life and capacity. Authentic witness of the good news of salvation prominently achieves the objective of her mission, which is to make all nations come to the knowledge of God.

Although Psalm 67 was composed in a culture and time different from ours, its message as the word of God is perennially alive and active. Members of the church live this message daily in their lives when they, like the psalmist, implore God's blessings for themselves and for non-believers and invoke God in their prayers with the same words: *yôḏûḵā ʿammîm ʾĕlōhîm yôḏûḵā ʿammîm kullām* ("let the peoples praise you, O God; let all the peoples praise you").

BIBLIOGRAPHY

Alonso Schökel, Luis. *A Manual of Hebrew Poetics*. Subsidia Biblica 11. Roma: Editrice Pontificio Istituto Biblico, 1988.

Alonso Schökel, Luis, and C. Carniti. *I Salmi*. Vol. 1. Roma: Edizioni Borla, 1992.

Amzallag, Nissim. "Psalm 67 and the Cosmopolite Musical Worship of YHWH." *Bulletin for Biblical Research* 25, no. 2 (2015) 171–85.

Benedict XVI. *Post-Synodal Apostolic Exhortation, Verbum Domini on the Word of God in the Life and Mission of the Church*. Rome: Libreria Editrice Vaticana, 2010.

Bullinger, E. W. *Figures of Speech used in the Bible*. Grand Rapids: Baker Book House, 2003.

Clemens, R.E. "*gôy*." In *TDOT*, 2:426–433. Grand Rapids: Eerdmans, 1999.

Clifford, Richard J. "Genesis." In *The New Jerome Biblical Commentary*, 8–28. London: Geoffrey Chapman, 1992.

Coniglio, Alessandro. "'Gracious and Merciful is YHWH . . . ' (Psalm 145:8): The Quotation of Exodus 34:6 in Psalm 145 and Its Role in the Holistic Design of the Psalter." *Liber Annuus* 67 (2017) 29–50.

Freedman, D. N. "*ḥānan*." In *TDOT* 5:22–36. Grand Rapid: Eerdmans, 1996.

Gerstenberger, Erhard S. *Psalms Part 2 and Lamentations*. The Forms of the Old Testament Literature XV. Grand Rapids: Eerdmans, 2001.

Girard, Marc. *Les Psaumes redécouverts: de la structure au sens 51–100*. Québec: Éditions Bellarmin, 1994.

Gunkel, Herman, and Joachim Begrich. *Introduction to Psalms: The Genres of the Religious Lyric of Israel*. Macon, GA: Mercer University Press, 1998.

Hartley, John E. *Leviticus*. WBC 4. Dallas: Word Books, 1992.

Hulst, A. R. "ʿam, gôy." In *Theological Lexicon of the Old Testament*, 2:896–919. Peabody, MA: Hendrickson, 1997.

John Paul II. *Redemptoris Missio*: Encyclical Letter on the Church's Missionary Mandate. Rome: Libreria Editrice Vaticana, 1990.

———. *Psalms and Canticles: Meditations and Catechesis on the Psalms and Canticles of Morning Prayers*. London: Catholic Truth Society, 2004.

Joüon, Paul, and T. Muraoka. *A Grammar of Biblical Hebrew*. Subsidia Biblica 27. Rome: Editrice Pontificio Istituto Biblico, 2006.

Keel, Othmar. *The Symbolism of the Biblical World: Ancient Near Eastern Iconography and the Book of Psalms*. Winona Lake, IN: Eisenbrauns, 1997.

Kraus, Hans-Joachim. *Psalms 60–150: A Continental Commentary*. Minneapolis: Fortress, 1993.

Luurtsema, Dean. "Psalm 67: The Challenge of Verbal Tense." Available at https://www.academia.edu/17173102/Psalm_67_The_Challenge_of_Verbal_Tense.

O'Brien, Mark, and Anthony Campell. "1–2 Kings." In *The International Bible Commentary: An Ecumenical Commentary for the Twenty-First Century*, 661–96. Bangalore: Theological Publications in India, 2015.

Okure, Teresa. "President's Welcome Address and Elaboration of Conference Theme." In *The Bible on Faith and Evangelization*, 6:xvii–xxviii. Edited by A. Ewherido et al. Acts of the Catholic Biblical Association of Nigeria. Port Harcourt: CABAN Publications, 2015.

———. "Gospel and Faith in the Parable of the Prodigal Son (Luke 15)." *The Bible on Faith and Evangelization*, 6:169–95. Edited by A. Ewherido et al. Acts of the Catholic Biblical Association of Nigeria. Port Harcourt: CABAN Publications, 2015.

Ravasi, Gianfranco. *Il Libro dei Salmi: Commento e attualizzazione*. Vol. 2. Bologna: Edizioni Dehoniane, 1996.

Tate, Marvin E. *Psalms 51–100*. WBC 20. Dallas: Word Books, 1990.

Terrien, Samuel. *The Psalms: Strophic Structure and Theological Commentary*. Grand Rapids: Eerdmans, 2003.

The Catechism of the Catholic Church. Nairobi: Paulines Publications Africa, 2011.

The Pontifical Biblical Commission. *The Jewish People and Their Sacred Scriptures in the Christian Bible*. Roma: Libreria Editrice Vaticana, 2002.

Vatican II. *Decree on the Church's Missionary Activity (Ad Gentes Divinitus)*. Edited by Austin Flannery. Northport, NY: Costello Publishing Company, 1980.

Watson, W. G. E. *Classical Hebrew Poetry: A Guide to Its Techniques*. Sheffield: Sheffield Academic Press, 1995.

Watts, John W. *Isaiah 34–66*. WBC 25. Nashville: Thomas Nelson, 1987.

Wenham, Gordon I. *Genesis 1–15*. WBC 1. Nashville: Thomas Nelson, 1987.

Wilson, Gerald H. *The NIV Application Commentary: Psalms*. Vol.1. Grand Rapids: Zondervan, 2002.

CHAPTER 5

Amos' Polemical Mission against Religious Hypocrisy (Amos 5:21–27)
In African Context

PILANI MICHAEL PAUL

INTRODUCTION

Religion in the Hebrew Scripture was always meant to affect and influence how the people must interact in their day-to-day life. This was all about how ethics and morality in life should be a reflection of one's encounter and relationship with YHWH. Thus, the saying was always true for them that "like God, like worshiper." If YHWH is a just and righteous God, then his worshipers must reflect his character. But when the lifestyles of his worshipers are at variance with these moral and ethical demands, then their authenticity as YHWH's followers is under threat. But this is precisely what the adherents of YHWH's religion in Israel were victims of in the eighth century BC. They all seemed perfect in their external displays of worship, prayer, and sacrifices. But they lacked justice and righteousness—the two virtues that positively influence human interactions. Whatever they did in the name of religion, they were all "hypocritical worship gestures for their own benefit."[1] Thus, in Amos 5:21–27, the prophet is all fire and brimstone against such worship and religion. In fact, "The section in Amos 5:21–27 is generally included in studies focusing on the prophetic critique of ritual and cult of the Hebrew Bible."[2] This present study envisages that Amos' mission as reported in the text can pose as critique and challenge for modern men and women

1. Udoekpo, *Israel's Prophets*, 30.
2. Klingbeil and Klingbeil, "The Prophetic Voice of Amos," 171.

who practice a kind of religion that is devoid of justice, ethics of life, and other moral conducts. It is a critique of such religions that rather permit or even promote permissiveness, violence, and many forms of man's inhumanity to man, since "it is useless to perform religious acts without authenticity."[3]

THE TEXT

> 21 "I hate, I despise your feasts, and I take no delight in your solemn assemblies. 22 Even though you offer me your burnt offerings and cereal offerings, I will not accept them, and the peace offerings of your fatted beasts I will not look upon. 23 Take away from me the noise of your songs; to the melody of your harps I will not listen. 24 But let justice roll down like waters, and righteousness like an ever-flowing stream. 25 "Did you bring to me sacrifices and offerings the forty years in the wilderness, O house of Israel? 26 You shall take up Sakkuth your king, and Kaiwan your star-god, your images, which you made for yourselves; 27 therefore I will take you into exile beyond Damascus," says the Lord, whose name is the God of hosts.

Form and Setting of Amos 5:21–27

The form of Amos 5:21–27 is a denouncement and judgement which can best be described as a prophetic cult critique. Couched in poetic language of irony and reversal,[4] the text presents a woe/funerary[5] oracle as a direct speech by YHWH in the first person singular, criticizing the basic elements of the Israelite cult. Meanwhile, from the historical point of view, the text (Amos 5:21–27) emerges as a response to a sociopolitical as well a religious situation of the northern kingdom of Israel. It happened at this period that Jeroboam II (793–753 BC), who is generally considered by scholars to be the hero-king of the Jehu dynasty, bolstered the control of Israel over a major trade route in the region. This was possible as, through military prowess, he was able to occupy the Transjordan and Judah after annexing the area of Gilead. But then as Bruce E. Willoughby would rightly say, "The most important annexation for Israel was Gilead and the Transjordan cities of Lo-debar and Karnaim . . . The King's Highway, the major trade route from the Tigris-Euphrates river valley to the Gulf of Aqaba and Egypt, ran through Gilead and the Transjordan."[6] The attendant benefit of this was that there was great proliferation of wealth in Israel. It was also a period of peace and expansion for Israel and even Judah since "The wars that threatened the two kingdoms during the reigns

---

3. Groenewald, "But let justice roll down like waters," 6.
4. Sweeney, *The Twelve Prophets*, 240.
5. Pitts, *An Exegesis of Amos 5:18–27*, 7.
6. Willoughby, "The Book of Amos," 205.

of the predecessors of Jeroboam and Uzziah were over. Assyria to the NE and Egypt to the S were both on the decline."[7] Summarily, therefore, and as Shalom Paul puts it, at this "silver age of Israelite history, Israel reached the summit of its material power and economic prosperity as well as the apogee of its territorial expansion, comparable only to the era of David and Solomon, the Golden Age."[8]

In the face of this, however, and as Philip Igbo affirms, the great prosperity had a corresponding corruption (2 Kgs 14:23–29).[9] This was so because "wealth was concentrated in the hands of a few; there was a wide gap between the rich and the poor. The rich took advantage of the poor at every given opportunity (2:6; 5:11), amassing wealth by dishonest means without regard for the rights of the poor (Amos 8:4–6)."[10] The archeological evidence of the objectionable disparity between the rich and the poor is reported by Willoughby, who states that "by the 8th century, one section of the city contained large houses, evidence of prosperity, while the other section contained the small houses of the poor."[11] In the midst of all these, the people suffered the misfortune of the presumption that all was well as they thought that peace, security, and wealth were visible indicators that YHWH was pleased with their moral, religious, and devotional activities. "They assumed that their steadfast devotion to cultic ritual exempted them from the requirements of righteousness and social justice and from the consequences of wrongdoing. Through sacrifice, they could guarantee divine favor and their own survival."[12] However, for YHWH, this was an intolerable shortcut. Thus, the pursuit of wealth under the façade of superfluous and unethical religion was disgusting to YHWH, who would rather they pursue righteousness. It is in this regard that Amos the prophet in 5:21–27 presents God as rejecting their worship, sacrifices, and offerings because they are meaningless and empty.[13] Additionally, in it, YHWH suggests better ways of approaching religion while threatening impending destruction for defaulters.

Delimitation and Organization of the Text

Some scholars such as Klaus Koch have proposed a four-part division for the book of Amos, namely chapters 1–2, 3–4, 5:1–9:6, and 9:7–15.[14] The text of this present study (5:21–27) falls in the third division, which contains prophetic oracles against Israel and predictions of the latter's destruction, which has led many scholars to think that

---

7. Willoughby, "The Book of Amos," 205.
8. Paul, *Amos: A Commentary*, 1.
9. Igbo, *Introduction*, 331.
10. Igbo, *Introduction to the Old Testament Books and Pseudepigrapha*, 331.
11. Willoughby, "The Book of Amos," 205.
12. Willoughby, "The Book of Amos," 206.
13. Boadt, *Reading the Old Testament*, 279.
14. Koch et al., *Amos*, 30.

the section, together with portions of chapter 6, contain the actual words of Amos.[15] More specifically, Amos 5:21–27 falls within a presentation of a series of woes in connection with: (i) the day of atonement (5:18–20), (ii) the cult (5:21–27), (iii) the military security of the nation (6:1–3), (iv) the *marzēaḥ* feast (6:4–7), and (v) the impending destruction (6:8–14).[16] However, the shift into direct speech in the first person singular in Amos 5:21–27a, as distinct from reported speech in the verses before and after, isolates the text and accords it a status worth attention in this study. It is clear therefore that Amos 5:21–27 is an independent unit that deals with questionable cult practices, which are at variance with the expectations of YHWH. "Here he [Amos] levels his most uncompromising attack against the lavishness of the official monotheistic cult. He upbraids, in no uncertain terms, Israel's extensive ritual praxis, rejecting it in toto: holidays, festival gatherings, and sacrifices, along with their accompanying hymns, melodies, and musical instruments."[17] In it, one sees "YHWH's critique of cultic action that is not accompanied by justice."[18] As a unit dealing with pretentious religious worship, Amos 5:21–27 can be broken down into the following literary structure:

A. vv. 21–23—YHWH's rejection of their worship

  i. v. 21—their religious feasts and assemblies are loathsome to YHWH

  ii. v. 22—their offerings are loathsome to YHWH

  iii. v. 23—their music is loathsome to YHWH

B. v. 24—YHWH rather requires justice and righteousness

C. vv. 25–26—denouncement of their false worship

  i. v. 25—denouncement of false worship in the desert

  ii. v. 26—denouncement of idolatry

D. v. 27—declaration of their exile

Exposition of the Text

Amos 5:21–27 opens with the theme of contrast and dramatic reversal in reference to the Day of the Lord in the previous verses. The people had celebrated in anticipation for the Day of the Lord. "Their expectation as God's elect was that of victory and blessing, triumph over foes and the recovery of political power from foreign nations."[19] Unfortunately, "The people have substituted the law and covenant acts of the Lord

---

15. Willoughby, "The Book of Amos," 208.
16. Willoughby, "The Book of Amos," 208.
17. Paul, *Amos: A Commentary*, 188.
18. Sweeney, *The Twelve Prophets*, 239.
19. Opade, "The Nexus Between Religious Practices," 70.

for ritual: His 'day,' when it comes, will be far from their expectations, and the zealous observance of religious ritual will not spare them from the impending doom. He will consign them to exile for their disregard of moral obligations."[20]

Thus, v. 21 opens with YHWH's expression of his active disgust for the formal religious services practiced by his people.[21] YHWH states: *Sänë°'tî mä'a°sTî HaG-Gêkem wülö' 'ärî ͣH Bü`accürö|têkem* ("I hate, I despise your feasts, and I take no delight in your solemn assemblies"). The designation *HaGGêkem* ("your feast") is the official description of the three major events in the cultic and agricultural year of the people of Israel. These said events are, first, *Pesach*, otherwise called Passover, which is the festival held at the beginning of the grain harvest. *Shavout* is the second one, and it is also referred to as Weeks or Pentecost, and it is a festival in honor of the conclusion of the grain harvest. The third one, *Sukkoth* or Booths or Tabernacles, is the conclusion of the grape and olive harvest and the beginning of the rainy season.[22] In the Hebrew Bible, references to these festivals are respectively found in Exodus 23:14–19; 34:22–26; and Deuteronomy 16:13–17.

Meanwhile, YHWH's reference to "your solemn assemblies" (`accürö|têkem) concerns the last (seventh) day of *Pesach* as well as the eighth day of *Sukkoth*, being also the latter's last day. The two "are special holidays that mark the conclusion of each festival."[23] These too are attested to in the Old Testament respectively in Deuteronomy 16:8; Leviticus 23:36; and Numbers 29:35. Thus, these feasts and their specifics are in the Old Testament as part of the cultic life of the Israelites, yet YHWH states that he "hates" and "despises" them—two strong rejection verbal terms. The term "hate" (*Sānē'*) is employed here in the qal perfect. Earlier on in v. 10, Amos had employed its use in reference to those who "hate injustice."[24] Billy K. Smith and Franklin S. Page have noted that it "is used three times in Amos, all in this chapter. Rather than hating evil (v. 15), Israel hated advocates of righteousness. Therefore God hated their presumptuous worship (v. 12)."[25]

Used alongside "despise" (*mā'as*), which basically means to "reject," "abhor," "refuse," or "loath,"[26] the expression portends the degree of YHWH's disapproval and contempt and how repulsive they appear to him. As Garret puts it, "The anarthrous seconding of the first verb [hate] with another [reject], near synonymous verb eloquently expresses the disgust of someone who is weary of something tedious and

---

20. Driver and Lanchester, *Joel and Amos*, 188.
21. Klingbeil and Klingbeil, "The Prophetic Voice of Amos," 172.
22. Sweeney, *The Twelve Prophets*, 240.
23. Sweeney, *The Twelve Prophets*, 240.
24. Udoekpo, *Rethinking the Prophetic Critique of Worship in Amos 5*, 99.
25. Smith and Page, *The New American Commentary*, 111.
26. Fabry, "*mā'as*, 48.

irksome."²⁷ Thus, the degree of YHWH's rejection and contempt of their festival is extreme, to say the least.²⁸

Indeed, the level of rejection and repudiation is extended to the next part of the verse. It states that "I take no delight in your solemn assemblies" (v. 21b). The term, which literally means "smell, enjoy the smell of," refers to the original intention of the cultic offering—namely, to give pleasure and joy to YHWH. But, as it were, they have failed at this. This "rejection of the entire panoply of the cult is expressed by its not being acceptable to the different senses—smell, v. 21; sight, v. 23; hearing, v. 23. God's disgust is completely sensible."²⁹

In v. 22 the denouncement of religious services continues. Both terms "burnt offerings (ʾōlôt) and "your grain offerings" (minHōtêkem) are technically referring to the meat and grain offerings which daily take place in the temple as prescribed in Leviticus 1 and 2. The term šeʿlem appearing in singular is a *hapax legomenon* occurs only here in Amos 5:22.³⁰ However, as a description, šeʿlem mürîʾêkem, which is "peace offering," is recorded in the Old Testament,³¹ which "was prescribed for special occasions and eaten by both priests and lay people.³² In this regard, YHWH continues to refuse to look upon them. Again, this is due to their abuse of cultic life. Amos thus "cautions against sacrifice that may be presented with spiritual ignorance and a false sense of security.³³

Verse 23 concludes with the repudiation of the charade of worship by the people. This time around, it concerns rejection of songs and melodies. Sweeney has inferred that "music including the playing of instruments and the singing of psalms, was a regular part of Temple worship . . . Indeed, the book of Psalms is thought by many to represent the hymnbook of the Jerusalem Temple."³⁴ However, the usefulness of songs and melodies notwithstanding, YHWH expressly repudiated it as in the case of the Israelite worship.

Conversely, v. 24 picks up an entirely different tone, which is a prescription of what true religion or integral worship is about. The verse is built around the two significant elements regarding prophetic cult critique, namely justice (mišPäṭ) and righteousness (cüdäqâ).³⁵ It opens with adversative wü (but) and a nifal imperfect gālal (yiGGal, "let roll down), presented with a jussive force.³⁶ The expression with

27. Garret, *Amos*, 168.
28. Osuagwu, *An Ideological-Critical Interpretation of Justice and Righteousness in Amos 5*, 109.
29. Paul, *Amos*, 189.
30. de Vaux, *Ancient Israel*, 427.
31. See Lev 3; 7:15, 28–34; also cf. 1 Sam 10:8; 11:15; 2 Sam 6:17–18.
32. Sweeney, *The Twelve Prophets*, 240.
33. Udoekpo, *Rethinking the Prophetic Critique of Worship in Amos 5*, 9.
34. Sweeney, *The Twelve Prophets*, 240.
35. Klingbeil and Klingbeil, *The Prophetic Voice of Amos*, 172.
36. Garret, *Amos*, 172.

the nouns "justice" and "righteousness" bound to it contrasts their empty religiosity that is poignant to YHWH with an alternative—namely, preferred ethical and moral actions. They are demanded to let *mišPäṭ* ("justice") and *cüdäqâ* ("righteousness")[37] to roll down like water and like an ever-flowing stream, respectively.

Finley opines that in the context in which they are used here, justice "encompasses reparation for the defrauded, fairness for the less fortunate, and dignity and compassion for the needy," while righteousness "indicates the conditions that make justice possible: attitudes of mercy and generosity, and honest dealings that imitate the character of God as He has revealed Himself in the law of Moses."[38] Meanwhile,

> The notion that justice and righteousness are required of the people is reflected in the people's constant request of YHWH that he judge between them and whichever foreign nation happens to be threatening them at the moment. If the people expect YHWH to act in their favour, they too are required to act justly towards each other.[39]

YHWH's demands for justice and righteousness are couched in water imagery. Water, in the words of Sweeney,

> is an important feature of Temple worship at the time of Sukkoth as the festival marks the beginning of the rainy season and represents YHWH's commitment to provide life and fertility for the land. The Jerusalem liturgy and psalms frequently make reference to the gushing forth of springs and rivers (Pss 104:10–17; 107:35–38), and the northern shrines would have a similar concern with water and fertility (1 Kings 18: cf. Judg 5:19–21).[40]

In this connection, Amos in v. 24 "draws upon a long tradition in which fertility for the land and justice for the people are considered together with the cultic worship of G-d (sic) [Psalms 40; 50; 68; 72; 147] as both are necessary for the sustenance of human life."[41] While still building on the preceding verses, the import of v. 24, therefore, is that the refutation of Israel's worship is not because it is merely cultic; rather, it is because it lacks justice and righteousness.[42] In all, due to the absence of these cultic elements of justice and righteousness, "the existing cultic practices are called sinful (4:4–5), useless (5:21–23) and doomed (5:4f)."[43]

---

37. In the OT, it is normal for the Hebrew pair to appear together frequently. Handy examples are to be found in 1 Kgs 10:19; 1 Chr 18:14; 2 Chr 9:8; Ps 99:4; Isa 9:7; 32:16; 33:5; 59:14; Jer 4:2; 9:24; 22:3; 33:15; Ezek 18:5, 9, 21, 27; 33:14, 16, 19; 45:9; Amos 5:7, 24.

38. John, *Joel, Amos, Obadiah*, 251.

39. Veronica, *The Prophetic Critique of the Priority of the Cult*, 68–69.

40. Sweeney, *The Twelve Prophets*, 240.

41. Sweeney, *The Twelve Prophets*, 241.

42. Groenewald, "'But Let Justice Roll Down Like Waters," 6.

43. Groenewald, "But Let Justice Roll Down Like Waters," 6.

Employing a rhetorical question, v. 25 recollects the subject of sacrifice earlier seen in v. 22. The verse asks: *hazzübäHîm ûminHâ hi|GGašTem-lî bammidBär ´arBä`îm šänâ Bêt yiSrä´ël* ("Did you bring to me sacrifices and offerings the forty years in the wilderness, O house of Israel?"). From the onset, the question in this verse anticipates a negative answer to the effect that the people did not offer such sacrifices in the desert.[44] However, this interpretation creates a canonical tension—namely, the presupposition in this verse as also in Jeremiah 7:22–23 and that of the records in the Pentateuch.[45]

In this regard, "The narratives in the Torah point to the fact that sacrifices were offered during the 40 years in the wilderness (cf. Ex 24; Ex 32; Lv 9 etc.)."[46] Mays, however, offers an alternative approach to the dilemma. In his words, the "opening question is a denial that the sacrifice and offering were the mode of Israel's relation to Yahweh during the wilderness years. Seen in connection with v. 24 it implies that in those normative original years Israel responded to Yahweh with obedience, and produced justice and righteousness instead of presenting sacrifice."[47] Groenewald has also attempted to resolve the problem by adopting an approach that discusses the dating of the text in question. "The statement, in v. 25, thus would only make sense if it is dated in an exilic or post-exilic setting as it relativises the significance of the sacrificial cult in a situation in which large groups of YHWH worshippers could not get access to a 'legitimate' temple."[48]

This having been said, it suffices to state that the idea here in v. 25 suggests that during the formative years of the nation, God's relationship with the people did not depend on any form of sacrifice but faithfulness to YHWH.[49] As Sweeney would say, "It would appear then that YHWH cites the sacrifices of the wilderness period as an indication that sacrifice alone does not constitute a proper relationship to YHWH, especially when the people reject YHWH and turn to other gods."[50] If this is so, they should not presume that sacrifices are necessarily fundamental as against the high premium YHWH places on justice.

Verse 26 takes the cult critique and accusation further: "You shall take up Sakkuth your king, and Kaiwan your star-god, your images, which you made for yourselves." However, the obscure nature of the accusation has engendered debates on its meaning. To begin with, the ‚astral deities in question *siKKût* and *Kiyyûn* are most likely Assyro-Babylonian gods.[51] In this connection, Hadjiev infers that "Most scholars see in v. 26 reference to two Mesopotamian deities: Sakkuth and Keiwan though

---

44. Groenewald, "But Let Justice Roll Down Like Waters," 6.
45. Leclerc, *Introduction to the Prophets,* 188. See also De Vaux, *Ancient Israel,* 428 on this.
46. Groenewald, "But Let Justice Roll Down Like Waters," 6.
47. Mays, *Amos,* 111.
48. Groenewald, "But Let Justice Roll Down Like Waters," 6.
49. Tchavdar, *Book of Amos,* 167.
50. Sweeney, "*The Twelve Prophets,*" 241.
51. Opade, "The Nexus Between Religious Practices And Human Value," 71.

it continues to be a mystery why these particular gods should have been singled out for mention in Amos."[52] Opade, on his part, opines that the reference to astral deities may suggest that they probably might have constituted part of Israelite contemporary worship.[53] If this is to be accepted, then the following verse (v. 27) would naturally flow as a consequence of the idolatrous worship of the people, aggravated by the lack of righteousness in the preceding verses. Verse 27 states: "'Therefore I will take you into exile beyond Damascus,' says the Lord, whose name is the God of hosts."

The "therefore" that opens the verse is employed to signal the relationship of cause and effect. Thus, the verse may have to be rendered that, as a result of the Israelites' unrepentant hypocrisy of worshiping idols while bringing religious sacrifices and offerings before the Lord, he says that he will send them into exile beyond Damascus.[54] "Most interpreters take this as a cryptic reference to Assyria, although Amos never mentions Assyria in the book."[55] Speaking about exile, its mention here may just be an implicit critique of the Israelites' propensity to go into relationship with other nations.[56] Hajiev thinks that there seems to be an implicit tension between the need for justice to flow like a river in v. 24 and the impending exile in v. 27. "The call in v. 24 implies a possibility for change, the announcement in v. 27 assumes exactly the reverse."[57] This opinion, however, is subject to debate since the call for justice and righteousness can conveniently be interpreted as YHWH's invitation for repentance. For Menezes, however, the text implies that Israel's exodus from bondage in Egypt (Exod 19:4) was YHWH's doing, but if Israel continues their hollow cultic practices, this time around "Israel's idols will be carried by Israel into Exile."[58]

Summarily, the foregoing discussion shows how the prophet Amos strongly disapproves of hypocritical worship, the type of worship that fools the society to the detriment of its poor, vulnerable members. However, this does not mean that "all forms worship are useless and objectionable in themselves. Neither does God seem to declare that rituals and religious songs as a whole have no value. They have value but must conform with a spirit of prayer, justice, and charity to one's neighbour."[59] At the end of the day, what Amos advocates for is that "justice should be sought at all levels irrespective of economic or political status of the persons involved. Irresponsible conducts, whether within or without the rreligious structures, adversely affect the society, and are a sin against God."[60]

---

52. Hadjiev, *A Composition and Redaction of the Book of Amos*, 167.
53. Opade, "The Nexus Between Religious Practices And Human Value," 71.
54. Pitts, *An Exegesis of Amos 5:18–27*, 2022.
55. Sweeney and Sweeney, *The Twelve Prophets*, 241.
56. Sweeney and Sweeney, *The Twelve Prophets*, 241.
57. Hadjiev, *Book of Amos*, 168.
58. Menezes, *Amos*, 1138.
59. Udoekpo, *Rethinking the Prophetic Critique of Worship in Amos 5*, 112
60. Igbo, *Introduction*, 334.

Theological Considerations in Amos 5:21–27

Even a cursory glance at the book of Amos would reveal that its theological import can never be overemphasized. If this assertion is true for the whole book, it is much more true for its fifth chapter. This is so because, as earlier stated, "The section in Amos 5:21–27 is generally included in studies focusing on the prophetic critique of ritual and cult of the Hebrew Bible."[61] In this regard, one can say that some theological significance of Amos 5:21–27 can be considered under three subsections:

1. Social Sin: The Undoing of Religious Practices
2. Humanitarian Acts Are Better Than Empty Ritual Acts
3. Sin against Social Justice Attracts Punishment

Social Sin: The Undoing of Religion and Its Holy Practices

The first theological motif in Amos 5:21–27 is the critique against social sin. In the face of all the external displays of religious activities, Amos "observes that Israel's worship is not accompanied by justice and respect of all human persons, especially the poor."[62] This is precisely what constitutes social sin, and this social sin in turn becomes the undoing of all religious practices that ordinarily should attract God's favors. Thus, Amos says, the festivals (v. 21), sacrifices (v. 22), the noisy music (v. 23), and proliferation of cultic activities (v. 25) are conveniently hated, despised, rejected by YHWH, precisely because they are external displays that are rather a façade that covers the life of social sin among the people. Therefore, "Amos' critique was meant to remind his contemporaries that traditional worship functioned to maintain the rapport between Israel and God."[63] In this way, "Amos vehemently attacked the sins of the society as sins against Yahweh, and warned of the coming judgment."[64] This brings out a strong clarion call that if religion must be true and its practices acceptable to God, then the adherents of such religion must develop and maintain the principle of total exclusion where social sin is concerned.

Humanitarian Acts Are Better Than Empty Ritual Acts

The face of the forgoing discussion on the theology of Amos 5:21–27 makes it clear that a true and sincere religion and all the rituals that it involves must always bear in mind the call to promote humanitarian acts best described as justice and righteousness in the text under study. Udoekpo insists that "Justice is vital for all generations

---

61. Klingbeil and Klingbeil, "The Prophetic Voice of Amos," 171.
62. Udoekpo, *Rethinking the Prophetic Critique of Worship in Amos 5*, 98.
63. Udoekpo, *Rethinking the Prophetic Critique of Worship in Amos 5*, 101.
64. Igbo, *Introduction*, 333.

and groups who have labored to define not just its meaning but also its importance for healthy society."⁶⁵ In fact, what is at issue here is abuse of piety to cover those who hide from their wicked ways. It is in this regard that Amos 5:21–27 is seen in this study as a call to all adherents of religions to be involved in mission to practice and promote humanitarian acts. Indeed, although rituals and cultic practices in religion are important and they help express the sentiment of devotion of the worshiper, they must come only after men and women have lived lives that put into consideration the needs and dignity of their fellow humans, especially the weak and vulnerable (Exod 22:21).⁶⁶ As Udoekpo states, "When worship was conducted properly and devotedly with a sense of love, gratitude, justice, righteousness, and respect, for the dignity of people—especially the weak and the poor—it was acceptable to God for the atonement of sins (Lev 1:4)."⁶⁷ Unfortunately, there is no room for double standards, and this echoes the prophecy of Hosea, "I desire steadfast love and not sacrifice, the knowledge of God, rather than burnt offerings" (Hos 6:6 RSV), and echoed by Jesus in Matthew 9:13. "If the Israelite behavior in the market place were characterized by love, justice, righteousness, and compassion, then their festivals, offerings, pilgrimages, and songs would be ideal of authentic worship dedicated to God."⁶⁸

Sin against Social Justice attracts Punishment

For Amos the prophet, if the hypocritical worship of the people with its concomitant oppression of the weak and the poor was left unpunished, then his prophecy would have been a futile endeavor. However, the consolation for the prophet is that such acts can never go unpunished. This theological motif in Amos 5 is an apt message for all religious adherents to note that one's unjust and unethical treatment of their weak and vulnerable neighbor will always come with consequences. Men and women with financial advantages and political influence who put up external religious displays but molest, kill, and maim the underprivileged in the society would always have to own up to their crime before the divine being, the author of all creatures.

AMOS 5:21–27 IN AFRICAN CONTEXT

Igbo, in his work, aptly captures the subject matter of this subunit of the study. In his words,

> Although Amos addressed his message originally to the Israelites of hos day, his message has an enduring value for all times. The ills denounced by Amos

---

65. Udoekpo, *Rethinking the Prophetic Critique of Worship in Amos 5*, 105.
66. Igbo, *Introduction*, 333.
67. Udoekpo, *Rethinking the Prophetic Critique of Worship in Amos 5*, 101.
68. Udoekpo, *Rethinking the Prophetic Critique of Worship in Amos 5*, 112.

in the 8th century are almost the same in our contemporary times: exploitation of the poor by the rich and upper class of the society, corruption in the courts of law (justice given to the highest bidder), and religious formalism.[69]

That this assertion is not an exaggeration can easily be confirmed even by either looking at social media and internet stories, picking up newspapers, reading academic articles, or casually viewing news from media houses.

Proliferation of Religious Centers for Hypocritical Worshipers

Every day, one wakes up to stories of injustice and man's inhumane treatment of other citizens, especially in Africa. This happens despite the fact that, as John Mbiti would say, Africans are "notoriously religious."[70] Additionally, everyday religious houses and worship centers are proliferating all over Africa. Using Christianity as an example, Agnes Acha avers that churches multiply every day and their members are steadily on the increase.[71] In another article, Acha affirms that "Religious centres, mostly churches and mosques are all over the places. In fact, all evidence points to the fact that new ones are still springing up almost on daily basis and most of these centres are never lacking in members as they are almost always filled to the brim."[72]

Notwithstanding this, Luke Ijezie decries the fact that the religious presence has not helped to breed good conduct among their adherents. He insists that "Religion is a great force in Nigeria today but one cannot but marvel at the alarming hypocrisy and contradictions in the social life of the worshippers."[73] Acha in her article corroborates this when she writes that "if the multiplication of churches remains on constant increase just as their members increase, and the rate of crime remains as high as it is with its accompanying social chaos and disorder, then some is certainly wrong somewhere."[74] Yet it is a reality that Africans are in bondage of every kind of evil at the hands of worshipers of different religions.[75]

Injustice Perpetrated by Worshipers

First, there is a high rate of social injustice. The poor are oppressed and denied their rights by the rich, who themselves flock worship centers on a daily basis. In this connection, Cletus Obijiaku asserts that scholars are unanimous that injustice manifested

---

69. Igbo, *Introduction to the Old Testament Books and Pseudepigrapha*, 334.
70. Mbiti, *African Concept of God*, 1.
71. Acha, "'These People Honour Me with Their Lips,'" 49.
72. Acha, "Jeremiah 7:1–15: A Call to Religious Integrity," 68.
73. Ijezie, "Freedom and Righteousness," 69.
74. Acha, "These People Honour Me with Their Lips," 49.
75. Ijezie. "Freedom and Righteousness," 69.

in the oppression of the poor is widespread in society. "This opinion cuts across both Christians and Muslims who form the majority of the population."[76] It is obvious that the injustice is first perpetrated by the few who are economically and politically empowered.[77] Talking from the point of view of Islam, for example, Ibrahim Abdulsalam decries that although Islam upholds social justice under the auspices of *Tawlid*, there is however so much injustice among highly placed Muslim worshipers against the weak, the poor, the sick, the needy, and even the orphans.[78] The point at issue here is that the perpetrators of this unethical conduct are seen to be practicing religion profusely, pretending all the while to be doing the right thing.

Corruption Practiced by Worshipers

Corruption and its proliferation is another indicator of unethical religion in Africa. Udoekpo, in this regard, states that Africans and especially Nigerians are "dominated by all kinds of shameless corruption, violence, inordinate pursuit of wealth."[79] These acts of corruption are highly practiced by the elite themselves who are obviously helpless in finding a true cure for this endemic disease. Udoekpo argues that the reason for corruption, the victims of which are the poor masses, is that the perpetrators "lack fear of the Lord, proper accountability, a sense of shame, concern for the common good and ethical responsibility."[80] But like the people of Israel, these vandals go to worship centers and still keep straight faces. In fact, Acha has rightly noted that they display different forms of piety, including donating huge sums of money and giving tithes, seed sowings to bishops, priests, pastors, Imams, or key leaders of religions.[81] Similarly, Teresa Okure writes that "in Nigeria, some politicians and civil servants embezzle public funds and from them they pay fat tithes and make huge donations to the church."[82] The bottom line here is that many contemporary worshipers belonging to the different religions are comfortable practicing religion without ethics, which includes the dynamics of hypocrisy and corruption, the very subject matter at issue in Amos' polemics in 5:21–27.

Crimes and Violence among Worshipers

For Africa, as a continent, the inhabitants of which are notoriously religious, one expects that "peace" and "tranquility" would be a glaring state. On the contrary, however,

---

76. Obijiaku, "Social Injustice and Its Corollary in Amos 8:1–14," 53.
77. Ucheaga, "Social Justice in Nigeria," 31.
78. Abdulsalam, "Social Justice In Nigeri," 2022.
79. Udoekpo, "Corruption in the Household of Micah," 17.
80. Udoekpo. "Corruption in the Household of Micah," 17.
81. Acha, "Jeremiah 7:1–15: A Call to Religious Integrity," 68.
82. Okure, "Integrity and Corruption," 150.

African nations are also notorious for increasing violence and crimes. In Nigeria, for example, since the early 2000s, crime and violence perpetrated by people who go to mosques and churches have proliferated to an extent where security of life and property is only possible under probability. In this connection, Acha insists that:

> Still among those who frequent these worship centres and churches, particularly, are those who have been involved in all sorts of crimes against humanity ranging from embezzlement of public funds, involvement in ritual killings, kidnapping, cheating at work places, bribery and corruption. These too make massive offerings, make thanksgiving and even give tithe, all from the proceeds of the illegal and evil funds realized through the terrible things they do.[83]

Indeed, although many forms of crime and violence are engendered or motivated by economic hardships, and others are politically motivated, in Africa and especially in Nigeria, many other forms of crime and violence have religious backgrounds. Hans Küng has argued that "Armed conflicts in which religion, often accompanied by ethnic differences, plays a part have proliferated in recent decades in various parts of the world: Northern Ireland, the Balkans, Sri Lanka, India, Nigeria."[84] To bring it home, Omotosho avers that "within the last two decades Nigeria has witnessed a variety of disturbances some of which have threatened the existence of the country as a nation. Some of these disturbances could be described as intra-religious while the others are interreligious."[85] While this is true of Nigeria, it is also true of many African countries. It is therefore not an undue exaggeration to state that in many African countries, "religion and violence are hardly strangers."[86] The contradiction here is that these violent acts against humanity are perpetrated by worshipers who are always seen in centers for worship, where it is understood generally that religion is "a vessel of peace, both inner and social."[87] This is precisely what set the prophet Amos on the mission for polemics against such adherents of religion. Thus, Amos 5:21–27 would continue to be relevant in the African nations and even beyond as long as violence and crimes continue to be promoted by worshpers of various religions.

Immoral Conducts among Worshipers

Almost all the major religions, including native ones, have strong codes of conduct concerning lifestyle and sexual practices. However, it has become evident that while people keep straight faces in places of worship and listen to sermons that emphasize these moral values, many go behind and indulge in them. These range from sexual

---

83. Acha, "Jeremiah 7:1–15: A Call to Religious Integrity," 69.
84. Küng, "Religion, Violence and 'Holy War,'" 253.
85. Omtosho, "Religious Violence in Nigeria," 15.
86. Hall, "Religion and Violence," 1.
87. Hall, "Religion and Violence," 1.

immorality and deviant sexual orientations to abortions and the like. In this connection, speaking in particular of incest, Peter Onwuka insists that "Incest is a phenomenon that is in increase both among Christians and non-Christians in Nigeria. Since sexual matters are usually shrouded in secrecy, so many of such activities go unreported."[88] Going further, Onwuka argues that other forms of sexual immoralities such as abuse of minors and rape continue to enjoy patronage. However, "Very worrisome are the ones perpetuated by the Christian leaders or ministers. Sexual immorality involving pastors and ministers of some denominations in Nigerians become a recurrent news in Nigerian newspapers."[89] In the face of all these, one is left with no choice but to argue that Amos 5:21–27 is still relevant even as it indicts the hypocrisy of religious people who live Janus-faced lives.

CONCLUDING THOUGHTS

In the foregoing study of Amos 5:21–27, it became clear that the prophet strongly criticized and condemned the hypocritical lives of those who worshiped YHWH but suffered moral bankruptcy. Most importantly, the prophet insisted that such lives of double standards have corresponding consequences. As it stands, this study has shown that the text remains relevant for many modern societies, especially in Africa. Accordingly, the study recommends that these Africans who flock into worship centers but live lives that are at variance with the tenets of the religion adopt the message of Amos: repent or suffer the consequences. This is more so because, as Acha would say, if religion is truly what it is, then its adherents should be able "to 'leaven the yeast' of the corruption, evil and disorder in our society today."[90]

Arguing in favoa r of ethical lifestyle in a society where religion is a great force, Ijezie expresses dismay at the contradictions and hypocrisy in social life. He insists that "As justice is the state of affairs brought about by the doing of righteousness, the lack of righteous relationships bring about a whole host of social evils."[91] But precisely because social evils are destructive, modern worshipers must desist from them for the society to be a better home for all. To ensure this, it is expected that citizens of all times should ensure that justice is always enthroned in all facets of the society. Using the Christian worshipers as an example, Obijiaku affirms that "Christian communities should strengthen their agents that work for justice and peace."[92] If this is true for the Christian worshipers, it should be true for all adherents of other religions, since social justice is needed for and by all.

---

88. Onwuka, "Sexual Immorality and Church's Discipline," 181.
89. Onwuka, "Sexual Immorality and Church's Discipline," 182.
90. Acha, "These People Honour Me with Their Lips," 49.
91. Ijezie, "Freedom and Righteousness," 69.
92. Obijiaku, "Social Injustice and Its Corollary in Amos 8:1–14," 59.

As regards corruption, this study challenges all Africans to reflect deeply on their actions and conscientiously turn to the divine beings they worship for help in order to discard corruption in society.[93] Additionally, since crimes and violence deprive citizens of peace and tranquility, Africans must strive to reflect the face of the God/gods they worship since all religions claim they uphold and preach peace, at least theoretically. Indeed, the adage should be put into practice that says: "Like god, like worshipers." Finally, since purity is preached by the different religions, moral decadence, especially those that come with abuse and molestations that are at variance with the tenets of these religions, should be shunned. By and large, then, Africans, who are said to be notoriously religious, ought to avoid Janus-faced lives; they ought to learn to be consistent in trying to synchronize their religions with their social lives. In this regard, Amos 5:21–27 would always be a relevant gadfly, the patronage of which would be needed to sting people's consciences into consciousness.

BIBLIOGRAPHY

Abdulsalam, Ibrahim K. *Social Justice In Nigeria: An Appraisal of the Role of the Muslim Ummah*, Bayero University, Kano. Accessible at: https://www.google.com/search?q=www.academia.edu%2F1151836%2Fsocial+justice+in+nigeria%3A+an+appraisal+of+the+role+of+the+MUslim+ummah&].

Acha, Agnes. "'These People Honour Me with Their Lips:' A Study of Isa 29:13 and Its Implication for Faith and Evangelization in Nigeria." In *The Bible on Faith and Evangelization*. Edited by Bernard Ukwuegbu et al. Acts of the Catholic Biblical Association of Nigeria (CABAN) 6. Port Harcourt: CABAN, 2015.

———. "Jeremiah 7:1–15: A Call to Religious Integrity." In *Integrity and Corruption in the Bible*. Edited by Bernard Ukwuegbu et al. Acts of the Catholic Biblical Association of Nigeria (CABAN) 12. Port Harcourt: CABAN, 2020.

"Amos 5:25-27—An Analysis." Bible Gateway. https://www.biblegateway.com/passage/?search=Amos%205%3A25-27&version=NET.

Anderson, Francis I., and David Noel Freedman. *Amos*. Anchor Bible Series 24A. New York: Doubleday, 1989.

Arnold, Bill T., and John H. Choi. *A Guide to Biblical Hebrew Syntax*. New York: Cambridge University Press, 2003.

Averbeck, Richard E. "Šelem." In *New International Dictionary of Old Testament Theology & Exegesis*. Edited by Willem Van Gemeren. Grand Rapids: Zondervan, 1997.

BibleWorks—[c:/program files (x86)\bibleworks 9\ini\bw900.swc] on Amos 5:23.

Boadt, Lawrence. *Reading the Old Testament: An Introduction*. New York: Paulist Press, 2012.

Brown, Walter E. "Amos 5:26: A Challenge to Reading And Interpretation." *The Theological Educator* 52 (1995).

Buber, Martin. *The Prophetic Faith*. New York: Collier, 1949.

Chisholm, Robert B., Jr. *Handbook on the Prophets: Isaiah, Jeremiah, Lamentations, Ezekiel, Daniel, Minor Prophets*. Grand Rapids: Baker Academic, 2002.

---

93. Udoekpo, "Corruption in the Household of Micah," 19.

Coffman, James Burton. "Commentary on Amos 5." In *Coffman's Commentaries on the Bible*. Abilene, TX: Abilene Christian University Press, 1983–1999. https://www.studylight.org/commentaries/eng/bcc/amos-5.html.

De Menezes, Rui. "Amos." In *The International Bible Commentary*. Edited by William R. Farmer. Minnesota: Liturgical Press, 1998.

De Vaux, Roland. *Ancient Israel: Its Life and Institutions*. Translated by John McHugh. Great Britain: Redwood Press Limited, 1997.

Driver, S. R, and H. C. O Lanchester. *The Books of Joel and Amos*. Cambridge: Cambridge University Press, 1915.

Elwell, Walter A., and Philip Wesley Comfort. *Tyndale Bible Dictionary*. Tyndale ReferenceLibrary. Wheaton: Tyndale House Publishers, 2001.

Eriye, Festus. "APC and Its Presidential Headache." *The Nation*. November 9, 2014.

———. "Presidency 2015: Neither Religion Nor Ethnicity." *The Nation*. November 30, 2014.

Fabry, Heinz-Josef. "mā'as." In *Theological Dictionary of the Old Testament (TDOT)*. Vol. 8. Edited by G. Johannes Botterweck et al. Grand Rapids: Eerdmans, 1999.

Familusi, O. O. "Religious Politics and its Implications for Sustainable Development in The Post Independence Nigeria." *Journal of Sustainable Development in Africa* 12, no. 5 (2010).

Fawole, Alade. "Religion and Political Contestation in Nigeria." *Nigerian Tribune*, October 28, 2014.

Finley, Thomas John. *The Wycliffe Exegetical Commentary: Joel, Amos, Obadiah*. Chicago: Moody Press, 1990.

Freston, Paul. *Evangelicals and Politics in Asia, Africa and Latin America*. Cambridge: Cambridge University Press

Garret, Duane A., *Amos: A Handbook on the Hebrew Text*. Michigan: Baylor University Press, 2008.

Gevirtz, Stanley. "A New Look at An Old Crux: Amos 5:26." *Journal of Biblical Literature* 87, no. 3 (1968).

Gitay, Yehoshua. "A Study of Amos's Art of Speech: A Rhetorical Analysis of Amos 3:1–15." *Catholic Biblical Quarterly* 42 (1980).

Groenewald, Alphonso. "'But Let Justice Roll Down Like Waters, and Righteousness Like an Ever-Flowing Stream' (Am 5:24): Social Justice Versus Cult Criticism in Amos (5:21–24) and Isaiah (1:10–20); A Trauma Perspective." *HTS Teologiese Studies/Theological Studies* 75, no. 3 (2019).

Hall, John R. "Religion and Violence: Social Processes in Comparative Perspective." In *Handbook for the Sociology of Religion*. Cambridge: Cambridge University Press, 2003.

Harper, William Rainey. *A Critical and Exegetical Commentary on Amos and Hosea*. New York: C. Scribner's Sons, 1905.

Igbo, Philip M. *Introduction to the Old Testament Books and Pseudepigrapha*. Enugu: Claretian Publications, 2020.

Ijezie, Luke E. "Freedom and Righteousness as Conditions for Good Citizenship: The Perspective of the Sabbath Regulation in the Old Testament." In *Good Citizenship and Leadership in the Bible*. Edited by Bernard Ukwuegbu et al. Acts of the Catholic Biblical Association of Nigeria (CABAN) 3. Port Harcourt: CABAN, 2014.

United Nations Office for the Coordination of Humanitarian Affairs 2001. "IRIN Web Special on Nigeria." IRINnews.org. 2003.

Ironside, H. A. "Commentary on Amos 5." StudyLight.org. https://www.studylight.org/commentaries/eng/isn/amos-5.html. 1914.

Jörg, Jeremias. *The Book of Amos: A Commentary*. Translated by Douglas W. Stott. Old Testament Library. Louisville: Westminster John Knox Press, 1998.

Kaiser, Walter C., Jr. *The Promise-Plan of God: A Biblical Theology of the Old and New Testaments*. Grand Rapids: Zondervan, 2008.

Kaiser, P. J. *A Comparative Government and Politics: Nigeria*. Briefing Paper, College Board, 2005. Available at: apcentral.collegeboard.com.

Keil, Carl Friedrich, and Franz Delitzsch. *Commentary on the Old Testament*. Vol. 10. Peabody: Hendrickson, 1996.

Klingbeil, Gerald A., and Martin G. Klingbeil. "The Prophetic Voice of Amos as a Paradigm for Christians in the Public Square." *Tyndale Bulletin* 58, no. 2 (2007).

Koch, Klaus, et al. *Amos: Untersuchtmit den MethodeneinerstrukturalenFormgeschichte [Alter Orient und Altes Testament]*. Neukirchen-Vluyn: Butzon & Bercker, 1976.

Kukah, M. H. "Contemporary Religious Dynamics in Nigeria." Federal News Service Inc. Washington, DC: 2007

Küng, Hans. "Religion, Violence and 'Holy War.'" *International Review of the Red Cross* 87, no. 858 (2005).

Lafferty Veronica T. *The Prophetic Critique of the Priority of the Cult: A Study of Amos 5:21–24 and Isaiah 1:10–17*. Unpublished doctoral thesis submitted to the faculty of the School of Theology and Religious Studies of the The Catholic University of America, 2010.

Leclerc, Thomas. *Introduction to the Prophets: Their Stories, Sayings, and Scrolls*. New York: Paulist Press, 2007.

Mays, J. L. *Amos*. London: SCM Press, 1985.

Mbiti, John. *African Concept of God*. London: SMC, 1970.

Mulzac, Kenneth D. "Amos 5:18–20 in its Exegetical and Theological Contexts." *Journal of the Adventist Theological Society* 13, no. 2 (2002).

Obijiaku, Cletus U. "Social Injustice and Its Corollary in Amos 8:1–14: Lessons for Nigerian Christians." In *Mercy and Justice in the Bible*. Edited by Bernard Ukwuegbu et al. Acts of the Catholic Biblical Association of Nigeria (CABAN) 9. Port Harcourt: CABAN, 2017.

Odey, Simon R., and Eric Ndoma B. *Religious Hypocrisy and Fanaticism in Nigeria: The Apex Problem of a Religious Nation; The Contemporary Religions and Religious Issues*. Makurdi, Nigeria: Ebonyi State University—New Frontier Ind. Research and Publications Int'l, 2017.

Okure, Teresa, "Integrity and Corruption in the Parable of the Shrewd Manager (Luke 16:1–8): A Contextual Study." In *Integrity and Corruption in the Bible*. Edited by Bernard Ukwuegbu et al. Acts of the Catholic Biblical Association of Nigeria (CABAN) 12. Port Harcourt: CABAN, 2020.

Omtosho, A. O. "Religious Violence in Nigeria—the Causes and Solutions: An Islamic Perspective." *Swedish Missiological Theme* (2003).

Onwuka, Peter C. "Sexual Immorality and Church's Discipline in 1 Cor 5:1–5: Implications for the Nigerian Church." In *Integrity and Corruption in the Bible*. Edited by Bernard Ukwuegbu et al. Acts of the Catholic Biblical Association of Nigeria (CABAN) 12. Port Harcourt: CABAN, 2020.

Opade, Faith O. "The Nexus Between Religious Practices And Human Value: Lessons From Amos 5:18–27." *International Journal of Innovative Social Sciences & Humanities Research* 9, no. 2 (2021).

Osuagwu, Tochukwu. *An Ideological-Critical Interpretation of Justice and Righteousness in Amos 5*. Unpublished MA degree thesis in the Faculty of Theology, University of Pretoria, 2016.

Paul, Shalom M. *Amos: A Commentary on the Book of Amos*. Minneapolis: Fortress Press, 1991.

Pitts, Roderick. "An Exegesis of Amos 5:18–27," 2012. Available at https://www.academia.edu/8901282/An_Exegesis_of_Amos_5_18_27.

Smith, Billy K., and Franklin S. Page. *The New American Commentary: Amos, Obadiah, Jonah*. Vol. 19B. Nashville: Broadman & Holman, 1995.

Sweeney, Marvin A. *The Twelve Prophets: Berit Olam*. Vol. 1. Minnesota: Liturgical Press, 2000.

Tchavdar, Hadjiev S. *A Composition and Redaction of the Book of Amos*. Berlin: Gruyter GmbH and Co. KG., 2009.

Ucheaga, Dorothy N. "Social Justice in Nigeria: The Dialectics of Ideas and Reality." *Humanities Review Journal* 1, no. 2 (2001).

Udoekpo, Michael U. "Corruption in the Household of Micah (Judges 17:1–6) in the Nigerian Context." In *Integrity and Corruption in the Bible*. Edited by Bernard Ukwuegbu et al. Acts of the Catholic Biblical Association of Nigeria (CABAN) 12. Port Harcourt: CABAN, 2020.

———. *Israel's Prophets and the Prophetic Effect of Pope Francis: A Pastoral Companion*. Eugene: Wipf & Stock, 2018.

———. *Rethinking the Prophetic Critique of Worship in Amos 5 for Contemporary Nigeria and USA*. Eugene: Pickwick Publications, 2017.

Willoughby, Bruce E. "The Book of Amos." In *The Anchor Bible Dictionary*, vol 1. Edited by David Noel Freedman et al. New York: Doubleday, 1992.

Chapter 6

The Prophetic Mission of Obadiah
in the Context of African Christianity

Michael Ufok Udoekpo

INTRODUCTION

The prophecy of Obadiah is the shortest book in the Hebrew Bible. It has only twenty-one verses, but those verses are rich. It reviews the ancient familial conflict between Esau and Jacob (Gen 25:29–30; 36; Jer 49:7–22). It conveys Obadiah's missionary voice, which speaks about such topics as divine judgment (vv. 1–4), the taunting of Edom (vv. 5–8), divine indictment (vv. 12–14), the Day of the Lord (vv. 15–18), and the theology of hope and Israel's restoration (vv. 19–21)—topics that are relevant for the church in Africa, or African Christianity, today. This church, of course, is widely and popularly acknowledged as a "Family of God's People," distinguishable from all other African human communities by its listening faith, hope, and love, which derives prophetically from, and centers on, Jesus and his redemptive work.[1] Historically, this church-family in Africa has already been blessed in many ways: in her sacramental life, her deep sense of the sacred, her sense of the mission and existence of God, her lively liturgical celebrations, and her deep-cherished sense of family values.[2] Such blessings notwithstanding, her numerous challenges and yearnings include poverty, political instability, social disorientation, misery, war, injustice of all forms, terrorism,

---

1. In this category belongs the Catholic "Church" in Africa as well as other "church" denominations, particularly in Nigeria. For discussion of the long history and state of Christianity in Africa, which is beyond the scope of this present study, see Isichei, *A History of Christianity in Africa*, 1995; Muli, "The State of Christianity in Africa," 2:312–18.

2. For details of how the church in Africa is characterized as a family, see Udoekpo, "Becoming a Church-Family in Africa," 171–92.

division, anthropocentrism and ethnocentrism, selfishness, tribalism, the inordinate urge for material things, syncretism, family and ethnic conflict, violence, betrayal, jealousy, and gloating over one another and ones' neighbors. Similar challenges were seen during the time of the biblical prophet Obadiah, which is the focus of this contextual and theological essay.[3]

This essay exegetically and historically explores two important topics inherent in the prophecy of Obadiah, one of the Twelve Minor Prophets whom God chose and sent: first, the sacredness of global family obligations, and second, the tragic consequences of tension and indifferent attitudes among family members.[4] While this work honors Teresa Okure, SHCJ, an outstanding missionary who has worked tirelessly to reach out to territories and persons for conversion as well as to "effect passage over the boundary between faith in Jesus and its absence," it equally passionately appeals to the listening ears of today's church and Christian communities in Africa.[5] Our essay consciously aims at actualizing, contextualizing, and relating the theological findings of the prophecy of Obadiah to the daily life situations of religious communities and church-families in African nations and beyond.

OBADIAH IN RETROSPECT

Some relevant background information is worth mentioning to provide a historical backdrop for the rest of our study, including information on the prophet Obadiah himself, as well as information on the book's situational and historical setting, audience, and relationship with other prophetic books, especially Jeremiah 49:7–22 and the Twelve Minor Prophets, as well its theology, text, and working structure.

---

3. Cf. John Paul II, First African Synod, *Ecclesia in Africa*; 1995; Benedict XVI, *Africae Munus*, 2011, and the *Instrumentum Laboris* of the SECAM Golden Jubilee Year July 2018–July 2019. For some of the challenges facing the church in Africa, see Oobator, ed., *Reconciliation, Justice and Peace*, 2011, which contains eighteen articles that reflect the yearnings of African scholars for African Christianity or the church in Africa.

4. In addition to exploring Obadiah within the context of the Twelve Minor Prophets (MT ordering: Hosea, Joel, Amos, Obadiah, Jonah, Micah, Nahum, Habakkuk, Zephaniah, Haggai, Zechariah, and Malachi; LXX ordering: Hosea, Amos, Micha, Joel, Obadiah, Jonah, Nahum, Habakkuk, Zephaniah, Haggai, Zechariah, and Malachi), the following works emphasize the importance of contextual or "inculturation hermeneutics" and theology: Ukpong, "Inculturation Hermeneutics," 17–32; Schreiter, *The New Catholicity*, 1997; and the entire work of his student Bevans, *Models of Contextual Theology*, 2002.

5. This definition or description of mission is drawn from the "preface to the ASM Series" in Okoye, *Israel and the Nations*, 2006, and Bevans and Gros, *Evangelization and Religious Freedom*, 2009. The basic functions of Christian proclamation, dialogue, witness, teaching, writing, worshiping, and reaching out to persons and territories—seen in ancient Obadiah and in Okure, a religious woman, and others today—fall under this definition and description of mission by missiologists and in Vatican II documents, including *Ad Gentes*, 6; *Lumen Gentium*, 16; and *Gaudium et Spes*, 22. By analogy, see also Okure's "Survey of Major Approaches to Mission in John's Gospel in the Twentieth Century," 7–35.

Obadiah is the shortest book in the Bible—so short, in fact, that it has no chapters.[6] As such, references provided for reading and studying contain only verse numbers. Obadiah is fundamentally focused on the "Day of the Lord" (*yôm ădōnay*) and the Lord's divine sovereignty, similar to Joel, Amos, and other minor prophets—a point we will discuss further.

The name Obadiah (*ōbadyâ*) translates as "one who serves Yhwh" or "servant of the Lord." Not much is known about the prophet Obadiah; the superscription provides no information other than the name, simply stating, "the vision of Obadiah" (*ḥăzôn ōbadyâ*). But we know that there are eleven other persons in the Old Testament with a similar name holding rich symbolic meaning. Like African names, Hebrew names were not empty labels. Names in both African and Hebrew culture can express prayer, honor a deity, or allude to a historically significant event.[7] In this study, we recognize that Obadiah's name is a highly symbolic and anticipatory reminder of the ministering role and missioning services that belong to the church-family in Africa and beyond. This symbolism notwithstanding, "Some scholars do suggest that this is a name assigned to an otherwise anonymous block of material to bring the number of the minor prophets to the significant number of twelve (corresponding to the twelve tribes of Israel)."[8] Others, however, believe Obadiah to be an actual individual. They suggest that the prophet Obadiah may have been closely associated with the mission in the temple area or a learned prophetic-scribe endowed with wisdom traditions.[9]

HISTORICAL AND SITUATIONAL SETTING

As we examine Obadiah's contextual, situational, and historical setting, we must remember that the Bible is a great code for cultures that stands the test of time and culture.[10] This is why many, including Daniel J. Simundson, agree that "Edom is the central focus of the book."[11] At the time Obadiah was written, Edom, a small country located in present-day southern Jordan, east of the area of the Dead Sea, held a strategic location for business along an ancient trading route. Edom ("red region") was well fortified and protected against potential enemies' militaries.[12] The ancient city of Petra ("rock"), visited by so many tourists today, is located within the vicinity of

---

6. See Pagan, "The Book of Obadiah," 5:611.
7. See Musopole, "Obadiah," 1041.
8. Leclerc, *Introduction to the Prophets*, 274.
9. Leclerc, *Prophets*, 274.
10. Benedict XVI, *Verbum Domini*, n. 110.
11. Simundson, *Obadiah*, 243.
12. The name Edom is further explained in Pagan, "Obadiah," 613, who says, "a characteristic of the region is the reddish color of its rocks and mountains; that geological trait may explain its name: *mwda* (*ēdôm*) signifies this red region."

Edom. Towns such as Sela (v. 3) and Teman (v. 9) are likewise found in the territory and neighborhood of Edom.[13]

The long history of conflict and misunderstanding between Israel and Edom is first introduced in Genesis 25. The conflict we see between these two peoples is comparable to such prevalent conflicts we see in modern societies in Africa, Nigeria in particular, today. Genesis 25:30 identifies Esau, the twin brother of Jacob, with Edom. These two brothers began fighting when they were still in their mother's womb (Gen 25:19–26), and their rivalry intensified when Jacob treacherously received from their father Isaac the blessings which should have customarily gone to his brother, the firstborn son Esau (Gen 27; cf. Gen 32–33; 36; Num 20:14–21; Deut 2:4–8; 23:7; Jer 49:7–11; Amos 1:11–12; Mal 1:2–4). Stories of conflicts between the two peoples are recorded during the time of David (2 Sam 8:13–14); they appear, in fact, as early as the time of King Saul, when Edom was listed among Israel's enemies (1 Sam 14:47). The conflict persisted through the time of the destruction of Jerusalem by the Babylonian military in 586/7 BCE (2 Kgs; Obad 11–14). Of course, when Obadiah speaks of Israel or the houses of Jacob and Joseph, he is referring to Judah, the only nation of God's people left to carry on the traditions. During the exile, both nations were politically weakened. After the exile, a group of Edomites migrated to the south of Palestine to protect it from Nabataean Arabs in the area that was later known as Idumea (Mark 3:8)—a region connected with Herod the Great, an Idumaen.[14] The terms "Idumea" and "Idumean," Danial I. Block argues, communicate not only the hostility of the Jews toward the Edomites and their resentment toward Herod, but that "the message of the prophet would have offered hope to the Judeans (and beyond) long after Obadiah had delivered these oracles."[15]

Although it may be difficult to determine precisely when Obadiah was written, and to whom, let alone the full historical or situational circumstances surrounding his preaching and mission work, all the details in the book seem to place Obadiah sometime in the exile, or after 586 BCE, when the people of Judah's remembrance of their humiliation at the hand of the Babylonian military was made worse by their memory of how Edom had not been there to render help; in contrast, the Edomites had even enjoyed their defeat, gloating, mocking, and remaining idle as they watched them suffer—a reaction that is common in our contemporary communities and neighborhoods today.[16]

---

13. Simundson, *Obadiah*, 243.

14. See the synopsis of this mutual hostility in Pagan, "Obadiah," 613 and Simundson, *Obadiah*, 243.

15. Block, *Obadiah*, 22–23.

16. For various theories and proposals regarding the dating and circumstances around Obadiah's preaching and mission, see Block, *Obadiah*, 23–24; Pagan, "Obadiah," 612; Simundson, *Obadiah*, 243–44; and Sweeney, *Twelve Prophets*, 280–81.

OBADIAH'S RELATIONSHIP WITH OTHER PROPHETS

In a study of this magnitude, it is imperative that we offer brief comments on the literary and thematic relationship of Obadiah to other prophets, especially Jeremiah and the other eleven Minor Prophets, as well as its text, overall message, and structure.[17] Scholars often point out the similarities and differences between Obadiah 1–7 and Jeremiah 49:7–22. Some argue that Obadiah was influenced by Jeremiah's prophecy in his preaching and mission, while others believe Jeremiah borrowed texts from Obadiah, suggesting both relied on each other.[18]

Comparatively, Jeremiah 49:7–22 and Obadiah 1–7 share a great deal of common language. Both, however, presuppose different contexts or situations. Jeremiah 49:7–22 condemns Edom and stresses the fear that Edom exudes (Jer 49:16). In pointing to YHWH'S future punishment of Edom, Jeremiah's prophecy, unlike Obadiah (vv. 12–14), does not provide specific grounds for punishment, nor does it envision concrete action other than vague threats of YHWH'S warfare against the Edomites.[19]

Obadiah points to Edom's being betrayed by its own allies (Obad 7) and calls for punishment against Edom not only by YHWH (Obad 1–7, 8), but also by northern Israel acting on behalf of Judah (Obad 16–18) or by both Israel and Judah (Obad 19–21). While the prophecy of Jeremiah concerning Edom (Jer 49:7–22) reflects the lamentation of a prophet whose people are defeated and can do nothing about the Edomites except to appeal to the God of Israel, Obadiah "envisions a course of action in which either a restored Israel or a restored Israel and Judah can take action for themselves together with YHWH."[20]

Obadiah 1–7 appears to be a more organized text than or a reworking of Jeremiah's prophecy concerning Edom. Jeremiah's messenger formula, "thus says the Lord," appears in the middle of the prophet's discourse (Jer 49:12), while that of the elected Obadiah, *kō-'āmar 'ădōnāy yhwh le'ĕdōm* ("Thus says the Lord God concerning Edom"), appears in Obadiah 1b, confirming that he was a prophet who was chosen and sent on mission. Likewise, the summons to fight, "Rise up for battle!" appears in Jeremiah 49:14, while Obadiah places his in verse 1d, setting up the entire prophecy as a challenge to Edom's indifference or uncharitable behavior toward its brother, its neighbor—especially when the Edomites' neighbors were most in need of their help.[21]

---

17. See Allen, *The Books of Joel, Obadiah, and Micah*, 133–43; Pagan, "Obadiah," 615; Sweeney, *The Twelve*, 283; Simundson, *Obadiah*, 245; Block, *Obadiah*, 38–41; Sweeney, "Sequence and Interpretation in the Book of the Twelve," 49–62; and Udoekpo, *Rethinking the Prophetic Critique of Worship in Amos 5*, 43–59, where much focus, study, and research has been placed on the relationship between Obadiah and other prophets

18. Pagan, "Obadiah," 615; Block, *Obadiah*, 38–39.

19. Sweeney, *Twelve Prophets*, 283.

20. Sweeney, *Twelve Prophets*, 283.

21. For additional and detailed comparative analysis of Jeremiah 49:7–22 with Obadiah's prophecy, see Sweeney, *Twelve Prophets*, 282–84; Block, *Obadiah*, 38–39.

Apart from Obadiah's relationship with Jeremiah, it is widely acknowledged in recent studies that Obadiah also has a literary (e.g., inclusio, repetition, catchwords, framing devices, motifs) and thematic (the Day of the Lord, worship, justice, righteousness, etc.) relationship with other prophetic works, especially the Twelve (of which Obadiah forms a part).[22]

In the Masoretic version (MT), Obadiah stands as the fourth book of the Twelve (Hosea, Joel, Amos, Obadiah, Jonah, Micah, Nahum, Habakkuk, Zephaniah, Haggai, Zechariah, and Malachi), while in the Septuagint (LXX) version, it is the fifth book of the Twelve (Hosea, Amos, Micah, Joel, Obadiah, Jonah, Nahum, Habakkuk, Zephaniah, Haggai, Zechariah, and Malachi). Given that Obadiah communicates a clear message of judgment against Edom and a message of hope for Judah, some commentators argue that Obadiah is deliberately positioned after Amos in the MT so as to build upon Amos's imagery of the restoration of the Davidic kingdom and its possession of the remnant of Edom (Amos 9:11–12).[23] Indeed, Amos and Obadiah bear many connections. For example, Obadiah 1–5 seems to quote Amos 9:1ff.[24] Additionally, a substantial number of changes in the prophecy of Obadiah are best classified as structural alterations on the basis of Amos 9 in order to announce judgment upon Edom in terms of the parallel judgment upon Israel in Amos 9:1ff. Obadiah strengthens the description: in Amos, the promise of judgment on Edom (vv. 11–15) is in opposition to the judgement against Israel (vv. 1–4); in Obadiah, Edom receives no such reprieve.[25] An additional connection between Obadiah and the Twelve, particularly Amos, can be seen in the superscription, where the introductory element in Obadiah 1, "*ḥăzôn*" ("the vison"), rhymes with that of Amos 9:1. Additionally, the phrase "I will bring you down" commonly appears in both. Some scholars also believe that Obadiah 5 functions as a thematic summary of Amos 9:7–10, which is characterized by the themes of destruction and remnant.[26]

---

22. Some studies to which I would refer for further detailed study on Obadiah's relationship with the Twelve include: Weimer, "Obadja: eine redaktionskritishche Analyse," 35–99; Bosshard-Nepustil, "Beobachtungen zum Zwölfprophetenbuch," 30–62; House, *The Unity of the Twelve*, 1990; Bosshard-Nepustil and Reinhold Gregor Kratz, "Maleachi im Zwölfprophetenbuch," 27–46; Steck, *Der Abschluss de Prophetie im alten Testament*, 1991; Collins, *The Mantle of Elijah*, 59–87; Nogalski, *Literary Precursors*, 1993; Nogalski, *Reactional Process in the Book of the Twelve*, 1993; Coggins, "The Minor Prophets—One Book or Twelve?" 57–68; Jones, *The Formation of the Book of the Twelve*, 1995; Barton, "The Canonical Meaning of the Book of the Twelve," 1996; Watts and House, eds., *Forming Prophetic Literature*, 1996; Bosshard-Nepustil, *Reception von Jesaja 1–39 im Zwölfprophetenbuch*, 1997; Zapff, *Redaktionsgeschichtliche Studien zum Michabuch im Kontext des Dodekaprophetons*, 1997; Schart, *Die Enstehung des Zwölfprophetenbuchs*, 2000; Udoekpo, *Re-thinking the Day of YHWH and Restoration of Fortunes in the Prophet Zephaniah*, 230–34; Ko, "Ordering of the Twelve as Israel's Historiography," 315–32.

23. Sweeney, *The Twelve Prophets*, 279. See also Sweeney, "Sequences and Interpretation in the Book of the Twelve," in *Reading and Hearing the Book of the Twelve*, 49–64.

24. Nogalski, "Intertextuality in the Twelve," 103–6.

25. Nogalski, *Redactional Processes*, 64; Udoekpo, *Worship in Amos 5*, 46.

26. Nogalski, *Redactional Processes*, 66; Udoekpo, *Worship in Amos 5*, 46.

THEOLOGY, TEXT, AND STRUCTURE

In addition to what has been said, many themes in Obadiah's theology are echoed in the other books of the Twelve and Jeremiah, including Obadiah's presumption of the existence of obligations on the part of one nation toward another, judgment for Edom and the nations, the Day of the Lord, divine justice, and hope for the remnant. When discussing the MT text of Obadiah, which in the most part is well preserved, scholars refer to Jeremiah 49—especially the LXX version—to interpret and amend difficult sections in Obadiah (vv. 1–5).[27] Textual corrections made in Obadiah include an amendment of the plural word *neḥppəśû* ("ransacked," in my translation from MT) to the singular form in verse 6, and the re-vocalization of other words to clarify the sense of the text in verses 7, 13, 17 , 20, and 21. A number of words in Obadiah's text may also have suffered transposition during the course of the text's transmission. This is obvious in verse 15. It is also argued that verses 19–20 were probably added in an early stage of the text.[28]

This amplifies many other probabilities proposed by scholars in terms of Obadiah's literary structure, details of which are beyond the scope of this essay.[29] A common proposed structure divides the book into two parts: The first part (vv. 1–15) communicates the historical circumstances surrounding the destruction of Jerusalem as well as Edom's punishment, and the second part (vv. 16–21) communicates God's judgment and hope. The following text of this essay, with its contextual exegesis for the church in Africa and beyond, considers Obadiah as a literary unit in which we see the following interrelated themes: Obadiah's voice of divine judgment (vv. 1a–4b); Edom's sins (vv. 5–9); divine indictment (vv. 10–14), the Day of the Lord (vv. 15–18), and the restoration of Israel's remnant (vv. 19–21).

Obadiah's Vision and Voice of Divine Judgment (vv. 1a–4b)

At the first reading, the reference to Obadiah's "vision"(*ḥăzôn 'ōbadyâ*) in verse 1a may seem misleading to many contemporary readers and listeners, especially those in Africa, and Nigeria in particular, where visionaries, seers, or diviners are not only influential but are seen all over the place. These so-called visionaries commonly appear in "commercial worship centers," where they are fueled by fundamentalism, poverty, and the desire to exploit others for material benefits. Ironically, many of these visionaries do not in fact know or worship the sovereign, just, powerful, and merciful Lord God (*ădōnāy yhwh*) of Israel, whom Obadiah represented as a prophet and missionary. The vision in Obadiah is not a visual picture but the Word of the Lord (*verbum domini*) concerning Edom (*le'ĕdōm*) and Judah.

---

27. Pagan, *Obadiah*, 616.
28. Pagan, *Obadiah*, 616.
29. For additional studies, see Pagan, *Obadiah*, 613–14.

The plural pronoun "we" in the phrase "we have heard" (šəmûâ šāma'nû) in verse 1c has a special implication beyond Obadiah, drawing in other nations, including African nations today. The identity of those referred to as "we" is not explicit.[30] But, as noted by Augustine Musopole in *African Bible Commentary*, people all over the world, especially Africans and Nigerians, need to be brought to know more about this God; they need to listen to the Lord God of history, the judge of the world. Everyone is invited to hear, convey, spread, teach, preach, and write God's words, as did Obadiah and our honoree, in order to be set free from the influence of other diviners or seers, from the rise of violence, wars, and division, from enthnocentrism and greed, from an inadequate sense of patriotism, from the betrayal of fellow citizens and the disorderliness facing Africa today (v. 1d).[31]

In verse 2a, the *hinnēh* ("behold") particle introduces the surprising and unavoidable punishment that the Lord God will dish out to the Edomites for abandoning their brothers and sisters, the Judeans (Jacob in v. 10), in their time of need during the fall of Jerusalem in 586/7 BCE. Of course, the Lord God will surely humiliate the proud Edom (Esau) and certainly make the kingdom look small among other nations (*qāṭon nətattîkā*) and despised (*bāzûy 'attâ mə'ōd*).[32] But in what does the greatness of a nation or a continent lie? Obadiah's listeners in Africa may ask. Is it in geographical, topographical, or demographical size? In military or economic might? In its skillful corruption and abuse of power or authority? Or does it perhaps lie in its industrialization, its embrace of true democracy and inclusiveness, its willingness to listen to one another, its synodality and ecumenism, and its unity of purpose and sense of patriotism and the common good, love of fellow citizens, and willingness to be a brothers' and sisters' keeper?

Verse 3a–c describe Esau's delusional self-confidence, self-worth, and unnecessary presumptuousness, as well as its sense of imperviousness, all of which results in proudness of heart (*zədôn libkā*). Of course, we know the term "heart" (*lēb*, *kardia*) generally refers to the seat of emotions, the will, thoughts, speech, actions, attitudes, and dispositions (v. 3c).[33] How we treat one another originates from our hearts (Matt 15:11–20). How one nation treats another nation has its origin in the heart. Pride can lead us to develop a distorted estimation of ourselves as individuals and as groups, thus encouraging exaggerated ambitions (economic, military) that threaten other nations, tribes, and territories, as was the case with the ancient biblical Edom. The Edomites also thought of themselves as invincible because they were living in clefts of rocks and impenetrable fortresses (consider, for example, the present-day Petra in

---

30. See Sweeney, *the Twelve Prophets*, 288.

31. Musopole, *Obadiah*, 1040.

32. The perfect verb used here, *nətattîkā* ("have made"), is seen as a "prophetic perfect" implying certainty and should be considered done. On the prophetic, see Rogland, *Alleged Non-Past Uses of Qatal in Classical Hebrew*, 53–114.

33. Block, *Obadiah*, 60.

Jordan). We too, within and outside of Africa (and Nigeria in particular), have things we rely on for false security, including modern nuclear and chemical weapons, money, charms, crude oil, our ethnic or tribal identity, witchcraft, cultural ideologies of male power and domineering attitudes, abuse of religious powers, and political powers beyond the limits of divine (the Lord God of Obadiah manifested in the Johannine Jesus of our honoree) approval.

Verse 4a–b contradicts Edom's false sense of invincibility: "Even though you soar like an eagle, and your nest is set among the stars . . . I shall bring you down, says the Lord" (*'im-tagəbbîah kannešer wə'im-bên kôkābîm śîm qinnekā, miššām 'ôrîdəkā nə'um-'ădōnāy/yhwh*). An eagle, as captured in this verse, is a symbol of pride as it soars aloft, scanning the earth with its keen vision and building its nest in a secluded place.[34] In this case, Edom foreshadows many contemporary nations, towns, villages, and individuals who may have power but, ironically, lack deeper vision to realize that their high flights and hidden nests—or homes under rocks (v. 3b)—cannot match the sovereignty of the Lord God of Israel, who has spoken through the voice and vision of Obadiah concerning Edom (v. 4b).

Edom's Punishable Sins (vv. 5–9)

God's sovereignty, as displayed in the initial verses of Obadiah's prophecy (vv. 2–4), is intensified in these verses discussing Edom's nature and the process of the punishment the nation will receive (vv. 5–9). In verses 5–9, other nations, including Edom's former allies, are God's instrument for teaching Edom a bitter lesson about their indifference toward their brothers and sisters in Judah.[35] Thieves will come to plunder their properties at night (v. 5a). They will destroy and steal all they want (v. 5b–c), and they will ransack or unearth Esau's hidden treasures (v. 6). Edom's allies will be actively involved (v. 7a–d)—a reminder that those with whom we eat can become our bitter enemy, or betray us, but not for the grace of the Lord God of Israel. Verses 8–9 conclude Edom's punishment, which extends to the destruction of the wise, intellectual, and learned people in Edom (v. 8), as well as its notable warriors and soldiers in Teman, one of Edom's major towns (v. 9). This may be premature to ask, but we must consider: What lessons can those Africans who downplay or disregard their intellectuals, teachers, and professors learn from Obadiah 5–9? We cannot overemphasize the importance of African or Nigerian intellectuals, besides soldiers and strong-standing armies in Africa. Intellectuals offer, among other things, leadership and a sense of direction for the development of civilization and culture. Any nation denied or robbed of its male and female intellectual leadership is left with cultural, spiritual, economic, social, and political starvation.

---

34. Musopole, *Obadiah*, 1042.
35. For detailed commentary on vv. 5–9, see Pagan, "Obadiah," 620.

Divine Indictment with Reasons (vv. 10–14)

While we contemplate the lessons of Obadiah 5–9, we finally find in verses 10–14 the reason for the discussed destruction and divine indictment against Edom: Esau's inhumane and violent treatment of Jacob or Judah on "that day" (v. 10). Edom failed to intervene on behalf of Judah when Jerusalem was being ransacked by strangers (*zārîm*) and foreigners (*nokrîm*). In fact, Esau was indifferent. He stood aloof on "that day" (v. 11a–b). Speaking through Obadiah, God points out in verses 12–14 what Edom should not have done on the "day of Jacob," as follows:

MT transliteration	Working Translation
v. 12. *wə'al-tēre' bəyôm-'āḥîkā bəyôm-nākərô*	and you should not have gloated over your brother on the day of his misfortune
v. 12b. *wə'al-tiṣmaḥ libnê-yəhûdâ bəyôm 'ābdām*	you should not have rejoiced over the Judeans on the day of their ruin
v. 12c. *wə'al-tagddēl pîkā bəyôm ṣārâ*	you should not have boasted on the day of distress
v. 13a. *'al- tābô' bəša'ar-'ammî bəyôm 'êdam*	you should not have entered the people's gate on the day of their calamity
v. 13b. *'al-tēre' gam-'attâ bətâ'âtô bəyôm 'êdô*	you should not have joined others in gloating over their disaster on the day of calamity
v. 13 c. *wə'al-tišəlaḥnâ bəḥēlô bəyôm 'êdô*	you should not have looted his goods on the day of calamity
v. 14a. *wə'al-ta'ămōd 'al-happereq ləhakərît 'et-pəlîttaiw*	you should not have stood at the crossings to cut off his fugitives
v. 14b. *wə'al-tasəggēr śərîdâiw bəyôm ṣārâ*	you should not have handed over his survivors on the day of distress

Indeed, the "day of Jacob," the fall of Jerusalem, was not just a day of misfortune (*yôm nokrô*), but also a day of ruin (*yôm 'obədām*), distress (*ṣārâ*), calamity (*'êdam*), and doom (*'êdô*). Unfortunately, on this sad day, Esau gloated (*rā'â*), rejoiced, or celebrated (*śāmaḥ*). He boasted when Jacob fell (*higdîl peh*); he invaded (*bô'*), looted (*šālaḥ*), cut off (*karat*), and handed over (*hisgîr*) the survivors of Jacob to the enemy military. In fact, pride, greed, corruption, ethnocentrism, lack of foresight, sectional discrimination, overestimation of self-worth, and the desire for revenge ruled the behavior of Edom, just as today these same characteristics affect tribalism, division, violence, and wars in different parts of Africa. Many African scholars, including our honoree Teresa Okure, SHCJ, have acknowledged that "ethnic pride and solidarity have led to ethnic conflicts and cleansing that pose a real threat to peace and stability on the continent."[36] We also see a lack of concern for the plight of many refugees and

---

36. See Musopole, *Obadiah*, 1043; Nwachuckwu, ed., "Neither Jew nor Gentile," 27–43; and Okure, "Gospel-Based Personal Identify and Life as Recipe for Racism-Free Leadership in the Church," 45–67.

displaced persons.[37] In the case of Edom, as it would be applicable to other nations, the Day of the Lord (*yôm-yhwh*) was not far off (v. 15a).[38]

The Day of the Lord (vv. 15–18)

Obadiah's mission of proclaiming God's judgment on the Day of the Lord (*yôm-yhwh*) applies to every nation, especially Edom: "*kî-qârôb yôm-yhwh/ 'al-kāl-haggôyîm*" ["for the day of the Lord is near against all nations"] (15a); "*ka'ăšer 'āśîtā yē'āśeh lāk gəmuləkā yāšûb bərōšekā*" ["and as you have done it, it shall be done to you, your deeds shall return to you"] (15b)." While "the day" in verses 12–14 referred to the historical events of the attack on Jerusalem in 586/7 BCE, verse 15a picks up from verse 8a, which says, "Behold, on that day, thus says the Lord" (*hălô' bayyôm hahû' nə'um-ădōnāy/yhwh*), and stresses the eschatological day of God's final judgment, which is a common traditional theme in other Minor Prophets.[39] In this way, and as rightly noted by Samuel Pagan, "The prophet ties the historical moment of Babylonia's triumph over Israel, with the day of divine judgment at some indeterminate future time."[40]

Obadiah 15b is retributive in nature. This is literarily indicated by the introductory "*kis*" (vv. 15–16).[41] Obadiah proclaims, "As you have done, it shall be done to you; your deeds shall return to you" (*ka'ăšer 'āśîtā yē'āśeh lāk gəmuləkā; yāšûb bərōšekā*), referring to Edom's violence toward Jacob as well as its gloating over Judah's distress. Other nations shall be punished for this as well, according to Obadiah, on the Day of the Lord. Obadiah's announcement of the universal nature of the Lord's Day is meant to inspire hope to all peoples, especially the Judeans. Obadiah 16 shifts attention from retributive to distributive justice, promising that the tables will turn and, ultimately, the fate once experienced by the Judeans will be shared by other nations. Stressing such reversal of fortune, Obadiah says, "For as you have drunk on my holy mountain, all the nations around you shall drink" (*kî ka'ăšer šətîtem 'al-har qādəšî yîšttû kōl-haggôyîm tāmîd*) (v. 16a); "they shall drink and gulp down, and shall be as if they never been" (*wəšātû wəlā'û wəhāyû kəlô' hāyû*) (v. 16b). Obadiah keeps his audience focused on drinking by repeating the verb *šātâ*, "to drink" (vv. 16a–b). The association of divine fury with drinking has a long history in Israel and in contemporary biblical interpretation, though further detail is beyond the scope of this essay (Deut 32:32–33; Jer 25:17, 21; Ezek 23:32–34). Block points out that although Obadiah does

---

37. Musopole, *Obadiah*, 1043.

38. See the Day of the Lord tradition in Isaiah 3, Ezekiel 30:1–19; Joel 2, and especially in Amos 5:18–20 and Zephaniah 1.

39. For a detailed study of this eschatological concept in the OT and prophetic traditions, especially the Twelve, see Udoekpo, *Day of YHWH*, 197–234; Udoekpo, *Worship in Amos 5*, 50–56.

40. Pagan, *Obadiah*, 625.

41. See the analysis of the retributive nature of this verse in Block, *Obadiah*, 84–85, which states that "the phrase, '*yāšûb bərōšekā*' (your deeds shall return to you/your head) involves a standard of expression for retribution (Num 5:7; Judg 9:57; 1 Sam 25:39; I Kings 2:33, 44; Neh 3:36; Joel 4:4)."

not specify what is drunk (wine, water, petrol, kerosene, tea, milk, *brukutu*, coffee, palm wine), "you must drink" (*kî ka'ăšer šətîtem*) serves as "a shorthand expression for consuming the wrath of YHWH."[42]

In addition, Sweeney thinks Obadiah 16 is initially referring to Edom's treaty with Israel/Jerusalem, which would have been sealed with feasting and drinking on Mount Zion (2 Sam 8:13-14; 1 Kgs 11:14-22; 2 Kgs 3:9-27), or to Edom's alliance with Judah (Jer 27:3). Then, the prophet expanded the reference to include other nations' alliances with Israel and Judah that were never kept, resulting in God's judgment of all nations, including Edom, who failed to support Israel and Judah when they were attacked.[43] Others think the references to drunken celebration are literary images of the conquerors' drunken victory celebrations as they became drunk on the alcoholic beverages the armies looted. Or it may simply and metaphorically refer to God's judgment on Babylon, Edom, Israel, and all other nations for failing to help one another— for failing to be their brothers' and sisters' keepers in times of trouble—since YHWH is the sovereign of all creation and the Lord of history. Significantly, all this must take place on "my"—that is, God's—"holy mountain" (*'al-har qādəšî*), referring to the section of Jerusalem (an important religious city, 2 Sam 5:7; Cant. 2:6; Isa 1:8) where the temple is located.

Obadiah offers in verses 17-18 what Daniel Block calls "the contrasting fate of Jacob."[44] Verse 17a reads: "But on Mount Zion there shall be those that escape, and it shall be holy" (*ûbahar ṣiyyôn tihəyeh pəlêṭâ wəhāyâ qōdeš*). Notice that "those who escape" (*pəlêṭâ*) will constitute a holy remnant of Israel on Zion that will enable the house of Jacob to regain "their possessions" (*wəyōrəšû bêt ya'ăqōb 'ēt môrāšēhem*) in 17b. Many exegetes—including the translators of the *NRSV*, as timely observed by Sweeney, followed closely in this study—read *môrāšēhem* ("their possessions") as *môrišēhem* ("those who dispossessed them") with the LXX, the *Qumran Murabba'at Scroll*, and other versions to emphasize Israel's vengeance against Edom and the nations, as stressed in verse 18.[45] But the MT reading of *môrāšēhem* ("their possessions") in verse 17 is quite all right as it stands. More light for understanding Obadiah 17-18 can be drawn from Joel 3:5 (NRSV 2:32; cf. Joel 2:3), which says, "For in Mount Zion and in Jerusalem there shall be those who escape," and Jerusalem shall be holy (Joel 4:17[3:17]).[46] That is to say, while Edom and other inhumane nations will be judged and reduced to stubble, the house of Jacob will become God's consuming fire or instrument. This means that Judah as a metaphorical fire and flame will not only burn down their enemy, reducing them to stubble and ashes, with no survivors, but, in

---

42. Block, *Obadiah*, 86-87.

43. Sweeney, *Twelve Prophets*, 295.

44. For extended exegesis or analysis of these verses, see Block, *Obadiah*, 89-93.

45. Sweeney, *Twelve Prophets*, 295; Wolff, *Obadiah and Jonah*, 60; Rudolph, *Joel-Amos-Obadja-Jona*, 311.

46. Sweeney, *Twelve Prophets*, 295.

the process of such holy war, Judah will repossess its inheritance, or claim its ancient territory (vv. 17–18). Obadiah's prophetic source is no other person but the Lord God of Israel, the restorer of the remnant and balancer of the scale of justice against oppressors, who has spoken (*kî yhwh dibber*) through Obadiah and continues to speak through his Son Jesus Christ, the church, and all missionaries today.

Restoration of the Remnant (vv. 19–21)

Obadiah goes on to prophesy hope and the restoration of the remnant (vv. 19–21). The Lord will guarantee Israel's restoration and the occupation of the land promised. The Lord is the universal king. The people of Negev (a desert region of southern Judah which the Edomites often targeted) would move into Edom, while those from the hills west of Hebron (Judah) would move into the land of the Philistines, possessing the fields of Ephraim and Benjamin (v. 19). Returning exiles from both the northern and southern kingdoms of Israel will settle in Negev in the south to as far as Zaraphath in the Sidonian territory (v. 20).[47] Finally, the Edomites, who were once indifferent and uncharitable toward the Judeans, will be governed from Jerusalem by the "*môšiʿîm*" deliverers (v. 21). They will be acting on behalf of Yhwh, the sovereign of all creation and kingdoms. Their victory will be an ultimate triumph over those who oppose the divine will and the calling to treat one another well, with love and compassion.

CONTEXTUAL AND THEOLOGICAL CONCLUSIONS

Reflecting on the preceding discussion and missionary review of Obadiah for Africa, it is evident that Obadiah's prophecy challenges us and illumines important issues for the community of believers that comprise today's church in Africa. It presents a somber criticism of the lack of unity, communion, solidarity, and fraternity among Africans, which Pope Francis equally highlighted in his January 1, 2014 message celebrating the World Day of Peace, "Fraternity, the Foundation and Pathway to Peace."[48] What we have discussed in honor of Teresa Okure, SHCJ, offers those of us in Africa a reminder of our commitment or obligation to meet human needs and to call all creation and nations into communion. It reminds us of God's judgment on his Day, of the sacredness of family life, of God's kingdom, and of hope for the future.

In spite of the numerous blessings God has bestowed upon the church in Africa, she continues to face numerous challenges, including poverty, political instability, misery, war, injustices violence, terrorism, division, ethnocentrism, jealousy, indifferent behavior and gloating toward others, ethnic and family conflict, and neglect of the poor and the minority—all challenges renounced by Obadiah in regard to the

---

47. See Ray L. Roth, "Zeraphath," *ABD* VI:1041.
48. See Pope Francis, "Message of His Holiness Francis for the Celebration of the World Day of Peace: Fraternity, the Foundation and Pathway to Peace" (Vatican City, January 1, 2014).

Edomites. The Judeans were suffering while the Edomites, as we saw, were rejoicing and gloating. Rather than responding to the needs of their neighbors, the Edomites betrayed them in a disgraceful way by collaborating with the Babylonians. As a church on mission in Africa, what theological and political posture are we to assume in the face of the above listed African problems? God's response to the Edomites challenges the church in African and African Christian communities and theologians to respond to God's people's needs with a sense of responsibility and solidarity, since contextual and mission theology—which Okure, our honoree, has taught for years—must not just be an academic exercise divorced from the everyday life situations and needs of the people.[49] Prayer is important and welcome when "it is accompanied by tangible acts of love that eliminate the causes that foment, favor, and perpetuate conditions of injustice among the destitute."[50] Obadiah's prophecy challenges believers in Africa and beyond to address real problems, some of which have been mentioned, particularly the oppression of socially excluded groups, such as ethnic minorities and homeless persons in Africa, Nigeria in particular. The church and Christian communities in Africa must themselves be transformed by the values of the kingdom of God taught by Obadiah. To ignore or remain indifferent to the plight of the indigent is one of the reasons why God judged Edom and other nations on his Day (Obad v. 8).[51]

Truly enough, the church in Africa, as affirmed throughout this essay, has always been modeled as a "Family of God's People." Obadiah illustrates the tragic consequences of tensions among family members, who have both the privilege and the responsibility of uniting and caring for one another, which the church in Africa should note. Neglect of family members, in the words of Joan E. Cook, "is even more tragic than neglect of people who are not related to us."[52] Finally, Obadiah in his mission reminds us of God's promises of hope. He looks forward to a future time when the evils and the challenges of the present will be transformed, and God's reign will prevail in Africa and beyond. Ancient Edom (a symbol of oppressors, tyrants, dictators, cynics, and faithless warmongers) will be overtaken by the Judahites (the faithful remnant). Mount Zion (a place, continent, or nation of peace, joy, inclusiveness, respect for divergent opinions, and compassion for the poor) will be the new center from which

---

49. See Okure, *Johannine Approached to Mission*, xv, where she calls contextualization the "revival of interest" in biblical scholarship that is mainly inspired by changing situations in mission lands, where previously silent and passive recipients of mission have now become its active agents, either in their countries or in their lands, reaching out to peoples and territories through prophesying, writing, teaching, witnessing, preaching, evangelizing, or proclaiming the gospel. For Okure, there is a need to make biblical passages, including Obadiah, relevant to the reader's faith context—a challenge which this essay has strived to meet throughout. Additional voices include: Ukpong, "Inculturation Hermeneutics," 17–32; Robert J. Schreiter, *The New Catholicity,*1997; Bevans, *Models of Contextual Theology*, 2002; Bevans and Tahaafe-Williams, *Contextual Theology*, 2011; Evans and Schroeder, *Prophetic Dialogue*, 2011.

50. See Pagan, *Obadiah*, 628.

51. See Pagan, *Obadiah*, 628.

52. Cook, *Hear, O Heavens and Listen*, 217.

the sovereign Lord will inspire missionaries in the likes of Obadiah and our honoree Teresa Okure, SHCJ, and the Lord will continue to rule over Africa and beyond. Hopefully, from here, Christian and religious communities will share their love of God and the benefits of the goonews of salvation with as many people as possible.

BIBLIOGRAPHY

Allen, Leslie C. *The Books of Joel, Obadiah and Micah*. NICOT. Grand Rapids: Eerdmans, 1976.

Anderson, Bernhard W. *Understanding the Old Testament*. Hoboken, NJ: Prentice-Hall, 1986.

Barton, John. "The Canonical Meaning of the Book of the Twelve." In *After the Exile*, 59–73. Edited by J. Barton and D. J. Reimer. Macon, GA: Mercer University Press, 1996.

Benedict XVI. "*Africae Munus* Post-Synodal Apostolic Exhortation on the Church in Africa in Service to Reconciliation, Justice and Peace, "You are the Salt of the Earth. . .You are the Light of the World (Matt 5:13–14)." Vatican City: Libreria Editrice Vaticana, 2011.

Bevans, Stephen B. *Models of Contextual Theology*. Maryknoll, NY: Orbis, 2002.

Bevans, Stephen B. , and Jeffrey Gros. *Evangelization and Religious Freedom: Ad Gentes, Dinitatis Humanae*. New York: Paulist Press, 2009.

Bevans, Stephen B., and Roger P. Schroeder. *Prophetic Dialogue: Reflections on Christian Mission Today*. Maryknoll, NY: Orbis, 2011.

Bevans, Stephen B., and Katalina Tahaafe-Williams. *Contextual Theology for the Twenty-First Century*. Eugene, OR: Pickwick Publications, 2011.

Blank, Sheldon. "Prophet as Paradigm." In *Essays in Old Testament Ethics: J. Philip Hyatt, in Memoriam*, 111–30. Edited by J. L. Crenshaw and J. T. Willis. New York: Ktav, 1974.

Block, Daniel I. *Obadiah: The Kingship Belongs to YHWH*. Grand Rapids: Zondervan, 2013.

Bosshard-Nepustil, Erich. "Beobachtungen zum Zwölfprophetenbuch." *BN* 40 (1987) 30–62.

———. *Reception von Jesaja 1–39 im Zwölfprophetenbuch*. OBO 154. Göttingen: Vandenhoeck & Reprecht, 1997.

Bosshard-Nepustil, Erich, and Reinhold Gregor Kratz. "Maleachi im Zwölfprophetenbuch." *BN* 52 (1990) 27–46.

Brueggemann, Walter. *The Prophetic Imagination*. Minneapolis: Fortress Press, 2001.

Coggins, R. J. "The Minor Prophets—One Book or Twelve?" In *Crossing the Boundaries: Essays in Biblical Interpretation in Honour of Michael D. Goulder*, 57–68. Edited by S. E. Porter, P. Joyce, and D. E. Orton. Biblical Interpretation Series 8. Leiden: Brill, 1994.

Collins, Terence. *The Mantle of Elijah: The Redaction Criticism of the Prophetical Books*. Biblical Seminar 20. Sheffield: JSOT Press, 1993.

Cook, E. Joan. *Hear, O Heavens and Listen, O Earth: An Introduction to the Prophets*. Collegeville, MN: Liturgical Press, 2006.

Francis. "Message of His Holiness Pope Francis to All Consecrated People on the Occasion of the Year of Consecrated Life." Vatican website. November 21, 2014. https://w2.vatican.va/content/franccesco/en/apost_letters/documents/papa-francesco_lettera-ap_20141121_lettera-consecrati.html.

Hays, Daniel J. *The Message of the Prophets: A Survey of the Prophetic Apocalyptic Books of the Old Testament*. Grand Rapids: Zondervan, 2010.

Heschel, Abraham. *The Prophets*. New York: Harper & Row, 1962.

Holladay, William L. "The Background of Jeremiah's Self-Understanding: Moses, Samuel and Psalm 22." *JBL* 83 (1964) 156–64.

House, Paul R. *The Unity of the Twelve*. Bible and Literature Series 27. JSOTSup 97. Sheffield: Almond Press, 1990.

Isichei, Elizabeth. *From Antiquity to the Present: A History of African Christianity*. Grand Rapids: Eerdmans, 1995.

John Paul II. *I Will Give You Shepherds, Post-Synodal Apostolic Exhortation, Pastores Dabo Vobis*. Vatican City: Libreria Editrice Vaticana, 1990.

———. "First African Synod, *Ecclesia in Africa*; Post-Synodal Apostolic Exhortation on the Church in Africa and Its Evangelizing Towards the Year 2000, 'You Shall be My Witnesses (Acts 1:8).'" Vatican City: Libreria Editrice Vaticana, 1995.

Jones, Barry Alan. *The Formation of the Book of the Twelve: A Study of Text and Canon*. SBLDS 149. Atlanta: Scholars Press, 1995.

Ko, Grace. "Ordering of the Twelve as Israel's Historiography." In *Prophets, Prophecy and Ancient Israelite Historiography*, 315–32. Edited by Mark J. Borda and Lissa M. Wray Beal. Winona Lake, IN: Eisenbrauns, 2013.

Laclerc, Thomas L. *Introduction to the Prophets: Their Stories, Sayings, and Scrolls*. New York: Paulist Press, 2007.

Laniak, Timothy S. *Shepherds After My Own Heart: Pastoral Tradition and Leadership in the Bible*. Downers Grove: Intervarsity Press, 2006.

Musopole, Augustine. "Obadiah." In *African Bible Commentary*, 1041–44. Edited by Totunboh Adeyemo. Kenya: World Alive Publishers, 2006.

Nogalski, James. *Redactional Processes in the Book of the Twelve*. BZAW 218. Berlin: de Gruyter, 1993.

———. *Literary Precursors to the Book of the Twelve*. BZAW 217. Berlin: de Gruyter, 1993.

———. "Intertextuality in the Twelve." In *Forming Prophetic Literature: Essays on Isaiah and the Twelve in Honor of John D. W. Watts*, 103–06. Edited by James W. Watts and Paul R. House. JSOTSup 235. Sheffield: Sheffield Academic, 1996.

Nogalski, James D., and Marvin A. Sweeney, eds. *Reading and Hearing the Book of the Twelve*. Atlanta: Society of Biblical Literature, 2000.

Obinwa, Ignatius M. C. *"I Shall Feed Them with Good Pasture" (Ezek 34:14): The Shepherd Motif in Ezekiel 34; Its Theological Import and Socio-Political Implications*. Forshung Zur Bibel, Band 125. Würzburg: Verlag, 2012.

Okoye, James C. *Israel and the Nations: A Mission Theology of the Old Testament*. American Society of Missiology Series 39. Maryknoll, NY: Orbis, 2006.

———. *Genesis 1–11: A Narrative-Theological Commentary*. Eugene, OR: Cascade Books, 2018.

———. *Genesis 12–50: A Narrative-Theological Commentary*. Eugene, OR: Cascade Books, 2020.

Okure, Teresa. *The Johannine Approach to Mission: A Contextual Study of John 4:1–42*. Wissenschaftliche Untersuchungen zum Neuen Testament 2. Reihe; Tübingen: J.C.B. Mohr/Paul Siebeck, 1988.

Orobator, Agbonkhiameghe E., ed. *Reconciliation, Justice and Peace: The Second African Synod*. Maryknoll, NY: Orbis, 2011.

Rogland, Max. *Alleged Non-Past Uses of Qatal in Classical Hebrew*. Studia Semitica Neerlandica 44. Assen: Van Gorcum, 2003.

Rudolph, Wilhelm. *Joel-Amos-Obadja-Jona*. Kommentar Zum Alten Testament, Bd. XIII, 2. Gütersloh: Gerd Mohn, 1971.

Schart, Aaron. *Die Enstehung des Zwölfprophetenbuchs*. BZAW 260. Berlin: de Gruyter, 1998.

Schneiders, Sandra M. *Prophets in their Own Country: Women Religious Bearing Witness to the Gospel in a Troubled Church*. Maryknoll, NY: Orbis, 2011.

Schreiter, Robert J. *The New Catholicity: Theology Between the Global and the Local*. Maryknoll, NY: Orbis, 1999.

Simundson, Daniel J. *Hosea, Joel, Amos, Obadiah, Jonah, Micah*. Abingdon Old Testament Commentaries. Nashville: Abingdon Press, 2005.

Steck, Odil Hannes. *Der Abschluss de Prophetie im alten Testament: Ein Versuch zur Frage de Vorgeschichte des Kanons*. Biblisch-theologishche Studien 17. Neukirchen-Vluyn: Neukirchener, 1991.

Sweeney, Marvin A. *The Twelve Prophets, Volume 1: Hosea, Joel, Amos, Obadiah, Jonah*. Berit Olam Studies in Hebrew Narrative & Poetry. Edited by David W. Cotter et al. Collegeville, MN: Liturgical Press, 2000.

———. "Sequence and Interpretation in the Book of the Twelve." In *Reading and Hearing the Book of the Twelve*, 49–62. Edited by James D. Nogalski and Marvin A. Sweeney. Atlanta: Society of Biblical Literature, 2000.

Udoekpo, Michael Ufok. *Re-thinking the Day of YHWH and Restoration of Fortunes in the Prophet Zephaniah: An Exegetical and Theological Study of 1:14–18; 3:14–20*. Das Alte Testament im Dialog 2. Berlin: Peter Lang, 2010.

———. *Rethinking the Prophetic Critique of Worship in Amos 5 for Contemporary Nigeria and the USA*. Eugene, OR: Pickwick, 2017.

———. *Israel's Prophets and the Prophetic Effect of Pope Francis: A Pastoral Companion*. Eugene, OR: Wipf & Stock, 2018.

———. "Biblical Traditions in the Johannine Prophetic Shepherd-Leadership of Bishop Camillus Umoh." In *That they May Have Life: A Festschrift in Honour of Most Rev. Dr. Camillus Raymond Umoh*, 25–30. Edited by Idara Out and Valentine Umoh. Nigeria: Pauline Publication, 2021.

———. "Becoming a Church-Family in Africa that Witnesses the Gospel to Everyone: Perspectives from Luke 3:4–6 and Isaiah 40:4–5." In *Becoming Church As the Family of God in Africa: Graces, Challenges and Prospects*, 171–92. Edited by Nwagwu Gerald et al. CIWA Theology Conference, 2019.

Ukpong, Justine. "Inculturation Hermeneutics: An African Approach to Biblical Interpretation." In *The Bible in Word Context: An Experiment in Contextual Hermeneutics*, 17–32. Edited by Walter Dietrich and Ulrich Luz. Grand Rapids: Eerdmans, 2002.

Umoh, Camillus R. *The Plot to Kill Jesus: A Contextual Study of John 11:47–53*. Frankfurt am Main: Peter Lang, 2000.

Watts, James W., and Paul R. House, eds. *Forming Prophetic Literature: Essays on Isaiah and the Twelve in Honour of John D. W. Watts*. JSOTSup 235. Sheffield: Sheffield Academic Press, 1996.

Weimer, Peter. "Obadja: eine redaktionskritishche Analyse." *ZAW* 27 (1985) 35–99.

Weter, Peter. "Leiden und definitional im Buch Jeremia." *KTZ* 74 (1977) 123–50.

Wifall, Walter. *Israel's Prophets: Envoy of the King*. Chicago: Franciscan Herald, 1974.

Wolff, Hans Walter. *Obadiah and Jonah: A Commentary*. Translated by Margaret Kohl. Minneapolis: Augsburg Publishing House, 1986.

Zapff, Burkhard M. *Redaktionsgeschichtliche Studien zum Michabuch im Kontext des Dodekapropheton*. BZAW 256. Berlin: de Gruyter, 1997.

Chapter 7

An Unsung Faith Heroine and an Unrecognized Evangelizer
Another Look at the Encounter between Jesus and the Samaritan Woman in John 4:1–42

Bernard O. Ukwuegbu

INTRODUCTION

The narrative of Jesus and the Samaritan woman in John 4:1–42 is an example of how Jesus, for the sake of his mission, crossed all barriers of his time to reach out to the Samaritans and therefore issued a pattern which is to be followed by his followers.[1] As the narrative develops (4:27–30), the woman goes into the town to bring her people to Jesus, the Messiah, in a manner consistent with the pattern established in other Johannine discipleship stories (cf. 1:40–49). Notwithstanding the self-evident missionary import of this passage and the Samaritan woman's role therein, the long history of its interpretation has proceeded not just in oblivion of the missionary import, but also in a sarcastic derogation of the heroine of the story.[2]

---

1. I share the view that the Fourth Gospel was a missionary document (*eine Missionsschrift*) addressed to non-believers to win them to faith in Jesus as opposed to those who see the Gospel as primarily a community document (*eine Gemeinde-Evangelium*) addressed to those already converted to strengthen their faith in Jesus. For an extensive discussion on these two views on the character and purpose of the Gospel, see Okure, *Johannine Approach to Mission*, 9–16.

2. Spencer, "Feminist Criticism," 289–385, for a good summary of the different views of some church fathers as follows: "Augustine interprets the woman's entanglement with five husbands as allegorical evidence of her sensual or carnal understanding of the world . . . John Chrysostom takes the Samaritan woman's marital history as a record of her sexual immoral past . . . Thomas Aquinas offers the Samaritan woman a backhanded sexist compliment. He is amazed that she converses so wisely

The reason for this sarcasm and this derogation is obvious. The Samaritan woman belongs to two levels of marginalization in the then patriarchal world. She is a woman in a male-dominated society, and a Samaritan in a world where salvation is of the "Jews."[3] It is therefore little wonder that a more positive reading of this story that emphasizes the embedded missionary significance is coming from those who experience prejudices today similar to those the woman experienced then,[4] primary among whom belongs the woman in whose honor this Festschrift is dedicated.

This essay is in continuation of this reading of the pericope coming from the margins. It employs the narratological analysis methodology, defined by Bal as "the ensemble of theories of narratives, narrative texts, images, spectacles, events; cultural artifacts that 'tell a story'. . . in a way that help the reader to understand, analyse and evaluate narratives."[5] Among the advantages of employing this method in biblical scholarship is that it helps to interpret biblical stories with insights drawn from the secular field of modern literary criticism in order to determine the effects that the stories are expected to have on their audience.[6] Combining this with a detailed literary exegesis of the text, the essay sheds light on the meaning of the text in its original context as well as highlights what the text has to say about the mission of the contemporary church as it concerns the crossing of boundaries and making the kingdom of God accessible to all people.

The need to do this in contemporary biblical scholarship is among the lessons that the *heroine* of this Festschrift has always strived to *hand down* to her numerous mentees who, like herself, come from the *margins* of contemporary biblical scholarship. In her review of Michael Legaspi's *The Death of Scripture and the Rise of Biblical Studies*,[7] Okure shares the latter's fundamental dissatisfaction with the presuppositions underlying most contemporary biblical methodologies[8] that seemed to have

---

with Jesus . . . since the fairer sex is generally considered curious and unproductive . . . Musculus gives her a limited credit. She is no chosen apostle . . . but merely a woman, a person of inferior sex and a private citizen not called to the ministry of the word . . . John Calvin is slightly charitable to the Samaritan woman . . . Branding her a poor woman, a common woman, unhappy woman, prostitute and hussy who did not deserve Jesus to speak to her at all" (319–21).

3. From this perspective, the Samaritan woman might have been a victim of the cultural practices of her day. Cf. Stibbe, *John Readings*, 70.

4. Kim points out that "the dialogue between Jesus and the Samaritan woman has caught the attention of third world scholars because of their experience of multi-layer victimization similar to that of the Samaritan woman in the story" in Nelavala, Surekha, *Liberation Beyond Borders*, 178.

5. Ball, *Narratology: Introduction to the Theory of Narratives*, 3, 5. For its application in reading Gospel biblical narratives, see Arde, "Narrative Criticism," 383.

6. Cf. Abia, *A Missional Perspective of John 4:1–42*, 10.

7. Legaspi, *The Death of Scripture and the Rise of Biblical Studies*, 2010, and my review of the book in *RBL* 02/2012.

8. This contention formed the "thesis" of Okure's study, "'I will open my mouth in parables' (Matt 13:35)," 445–63; commissioned by the SNTS at its first ever meeting in the southern hemisphere in Johannesburg, South Africa, in 2000.

emptied Scripture of its meaning by divorcing it from life.[9] In what she explained as "the exegetical method of Jesus Christ based on the exposition of the Scripture from the Law to the Prophets,"[10] she cautions against fixation on methods that demand that the biblical studies should concentrate only on the text and its redaction and sources, for instance, and ask no life questions of the authors and the audience to which the texts were addressed for life-transforming responses.[11] Continuing, Okure admonishes students of the Bible to guide against the two extremes of slavishly espousing existing corrupt biblical methodologies, on the one hand, and introducing other types of corrupt biblical methodology, on the other. We do this when we ignore the meaning of the text as addressed to its original audience or when we bypass the social context and life situation of the audience to which the text was addressed to make it say what we want it to say to please our audience.[12] Since the church is clear that inspiration in Scripture lies primarily "in the meaning which the sacred writers really had in mind,"[13] efforts to discover their message as addressed to their covenanted community constitute the primary level of integrity in biblical exegesis. Only when we study Scripture in this way can we help the church "to grow and mature in its understanding of Scripture."[14]

This, and not any mechanical adoption of or adaptation to the hegemonic tyranny of any of the mainstream methods in contemporary biblical scholarship, is the overarching method adopted in this essay. I am particularly delighted to write it as a contribution to a Festschrift dedicated to honoring an individual who is not only a mentor to most of us from this part of the globe in biblical scholarship, but also one whose career in biblical studies was launched by her seminal work on this pericope and one who helped in stamping her imprint in giving its interpretation a missionary focus.[15]

---

9. Okure, "Integrity and Corruption," 33–35.

10. These were her exact words in an oral response to the question as to the methodology undergirding her approach to interpreting the Scriptures.

11. While acknowledging that "the historical critical method clearly did much to liberate the Church exegesis from . . . the tendency to moralise and spiritualise the reading of the biblical works in an anthological approach that ignored the historical contexts of the texts," Okure ("Integrity and Corruption," 35) points out that "in the process it did worse in many ways by introducing what one might call atheism into biblical studies, that is, a study of Scripture that does not ask or concern itself with faith questions."

12. Okure, "Integrity and Corruption," 35.

13. The Second Vatican Council, *Dei Verbum*, no. 12.

14. Pope Francis, *Evangelii Gaudium*, no. 40.

15. The role of Teresa Okure in arguing for a shift in the reading of this pericope has been widely recognized and acknowledged. See, for instance, the following observation from Abia, *A Missional Perspective of John 4:1–42*, 6: "Unlike other authors, Okure . . . develops the missional perspective of John's Gospel and . . . considers John 4 as being the most overtly concerned with mission in the Gospel."

LOCATING THE PERICOPE WITHIN THE BOOK OF SIGNS

Jesus' encounter with the Samaritan woman and through her with the people of Samaria occupies a central place in the Book of Signs. After the first sign at Cana (2:1–12), there was a strong concentration on the response of the Jewish people to the word of Jesus (2:13–3:36). The mother of Jesus displayed an unquestionable acceptance of the word of Jesus, and this act of faith led to the first of Jesus' signs, the manifestation of his glory and the perfection of the former gift of glory at Sinai (2:1–12). The criterion of acceptance of the word of Jesus was established after Jesus' criticism of the limited faith of the first disciples (1:35–51). Based on this criterion, Jewish characters manifested no faith ("the Jews"), limited faith (Nicodemus), and authentic Johannine belief in the word of Jesus (John the Baptist).[16] The episodes that follow (4:1–42) take place in Samaria.

The focus on Samaria is highlighted by the fact that the encounters between Jesus and the Samaritans happen in one place, with only a slight displacement at the end of the passage (v. 40). The time sequence of the narrative is linear. As the disciples go to buy food (v. 8), Jesus talks with a Samaritan woman. As the disciples come back, she returns to the village (v. 28), and her fellow villagers begin to come toward Jesus (v. 30). While they are on the way, Jesus speaks to the disciples (vv. 31–38). The Samaritans arrive, invite him to stay with them (v. 40), and eventually come to faith in him. After his two days' stay with them, he departs to Galilee (v. 43). Except for the brief discourse that Jesus delivers to his disciples (vv. 31–38), all the characters who encounter Jesus are Samaritans: the Samaritan woman (4:1–15, 16–30) and the Samaritan villagers (vv. 39–42). After v. 42 Jesus departs to Galilee and there encounters a royal official (vv. 43–54).

SETTING THE STAGE (JOHN 4:1–6)

Jesus moves away from Judea on a journey to Galilee via Samaria.[17] The journey, according to Josephus, takes about three days.[18] The motivations are given for Jesus' departure from Judea (v. 1) and for his presence in Samaria: "He left Judea and started back to Galilee. But he had to pass *edei*[19] through Samaria" (vv. 3–4).[20] Reading the *edei* of 4:4 in the context of what is about to happen in Samaria suggests a deeper meaning than a mere change in geographical setting. Considered on the macro level

---

16. Moloney, *John*, 113.
17. Cf. Olson, *Structure and Meaning*, 124.
18. Josephus, *Life*, 52.269.
19. See the various translations given to *edei* ranging from: "he must" (KSV) to "he had to" (NLT)
20. According to Moloney (*John*, 116): "The motivation for Jesus' journey through Samaria is some constraint under which Jesus acts out his story. Although it is not clear, at this stage, why this should be the case, Jesus' presence in Samaria is the result of divine necessity. He *must* move into the world beyond Israel."

of the narrative of the Fourth Gospel, *edei* is mostly connected with Jesus' saving mission (3:14; 9:4; 10:16: 12:34; 20:9). This implies that if Jesus goes to Samaria out of necessity, this necessity must have to do with his divine mission.[21]

The time and place of the encounters that will fill vv. 7–42 are provided (vv. 5–6). The precise scene of encounter, Sychar, is subject to debate, but the narrator's description of the city as "near the field that Jacob gave to his son Joseph" (v. 5) introduces a biblical and Jewish theme of the gift of water that Jacob gave (cf. Gen 33:10; 48:22; Josh 24:32)[22] and provides important background to Jesus' discussion with the woman over wells and the gift of water in vv. 7–15[23] as well as the basis for the symbolism in which Jesus proves greater than Jacob.[24]

Episode 1: Jesus' First Encounter with the Samaritan Woman (John 4:7–15)

As Jesus sits beside a well, the woman comes to draw water. It is natural that the woman comes to the local well with her jar, looking for the water she needs for daily life.[25] What is, however, awkward is the time of the day that she appeared. Whereas such trips by women usually take place in morning and evening times (cf. Gen 24:11; 29: 7), this woman comes at noontime. While attempts have been made to read this, together with the woman's marital status, as indicative to her character as a notorious sinner,[26] this does not seem to be the primary focus of the narrative.[27] More important in the narration is that the "woman" is a "Samaritan" and that she comes to draw "water,"[28] themes that will dominate the rest of the story

Jesus initiates a dialogue with the woman through the use of an imperative (v. 7: *dos mi pein*: "give me to drink," using the imperative aorist active second person singular from *didōmi* = "to give"). It is extraordinary that Jesus should speak to the woman. Ordinarily, he should not do so on two accounts. First, she is a woman,[29] and

---

21. For O' Day, "The Gospel of John," 563–71, "It is best to see the necessity as both geographical and theological. Jesus' itinerary must have been governed by geographical expediency, but his stay in Samaria was governed by the theological necessity of offering himself to those whom social convention deemed unacceptable" (565). Okure, *Johannine Approach*, 85, reads this in the light of Jesus' commitment to fulfilling the will of the Father as the Savior of the world (3:16).

22. Moloney, *John*, 116.

23. O' Day, *Revelation in the Fourth Gospel*, 56.

24. Abia, *A Missional Perspective of John 4:1–42*, 23.

25. Koester, *The Word of Life*, 61.

26. See for instance Malina and Rohrbaugh, *Social-Science*, 98

27. Spencer, "Feminist Criticism," 307–8.

28. O' Day, *Revelation in the Fourth Gospel*, 58.

29. Barclay, *Gospel of John*, 151, points out the oddity of this encounter: "The Strict Rabbis forbade a Rabbi to greet a woman in public . . . For Rabbis to be seen talking to a woman in public was the end of his reputation—and yet Jesus spoke this woman. Not only was she a woman; she was also a woman of a notorious character. No decent man, let alone a Rabbi would have been seen in her company, or even exchanging a word with her—and Jesus spoke with her."

second, she is a Samaritan. The woman's response highlights the irregularity of the encounter. It also has a nuance of mockery:[30] "How is it that you, a Jew (*Joudaios*), ask a drink of me, a woman of Samaria?" Her response is informed by the strained relationships between Jews and Samaritans.[31] That such hostility has some historical basis is confirmed by Josephus's report of a serious clash in 52 BCE between the two groups which even required Roman intervention to quell.[32]

Jesus does not answer the woman's question. Instead he announces that if she knows two truths, the gift of God (*tēn dōrean tou theou/*) and he "who is speaking to you" (*tis estin ho legōnsoi*), she would need only to ask the one speaking, and "living water" would be given to her (v. 10). The playful turn in the conversation makes one wonder who really is thirsty. The woman comes looking for ordinary water and is now told about the water that quenches a thirst she did not even know she had.[33] The two elements that form v. 10a serve as the basis for the entire discussion between Jesus and the woman.

The Living Water Debate (John 4:10–15)

The first "living water" is open to two meanings. On the one hand, it can mean flowing water of a cistern or a pond. But the expression also has a long history in biblical tradition that points beyond the physical reality of water to symbolically represent the gift of God that is eternal life.[34] In the Old Testament, God himself is the "fountain of living water" (Jer 2:13; 17:13; Ps 36:8). So, if God is the fountain of living water and Jesus claims to be the giver of that which is divine, then he is the true revealer of God.[35] He alone makes God known (John 1:18; 3:13) and thus offers the possibility of eternal life to those who are born again of water and the Spirit (3:16).

With this, Jesus draws the attention of the woman (and the reader as well) to his identity. But not only is she unable to reach beyond the physical understanding of "living water,"[36] she is also still locked within her own traditions.[37] She is only able to explain the origins of the water in terms of the Jacob tradition she knows,[38] and

---

30. Moloney, *John*, 117.

31. Luke 9:51–55 refers to an episode in which Jesus and his disciples were refused hospitality by a Samaritan village.

32. Cf. Josephus, *Antiquities*, 20.6.1–3, 118–36; *Jewish Wars* 2.12.3–5.232–46

33. Okure, *Johannine Approach*, 93, is therefore right in her remarks that the statement "Give me to drink" (4:7) is actually an "offer made in form of a request" and that what Jesus was asking from the woman was receptivity on the woman's part

34. MacRae, "Invitation to John,," 347.

35. Abia, *A Missional Perspective of John*, 61.

36. Koester, *The Word of Life*, 11.

37. Okure, *Johannine Approach*, 99.

38. Genesis 33:19 and 48:22 speak of Jacob giving Shechem to Joseph together with its well. He himself, his family, and his entourage drank from it and they were satisfied with its water. Later legends

she challenges Jesus' claim based on this, her own tradition. Convinced that the giver of the gift was Jacob, she cannot imagine that Jesus might be greater than Jacob and shows no openness or acceptance of Jesus' promise of the gift of God.[39]

The woman's inability to accept the word of Jesus becomes more evident in Jesus' further promise in vv. 13–14, and her reply in v. 15. Jesus responds that he is not only "greater than" Jacob, but that he supplants the reality that had been described in the Old Testament (6:49–51; 11:9–10). Unlike in the preceding discussion where Jesus spoke to the woman, Jesus' development of this promise here addresses a universal audience. Beginning his words with reference to everyday water, Jesus points out that while everyone who drinks of the water from that well will eventually be thirsty again (v. 13), whoever drinks of the water that he will give will never thirst, because the gift that Jesus gives will be a spring of water welling up to eternal life (v. 14).[40] The gift that Jesus promises is associated with some future moment in the story of Jesus. He "will give" (*dōsō*) it and "it will become in them (*genh,setai evn auvtw/|*) a spring of water welling up to eternal life" (v. 14). The promise of Jesus transcends this person, this place, this water, this well, and this time. It is not this time that determines the gift Jesus must give, but sometime in the future when he will give a gift of water welling up to the eternal life.

The woman's response in v, 15, "Sir, give me this water (*kurie dos moi touto to hudōr*), so that I may never be thirsty or have to keep coming here (*mē duerchōma entarde*) to draw water," suggests that she thinks of it as a plumbing miracle, which will eliminate the need to haul water from the well each day.[41] She takes Jesus' words on the gift of water and the spring in v. 14 and makes them her own. However, in doing so she transforms the words of Jesus from the promise of a future gift of water welling up to eternal life into her own agenda of this well, this place, and this water, satisfying her thirst. In this way, the woman misunderstands Jesus' words in a physical and selfish sense[42] in a way that parallels the response of the Jews in 2:20.[43] She too

---

about the patriarch Jacob associated him with a "travelling well." Cf. Moloney, *John*, 118.

39. Okure, *Johannine Approach*, 99. It is worth noting here that Jesus' assertion that he can grant access to the source of living water leads to the first christological insight of the passage—Jesus is greater than Jacob. Ironically, the woman is asking more than she realizes with her question: "Are you greater than our father Jacob" (v. 12)? John 8:53 had the Jews repeating the same question in connection with Abraham. Cf. Edward, *John*, 56.

40. Permanent possession of "living water" within a Jewish symbolic system could either refer to the purifying of God's Spirit in the righteous community (1QS 4:21); to God the "fountain of living waters" (Jer 2:13), from which worshipers drink (Psa 36:8), or to Wisdom, who says of herself: "He who eats of me will hunger still, he who drinks of me will thirst for more" (Sir 24:23–29). Jesus' saying may even be a deliberate reversal of Wisdom's claim.

41. Koester, *The Word of Life*, 61.

42. Okure, *Johannine Perspective*, 103.

43. A similar understanding of Jesus' message is also seen in 6:60–66 with reference to the Bread of Life discourse.

is presented, at the conclusion of this first moment of her encounter with Jesus, as having no faith.[44]

However, there is a contrast between "the Jews" and the Samaritan woman. The end response of the two characters might be the same, as Jesus' words are rejected, but the hostility of "the Jews" is not found in the woman. Indeed, there are signs of a growing respect. The mocking title, "a Jew" (v. 9) is replaced by "Sir" (vv. 11, 15).[45] The Jews disappeared from the narrative after 2:13–22, but they will return, publicly hostile, in 5:16–18. The Samaritan woman remains in the narrative. Her rejection of the word of Jesus does not bring her role to a conclusion.

The Second Episode: The Messiah-Prophet Dialogue (John 4:16–26)

Jesus' Divine Insight (John 4:16–19)

The conversation shifts to the woman's personal life with Jesus' demand in v. 16: *hupa ge phōnēson ton andra souk a elthe enthaide* ("go, call your husband, and come back"). Stibbe explains this shift in terms of what he calls a "technique of deliberate transcendence," a technique employed by Jesus in the Fourth Gospel to draw attention to his supernatural knowledge.[46] Here, it is used to draw attention to the fact that Jesus knows about the woman's past life even though he is—in her view—a complete stranger from a rival territory.[47] When Jesus asks the woman to go and call her husband, he knows already that she has no husband, that she has been five times married, and that the man she is living with is not her husband.

There are two possible ways to understand the woman's response in v. 17a that she has no husband. She may be telling a lie since she really does not want to be bothered further by Jesus on her private life. Or she may truly mean that she has no husband, which means that she does not consider herself married to the man with whom she is living.[48] In this case, she is speaking the truth, as Jesus' reply in v. 17b confirms.[49] While this may lead to the inference that the woman's past would be considered sinful, the fact that the implication of the woman's moral status was not further pursued shows that her sinfulness is not the point of the narrative.[50] Rather, the marital theme

---

44. For more on this line of argument, see Moloney, *John*, 118–19.
45. O' Day, "The Gospel of John," 64; Okure, *Johannine Perspective*, 108.
46. Cf. Stibbe, *John's Gospel*, 18.
47. O' Day, *Revelation in the Fourth Gospel*.
48. Moloney, *John*, 127.
49. According to Okure, *Johannine Approach*, 109, "The woman is telling the truth, but with her tongue in her cheek, because she wants to get rid of Jesus." Moloney (*John*, 248) also confirms the veracity of this from the fact of the woman's later admission to her townspeople in 4:29, 39 that Jesus told her everything she ever did.
50. Moloney, *John*, 148. However, the Jacob theme may still be implicit in this passage since the well is the place of courtship in the Jacob story. Jesus replaces the numerous husbands which the woman has had.

is introduced with a view to letting the woman know how much Jesus knows about her own private life.[51]

The impact of Jesus' reply in v.17b–18 must indeed be overwhelming to the woman's defensive stance hitherto sustained throughout the preceding part of the conversation. His claim to give living water was beyond her grasp, but a person who tells her about the secrets of her life commands attention.[52] Jesus' somewhat ironic but deeply respectful emphasis on how "well" and "truly" she has spoken becomes more significant. This affirmation discloses Jesus' tactful manner of appealing to the woman to drop her resisting stance. The same tone of appeal continues through vv. 21–24 (*pisteu moi gunai*, "Woman, believe me"), and it finally works.

Up to this point, the woman has been trying to block the conversation, and her rejoinders have not revealed any genuine interest on her part in the conversation. Her questions have been calculated in the main to annoy Jesus, though in vain. Her quarrelsome attitude is evident, for instance, from the taunting question in vv. 9 and 11 and from the rhetorical question in v. 12. Now, however, and for the first time, she not only shows a genuine interest in Jesus' statement in vv. 17b–18, she also takes the initiative in advancing the conversation. She, who has been suspicious of Jesus all this while (4:9), is now ready to receive him as a prophet: "Sir, I perceive that you are a prophet" (v. 19).[53]

The Locus of Worship Debate (John 4:20–24)

Although the woman's declaration that Jesus is a prophet[54] reflects a growth in her progressive understanding of the identity of "he who it is that is speaking to you," the term *prophētēs* here is to be understood in a very generic sense of a person endowed with supernatural power and to whom one could turn to hear the word of God. This interpretation is supported by the woman's assertion in v. 20: "Our fathers worshiped on this mountain;[55] and you say that in Jerusalem is the place where men ought to worship." The juxtaposition of "our fathers" and "you" shows that in the woman's mind, Jesus remains essentially a Jew—a Jewish prophet, no doubt, but a Jew nonetheless.

When exactly the Samaritan schism started is a matter of dispute. But that the Samaritans held to the sanctity of Gerizim, at least as much as Jews held to that of

---

51. The reader of the Gospel is not surprised at Jesus' unique insight into persons. In a sense, v. 18 functions in much the same way as 1:48b, where Jesus gives evidence of his divine knowledge to Nathanael by claiming the knowledge of him, specifically under the fig tree, prior to his being called by Philip, and hence to their first meeting (cf. also 1:42; 2:24–25). As the story proceeds, Jesus' revelation of his divine knowledge to the woman has an effect on her similar to that which it had on Nathanael. Cf. Okure, *Johannine Approach*, 110–13.

52. Stibbe, *John Readings*, 66.

53. Hakola, *Identity Matters*, 101.

54. Koester, *The Word of Life*, 61.

55. Ridderbos, *John*, 161.

Jerusalem, is not disputed.[56] For the Samaritans, not only was Gerizim the place of the sacrifice of Isaac; next to Sinai, it was the mountain of revelation, the eternal hill, the point of entry into the invisible, the new Eden of the end-time. By the time of Jesus, a typical Samaritan tradition expected "the prophet" to uncover the lost temple vessels and to vindicate its own tradition of worship, not in Jerusalem but on Mount Gerizim, which they took to be the location of Jacob's heavenly vision in Genesis 28:16–18. Jewish traditions, on the other hand, enlisted Jacob's vision as a legitimation for the Jerusalem cult. *Jubilees* 32:21–26 has the angel who shows Jacob the heavenly tablets warn against building a temple at Bethel. 4QPBless has Jacob foresee the coming of the messianic ruler from Judah along with the Interpreter of the Law. A Midrash on Genesis 27:27 has God show Jacob the building, destruction, and rebuilding of the Jerusalem temple (*Gen. Rab.* 65:23). The woman's words may be intended as a challenge to Jesus to state his opinion on this controversy as a prophet.

Jesus' response in v. 22, "You worship what you do not know; we worship what we know, for salvation is from the Jews," seems to acknowledge a sort of priority of Jews over Samaritans.[57] "From a Jewish perspective, Samaritan worship is directed away from God, not toward him. Although Jews and Samaritans shared some common traditions going back to Jacob and his predecessors (cf. 4:12), it was said that Samaritan worship included other deities, which had been introduced into the region centuries before (cf. 2 Kings 17:29–41). Their practice was considered a departure from true faith."[58] Jesus, here, is speaking as a Jew; and evaluating the Samaritan religion from a Jewish point of view, he somehow admits the superiority of Jewish worship to that of the Samaritans.[59]

But whatever overt support of the Jewish perspective on the locus of worship debate is quickly wiped away in what follows. Jesus does not say that the Samaritans should redirect their worship from their mountain to Jerusalem. By negating the claims of both sides, "neither on this mountain nor in Jerusalem," Jesus, rather than get bogged by the age-old rivalry, proclaims that in the messianic age, which has now dawned, worship of God will not be tied to a holy place.[60] As earlier he had refused to enter into the standing quarrel between the Jews and the Samaritans or to dispute the worth of Jacob's well (vv. 9–10, 11–14), so now he transposes the issue of worship to a completely different plane, that of eschatology. In this new sphere of reality, the issue of worship centers on the right manner or true meaning of worship, not on place. In

---

56. For a detailed discussion on the Jerusalem/Gerizim controversy and the diverse scholarly opinions, see Abia, *A Missional Perspective of John 4:1–42*, 70–71.

57. Moloney, *John*, 150–51.

58. Koester, *The Word of Life*, 62.

59. Hakola, *Identity Matters*, 105; Stibbe, *John Readings*, 66.

60. As Thettayi, *In Spirit and Truth,*, 225, observes: "The important issue being raised here is the contravention of boundaries that cannot be resolved by a shift in geographical focus. Jesus transcends the barrier of geography—this or that mountain (4:20) and reveals Himself as the new temple in whom the Father can be worshipped."

this order, both Jerusalem and Gerizim, the sacred places of Jews and Samaritans, have now become obsolete because God no longer resides in such places but only in his Son Jesus Christ.[61] He is the one through whom the whole world (Jews, Samaritans, and Gentiles) can come to the Father (cf. 4:42; 3:16; 14:6). It becomes clear that for Jesus the true standard of worship is belief in Jesus, a universal worship which is open to all people, all genders, and all races.[62] Jesus has already supplanted Jewish purification rites (2:6–11; 3:25–30); and the reader has been told that the "risen Lord" supplants the Jerusalem temple (2:21). Now he also is the proper locus of worship, understood as a "worship in Spirit and in truth,"[63] a worship that is available to all who are willing to abandon their former modes of worship.[64]

John understands "Spirit" to be the Spirit of God, which purifies the believer and is a permanent possession. God's truth can also be spoken as purifying the sinfulness and perversity of humanity (1QS 4:20–21). The Essenes described the Torah as a well dug by their teachers from which they drew their knowledge of truth (CD 6:2–5).[65] In the Fourth Gospel, "spirit and truth" are closely connected to the person of Jesus (1:14: 14:6, 17; 15:26; 16:7; 17:7). Worship "in spirit and truth," used to describe the quality of life which is proper to those who are born again of "water and the Spirit" (3:3, 5–8) or who are empowered to become "children of God" (1:12–13), can only take place through him. In the new age which Jesus has inaugurated, God's presence will no longer be localized on specific mountains because God is now to be found in the person of Jesus.[66]

Jesus Is Acknowledged as the Messiah (John 4:25–26)

The discourse reaches its conclusion when the woman suggests that Jesus might be the messianic prophet and Jesus responds, "I Am" (vv. 25–26). The important questions here concern the identity of the Messiah expected by the woman and the relationship between this Messiah and the one proclaimed by Jesus in v. 26, and which the woman later proclaims to her fellow Samaritans in v. 29. From all indications, it does seem that for the woman, "Messiah" is a generic term equivalent in Johannine terms to the

---

61. Brunner, *The Gospel of John*, 258.

62. Spencer, "Feminist Criticism," 310.

63. Though the importance of the cultic site has been relativized, worship has not. But there is a caveat: In the new age that Jesus is inaugurating, worship will be open to all people, including the old worshipers (both Jews and Samaritans). See Abia, *A Missional Perspective of John 4:1–42*, 74.

64. Hakola, *Identity Matters*, 108.

65. For John, Jesus is the truth since he is the revelation of God (8:45; 14:6; 17:17–19).

66. Abia, *A Missional Perspective of John 4:1–42*, 76. Kok, *Restoration of the Samaritan Woman in John*, 146, brings out the implications of this fact for mission in a very modern language thus: "God has moved from the localised materialistic to the 'glocal' (global and local) spiritualistic. With 'glocal' it is meant that God will be localised wherever Jesus is, but globalistic in the sense that Jesus is to be found not only with the Jews but also with the Samaritans (4:1–42) and even with the Gentiles (4:43–54)."

"one sent." It has no well-defined contours of nationality and descent as has that of the Jews in 7:27–36, 40–52. This comes out clearly when we recall that the woman uses the term *Messi,aj* without the article, in contrast to Andrew's *to.n Messi,an* (1:41), where the term receives a further specificity from Philip in v. 45. What matters is that he is expected and that he will teach and announce "everything."

If the woman had used the "messiah" to express her belief in the expectations of the time, Jesus' `Egw, eivmi* transcends such limited notion because it is not only a reference to the future ("the coming messiah who will show us things") but a hear and now reality ("I, who speak to you").[67] Though the context leads one to supply a predicate "Messiah" for Jesus' "I AM" response to the woman's question, any Johannine Christian would have recognized the absolute use of the expression "I Am" to indicate Jesus' divine being. This link will be made explicit when Jesus is shown to be greater than Abraham (8:24, 28). The basis for true worship in the Johannine community is the confession of Jesus as prophet, Messiah, Savior of the world, and equal to God.

Noteworthy in the entire Dialogue is the method by which Jesus' self-revelation and or self-identification is made. The identification grows out of this entire revelation in action as a process of discovery in which the woman plays an important role. Jesus does not start by telling the woman that he is the Messiah, worthy of belief. Rather, he acts like one in his attitude toward her, in his teaching, and in his supernatural knowledge of her own private life. The revelation of his divine knowledge in vv. 17b–18 is the leading light guiding the woman in this process of discovery as vv. 28–29 show. Okure sees here the attitude of humility in the exercise of mission that is proper to the missionary.[68]

The woman's final response is given in action: she abandons her water pot and goes into the city to spread the news of her encounter and discovery. Different interpretation has been given as to the reason behind the woman's action of abandoning her waterpot, ranging from the need to enable her speedily to reach her village to call her villagers,[69] through the fact that she plans to return to Jesus to continue the dialogue,[70] to a demonstration of her willingness to fulfill the first prerequisite of being a disciple: leaving everything behind to follow Jesus.[71] While all these and many more explanations are plausible, the one that is best supported by the textual narrative is her intention to return after the trip to the village, which she eventually did with the rest

---

67. The fact that this revelation is made to non-Jews and the confession elicited from them is a clear indication that the revelation which Jesus has brought is not only for the Jews but is universal (4:42) and as such transcends both the Jewish and the Samaritans' expectations of a future bringer of salvation. Cf. Abia, *A Missional Perspective of John 4:1–42*, 77.

68. In her own words: "Jesus' humility in approaching his audience was also seen in his deep respect for the Samaritan woman despite her sex, persona; history and nationality." Cf. Okure, *The Johannine Approach to Mission*, 290.

69. Okure, *Johannine Approach*, 135.

70. O' Day, *Revelation in the Fourth Gospel*, 75.

71. Stibbe, *John Readings*, 67; Edwards, *John*, 59.

of the villagers. She not only has to abandon her belief in the sanctity of Gerizim, but she accepts to do this on the revelatory word of a Messiah who is a Jew by nationality.[72]

Third Episode: The Dialogue with the Disciples (John 4:27–38)

Jesus' disciples return as the woman goes into the town to bring people to Jesus the Messiah (vv. 27–30). Her action reflects the pattern established in the discipleship stories (1:40–49). A series of proverbial sayings (with parallels in the agricultural imagery of the Synoptics) directs the disciples toward their own task in "harvesting" those who are yet to come. In v. 35, Jesus corrects a proverb about time between sowing and harvest by announcing that the field is already ripe, perhaps in preview of the approaching Samaritans in v. 30.[73] Verse 36 describes the wages received by sower and reaper as another sign of the new age. Leviticus 26:5 describes the ideal reward as a time in which wheat harvest, grape harvest, and sowing all follow consecutively (cf. Amos 9:13). In John the missionary "harvest" does not begin until the hour of Jesus' crucifixion/exaltation (e.g., 12:32). The phrase "for eternal life" added to "fruit" makes it clear that the "harvest" is conversion to belief in Jesus.

Jesus proceeds in vv. 37–38 to interpret another known proverb, "one sows another reaps," without its pessimistic overtones (cf. Mic 6:15). It is difficult to determine how the proverb is being applied to the disciples. Does it allude to a "mission" of the disciples during Jesus' ministry (e.g., they will reap what the woman has sown among the Samaritans)? Or does it refer to the post-resurrection "sending" of the disciples (e.g., 17:18; 20:21)? The narrative structure of the Gospel favors the latter.[74] The saying cautions the community against taking credit for its missionary success. It merely reaps the fruits of others' labor: primarily that of Jesus, but reference to the first generation of Christian missionaries could also be implied.[75]

The Final Episode: The Samaritans Come to Faith (John 4:39–42)

Jesus remains at the well, but the disciples disappear into the background as the Samaritans and the Samaritan woman come to Jesus. This brief passage is composed of four affirmations, three of them from the narrator and a final one from the Samaritans who address the woman, upon whose word they have come to Jesus (cf. vv. 29–30).

---

72. Koester, *The Word of Life*, 9.

73. A similar saying appears in Matt 9:37–38. Allusion has also been made here to the theme of harvest in Synoptic kingdom parables (Mark 4:3–9, 26–29, 30–32), where the contrasts are drawn in terms of the perilous conditions, hidden growth, or small seed and the abundance of the harvest.

74. John 17:20 has the departing Jesus pray for "those who will believe in me through their word," and John 20:29b has the risen Lord pronounce a blessing on those who have "not seen and (yet) believed."

75. Acts 8 distinguishes two phases in the conversion of Samaria, the preaching of Philip and the arrival of Peter and John to confer the Spirit to the new converts.

Brief but elegant, the episode serves as a climax to Jesus' presence in Samaria with non-Jews proclaiming him as a universal savior.

The Samaritans believe first based on the word of the woman who testified about Jesus with the question: "Can this be the Messiah" (v. 29). Worthy of note here is that the evangelist himself considers the woman's report here to be the word of a witness (*ton logon tēs gynaikos marturousēs*) on the grounds of which some of the Samaritans first believed (v. 39).[76] Motivated by their partial faith, they invite Jesus to stay with them. From all likelihood, the issue of the conflict between Samaritan and Jew (v. 9) appears to have been forgotten.[77] This attests not only to the degree of confidence Jesus had earned, but also to their conviction that he was nonetheless the promised Messiah. Jesus is reported as staying with them "two days," after which many more came to faith based on their own experience of Jesus' words.[78]

A distinction, already made clear by the narrator in vv. 39 and 41 between the "words" of the woman and the "word" of Jesus, is once more articulated by the Samaritans in the only direct speech found in the narrative. They disassociate themselves with their initial belief (v. 39) by telling the woman in v. 42 that they "no longer (*ouketi*) believe because of your word (*dia tēn sēn lalian*), for we have heard for ourselves."[79]

Classical literature uses the word *lalia.* to speak of "gossip, common talk," but it can hardly have that negative meaning here.[80] As a matter of fact, the use of *lalia.* in this passage is neither intended to dismiss nor minimise the woman's testimony as if it were "mere talk" or "chatter."[81] On the contrary, the Samaritans sought to embrace it and to make it their own. Not only did many of them believe on account of her words, but they also immediately left their town in search for Jesus (4:30). It is the woman's *lalia.* that prepared the way for the *lalia.* of Jesus which became available to the Samaritans when they invited Jesus to stay with them for two days.[82] And now that they have stayed with him, they now believe because of his *logoi*. There is only one revealing *logoi*, and it comes from Jesus. They believe because they themselves have had the experience of hearing (v. 42b: *akekoko*, "amen"). On the basis of this hearing they claim to know (*oidamen*) that Jesus is the savior of the world.

---

76. Okure, *The Johannine Approach to Mission*, 170.

77. Schnackenberg, *John*, 455.

78. Abia, *A Missional Perspective of John 4:1–42*, 92.

79. Okure, *Johannine Approach*, 170, observes the awkward nature of the introduction of this distinction: "It is generally noted that v. 39 is a discrepancy introduced by the Evangelist into a lost primitive story of Jesus' encounter with a woman . . . In this present context, v. 39 placed before vv. 40–42 indicates that the Samaritans believed *because of* the woman's word"

80. See Okure, *Johannine Approach*, 171, especially her remark that the position that *lalia.* means mere chatter as opposed to Jesus' substantial *lo,goj* runs into conflict with the evidence of the Gospel itself which uses *lalia.* and copiously, *lalei/n* the verb as a technical term to describe Jesus' own proclamation.

81. Contra Schnackenburg, *John*, 455.

82. Kreslet, *Picturing Christian Witness*, 97.

Rather than downplay the significance of the woman's role in the episode, this subtle distinction locates her missionary role along the line of other missionary heroes in the Fourth Gospel. In John 17:20, Jesus prays not just for the disciples, but for those who will come to believe "through their words" (*dia ton autōn*). So understood, the Samaritan woman is the first and only person during Jesus' earthly ministry through whose words of witness a group of people are brought to "come and see" and to believe in Jesus.[83]

This reading of the passage gains extra import if we recall that the narrator refers to the woman as "testifying" (*marturouses*). In the Fourth Gospel, *marturia* and the verbal form *marture,w* are important words used to describe the act of bringing people to Jesus so that they may believe and have life in his name (20:31),[84] a requirement which the *marturou,shj* of the woman has fulfilled (4:30, 39–42). I share here the conclusion of Abia's reading of this passage:

> In this regard, the missionary role of the woman can be compared to that of John the Baptist. Like the Baptist (1:35–35), her hearers leave and seek after Jesus (4:30, 39) and as she decreases (4:30), Jesus increases (4:42). Her role was merely to lead the townspeople into their encounter with Jesus like the Baptist did. In missiological terms, it means that there is a stage beyond a mere belief in Jesus on the basis of the witness of a believer, namely: that of personal encounter with Jesus through his revelatory word.[85]

Jesus Is Acknowledged as "The Savior of the World"

The first disciples claimed to have found the Messiah (1:41; 45), and Nathaniel claimed to "know" that Jesus was a teacher come from God (cf. 3:2), but their finding and knowledge were based on their own religious and cultural traditions. The knowledge of the Samaritans is based entirely on the *lo,goj* of Jesus. And in accordance with the degrees of faith reflected in the titles predicated of Jesus, the Samaritans go beyond "prophet" and "Messiah" to acknowledge Jesus as *avlhqw/j o` zōtēr tou/kosmou* ("truly the Savior of the world").[86]

The title "Savior" occurs only here in the Fourth Gospel and only once again in the Johannine corpus (1 John 4:14). It is infrequent as a title for Jesus in the earlier New Testament writings. It appears in the infancy narratives of Luke (2:11) and in reference to the exalted Lord as "Savior" in Acts (5:31; 13:23; Phil 3:20). The Fourth Gospel prefers to speak of Jesus coming or giving himself for the "life of the world" (cf. John

---

83. Nissen, *New Testament and Mission*, 91.
84. Scott, *Sophia and the Johannine Jesus*, 192.
85. Abia, *A Missional Perspective of John 4:1–42*, 94. The analysis of this section of the pericope is taken to a great extent from Abia's reading.
86. MacRae, "Invitation to John," 348.

1:29; 6:33, 51). *Zōter* appears in the LXX to translate Hebrew *phi (Am*, which is used of God (e.g., Isa 45:15, 21; Wis 16:7; Sir 51:1; 1 Macc 4:30). It was also current in the pagan world as a designation for deities, kings, emperors, and others who might be perceived to function as benefactors of the people. An inscription found at Ephesus from 48 BCE speaks of the deified Julius Caesar as "god manifest and common savior of human life." Philemon 3:20 uses "Savior" for the exalted Jesus when he comes in judgment at the Parousia. However, "Savior" appears to have become a common title for Jesus only toward the end of the first century, as is evident in its use in the Pastoral Epistles (e.g., 1 Tim 4:10; 2 Tim 1:10; Titus 1:4; 2:13; 3:4, 6; also 2 Pet 1:1, 11; 2:20; 3:2, 18).

In our context, "Savior" is not a title derived from the Samaritan expectations but might be intended to show that the Samaritans have transcended their particularized expectations just as the Jewish protagonists of Jesus are challenged to do in discourses that culminate with the Son-of-Man sayings. In other words, the title grows out of the Samaritans' personal experience of Jesus as the universal Messiah whose saving mission transcends Jewish national boundaries bolstered by sociocultic practices (vv. 9, 20, 22). Salvation does indeed take its departure point from the Jews, but it does not end with the Samaritans. The fruit of Jesus' mission is offered to any who are open enough to receive it (vv. 13–14). Boers is therefore right when he writes about this passage:

> Jesus, the Messiah, is neither the saviour of the Samaritans nor of the Jews— "an hour comes when neither on this mountain nor in Jerusalem will you worship the Father (v. 21)—but the saviour of the world—"the true worshippers will worship the Father in spirit and truth" (v. 23). True worship, worship in the spirit, constitutes a community beyond all earthly religious communities, a community of worship in which all of humanity is united. That is what the villagers recognise; it is the point of the story.[87]

The confession of the Samaritans is public as is that in 1:34; 6:69; 11:27; and it grows out of the joint witness of Jesus and the woman. This is the central confession sought in the Gospel (20:31), and whatever form it takes, it always focuses on what Jesus' mission means for the audience who so confesses him. In the case of John the Baptist, the confession (1:34) is preceded and followed by a public denial that he (the Baptist) himself is the Christ (1:20; 3:23), a denial which is all the more striking given the positive way in which the question is put to him by the envoy of the Pharisees. In our passage, the confession of the Samaritans, like that of the woman, is shown to be a response to Jesus' own self-revelation, given as a gift. Like John the Baptist, the Samaritans are open to the revelation of Jesus, and this openness leads to their recognizing and confessing him as the "Savior of the world." As John the Baptist heard the voice of the bridegroom and rejoiced to hear that voice, the Samaritans hear the words of Jesus and confess that this indeed is the savior of the world. As John the Baptist

---

87. Hendrikus, *Neither on This Mountain nor in Jerusalem*, 199–200.

was prepared to decrease that Jesus might increase, so are the Samaritans prepared to abandon all debates of Gerizim or Jerusalem and place their trust in Jesus as the savior of the world. The Samaritans' openness to the word of Jesus transforms them; they become examples of authentic Johannine belief.

CONCLUSION

The apparent success of Jesus' encounter with the Samaritans stands out in the Book of Signs. In almost all his encounters with Jews from Galilee to the north or Judea to the south, he meets with opposition to some degree. One can speculate whether the favorable response of the Samaritans rests on a historical role of Samaritans in early Christianity, but the evidence is too slight to be conclusive. What is more important in this carefully wrought story is the dynamic of coming to faith in response to Jesus' word—and the mission of Jesus' disciples.[88]

The narrative of 4:1–42 articulates a point of view about how one should respond to Jesus and the fruits of such a response (cf. 2:13–3:36). With the "word" of Jesus as the criterion, the story of Jesus' presence among the Samaritans points to the possibility of no faith (vv. 1–15: the Samaritan woman), partial faith (vv. 16–30: the Samaritan woman), and authentic Johannine belief (vv. 39–42: the Samaritan villagers). Not only does the Samaritan woman serve as an example of a disciple who goes out and brings people to Christ,[89] but the Samaritans' faith is also presented as an example of faith based on testimony without miraculous signs (cf. 20:20).[90]

These models of belief are closely associated with the Johannine message on the importance of belief in the revelation of God in and through the word of Jesus for life and salvation (cf. 4:13–14, 21–24, 34–38). Jesus has come to bring to perfection the work given to him by the Father, and he associates disciples with himself, as the fields are ripe for the harvest (vv. 31–38). Jesus' promise of 3:17, "For God sent the Son into the world, not to condemn the world, but that the world might be saved through him," is being acted out in the narrative. The concentration upon the characters *beyond the world of Judaism* indicates that no one, of whatever race, culture, or religion, is to be excluded in the Johannine community and in the Johannine theology of revelation and salvation.

On why this reading of the passage has not been normative in the history of the interpretation of this passage, despite its self-evident nature, the *heroine* of this Festschrift has this to say: "Strictly speaking, these are problems raised by contemporary scholarship, not by the Johannine data themselves; and they arise because of the restrictive meaning attached to mission in modern times, that is, primarily as outreach

---

88. MacRae, "Invitation to John," 348–9.
89. Witherington, *John's Wisdom*, 125.
90. Abia, *A Missional Perspective of John 4:1–42*, 28

to non-believers in 'the Third World' [and] arises only where mission is understood exclusively of the disciples, a conception which is certainly not Johannine."[91]

When read in its proper context, as we have tried to do in this essay, the passage, no doubt, has some implication for the members of the Johannine community. In the vision of the Gospel, the cycle of faith is incomplete without this open confession by the believer, a confession which, in turn, becomes a witness to its hearers. Indeed, genuine belief in Jesus is inseparable from a missionary impetus (cf. 1:38–46; 15:16). It is inconceivable then that the audience of the Gospel would have heard the story of Jesus' missionary activity in Samaria and yet not make any associations between this activity and their own experience of mission, especially since Jesus is here presented as *the* evangelizer of Samaria. The passage also has some implication for the contemporary church and her approach to mission. Listening to Jesus and the Samaritan woman, especially the way Jesus engaged and related to her, seems to call for an alternative way of disseminating the Gospel in an undiscriminating manner. In this narrative, the method of Jesus is fundamentally dialogical, the movement of the entire dialogue centers on the woman and her needs (4:10, 13–14), and while it climaxes in the self-revelation of Jesus, it becomes a journey of self-discovery for the woman.[92] Not only does Jesus supernaturally know about the woman's past, but he is also well conversant with Samaritan ways of thinking about things.[93] This suggests that mission work requires more than knowledge of the Bible, the church traditions, and doctrines. It also demands a good knowledge of the views and belief system of the persons to whom one is witnessing.[94] Milne rightly observes that among the failures in some modern approaches to evangelism are often failures in love because "people want to know that we care before they care about what we know."[95]

The Samaritan episode has shown that the mutual love that exists within the community of Jesus' followers extends beyond ancient hostilities like that of Jews and Samaritans. It challenges the contemporary church to engage in missionary journeys that will break down all barriers and cultural codes that limit the opportunities of sharing of resources among people. As Kok & Niemand aptly remark: "The way of Jesus as exemplified in this passage, when properly read, invites us to become missional-incarnated agents of healing and restoration bringing light where there is darkness, life where there is death . . . and hope where there is no hope."[96]

---

91. Okure, *Johannine Approach to Mission*, 292.
92. Nissen, *New Testament and Mission*, 91.
93. Abia, *A Missional Perspective of John 4:1–42*, 101.
94. Witherington, *John's Wisdom*, 123.
95. Milne, *The Message of John*, 86.
96. Kok and Niemand, "(Re) discovering a Missional-Ethos," 6.

BIBLIOGRAPHY

Abia, Peter. *A Missional Perspective of John 4:1–42: Hearing Jesus and the Samaritan Woman and Its Implications for the Mission of the Contemporary Church.* Pretoria: University of Pretoria Press, 2014.

Ball, M. *Narratology: Introduction to the Theory of Narratives.* Third Edition. Toronto: University of Toronto Press, 2009.

Barclay, William *The Gospel of John, Vol. 1.* Philadelphia: Westminster, 1975.

Boers, Hendrikus. *Neither on This Mountain nor in Jerusalem.* SBLMS 35. Atlanta: Scholars, 1988.

Brunner, F.D. *The Gospel of John: A Commentary.* Grand Rapids: Eerdmans, 2012.

Edward, M. *John.* Blackwell Bible Commentary. UK: Blackwell Publishing Company, 2004.

Hakola, R. *Identity Matters: John, the Jews and Jewishness.* Leiden: Brill, 2005.

Koester, Craig. *The Word of Life: A Theology of John's Gospel.* Grand Rapids: Eerdmans, 2008.

Kok, J. *The Restoration of the Samaritan Woman in John: And Its Implication for a Missionary Ecclesiology.* Nijmegen: Unibook, 2011.

Legaspi, Michael C. *The Death of Scripture and the Rise of Biblical Studies.* Oxford Studies in Historical Theology. Oxford: Oxford University Press, 2010.

MacRae, George W. "Invitation to John." In *Invitation to the Gospels,* 325–403. Edited by Paul J. Achtemeier et al. New York: Paulist Press, 2003.

Malina, B. J., and R. L. Rohrbaugh. *Social-Science Commentary on the Gospel of John.* Minneapolis: Fortress Press, 1998.

Milne, B. *The Message of John: The Bible Speaks Today.* Leicester, England: Inter-Varsity Press, 1993.

Moloney, Francis J. *The Gospel of John.* Sacra Pagina 4. Collegeville, MN: Liturgical Press, 1998.

Nissen, J. *New Testament and Mission: Historical and Hermeneutical Perspectives.* Frankfurt am Main: Peter Lang, 1999.

O'Day, G. R. "The Gospel of John: Introduction, Commentary and Reflection." In *New Interpreter's Bible,* IX:563–71. Nashville: Abington, 1995.

———. *Revelation in the Fourth Gospel: Narrative Mode and Theological Claim.* Philadelphia: Fortress, 1986.

Okure, Teresa. "'I will open my mouth in parables' (Matt 13:35): A Case for a Gospel-Based Biblical Hermeneutics." *NTS* 46, no. 3 (2000) 445–63.

———. "Integrity and Corruption in the Bible: President's Address and Presentation of the Convention Theme." In *Acts of the Catholic Biblical Association of Nigeria,* 33–35. Edited by Bernard Ukwuegbu, Mary Jerome Obiorah, Anthony Ehwerido, and Cletus Gotan. CABAN 12. Port Harcourt: CABAN Publications, 2020.

———. *The Johannine Approach to Mission: A Contextual Study of John 4:1–42.* Wissenschaftliche Untersuchungen zum Neuen Testament 2. Tuebingen: Mohr Siebeck, 1988.

Olson, B. *Structure and Meaning in the Fourth Gospel: A Textual-Linguistic Analysis of John 2:1–11 and 4:1–42.* Sweden: CWK Gleerup Lund, 1974.

Ridderbos, H. *The Gospel of John: A Theological Commentary.* Grand Rapids: Eerdmans, 1997.

Schnackenberg, R. *The Gospel According to John, vol. 1: Introduction and Commentary on Chapters 1–4.* New York: Cross Road, 1987.

Scott, M. *Sophia and the Johannine Jesus.* JSOTSup Series 71. Sheffield: University of Sheffield Press, 1992.

Skreslet, S.H. *Picturing Christian Witness: New Testament Images of Disciples in Mission.* Grand Rapids: Eerdmans, 2006.

Spencer, F. S. "Feminist Criticism." In *Hearing the New Testament: Strategies for Interpretation,* 289–385. Edited by J. B. Green. 2nd edition. Grand Rapids: Eerdmans, 2010.

Stibbe, M.W.G. *John Readings: A New Biblical Commentary.* England: JSOT, 1993.

———. *John's Gospel: New Testament Readings.* London: Routledge, 1994.

Surekha, Nelavala. *Liberation Beyond Borders: Dalit Feminist Hermeneutics and Four Gospel Women.* Treblin, Germany: Proquest, Umi Dissertation Publishing, 2011.

Thettayil, B. *In Spirit and Truth: An Exegetical Study of John 4:19-26 and a Theological Investigation of the Replacement Theme in the Fourth Gospel.* Leuven: Peeters, 2007.

Van Arde, A. G. "Narrative Criticism." In *Focusing on the Message: New Testament Hermeneutics, Exegesis and Methods,* 381–418. Edited by Du Toit. Pretoria: Protea Book House, 2009.

Witherington, B. *John's Wisdom: A Commentary on the Fourth Gospel.* Louisville: Westminster John Knox, 1995.

CHAPTER 8

The Request of the Mother of James and John in Matthew 20:20–28

Its Missionary and Masculinity Implications

GESILA N. UZUKWU, DMMM

INTRODUCTION

Most scholars would argue that the socio-cultural and religious practices of first century Jews greatly influenced the author of the Gospel of Matthew. According to Daniel J. Harrington, references to women in Matthew are patriarchally determined.[1] Adopting an androcentric perspective, Matthean scholars have not strictly given focused attention on the character of the mother and its implication. In exegetical-theological studies of Matthew 20:20–28, an analysis of the reason for her presence quickly drops out or gets marred by discussions on the general reason for the inclusion of women in the Gospel of Matthew. Or the focus becomes more on the sons than the mother. Such would justify the position of Albright and Mann, and also J. P. Meier, who hold that the mother of the sons was included to shed the sons on a positive light.[2] Thus in an attempt to depict the sons in a positive light, the mother now takes the blame.

The character of the mother of the sons of Zebedee has not received the proper attention it deserves. Addressing a variety of mother-son relationships in the Scripture and the import of patriarchal ideologies on women, I suggest that the mother's approach to Jesus in Matthew 20:20–28 evokes the oppressive sociopolitical situation of women in ancient Israel and how getting out of the situation was dependent upon

---

1. According to Harrington, "Problems and Opportunities in Matthew's Gospel," 420.
2. Albright and Mann, *Matthew*, 241; Meier, *Matthew*, 227.

the idea of having a son/sons. Here, I would develop an eschatological sociopolitical argument that Matthew 20:20–28 is the case of a mother who, in making request for her sons, is indirectly making a request for herself because she wants to be freed of the sociopolitics of male domination in the would-be kingdom to come.

2. SCHOLARLY MODELS OF INTERPRETING MATTHEW 20:20–28 AND THEIR IMPLICATIONS FOR UNDERSTANDING MATTHEW'S GOSPEL

Recent scholarship on Matthew 20:20–28 tends to focus on three major areas of interest. The first interest takes on the basic redaction-critical considerations about the passage in question. Here, some traditional scholarship has focused on the differences and similarities between Matthew and Mark's account (Mark 10:35–40), seeking to understand the reason for the addition or omission of the character of Zebedee's wife in the narrative.[3] Presuming that there is a certain level of dependency or connection between Matthew 20:20–28 with Mark 10:35–40, some scholars would easily read and situate the story of the mother of the sons of Zebedee in Matthew 20:20–28 as one of the few references to women in the Gospel of Matthew with little or no importance attached to her presence. According to D. A. Carson and P. J. J. Botha, for instance, there is little or no obvious theological motif for introducing the mother of the sons of Zebedee. It only functioned as "bridging scenes" or links to major narratives and themes.[4] Albright and Mann and many others hold that the mother of the sons was included to cast the sons in a positive light.[5]

The second interest looks at the reason for the presence of the mother of James and John in relationship with the narrative or the message of story. Here, emphasis is more on the main purpose and theological contributions of the text, based on the assumption that the special reference to the mother's intervention in Matthew 20:20 is indispensable for understanding the passage in question. Jane Korpas and Emily Cheney suggest that the request narrative is one of Matthew's openness to women and their pastoral-theological involvement in the ministry of Jesus. Korpas, for instance, speaks of Matthew's interest to change the status quo of women, from the marginalized state of women to greater involvement in the public ministry of Christ as leaders and disciples.[6]

Speaking of discipleship, Elaine Mary Wainwright has argued briefly on how the request speech of the mother of the sons of Zebedee is significant for understanding

---

3. See note on Rudman, "Whose Kingdom Is It Anyway?" 97–104, 99–100; Evans, *Matthew,* 353; Senior, *What are they Saying about Matthew?* 117–119.

4. Botha, "The Gospel of Matthew and Women," 514; Carson, *Matthew,* 431.

5. Albright and Mann, *Matthew,* 241; Matthew, *New Testament Message,* 227.

6. Kopas, "Jesus and Women in Matthew," 13–21; Cheney, "The Mother of the Sons of Zebedee (Matthew 27.56)," 13.

Jesus' teaching on discipleship. With the question of the mother of the sons and Jesus' response, she argues, the author of Matthew highlights that real discipleship in the messianic *basileia* involves renouncing family membership or family ties, receiving the gifts associated with the *basileia*, and finally doing the will of God.[7] Thus, family ties or religious ties, or even a mother's request on behalf of her sons, cannot guarantee one a place in the eschatological fulfillment in the *basileia*. They too, must receive the gifts of God and do the will of God.

Few others would suggest that the story of the mother of the sons of Zebedee shows the inclusive nature of Jesus' mission. It is evidence of the special interest Jesus had on those classified as the "the other," "the lowly," "the despised," or "the outsider."[8]

Aside from the question of the synoptic problem, the third interest emerges from studies on the issue of possible dependency or connection between Matthew 20:20–28 and any other passage in the sacred text. Interesting is Dominic Rudman's reading of Matthew 20:20–28 in light of the story of Bathsheba's petition to Solomon in 1 Kings 2 at the behest of Adonijah, who wants to marry Abishag, a woman formerly associated with David. According to Rudman, both narratives have clear parallels and contrast that work "to present James and John, the self-serving brothers, as antitypes for Adonijah."[9] It is interesting that Rudman articulates the message of Matthew 20:20–28 from the context of royal household narratives, especially the role of the queen mother in furthering the intention of the sons. As in previous studies, Rudman has paid so much attention to the character of the sons. While his insight could be informative for our study, this article takes its stance on the character of the mother. It will reveal how the peculiar relationship between mothers and their sons works in favor of the mothers. The mother may have made the request, but the request was indirectly for herself rather than the sons. It is our task then to see how Matthew 20:20–28 embodies the conscious but unspoken expectations of the mother in relation to the reality of the kingdom requested for.

3. THE SOCIO-RELIGIOUS AND POLITICAL CONTEXTS BEHIND MATTHEW 20:20–28

Scholarship in the period of formative Judaism has commonly maintained that in late antiquity, Jewish women had clearly a secondary position in relation to men, especially in the areas of power, prestige, influence, and status.[10] Patriarchal ideologies about the role and function of a woman shaped the life of women within the larger social order and household structure. Women cannot participate in politics, public,

---

7. Wainwright, *Toward a Feminist Critical Reading of the Gospel*, 119.
8. Carson, *The Gospel of Matthew*, 583; Brown, *The Birth of the Messiah*, 71–77.
9. Rudman, "Whose Kingdom Is It Anyway?" 97–104.
10. Swidler, *Women in Judaism,* accessed at file:///D:/STUFF/INFO/Religion/Women/Women_in_Judaism.mht.

and social life. Their main task is to take care for the daily needs of the home and their family members.

While women did not have recognizable public roles and experienced relatively low recognition in the social-public life, the birth and presence of a male child in the family made a woman more relevant and gave her a better sociopolitical and ideological space to function in the society. In the words of Stuart L. Love, "A woman's 'salvation' is through bearing children, many if possible, and especially sons. Therein she gains honor from her husband and standing within the family."[11]

It was a condition that gave women visibility, influence, a better opportunity, and status upgrade.[12] One of the rabbinic sources is quoted as saying, "It is well for those whose children are male, but ill for those who are female."[13] As soon as a woman gave birth to a male child, her status stepped up. The scorn of Hagar toward Sarah, and that of Sarah toward Hagar, is an example of what the birth of a male child could do to the status of a woman (Gen 16:1–6).

Sons could ask advice of their mothers. We have an example in Proverbs 31:1–9, where King Lemuel of Massa informed us of what was taught to him by his mother. It is of interest to note that the birth of a male child stands out in the sacred Scripture more than that of a female. Evidence can be seen from the fact that it is majorly the birth of a male child that is recorded and announced in both the Old and New Testament (confer the genealogy of Jesus Christ in Matt 1:1–17).

The possession of a male child gave a woman not only a sense of security in their households and society, but it was also a means through which a woman could exercise power, authority, and control over Israelite society. For instance, references can be made of the impact of queen mothers on the kings of Israel and how mothers ruled through the presence of their sons.[14] Certain leaders of Israel were known alongside with their mothers. The regnal formula "his mother's name" is given of seven queen mothers out of the ten queen mothers mentioned in the books of 1 and 2 Kings. In the regnal formula we have Hamutal (2 Kgs 24:18), Naamah (1 Kgs 14:2), Zibiah (2 Kgs 12:1), Jecoliah (2 Kgs 15:2; 2 Chr 26:3), Jehoaddin (2 Kgs 14:2; 2 Chr 25:1). Other queen mothers whose names did not occur with the regnal formula include Maacah (1 Kgs 15), Athaliah (2 Kgs 11), Bathsheba (1 Kgs 1–2), and Nehushta (2 Kgs 24).

---

11. Love, "The Household," 23.

12. Rabbinic tradition insisted on the duty of propagation, not just the obligation of procreation in marriage but of male offspring since male offspring are considered important for the continuity of the Jewish race. Confer the *Babylonian Talmud* (bYeb. 6, 6), cited in Swidler, *Women in Judaism*, 64.

13. Confer the Rabbinic Text *bKid* 82b, cited in Swidler, *Women in Judaism*, 64. Other citations include "at the birth of a boy all are joyful . . . at the birth of a girl all are sorrowful." (bNid. 31b). "When a boy comes into the world, peace comes into the world . . . When a girl comes, nothing comes" (Ber. 93; bBer. 31b; bB.M. 84b. Also, bNid. 71a), cited also in Swidler, *Women in Judaism*, 101n75.

14. Interesting discussions on the role of the queen mothers of Israel are found in Andreasen, "The Role of the Queen Mother in Israelite Society," 179–94.

As a result of the presence of their sons in the royal courts, the queen mothers had heritage of influence and authority. King Solomon, for instance had a throne brought for the king's mother, and she sat down at his right hand (1 Kgs 2:19). Queen mothers held significant positions within the palace and had such great influence upon their sons that they too were included in any form of "assessment of whether or not the king's reign conformed to divine standards."[15] Their statuses were elevated not only because they gave birth to royalties, but they could also influence the political, religious, and social decisions made by their sons for their people.

The queen mother Bathsheba, for instance, was instrumental in securing Solomon's succession to the throne (1 Kgs 1–2). We have also the example of Althalia, the "usurper queen," who wielded a lot of power from the throne in favor of her son. And when her son died, she arose and destroyed all the royal family and reigned for seven years.[16] In the case of Althalia, if the power relation gave rise to a collision of power, the son may eliminate the mother.[17]

With special reference to the New Testament, the role of women as wives is not as strongly emphasized as their roles as mothers.[18] Wives are not recognized in the same way as women who have given birth (especially to male children). In the context women are mentioned as mothers, their roles are majorly designated in association with their children, either in reference to Jesus or in reference to those who were Jesus' disciples or companions of the apostles (Matt 20:20; 27:56; Mark 15:47; 16:1; Luke 24:10; John 19:25; Acts 12:12; Rom 16:13, to mention a few).

The presence of the mothers alongside their sons enabled them to get closer to Jesus. It offered them opportunities to hear the message of Jesus, to experience transformation that ushers in a string of the vision of the kingdom to come (a beginning of the fulfillment of the beatific vision). It also granted them security and protection in the public spaces. Given that Jesus' ministry was a public affair, one could assess that the companionship of the sons gave the mothers both security and the opportunity to participate in Jesus' mission. Without their sons, the women could experience danger and misunderstanding in the society.

Like the queen mothers of the Old Testament, the special interest in mentioning the mothers of the disciples was because the women were also interested in what their son(s) stand to gain. One of the expectations of the disciples was that they assumed Jesus (the anointed one) was the royal descendant of David (Isa 9:7; 11:1; Pss 2; 89; 132) who had come to reestablish the earthly kingdom (Matt 19–23). Jesus chooses

---

15. Solvang, "Biblical Royal Mothers."

16. Mathys, "1 and 2 Chronicles," 297.

17. Confer also Brewer-Boydston, *Good Queen Mothers, Bad Queen Mothers*, 2016; Bowen, *Mothers and Son*, 2021.

18. Tammi Schneider has a similar view in her *Mothers of Promise: Women in the Book of Genesis*, but the focus of her study is on the women of the promise in Genesis. Cf. Schneider, *Mothers of Promise*, 11.

to define his kingship in a dramatic contrast to what the disciples expected—not in terms of earthly king or the warrior Messiah,[19] but one who has come to liberate his people from sin and darkness and lead them back to God. Even when the disciples acknowledged or realized that Jesus' kingdom was a future or an eschatological kingdom, they still longed and lobbied for a position in that kingdom.

MOTHERHOOD THROUGH THE SONS: A REQUEST FOR AN ESCHATOLOGICAL SOCIOPOLITICAL LIBERATION

Matthew 20:20–23 is clearly delineated from the text before and after it, as 20:17–19 situates the third passion prediction while 20:24–28 is a further focus on the missiological request, but at this time excluding the presence of the mother. At 20:21, the mother of the sons of Zebedee began her request with an aorist imperative statement "εἰπὲ ἵνα." The aorist imperative expression in this verse indicates a "one-time" command, exhortation, or entreaty for Jesus to perform the action implied in the verb—namely, that he permits her two sons to sit, one at his right hand and one at his left, in his kingdom.

The mother of the sons of Zebedee introduced her sons using the emphatic possessive pronouns οὗτοι οἱ δύο υἱοί μου ("these two sons of mine"). The most natural understanding of the expression would be that the woman is speaking exclusively of her own sons, referring not to other disciples or to other mothers. In addition to the above, the combination of both possessive (μου, "mine") and demonstrative (οὗτοι, "these") pronouns serves to stress emphatically the importance of the request. It is like saying, "You listen to me for I desperately need this favor." That the mother would be emphatic while presenting her sons to Jesus stresses the additional reason behind the request. In addition to identifying James and John as her sons, this woman is recognizing also that these two sons of hers are her heritage, her means of survival, and the only means of liberating her from the present suffocating masculine space in order to participate in the kingdom.

While the mother of the sons of Zebedee has come to Jesus to ask εἷς ἐκ δεξιῶν σου καὶ εἷς ἐξ εὐωνύμων σου ("one at your right and one at your left"), she makes a triple request: one for James, one for John, and one for herself. Thus, the request of Zebedee's wife for the sons overlaps with the personal request for herself. As already highlighted above, Matthew 20:20–28 is set within the context of typical ideas of patriarchal traditions. Yolanda Dreyer observes how the story of the mother of the sons of Zebedee and the stories of other women in the Gospel project the particular ideologies of male domination. According to Dreyer, the representation of the mother of James and John is interpretive of a male dominated society where "women's status depended on having sons and on how well their sons did in life."[20]

19. Keener, *The IVP Bible Background Commentary*, 233.
20. See Dreyer, "Gender Critique," 4.

We have already highlighted the point that the courage of the wife of Zebedee to come to Jesus can best be understood as reflecting patriarchal ideas that a woman's strength and security lies in her sons. Like the sons, the mother wants to be part of the kingdom Jesus taught. Or more so, she wants to be liberated from the "rigid, hierarchical, authority-centered social structure"[21] that largely characterizes her society to join Christ's kingdom since Christ preaches freedom. Living in a patriarchal society, the limitations placed on her prevent her from making a direct request for herself.[22] Thus, trapped in a man's world, this woman resorts to indirect and skillful means to achieve her ends.

In this specific instance, the mother of the sons of Zebedee is the one seeking to liberate herself through her sons. The mother of James and John may have been weighed down by the many limitations placed on her as a woman. In this case, she is now looking for something outside of her society, something heavenly. Invariably, it is like she is praying for her sons, but she is praying for herself. So even in heaven, she is making a request for herself.

Peculiar to Matthew is the way he employs subversive strategic elements in his narrative to project the struggles of women for liberation. Where a story revolves around the action of a woman, we discern the sense of a woman's struggle for liberation from the oppressive religious-cultural weight of a male-centered society. According to Jane Korpas, Matthew's women always appear as victims and survivors. They "always experience danger, loss of relationships and damage to their reputations, and yet they manage to prevail over the most trying circumstances and contribute to the future of Israel."[23]

The above can be said also of the woman with the flow of blood in 9:20–22. Her action was a silent but powerful way to discover Jesus and be healed. She would have been traumatized, living in a social cultural setting that has placed limited opportunities for her to be cured. Moreover, given her physical condition, she must have experienced chronic segregation from the society, since in the eyes of the community she would be constantly impure. But her ability to reach out to Jesus in the midst of the crowd (cf. Mark 5:24) symbolically expresses her feminine ability to push her struggle to the fringe in the midst of a patriarchally dominated system and environment.

---

21. Staurt Love maintains that Matthew's Gospel "presupposes a rigid, hierarchical, authority-centered social structure largely based on the paradigm of the household. Although exceptional or deviant gender behavior exists, it does not burst the societal boundaries of the household determined by an advanced agrarian mould." See Love, "The household," 22.

22. In context, it is assumed that the patriarchal structure in place did not provide women much avenue to express themselves, especially in the interactions with Jesus in his public ministry. This claim can be used to argue for the reason why the woman with flow of blood in 9:20–22 could not bodily meet Jesus for healing, why the woman could only anoint Jesus in the house in 26:6–13, and why Zebedee's mother could make request for the sons, even though the request is especially for her.

23. Kopas, "Jesus and Women in Matthew," 14.

The last segment of the request by the mother of James and John is the mentioning of the kingdom, ἐν τῇ βασιλείᾳ σου ("in your kingdom"). Interestingly, the portrayal of Jesus as a king in Matthew had a burning impact on the request of the mother of the sons of Zebedee. While the kingship of Christ was most prominently highlighted by the author of the Gospel of Matthew, the narrative about the sons of Zebedee and their mother highlights the peek of Jesus' acknowledgement of the existence of the kingdom.[24]

Thus, in the context of Matthew's Gospel, the strong emphasis on Christ's kingly glory may have left the disciples and their mother with a burning desire to be part of that coming kingdom.[25] Given the fact that the family of Zebedee were related to Mary the mother of Jesus (Salome was the sister to Mary), the mother of the sons of Zebedee would have thought that they had a special place in the kingdom, either through kingship ties or royal membership in Christ.[26] In addition, the family of Zebedee may have had certain popularity either in the circle of the disciples or in the society that must have made the mother take such leap of opportunity.[27]

Thus, that the mother of the sons of Zebedee has followed her sons to meet Jesus to make the missiological request of participating in Christ's kingship to come was a valuable asset for the mother. Through the sons, the mother of James and John is requesting for the possibility of a royal participation in the kingdom of Christ. The mother of the sons of Zebedee must be aware of the social system of Israel, that any possible ascension to the throne will liberate her and give her the authority and protection she desires.

The mother of the sons of Zebedee stood on the benefits and importance of her position to the sons to request a position for herself, since her position in relation to the sons will give her a chance to be on the throne with the sons. She was a playing a significant role in ensuring that her sons reign in the kingdom, alongside her. Like the queen mothers of the Old Testament, the mother of the sons of Zebedee assumes that a seat for her sons was a gain for her. It will grant her security, higher respect (since she is submitting two sons), power, political and religious influence and roles, and an official social position in the royal court of heaven. Thus, a reading of Matthew 20:20–28 within the conventional socio-religious system germane to the Matthean community makes clear how the missiological request of the mother of the sons of Zebedee recognizes the mother as the major suppliant.

---

24. According to Pennington, in his "The Kingdom of Heaven in the Gospel of Matthew," 44, "each of the Synoptics clearly portrays Jesus' ministry as one that focuses on the kingdom, but Matthew stands out among the Evangelists. At the basic level of vocabulary, we see that Matthew uses *basileia* some fifty-five times in a wide variety of phrases, including 'kingdom of heaven,' 'kingdom of God,' 'the Father's kingdom,' and simply, 'the kingdom.'"

25. France, *Matthew*, 281.

26. Mbabazi, "Christians as Members of a 'Royal Family,'" 101–14.

27. The family of Zebedee is one family name that reoccurred in all four Gospels (Matt 4:21; 10:2; 20:20; 26:37; 27:56; Mark 1:19, 20; 3:17; 10:35; Luke 5:10; John 21:2).

PATRIARCHAL STRUGGLES AND FEMININE SPACE IN MATTHEW 20:24–28

Jesus' response to the request of the mother of the sons of Zebedee in Matthew 20:24–28 evokes a number of issues. The first is that Jesus did not respond directly to the question posed by Zebedee's wife. From reproaching the mother and the sons of their ignorance about what they were asking for, Jesus moved to the question of "drinking the cup"—which is a statement that predicts the future suffering of Jesus and his followers ("You will indeed drink my cup, but to sit at my right hand and at my left, this is not mine to grant, but it is for those for whom it has been prepared by my Father," 20:23).[28]

Second, from teaching about his inability to grant the request of the mother of James and John, Jesus turns immediately to reproach the disciples for misunderstanding the intention behind the request. The disciples must have thought that the request was about position of power and greatness among them (which is at the heart of their quarrel). But they did not see the depth or deep content of the woman's request. In a deliberate irony, Jesus puts back to the disciples the very purpose the mother of James and John has approached him.

He remarks that the rulers of the Gentiles κατακυριεύουσιν αὐτῶν ("lord it over them") and their great ones κατεξουσιάζουσιν αὐτῶν ("exercise authority over them," 20:25). According to Carson, Jesus was alluding to the situation of the Romans since "power and authority characterized their empire."[29] It is no doubt that Jesus may be making a literal allusion to those in authority or power. But by using such an example for the disciples, it implies in a sense that the problems of power and authority shape the life of the disciples also.

The accusation of exercise of domination and oppression (κυριεύω, "to rule, to govern, to reign over"[30]) and of the exercise of authority (κατεξουσιάζω, "to rule or reign by exercising authority over"[31]) is a basic urge that drives and strives in a male-orientated society. The fact that Jesus attempted to use it to address the disciples means that the disciples, like their fathers, are under the same indictment. This issue of hierarchy and authority may allude to the toxicity of masculinity rivalry and hierarchical competition that can come as a result of the struggle for female attention, class, religion, and place of position. When such situations are not addressed, often women and children end up becoming the victims of masculine tussles.

The reproach also addresses the use of unrestrained masculine power and authority to oppress and dominate women. In a society where men make decisions for women, intimidate and control female actions, suppress femininity and its dignity, and uplift the status of women on the basis of the birth of a male child, Jesus attempts

---

28. Carson, *The Expositor's Bible Commentary*, 431–32.
29. Carson, *The Expositor's Bible Commentary*, 432.
30. Louw and Nida, *Greek-English Lexicon of the New Testament*, 477.
31. Louw and Nida, *Greek-English Lexicon of the New Testament*, 477.

to bring the attention of the disciples to these oppressive situations of women, which, in some details, must have been the reason for the mother of the sons of Zebedee to approach Jesus for liberation. Ironically, the disciples did not understand either the intention of the mother of the sons of Zebedee or Jesus' judgement of the situation. In their lack of knowledge, they indicted themselves of the same issue that brought the mother of James and John to Jesus, thereby affirming what the woman is running away from. Thus, even though a woman has brought the question, it ends up degenerating to masculine struggle for supremacy and the toxicity of male prejudice.

CONCLUSION

The author of the Gospel of Matthew has skillfully included and used the story of the mother of the sons of Zebedee to address the conventional societal structures that oppressed and reduced females' dignity at the time. In a world of male toxicity and patriarchal competition, women are not included. There is no space for the woman except through her sons. This is the reason why Zebedee's wife wants to escape by asking that her sons be part of the kingdom. Jesus is addressing the disciples to overcome the unrestrained use of masculine power over women. Therefore, in the request, "Grant that these two sons of mine will sit, one at your right hand and one at your left, in your kingdom," it is possible to understand it as a woman's missiological request that seeks liberation from a male-centered kingdom to a kingdom of greatness in Christ.

BIBLIOGRAPHY

Albright, W. F., and C. S. Mann. *Matthew*. The Anchor Bible 26. Edited by W. F. Albright and David Noel Freedman. Garden City, NY: Doubleday, 1971.

Andreasen, Erik A. "The Role of the Queen Mother in Israelite Society." *CBQ* 45 (Apr 1983) 179–94.

Botha, P. J. J. "The Gospel of Matthew and Women." *In die Skriflig* 37 (2003) 505–32.

Bowen, Brian. *Mothers and Sons: Queen Mothers of Judah and the Religious Trends that Develop During Their Sons' Reign*. Unpublished Diss. Olivet Nazarene University, 2021.

Brewer-Boydston, Ginny. "Good Queen Mothers, Bad Queen Mothers: The Theological Presentation of the Queen Mother in 1 and 2 Kings." *The Catholic Biblical Quarterly* Monograph Series 54. Washington, DC: The Catholic Biblical Association of America, 2016.

Brown, Raymond E. *The Birth of the Messiah: A Commentary on the Infancy Narratives in Matthew and Luke*. London: Chapman, 1977.

Carson, D. A. *The Gospel of Matthew*. In *The Expositor's Bible Commentary: Matthew, Mark, Luke, with the New international version of the Holy Bible* 8. Edited by Frank E. Gaebelein. Grand Rapids: Zondervan, 1984.

Cheney, Emily. "The Mother of the Sons of Zebedee (Matthew 27.56)." *Journal for the Study of New Testament* 68 (1997) 13–20.

Dreyer, Yolanda. "Gender Critique on the Narrator's Androcentric Point of View of Women in Matthew's Gospel." *HTS Teologiese Studies/Theological Studies* 67, no. 1, Art. #898. DOI: 10.4102/hts.v67i1.898, Page 4.

Evans, Craig A. *Matthew.* New Cambridge Bible Commentary. Cambridge: Cambridge University Press, 2003.

France, R. T. *Matthew: Evangelist and Teacher.* Exeter: Paternoster, 1989.

Harrington, Daniel J. "Problems and Opportunities in Matthew's Gospel." *Currents in Theology and Mission* 34 (2007) 417–23.

Keener, Craig S. *The IVP Bible Background Commentary.* Downers Grove: InterVarsity Press, 2014.

Kopas, Jane. "Jesus and Women in Matthew." *Theology Today* 47 (Apr 1990) 13–21.

Love, Stuart L. "The Household: A Major Social Component for Gender Analysis in the Gospel of Matthew." *Biblical Theology Bulletin* 23 (1993) 21–31.

Mathys, H. P. "1 and 2 Chronicles." In *The Oxford Bible Commentary.* Edited by J. Barton and J. Muddiman. Oxford: Oxford University Press, 2001.

Mbabazi, Isaac Kahwa. "Christians as Members of a 'Royal Family' in the Gospel of Matthew." *Africa Journal of Evangelical Theology* 30, no. 2 (2011) 101–14.

Meier, John P. *Matthew New Testament Message: A Biblical-Theological Commentary.* Wilmington, DE: Michael Glazier, 1980.

Pennington, Jonathan. "The Kingdom of Heaven in the Gospel of Matthew." *SBJT* 12, no.1 (2008) 44–52.

Rudman, Dominic. "Whose Kingdom Is It Anyway? The Sons of Zebedee as Antitypes for Adonijah in Matthew 20." *BN NF* 125 (2005) 97–104.

Schneider, Tammi J. *Mothers of Promise: Women in the Book of Genesis.* Grand Rapids: Baker Academic Publishing Company, 2008.

Senior, Donald. *What are They Saying about Matthew?* New York: Paulist Press, 1996.

Solvang, Elna K. "Biblical Royal Mothers." *Bible Odyssey.* Accessed April 3, 2022. https://www.bibleodyssey.org/en/people/related-articles/biblical-royal-mothers.

Swidler, Leonard. *Women in Judaism.* New York: Scarecrow Press, 1976.

Wainwright, Elaine Mary. *Toward a Feminist Critical Reading of* the *Gospel according to Matthew.* New York: Walter de Gruyter, 1991.

CHAPTER 9

The Samaritan Woman's Witness to Jesus in John 4:39 as an Evangelizing Model

ANTHONY IFFEN UMOREN, MSP

INTRODUCTION

Pope Paul VI defines evangelization as "the carrying forth of the good news to every sector of the human race so that by its strength it may enter into the hearts of men and renew the human race."[1] By this he means that the church accomplishes the task of evangelization "when, solely in virtue of that news which she proclaims, she *seeks to convert* other individual consciences of (people) and their collective conscience, all the activities in which they are engaged and, finally, their lives and the whole environment which surrounds them."[2] Such an understanding of evangelization is very much in line with the biblical call for *metanoi,a* ("conversion," "change of mind and attitude"), which is seen to be the very foundation and core of Jesus' preaching (Matt 4:17; Mark 1:15; Luke 5:32) and miraculous acts (Matt 11:20–24). Pope John Paul II affirms that in this task of evangelization, the church recognizes the participation of lay men and women, some to whom the origin of many churches can be traced.[3] In particular, he acknowledges and extols the active role of women in the church's evangelizing mission:

---

1. Paul VI, *Evangelii Nuntiandi*, no. 18.
2. Paul VI, *Evangelii Nuntiandi*, no. 18.
3. John Paul II, *Redemptoris Missio*, no. 71.

Here I would like to express particular appreciation to those women who are involved in the various areas of education extending well beyond the family: nurseries, schools, universities, social service agencies, parishes, associations and movements. Wherever the work of education is called for, we can note that women are ever ready and willing to give themselves generously to others, especially in serving the weakest and most defenceless. In this work they exhibit a kind of affective, cultural and spiritual motherhood which has inestimable value for the development of individuals and the future of society. At this point how can I fail to mention the witness of so many Catholic women and Religious congregations of women from every continent who have made education, particularly the education of boys and girls, their principal apostolate? How can I not think with gratitude of all the women who have worked and continue to work in the area of health care, not only in highly organized institutions, but also in very precarious circumstances, in the poorest countries of the world, thus demonstrating a spirit of service which not infrequently borders on martyrdom?[4]

Furthermore, the pope thanks God for the special gift of the feminine "genius":

The Church gives thanks for each and every woman: for mothers, for sisters, for wives; for women consecrated to God in virginity: for women dedicated to the many human beings who await the gratuitous love of another person; for women who watch over the human persons in the family, which is the fundamental sign of the human community; for women who work professionally, and who at times are burdened by a great social responsibility... The Church gives thanks for all the manifestations of the feminine "genius" which have appeared in the course of history, in the midst of all peoples and nations; she gives thanks for all the charisms which the Holy Spirit distributes to women in the history of the people of God, for all the victories which she owes to their faith, hope and charity: she gives thanks for all the fruits of feminine holiness.[5]

By the official recognition and value placed on the role of women in evangelization by these popes, the church's leadership has set the stage for the individual members of the church to play their different parts in appreciating, promoting, and placing a high value on the ministry of women in the church.

The church's stance in recognizing and appreciating the positive role of women who bear witness to Jesus in evangelization is in line with that of the author of John's Gospel. In John 4:39, the Greek verb *martyreō* ("to bear witness," "testify," or "give testimony") is used to describe the activity of a Samaritan woman who, having had an encounter with Jesus at Jacob's well, came to know, accept, believe in, and consequently bear witness to him as the Messiah, such that other Samaritans from her city also

---

4. John Paul II, *Letter of Pope John Paul II to Women*, no. 9.
5. John Paul II, *Mulieris Dignitatem*, no. 31.

came to believe in Jesus as the savior of the world. This paper undertakes an exegetical study of the Samaritan woman's witness to Jesus, as narrated in John 4:39. This is done with the aim of deepening an understanding of the nature and positive impact of her evangelizing role, especially within the Johannine literary and theological contexts. By focusing on the evangelizing role of the Samaritan woman in John 4:39 positively, this study decidedly adopts a specific feminist methodological principle of biblical interpretation, which seeks to highlight positive biblical traditions on women.[6]

Classified among the contextual approaches to biblical interpretation by the Pontifical Biblical Commission,[7] the Commission acknowledges that "feminist exegesis has brought many benefits. Women have played a more active part in exegetical research. They have succeeded, often better than men, in detecting the presence, the significance and the role of women in the Bible, in Christian origins and in the Church."[8] Resting on a consciousness that the Holy Bible has, through the ages, been oftentimes used as a tool in supporting and even enforcing the continuous subjugation of women throughout the world,[9] women today are increasingly making inroads into the biblical world in order to address the problem, with the hope of allowing the Bible to speak to both male and female as the true word of God and not be seen as some tool for a misogynist religion.[10] Accordingly, "Feminist hermeneutics moves women in the narrative from the margin to the center, a constructive phase of interpretation . . . as liberating proclamation for people in our world today."[11] This inclusive dimension reflects what Okure describes as the goal of "African Women's Hermeneutics,"[12] an inclusive approach to doing theology that seeks to promote a "human revolution" rather than just the liberation of women.[13]

The above chosen exegetical approach for this study, while employing "the current methods of exegesis especially the historical-critical method,"[14] here requires close examination of the positive aspects of the Samaritan woman's witness to Jesus in John 4:39 within its Johannine literary and theological contexts. By adopting the principle of feminist exegesis in this study, it is hoped that the witnessing activity

---

6. Feminists have fashioned the following three methodological principles toward fruitful feminist biblical hermeneutics: (1) Highlighting positive biblical traditions on women, (2) reinterpreting biblical traditions which are oppressive toward women, (3) and rejecting biblical traditions which are oppressive toward women. Cf. Sakenfeld, "Feminist Uses of Biblical Materials," 22–23. This paper adopts the first biblical hermeneutical principle.

7. The Pontifical Biblical Commission, *Interpretation*, 58–63.

8. The Pontifical Biblical Commission, *Interpretation*, 62.

9. Zikmund, "Feminist Consciousness," 22–23.

10. The efforts made so far is discussed by Lerner, "One Thousand Years of Feminist Bible Criticism," 138–66.

11. Mitchell, *Beyond Fear and Silence*, 42.

12. Okure, "Invitation to African Women's Concerns," 48.

13. Okure, "Invitation to African Women's Concerns," 42.

14. The Pontifical Biblical Commission, *Interpretation*, 61–62.

of this nameless first-century Samaritan woman would serve as a biblical model to inspire and guide modern women and men already engaged in, or who wish to engage in, evangelization and missionary apostolate.

John 4:39 in Relation to Its Literary Context

The passage under study, John 4:39, translated in the *New Revised Standard Version* (NRSV) as, "Many Samaritans from that city believed in him because of the woman's testimony, 'He told me everything I have ever done,'" is found within a larger pericope of John 4:1–42, which is normally captioned "Jesus and the Samaritan woman." Within this larger pericope, 4:39 is located at the beginning of what may be considered as the last unit of the pericope—4:39–42. This last unit deals with the faith of the Samaritans. While treating it as literarily related to its immediate contexts before and after, this study addresses 4:39 as a single, independent unit because of its unique, theologically relevant vocabulary and theme: that the Samaritans "believed" (*episteusan*) in Jesus on account of the "word" (*ton logon*) of the "woman" (*tēs gynaikos*) "witnessing" (*martyrousēs*) to them.

The immediate literary context before John 4:39 (4:1–38) and the immediate literary context after it (4:40–42) build up the full narrative about Jesus and the Samaritan woman. According to the narrative, which is dialogical in nature, Jesus was on his way to Galilee and stopped over by Jacob's well, near a Samaritan town. Contrary to Jewish ethics and purity rules, he spoke to a nameless Samaritan woman at the well, asking her for a drink of water. The woman's response, which made a reference to Jewish-Samaritan strained relationship, enabled Jesus to indicate to the woman that the water in the well was actually inferior to his own living water, which he could give to her on request. The woman misunderstood Jesus' play on the words "living water" and ironically compared Jesus to Jacob. Jesus taught her that his own living water brings eternal life. Convinced, the woman asked Jesus for this living water for herself, indicating thus her personal thirst or need for Jesus.

Then Jesus delved into the woman's personal life. By the revelation of the woman's life, Jesus revealed his own identity as well. And the woman, a symbol of wisdom, perceived that Jesus is a prophet. Her curiosity to know deeper truths led her to open a discussion about right worship. Jesus taught her again. Jesus must have been such a good teacher to the woman that it reminded her of the hope for the coming of a messiah-teacher whom the Samaritans were expecting. But Jesus in turn revealed himself to her as the long-awaited Messiah. Thereafter, she abandoned her water jar, went into the city, and invited the dwellers to come and see Jesus.

Meanwhile, the disciples of Jesus, who had been away to buy food, returned and were surprised to see Jesus talking with a woman. They couldn't persuade Jesus to eat the food they had brought. For Jesus, his food is to do the will of God. Then Jesus taught the disciples. Using the image of a harvest, he spoke about a spiritual harvest which the disciples are to participate in its reaping. The narrative draws to an end with the affirmation that "the Samaritans came to believe in Jesus as a result of the woman's testimony or witnessing to Jesus." The people invited Jesus to stay with them. He did so for two days, after which many more believed in him upon hearing directly from Jesus himself. They believed that Jesus is the savior of the whole world, much beyond the limited Samaritan expectation of a messiah-teacher intended for the Samaritans only.

From all indications, through her act of bearing witness to Jesus and the resultant believing effect or impact of this action, the narrative depicts the Samaritan woman as an evangelizer. This role resonates with the missionary undertones[15] embedded in the purpose of John's Gospel, as found in John 20:31, within the wider or remote literary context of John 4:39: "But these are written that you may believe that Jesus is the Christ, the Son of God, and that believing you may have life in his name."

This purpose of the whole Gospel of John, so stated, does seem to mark out missionary kerygmatic concerns in the Gospel. Such a missionary outlook, reflected in 4:39 and 20:31 through the word *pisteuō* ("belief"), indicates a literary and theological relationship between our text and the main thrust of the whole Gospel through a vocabulary and thematic affinity. Thus, just as the whole Gospel of John is written "that you may *believe*," so also John 4:39 is included in the Gospel to illustrate the fact that through a Samaritan woman's testimony, "many Samaritans from that city *believed* in (Jesus)" as the savior of the world (4:42).

In relation, therefore, to its immediate and remote literary contexts, John 4:39 is a prominent passage which highlights the positive outcome of a mission effectively and conclusively carried out. That the faith or belief of a community is linked to the witnessing role or word (*to,n lo.gon*) of a woman leads this paper to analytically investigate further possible literary and theological implications of the Samaritan woman's witness to Jesus, on account of which the Samaritans came to faith in Jesus.

THE SAMARITAN WOMAN'S WITNESS TO JESUS IN JOHN 4:39: LITERARY-THEOLOGICAL ANALYSIS

The Samaritans lived in the city or region of Samaria, capital of the Israelite northern kingdom. The name is also used to refer to members of a particular religious sect or community that is found in that area.[16] Those Samaritans referred to in John 4:39 lived in Sychar, near the well of Jacob (John 4:6). Mention of the well of Jacob has aided the possible identification of Sychar with Schechem, a city that is closely associated with Jacob in the Old Testament (Gen 33:18–20) and lies at the foot of Mount Gerizim, the mountain on which the Samaritans sited their temple (John 4:20).[17]

---

15. Heine, *Women and Early Christianity*, 134–135.
16. Gaster, "Samaritans," 90.
17. Brown, *The Gospel According to John I–XII*, 169.

Although historically the Jews and the Samaritans were considered one people until the religious schism that separated Israel and Judah (1 Kgs 12:1–20), the first-century-AD Jews did not regard the Samaritans as true Israelites. This was because the Samaritans were mixed-blood descendants from marriage that involved Israelites and Mesopotamians after the Syrian war in 722 BC.[18] Because of Jewish insistence on purity of blood in genealogy, and also because of many other historical disputes between them and the Samaritans (Ezra 4:7–24; Neh 4:1–13), the Jews had no regard for the Samaritans. They were regarded as worse than pagans (John 8:48). As a result, the Jews were reserved in their contact with them. John 4:9 indicates that a Jew was not even expected to ask a Samaritan for water to drink, not to mention other acts of hospitality like eating and staying under the same roof, actions which would be considered as breaching Jewish purity laws (Luke 9:51–55).

The Samaritans had their own beliefs, some of which were shared by the Jews. Gaster classified these beliefs into five: (1) belief in one God; (2) acknowledgment of Moses as the supreme apostle of God and as a unique being; (3) acceptance of the Torah (Pentateuch) as the only authentic law of God, probably because the prophets and the writings had not become normative writings as at the time of the schism; (4) recognition of Mount Gerizim as the chosen place of God, prescribed in Scripture; and (5) expectation of a final day of rewards and punishment.[19] The Samaritans, like the Jews, awaited a Messiah, but their concept of a Messiah was that he would be a teacher as found in Deuteronomy 18:18. It was to these Samaritans that one of them, a woman, bore witness about Jesus.

The verb used in John 4:39 to describe her witnessing role appears in our text as *martyrousēs* (present, participle, active, genitive, feminine, singular of *martyreō*—"of her witnessing," or "of her testimony"). This witnessing or giving testimony is not forensic or of historical facts but a witness to faith. A witness is one who has firsthand knowledge of the subject being witnessed about. The verb *martyreō*, used by John to refer to the witnessing activity of the woman, is a favourite Johannine verb which occurs thirty-four times in John's Gospel as against once in Matthew's Gospel, once in Luke's Gospel, and none in Mark's Gospel. For John, Jesus does not delight in bearing witness to himself (5:31). Rather, another bears witness on his behalf (5:32). However, even if Jesus bears witness to himself, there is nothing wrong about him doing so, since his witness is true (8:12–18). Jesus, therefore, did bear witness to himself as the "light of the world" (8:12; 12:46), the "bread of life" (6:35, 48) that came down from heaven (6:41, 51), the "Son of Man" (9:35–38), the "gate for the sheep" (10:7–9), the "good shepherd" (10:11, 14), the "resurrection and the life" (11:25–26), "the way, the truth and the life" (14:6), and the "true vine" (15:1, 5).

John also uses the word *martyreō* to refer to the true witness which John the Baptist bears to Jesus (5:32–33) as the Messiah whom he, John, was sent ahead of (1:19–26,

---

18. McKenzie, *Dictionary of the Bible*, 265.
19. Gaster, "Samaritans," 193.

30; 3:25–30), the "Lamb of God" who takes away the sins of the world (1:29), the one on whom the spirit descended from heaven like a dove and remained on (1:32), and the "Son of God" (1:34). The word *martyreō* is further used to refer to the witness that the works of Jesus bear of him as the one "sent by the Father" (5:36; 8:18); the Father himself bears witness to Jesus as the one whom "He has sent" (5:37–38); and the Scriptures bear witness to Jesus as the "source of eternal life" (5:39–40). Furthermore, the Advocate or Spirit of Truth will, when he comes, bear witness on behalf of Jesus (15:26); similarly, the disciples will bear witness to Jesus because they have been with Jesus from the beginning (15:27). However, it is only in John 4:39 that John uses the word *martyreō* to refer to the witnessing activity of a woman to Jesus.

The Samaritan woman bore witness to Jesus among her people in the city by inviting them: "Come and see a man who told me everything I have ever done! He cannot be the *Messiah*, can he?" (4:29). As a result, "Many Samaritans from that city *believed* in him because of the woman's *testimony* (*witness*), '*He told me everything I have ever done*'" (4:39). And "so when the Samaritans came to him, they asked him to stay with them; and he stayed there two days. And many more *believed* because of *his word*" (4:40–41). In the final analysis, the Samaritans "said to the woman, 'It is no longer because of what *you said* that we *believe*, for *we have heard* for ourselves, and *we know* that this is truly the *Saviour of the world*'" (4:42), an indication that their faith was reinforced by their having a personal encounter with Jesus through hearing from him, and this brought them to a new personal knowledge of him.

How did Jesus and the woman get to this point, such that the woman, according to John, "left her water jar and went back to the city" (4:28) to bear witness to Jesus among her people? John narrates that Jesus' initial simple request to the Samaritan woman was, "Give me a drink" (4:7), but the woman expressed surprise at such a request: "How is it that you, a Jew, as a drink of me, a woman of Samaria" (4:9). Then Jesus, knowing the woman's need or preference for living (spring) water over well water, said to her, "If you knew the gift of God and who it is that is saying to you, 'Give me a drink,' you would have asked him, and he would have given you living water" (4:10). Curious, the woman asked Jesus, "Where do you get that living water?" (4:11), a question that prompts Jesus to teach her about the special and spiritual nature of the living water that he was offering her: "Everyone who drinks of this water will be thirsty again, but those who drink of the water that I will give will never be thirsty. The water that I will give will become in them a spring of water gushing up to *eternal life*" (4:13–14). The woman, interested but definitely not yet knowing who Jesus was, and not fully understanding what he actually meant by "living water," a veiled reference to the Holy Spirit (see John 7:37–39), quickly made her request: "Sir, give me this water, so that I may never be thirsty or have to keep coming here to draw water" (4:15).

Obviously, according to Getty-Sullivan, "John uses the literary device of *misunderstanding* to guide the conversation and the readers to a new level of spiritual reflection. For example, the woman's lack of comprehension even of the physical or literal meaning of Jesus' questions serves as an opportunity for Jesus to teach her more, to open her up to more revelation."[20] This became possible because, despite the woman's rebuff at Jesus' request for a drink, Jesus ignored this and her further ironic query, whether Jesus was greater than Jacob, who gave them the well (4:12). In this way, he refused to be sidetracked but remained focused on his primary goal for engaging in the encounter with her: that of sharing who he is with her as the "gift of God" (4:10). Brown therefore notes that "Jesus does not answer her objection but responds in terms of what he can give her."[21]

It wasn't, however, until Jesus delved into the woman's personal life, relating with her at the level of a normal human person and revealing something about her life, that the Samaritan woman was "personally touched." She experienced what can be termed a "personal encounter" with Jesus, making her to convincingly affirm, "Sir, *I see* that you are *a prophet*" (4:19).[22] At that point, having personally come to know and accept Jesus as a prophet, the tone of their discussion changed, as the woman now became eager to learn about spiritual matters: "Our ancestors worshipped on this mountain, but you say that the place where people must worship is in Jerusalem" (4:20). Jesus begins his reply by inviting the woman to believe him: "Woman, believe me" (4:21), and went on to teach her many spiritual truths. And in the woman's desire for deeper spiritual knowledge, she said to him, "I know that Messiah is coming (who is called Christ); when he comes, he will proclaim all things to us" (4:25). This made Jesus reveal himself fully to her: "I am he, the one who is speaking to you" (4:26). Fully convinced, the woman left her water jar and went into the city to bear witness to Jesus.

The witnessing activity of the Samaritan woman finally generates a strong belief among the Samaritans in Jesus as the "Messiah" (*christos*) and the "savior of the world" (*sōtēr tou kosmou*) (4:29–30, 42). As savior of the world, Jesus is a universal savior, to whom the Samaritans also go for salvation. Prompted by the woman's witness, the Samaritans would rightly acclaim: "And we have seen and do testify that the Father has sent his Son as the Savior of the world" (1 John 4:14; see John 3:17). The Samaritan woman became an accomplished evangelizer because she had allowed herself to have a personal encounter with Jesus, listened to, and learned from him. She discovered who Jesus was for her, believed in him, and publicly bore witness to him among her people while leading them to go to Jesus to learn from him and confirm their faith. By this, she brought to full realization the purpose of all the words and signs of Jesus within the Johannine literary and theological contexts, thus rendering her witnessing role as a model of evangelization and mission in John's Gospel. Okure affirms: "The purpose of the woman's witness . . . is to lead the listener to believe in Jesus as the Christ. This

---

20. Getty-Sullivan, *Women in the New Testamen*, 97.

21. Brown, *An Introduction to the New Testamen*, 199.

22. It was also as a result of Thomas's personal encounter with the risen Jesus that made him exclaim, "My Lord and my God!" (John 20:26–28).

is the primary, even exclusive function of witness in the Gospel,"[23] a point which the stated theological purpose of John's Gospel in 20:31 brings clearly to the fore.

A well-known position of John is that faith or belief in Jesus can be as a result of the *sēmeia* ("signs") of Jesus (2:11, 23; 4:53; 7:31; 11:15, 42, 45; 12:27; 20:31). John, however, insists that faith, in reality, should not be as a result of having seen signs (2:18; 4:48; 6:26f, 30; 20:29). Authentic faith, rather, must emanate from the believer as an irresistible force toward Jesus primarily on the basis of the *logos* ("word") of Jesus, or the witnessing word of others about Jesus (1:7; 4:41f, 50; 5:24, 47; 8:30f; 17:20). It is, therefore, significant that in John 4:39 it is reported that the Samaritans believed (*episteusan*) in Jesus as a result of the Samaritan woman's word (*dia ton logon tēs gunaikos*). The noun *logos* ("word") here is used to refer to "proclamation, instruction, teaching, message"[24] borne out of personal faith and conviction. It is such *logos* (word as proclamation, instruction, teaching, message) that has the power or ability to convince another to believe in Jesus. In John 17:20–21, Jesus specifically prayed to the Father for the unity of the ones who will believe (*pisteuontōn*) in him on account of the *logos* (proclamation, instruction, teaching, message) of his disciples, that they may all be one, and one in him and the Father, just as the Father and himself are one.

John demonstrates, therefore, that the faith of the Samaritans was not based on miracles or signs but on hearing the word, first from the Samaritan woman. An even deeper faith is evoked from the Samaritans when they listen to Jesus himself for two days, "Many more believed because of his word" (*logos*), making the people to confess to the woman: "It is no longer because of what you said that we believe, for we have heard for ourselves, and we know that this is truly the Saviour of the world" (4:41–42). The Samaritans combine their faith with knowledge, a Johannine prerequisite necessary for attaining eternal life (John 17:3). Thus, the primary attraction to faith on account of another person's witness to Jesus, important as it may be, is only a signal of the beginning of faith. It is only when the seeker draws close to Jesus himself, listens to him through the Scriptures (2 Tim 3:15–17; 1 Thess 2:13; Heb 4:12), and thus comes to a deeper knowledge of him that faith becomes more perfect. Brown would have us contrast between "the unsatisfactory faith of the Jews in 2:23–25 based on a superficial admiration of miracles with the deeper faith of the Samaritans based on the word of Jesus."[25]

Okure is right that in John 4:39 there is a high value placed by the evangelist on the witness to Jesus by the Samaritan woman because, like the disciples of Jesus, she was taught by Jesus, she believed in Jesus, and she inspired that same belief in her hearers.[26] Having led the people to discover Jesus for themselves, the Samaritan woman had played her part. In line with Fiorenza's thinking, it is likely that that part may have

23. Cf. Okure, *Johannine Approach*, 170–71.
24. See Arndt and Gingrich, "*logos*," 477.
25. Brown, *The Gospel According to John I–XII*, 185.
26. Okure, *Johannine Approach*, 171.

remained indelible in the reminiscences of the Samaritan community which, when it grew larger (Acts 8:4–25), remembered with pride that it first believed in Jesus through the evangelizing or witnessing activity of one of their women.[27] She comments:

> The dramatic dialogue is probably based on a missionary tradition that ascribed a primary role to a woman missionary in the conversion of the Samaritans ... the woman's testimony motivates the Samaritans to come to him (4:39) ... the woman becomes a witnessing disciple because "he told me all that I ever did" (4:29). In 17:20 it is stressed that Jesus prayed not only for the disciples but also for "those who believe in him through their word." Using almost the same words, 4:39 states that many Samaritans believed in him "because of the words of the woman who testified." However, they come to full faith because of the self-revelation of Jesus.[28]

In like manner, Carmody remarks: "(The Samaritan woman) need not think of herself as a being condemned to haul water and pleasure men. She could be a witness to salvation, a sharer and proclaimer of great good news. In offering her this new set of possibilities, this fresh way of defining herself, Jesus was gambling that she had the wherewithal to catch his drift, the gumption to make a change . . . She is in the gospel as a model of faith."[29] Jesus accepted her in spite of her personal background, and even ignored his disciples who "were astonished that he was speaking with a woman" (John 4:27). Rather, by patiently teaching and spiritually guiding her along, Jesus brought to the fore the Samaritan woman's hitherto unimaginable potentials for evangelization. According to Carmody, the Samaritan woman, on account of the fact that "she was struck, dealt honestly with what she found, took it to heart, and acted upon it, through her witnessing role, becomes in the gospel of John 'a model of faith.'"[30] Such a positive affirmation about a Samaritan woman would hardly have been normative in first-century Palestinian patriarchal culture, where a woman's witness was never believed (Luke 24:9–11). No less positive is Edet, who insists that "indeed the Samaritan villagers believed, because of the woman's word (John 4:39, 42 *dia ton*

---

27. On this point, Elizabeth Schüssler Fiorenza has it that "exegetes agree that the Johannine community had a strong influx of Samaritan converts who might have been catalysts for the development of the high Christology of the Gospel. The present Johannine community reaps the harvest made possible by the missionary endeavours of a woman who initiated the conversion of the Samaritan segment of the community ... the woman is characterized as the representative of the Samaritan mission" (cf. Fiorenza, *In Memory of Her*, 327).

28. Fiorenza, *In Memory of Her*, 327–328.

29. Carmody, *Biblical Woman*, 105.

30. Carmody, *Biblical Woman*, 105. Other Johannine texts also portray women as models of faith in relation to Jesus. Thus in the story of the woman caught in adultery (John 8:3–11), her faith generates Jesus' forgiveness (8:11); in the story of the death and raising of Lazarus (John 11:1–45), Martha's and Mary's faith in Jesus (11:21–27, 32) leads to Martha acknowledging Jesus as the *Messiah*, the *Son of God* (11:27), and the raising of their brother from the dead (11:44). Furthermore women's faith in Jesus made some of them remain faithful to him even until death (19:25), enabling Jesus to commission a woman, Mary Magdalen to bear witness to his disciples concerning his resurrection (20:1–2, 11–18).

logon pisteuein) . . . To some extent she serves to modify the thesis that male disciples were the only important figures in Church founding."[31] John's positive picture of this woman is quite consistent with his positive picture of women in his Gospel, generally (2:1–11; 8:1–11; 11:17–27; 19:25–27; 20:1–18).

Lessons for Evangelization and Mission from John 4:39

From the above literary and theological analysis, some lessons can be learned for the church's evangelization and missionary apostolate from the Samaritan woman in her witness to Jesus in John 4:39. Since every Christian is called to participate in evangelization, Christians should:

i. *Exhibit a lively, personal curiosity to know Jesus intimately* and allow Jesus to teach them, just like the Samaritan woman did. This is necessary because, if a Christian is ignorant or merely partially knowledgeable about God, Jesus, the church, etc., he or she cannot be an effective evangelizer.

ii. *Have a personal, life-transformative encounter with Jesus,* which leads to one being *personally convinced of the truth of the faith,* just as the Samaritan woman was. It was actually because Jesus penetrated and changed her personal life that motivated or inspired the Samaritan woman's personal faith conviction, making her to know him, believe in him, and bear witness to him. This made her townspeople come to Jesus, accept him, listen to him, and also believe in him. In authentic evangelization, the old Latin adage *nemo dat quod non habet* ("You cannot give what you do not have") holds sway.

iii. *Be undaunted by socio-cultural obstacles and biases* when proclaiming the truth. Just as the Samaritan woman defied her patriarchal and personal backgrounds, and led the people to Jesus on account of her conviction that she had found the Messiah, so also Christians should be undaunted when proclaiming the truth which they believe in as a matter of conscience, whether they find themselves in the family, church, society, or place of work.

iv. *Imitate the attitude of Jesus* toward the Samaritan woman and the Samaritans by treating everyone, men and women, with respect, sincerity, and seriousness as Jesus did to the Samaritan woman, even when his disciples were astonished to find him speaking with her. Jesus also respected and accepted the Samaritans, whom the Jews despised as being demon possessed (John 8:48). Christian evangelizers should, like Jesus, be courageous enough to lovingly ignore and denounce oppressive societal, religious, and cultural tendencies and attitudes which are divisive rather than unitive of humanity created in God's image.

---

31. Edet, "Women and Evangelization," 129–30.

v. *Learn from the attitude of the Samaritan villagers* toward the Samaritan woman. Being part of a patriarchal community, the Samaritan residents of Sychar could have despised the woman and her witnessing activity and refused to believe her story (cf. Luke 24:10–11). But, as it turned out, they buried all pride, arrogance, and androcentrism and believed in Jesus on account of the woman's witness or testimony (John 4:40–42).

vi. *Direct people to listen to Jesus*, who continues to speak to people of all nations today through the Scriptures (2 Tim 3:15–17; 1 Thess 2:13; Heb 4:12) and the church (Luke 10:16; Rev 2:7, 11, 29).

Indeed, in the words of Okure, the story of the Samaritan woman's witness to Jesus

> Holds the key for understanding John's theology of and method in mission. Jesus' respectful attitude toward the woman and the Samaritans challenges all missionaries, that is, the entire Church, to learn from him the techniques of successful missionary undertaking. These include using the realities, traditions, and daily concerns of the people in proclaiming the gospel to them. True missionary work should break down age-old barriers of race, sex and class between peoples. At the end of the endeavor the people evangelized should grow in stature as the woman did. She became an effective apostle to her people. Jesus depended on her to introduce him to the Samaritans just as he depended on John the Baptist to introduce him to the Jews; but as John the Baptist faded out of the picture after he had done his work, so does the woman, and so should all true disciple-missionaries and witnesses to Jesus, so that Jesus and God may become all in all.[32]

CONCLUSION

Our study of John 4:39, using the feminist biblical hermeneutical principle of highlighting positive biblical traditions on women, has examined the significance of John the Evangelist's use of a reserved word *martyreō* ("to bear witness," "testify," or "give testimony"), to describe a Samaritan woman's witness to Jesus among her people. Her action—whereby she allowed herself to have a personal encounter with Jesus, listened to, and learned from him, discovered who he was for her, believed in him, and publicly bore witness to him among her people, while leading them to go to Jesus to learn from him and confirm their faith in him—undoubtedly served as a Johannine model for missionary evangelization. The capacity to lead others to believe in or have faith in Jesus, such that they draw close to God for eternal salvation, is the ultimate goal of all evangelization efforts, and such efforts can take the example of the Samaritan woman's witness to Jesus among the Samaritans as a model.

32. Okure, "John", 1512–1576, here 1543.

BIBLIOGRAPHY

Arndt, William F., and F. Wilbur Gingrich. "*Logos.*" In *A Greek-English Lexicon of the New Testament and Other Early Christian Literature*. Chicago: The University of Chicago Press, 1979.

Brown, Raymond E. *The Gospel According to St. John*. The Anchor Bible. Garden City, NY: Doubleday, 1966.

———. *An Introduction to the New Testament*. New York: Doubleday, 1997.

Carmody, D L. *Biblical Woman: Contemporary Reflections on Scriptural Texts*. New York: Crossroad Publishing Company, 1988.

Cunnigham, A., Susanne Breckel, and Rita Anne Houlihan, eds. *Women in Ministry: A Sister's View*. Chicago: NAWR Publications, 1972.

Edet, Rosemary. "Women and Evangelization: A New Testament Perspective." In *Evangelization in Africa in the Third Millennium: Challenges and Prospects*. Edited by Justin S. Ukpong et al. Proceedings of the First Theology Week of the Catholic Institute of West Africa, Port Harcourt, Nigeria, May 6–11, 1990.

Fiorenza, Elisabeth Schüssler. *In Memory of Her: A Feminist Theological Reconstruction of Christian Origin:* New York: Crossroad, 1984.

Gaster, T. H. "Samaritan." In *The Interpreter's Dictionary of the Bible*. Nashville: Abingdon Press, 1985.

Getty-Sullivan, Mary Ann. *Women in the New Testament*. Collegeville, MN: The Liturgical Press, 2001.

Heine, S. *Women and Early Christianity: Are the Feminist Scholars Right?* London: SCM Press, 1987.

John Paul II. Apostolic Letter, *The Dignity and Vocation of Women (Mulieris Dignitatem)*. Vatican City: Libreria Editrice Vaticana, 1988.

———. *Redemptoris Missio*, 1991.

———. *Letter of Pope John Paul to Women*, 1995.

Lerner, G. "One Thousand Years of Feminist Bible Criticism." In *The Creation of Feminist Consciousness: From Middle Ages to Eighteen-Seventy*. New York: Oxford University Press, 1993.

Link, A. "*Was Redest Du Mit 1hr?*" *Eine Studie Zur Exegese, Redaktions—Und Theologiegeschichte Von Jon 4: 1 –42*. Darmstadt: Verlag Friedrich Pustet, 1992.

McKenzie, J. L. *Dictionary of the Bible*. London: Geoffrey Chapman, 1978.

Mitchell, Joan L. *Beyond Fear and Silence: A Feminist—Literary Reading of Mark*. New York: Continuum, 2001.

Okure, Teresa. *The Johannine Approach to Mission: A Contextual Study of John 4:1–42*. WUNT 2/31. Tübingen: J. C. B. Mohr (Paul Siebeck), 1988.

———. "John." In *The International Bible Commentary: An Ecumenical Commentary for the Twenty-First Century*. Edited by William R. Farmer, Sean McEvenue, Armando J. Levoratti, and David L. Dungan. Bangalore: Theological Publications in India, 2013.

———. "Invitation to African Women's Concerns." In *Interpreting the New Testament in Africa*. Edited by Mary N. Getui, Tinyiko Maluleke, and Justin Ukpong. Nairobi: Acton Publishers, 2001.

Paul VI. *Evangelii Nuntiandi*, 1975.

The Pontifical Biblical Commission. *The Interpretation of the Bible in the Church*. Kenya: Paulines Publications, 1994.

Ringe, S. H. "A Gentile Woman's Story." In *Feminist Interpretation of the Bible*. Edited by Letty M. Russell. New York: Basil Blackwell, 1985.

Russell, L. M., ed. *Feminist Interpretation of the Bible*. Oxford: Basil Blackwell, 1985.

———. "Introduction: Liberating the Word." In *Feminist Interpretation of the Bible*. Edited by L. M. Russell. New York: Basil Blackwell, 1985.

———. "Authority and the Challenge of Feminist Interpretation." In *Feminist Interpretation of the Bible*. Edited by Letty M. Russell. New York: Basil Blackwell, 1985.

Sakenfeld, K. D. "Feminist Uses of Biblical Materials." In *Feminist Interpretation of the Bible*. Edited by Letty M. Russell. New York: Basil Blackwell, 1985.

Zikmund, B. B. "Feminist Consciousness in Historical Perspective." In *Feminist Interpretation of the Bible*. Edited by Letty M. Russell. New York: Basil Blackwell, 1985.

CHAPTER 10

Christology, Pneumatology, and Missiology in Luke 4:16-21

ROWLAND ONYENALI, CMF

1. INTRODUCTION

The opportunity to contribute a paper in honor of Theresa Okure is fascinating and intriguing at the same time. The fascination comes from the fact that she is one of the foremost female exegetes from Africa, who has devoted almost her entire life to the study of the Bible. She has remained dogged in her resolve to make the meaning of the sacred Scriptures come alive among those who read them with faith. It is intriguing also because of her method of biblical analysis. She has always made it known that a study of the Bible must bear in mind the meaning of a pericope in relation to the theology of the whole book under study. In other words, no passage in a book of the Bible should be studied in isolation. This fact is at least very clear in her inaugural PhD thesis submitted to the Fordham University and later published as *The Johannine Approach to Mission: A Contextual Study of John 4:1-42*.[1] Reading through the work, one understands that by "contextual study" she does not mean the interpretation of particular verses in relation only to their immediate context. Rather, it means a correlation between each passage and the context of the entire Gospel in which the passage is located. To be precise, she used the whole of the Fourth Gospel as her primary reference to explain the passage of John 4:1-42, leading her to the conclusion that "mission

---

1. Okure, *Johannine Approach*, 1988. Also, her study of John 1:12-14 led her to an exploration of the gift of divinization in the whole of John's Gospel. See Okure, "'He Gave Them Power to Become Children of God' (John 1:12-14)," 118–35.

for the evangelist means fundamentally persuading his readers that Jesus is the Christ, the son of God, the giver of life"[2] and that "in Johannine terms the document is a missionary document *precisely* because it is a community document."[3]

In this paper, as part of my tribute to this revered biblical scholar, I intend to make a narrative critical analysis of Luke 4:16-21. I consider this important since it has become normative in Lukan studies to suggest that the preaching of Jesus in the synagogue of Nazareth is programmatic for our understanding of the mission of Jesus in the Third Gospel. For instance, Obiora J. agrees that "the author of the Gospel according to Luke perceived, in Isa 61:1-2, an apt OT text for a programmatic passage of his gospel.[4] In the same way, Uzowulu sees the passage of Luke 4:16-19 as foreshadowing the account of the entire ministry of Jesus which will later evolve.[5] However, many scholars who have studied Jesus' preaching in Nazareth have dwelt so much on the entire pericope of Luke 4:16-30.[6] The justification for my choice of only vv. 16-21 is because they contain the core of the manifesto of Jesus. Verses 22-30 seem to have relevance for the Gentile mission which, though relevant in Lukan studies, will distract from my immediate concern in this study. Moreover, the difficulties involved in the thought sequence between v. 22 to v. 23, v. 23 to v. 24, and v. 24 to vv. 25-27 would naturally lead to source-critical issues which are not important to me in this paper.[7] The primary aim of the study is to see how the identity and mission of Jesus as laid down in this passage agree with the overall scheme of the Gospel according to Luke.

The task is made easier by the fact that only Luke reports both Jesus' reading from the scroll of Isaiah and the contextualization of this reading on himself in his preaching in the synagogue of Nazareth. Matthew and Mark simply remark that Jesus came to his hometown and preached, evoking questions regarding his lineage (Matt 13:54-58; Mark 6:1-6). For Luke's Synoptic mates, the highlight of the synagogue episode seems to be the unbelief of Jesus' home people, which made him unable to perform many miracles there (Matt 13:58; Mark 6:5f). Again, while Matthew and

---

2. Okure, *Approach*, 262.

3. Okure, *Approach*, 294, stress original. This could also be termed "composition criticism." See Moore, *Literary Criticism and the Gospels*, 4-7.

4. Obiora, "'The Spirit of the Lord God Is upon Me' (Isaiah 61:1)," 49.

5. Uzowulu, "The Spirit of the Lord in a Pentecostal Era," 94.

6. For a summary of scholarly discussion on Luke 4:16-30 thirty years ago, see Schreck, "The Nazareth Pericope," 399-471.

7. There are arguments concerning the relation between vv. 1-16 and vv. 22-30. For Crockett, the second half of the passage is disjointed from the first. If Jesus won the approval of all in the synagogue, as v. 22 suggests, the angry reaction of vv. 28-30 appears contradictory. See Crockett, *Luke 4:25-27 and Jewish-Gentile Relations in Luke-Acts*, 80. On the other hand, Combrink thinks that the event is narrated in a pendulum: Jesus reads and contextualizes the text and the audience reacts in the affirmative while some make reference to his ancestry. Jesus then interprets the text by incorporating Gentiles and the audience becomes angry. Combrink, "The Structure and Significance of Luke 4:16-30," 27-47. His conclusion is that "the rejection narrative forms a coherent whole, true to the style and literary method of Luke." Combrink, "Structure," 48.

Mark place the encounter at the center of the ministry of Jesus, Luke places it at the beginning of this ministry "to encapsulate major features of the ministry of Jesus."[8] There are indications that Luke has uprooted the text from its original position at the center of Jesus' ministry and inserted it right at the very beginning.[9] This means that it must have had a special interest in Luke's theological scheme.[10] One could argue that in the Lukan narrative, "the text is critical because it is the opening utterance by Jesus, which sought to give possible directions for His ministry ... It gives the criteria to evaluate the works of Jesus at the end of His ministry"[11] and possibly to evaluate the ministry of his followers.

2. THE METHOD OF NARRATIVE CRITICISM

To begin with, narrative criticism takes into consideration the narrative integrity of a text. The proponents of this method emphasize the inherent unity of the Gospel narratives in a bid to have a holistic reading of the Bible. In this sense, the meaning of a part of the text is made evident in the light of the wider unity of the whole.[12] The narrative method is much more of a synchronic approach rather than a diachronic one. Its goal is to interpret the text in its finished form,[13] since "portions of texts are ... meaningful units only when they manifest a link between their contents and the general sense of the text."[14] This method sees the author as a craftsman or architect. He determines the point of view from which the story is told as well as the perspective from which the story is read or heard. In the words of Rhoads and Michie, "The narrator speaks from an ideological point of view ... So the narrator is always there at the reader's elbow shaping responses to the story-even, and perhaps especially, when the reader is least aware of it."[15]

---

8. Nolland, *Luke 1–9:20*, 191. France notes that Luke has moved the story out of its natural place in the narrative in order to use it as a "frontispiece" for his account of the Galilean ministry. France, *Matthew*, 548. A representative list of some source reconstructions has been made by Schürman, "*Zur Traditionsgeschichte der Nazareth-Perikope, Lk 4, 16–30*," 195.

9. The remark in v. 23 about the deeds of Jesus in Capernaum is a pointer to this fact. See Marshall, *The Gospel of Luke*, 177.

10. For Combrink, since this section is of crucial importance to the understanding of the Gospel as a whole, "We may perhaps see Luke here at work in a manner illuminating for the rest of his Gospel." See his "Structure," 27. It could mean that, for Luke, the ministry of Jesus is the fulfilment of OT prophecies. Cf. Marshall, *Luke*, 178.

11. Aryeh, Anum, "Christology and Soteriology in Luke," 2.

12. See Olmstead, *Matthew's Trilogy of Parables*," 10.

13. Powell, *What Is Narrative Criticism?* 7.

14. Weinrich et al., *Textgrammatik der deutschen Sprache*, 29. See Stamps, *Rhetorical and Narratological Criticism*, 232.

15. Rhoads and Michie, *Mark as Story*, 39. See also Booth, *The Rhetoric of Fiction*, 20. For Bal, "Whenever events are presented, they are always presented from within a certain 'vision.'" Bal, *Narratology*, 142.

Although this is an accepted narrative-critical method of biblical analysis, critics of this method may regard it as being open to extrapolation or having the tendency to generalize conclusions.[16] Secondly, the secondary unity of the biblical materials is too evident. A simple experiment could make this clear. One could read the first two chapters of the Gospel according to Mark and try to imagine the literary unity of these chapters. It is evident that what we have is more of a patchwork unity than a seamless garment. Thirdly, a narrative-critical reading that does not pay attention to the prior history or the sources of the given text could lead to readings that are purely subjective and ahistorical.

However, the advantages of such a method cannot be overlooked. It is not to be supposed that the biblical writers wrote with the primary intention of comparing their document with their sources. Rather, it seems that the main aim of their writing was to communicate the deposit of faith to their communities, despite the sources at their disposal. Therefore, narrative criticism helps one to discover the self-conscious manner in which the author has crafted his story with his reader directly in view.[17] It assumes an internal textual connectedness or integration as corrective to form, tradition, and redaction criticism which may lead to atomizing of the biblical story into unrelated literary pieces. At the end, narrative criticism helps one "to discover and examine the textual components and to analyze how they work together to create a purposeful effect"[18] and to elicit a certain response from the reader.[19] This does not mean that narrative criticism does not consider the possible sources of a pericope. It does, in the hope of seeing how the editorial work of a particular author of a pericope serves the entire purpose of his writing. It allows each author of the biblical books to be seen as a theologian who has something to communicate to his audience rather than a compiler or editor of randomly collected theological data from his sources.

It is interesting to note that Jesus seems to have adopted this approach in explaining the Scriptures to the bewildered disciples on the way to Emmaus. Jesus even went beyond a single book of the Scriptures. He started with Moses and went through all the prophets to explain all the things written about him (cf. Luke 24:27).[20] That their hearts burned within them indicates that Jesus achieved the required response from his listeners.

---

16. See Painter, Review: "The Johannine Approach to Mission," 347–49.
17. Petersen, *Literary Criticism*, 58.
18. Porter, *Handbook*, 221.
19. Kingsbury, *Matthew*, 3.
20. In fact, Okure referred to this passage while responding to critiques to her beloved method of exegesis during her paper presentation at the 2020 conference of the Catholic Biblical Association of Nigeria, *CABAN*. Who could ever fault the exegetical method already employed by Jesus?

3. THE STRUCTURE OF THE TEXT OF LUKE 4:16-21

The aim of structural analysis is to visualize the flow of the argument which could help one to make preliminary decisions concerning the stress of the pericope.[21] To this effect, various structural paradigms have been suggested by different authors in the study of this important Lukan passage.[22] However, what I present here is the way I see the passage.

Introduction: and he came to Nazareth, where he had been brought up (v.16 a)
 1a. and he entered into the synagogue on the Sabbath day as he usually did (v. 16b)
  2a. he stood up to read (v. 16c)
   3a. and they handed him the scroll of the prophet Isaiah (v. 17a)
    4a. and unrolling the scroll he found the place where it is written (v. 17b)
     the spirit of the Lord is on me (v. 18a)
      for he has anointed me (v. 18b)
       to proclaim the good news to the poor
      he has sent me (v. 18c)
       to proclaim liberty to those in captivity and sight to the blind
     to send the oppressed to freedom
     to proclaim a year of the Lord's favour (v. 19
    4b. and he rolled up the scroll (v. 20a)
   3b. gave it (the scroll) back to the assistant (v. 20b)
  2b. and sat down (v. 20c
 1b. and all the eyes in the synagogue were fixed on him (v. 20d)
Conclusion: then he began to speak to them (v. 21a)
This text is being fulfilled today even while you are listening (v. 21b)

What is most evident in this structural presentation is the symmetry that exists between the first part (vv. 16–19) and the second part (v. 20) of the passage. This is especially so from the moment Jesus entered the synagogue (v. 16b) until the time he finished reading from the scroll and sat down (v. 20). The diagram above easily shows the symmetry between elements 1a and 1b (catchword: synagogue), 2a and 2b (stood up versus sat down), 3a and 3b (handed him the scroll versus gave back the scroll), as well as 4a and 4b (unrolling the scroll versus rolling up the scroll). However, this symmetry is broken by the lack of correspondence between the introduction and the conclusion. This is understandable judging from the fact that I only adopted a section of the whole episode presented by Luke. Had I considered the whole pericope to v. 30, Jesus' coming to Nazareth (v. 16a) would have had a correspondence with his leaving Nazareth (v. 30b).

---

21. See Fee, *New Testament Exegesis*, 41.
22. See, for instance, Combrink, "*Structure*," 29.

Nonetheless, of particular importance to the pericope are verses 18-19. This importance is shown not only by the amount of ink Luke has spent in penning these verses, but especially by the fact that it is here, more than in any other New Testament passage, that Jesus presents his manifesto in clear terms.[23] It seems that in these verses, Luke has consciously allowed the narrative tempo to drop so as to exhaust the full importance of the programmatic announcement of the person and mission of Jesus.[24] As the sketch above shows, the Isaianic quotation in vv. 18-19 is framed by a chiasmus formed by the verbs "stood up," "was handed," and "unrolled" in vv. 16-17 and "rolled up," "handed," and "sat down" in v. 20. In the quotation itself, there is a tripartite repetition of "me" ("is on me," "has anointed me," "has sent me"). This shows the centrality of the person of Jesus in the narrative. Moreover, the mission of Jesus, which is to evangelize the poor, is resolved into three parallel infinitive clauses: "to proclaim liberty," "to send the oppressed to freedom," and "to proclaim a year of favor." The anointing of Jesus by the Spirit and Jesus' mission to proclaim the good news to the poor all come to the fore in this segment. If the postulation is true that the mission of evangelizing the poor in v. 18b is expanded in v. 18c, it then means that we have a synonymous parallelism in the first clauses of these two verses. The anointing of Jesus is the same thing as the sending of Jesus.

The last verse of our passage makes mention that the prophecies of the old dispensation have been fulfilled in the life and mission of Jesus (v. 21b). This is quite revealing because, at the beginning of his narrative, Luke tells us that the focus of his writing is about the events that have been fulfilled among us (1:1). This shows that Luke is interested "in constructing a narrative that shows how God's purposes have been realized in those events. Luke is writing a purposeful theological narrative in which God is the primary actor."[25] Although God is the primary actor in the narrative, human collaborators have been incorporated in the mission of bringing the good news to the poor.

4. Pneumatology and Christology in Luke 4:16-21

As mentioned above, the central figure in the pericope under consideration is the person of Jesus. Whatever is said about the Spirit or about the missionary mandate has reference to Jesus. This is made clear by the threefold repetition of "me" in v. 18. The implication is that the spotlight of the Isaianic quotation is on Jesus. As Green has argued, this emphasis on "me" has to be read "against the background of the build-up

---

23. One could relate this to the reply Jesus gave to the question of the disciples of John concerning the person of Jesus. In Luke 7:22 Jesus referred to the healing of the sick and the proclamation of the good news to the poor.
24. See Obiora, "Spirit," 57.
25. Holladay, *A Critical Introduction*, 224.

of anticipation regarding Jesus' identity and public ministry."²⁶ Also the summary presentation of Jesus' contextualization of the text of Isaiah in v. 21 serves to "eliminate everything that would keep Jesus from center-stage and that would detract from a sense of his total command of the situation."²⁷ It is in his person that the prophetic utterances of Isaiah come to fulfillment.

However, the identity of this Jesus has to be worked out systematically. Before his birth, the angel reports that he is Son of the Most High (1:32) or Son of God (1:35). This is possible because his conception came about through the operations of the Holy Spirit. At the finding of the child Jesus in the temple, his response to Mary was that he must be about his Father's business (2:48f). While he was at prayer after his baptism, the heavens opened and the Spirit descended upon him (3:21), then the voice of God proclaimed that Jesus is the begotten Son of God (3:22). In this, we see a strong connection between the indwelling of the Spirit of God in Jesus and his identity as Son of God. One suspects that it is the operation of the Spirit of God in Jesus that qualifies him to be God's begotten.²⁸ Hence, we find in 4:18 Jesus' self-affirmation of the identity given him by the angel and by the heavenly voice. Jesus is the Son of God by virtue of the Spirit which has been given to him.

One could also argue that the pericope of Luke 4:16-21 has answered the tempter who wanted Jesus to prove that he is the Son of God. The first and third elements of the temptation of Jesus in Luke's presentation were couched in a conditional manner thus: "If you are the Son of God" (cf. Luke 4:3.9). In our present pericope, Jesus seems to affirm that he is the Son of God by virtue of the indwelling of God's spirit in him and by virtue of the mission which he is to accomplish in God's name. Hence, we are dealing with a high christological title known to the primitive church.

Ordinarily, "the mere title 'son of God' as such leaves matters open"²⁹ because divine sonship means being related to God in some special way and being commissioned by God to fulfill some vocation. However, one could read the title from the backdrop of its application to designate the Davidic king in the Old Testament.³⁰ The divine sonship of the Davidic king is related to his messianic mission. Again, the filial address to the king in these words "you are my son" (Psa 2:7) is received in the rabbis as a messianic title.³¹ Also the Qumran community has evidence of "son of God"

---

26. Green, *The Theology of the Gospel of Luke*, 77.

27. Haenchen, "Historie und Verkündigung bei Markus und Lukas," 294. Nolland, *Luke*, 196.

28. For Ezeani, the Holy Spirit is the connecting word and the motivating factor in the presentations in the first four chapters of the Gospel of Luke. See his *The Apologetic Revisited*, 126.

29. O'Collins, *Christology*, 113.

30. Cf. 2 Sam 7:14; 1 Chr 17:13; 22:10; 28:6; Jer 23:5-8; Ezk 37:21-23; Zech 3:8-10; 12:17-13:1; Hag 2:21-22, etc.

31. See b. Sukka 52a and 4Q Florilegium 1:11.

as having a messianic significance.³² If Luke understood it the same way, this could mean that the messianic import of the person of Jesus is in view in our passage.

When we turn to the Gospel of Luke, we see an emphasis on the relationship between the divine sonship of Jesus and its messianic significance. There seems to be an identification of "son of God" and "messiah" in 4:41. In this verse, Jesus had to rebuke the demons who were proclaiming him the son of God. He did this because they knew that he was the Messiah. Luke 4:18 could also be related to the answer which Jesus gave to the disciples of John who came to enquire from him whether he was the Messiah (7:18–20). Luke's editorial comment remarks that at that time, Jesus healed many people of their sicknesses, freed many from evil spirits, and gave sight to the blind (7:21). To concretize this identity through his mission, Jesus sends John's disciples back to John to announce that the blind see again, the lame walk, lepers are made clean, the deaf hear, the dead are raised to life, and the poor are given the good news (7:22). Just as "to evangelize the poor" in 4:18 is the summary of the mission of Jesus, which is then expanded into different elements,³³ the apex of the mission of Jesus in 7:22 is the "giving of the good news to the poor."

Again, since Jesus does not only herald the good news but also brings about salvation, he is not merely a prophetic figure. In other words, the concluding words of Jesus in our pericope (this text is being fulfilled today even while you are listening) are nothing short of a messianic self-affirmation. This seems to be well-understood by Peter in his acclamation that Jesus is the Messiah of God (9:20). This affirmation is carried out clearly in the episode of the judgment of Jesus before the Sanhedrin. In his presentation, Luke has compressed the whole scene into a few verses to focus on the question bothering on the divine sonship of Jesus and his messianic significance. The two-pronged question from the chief priest was to tell the Sanhedrin if he was the Messiah (22:67) and if he was the Son of God (22:70). The way that the question was couched indicates that the high priest understood the two terms to be one and the same. To this, Jesus responded with a resounding "Yes I am" (22:70). In other words, Jesus is God's Son, the Messiah.

These passages considered give the reader a deep insight into the person of Jesus which the whole Gospel goes on to emphasize. The picture that the passages present is first and foremost the picture of Jesus who is imbued with the Spirit of God. There is thus an intrinsic connection between pneumatology and Christology in our pericope of study.

The role of the Spirit of God seems to be an important part of the Gospel of Luke. In our passage, the Spirit appears as the principal agent of the mission of Jesus. Jesus first announces in the passage that the spirit of the Lord is on him (v. 18a). The import of the indwelling of the Spirit on him is for the sake of anointing him (v. 18b). That is the significance of *heineken* ("because"). It is this anointing that empowers him

---

32. See Evans, "The Recently Published Dead Sea Scrolls and the Historical Jesus," 549–51.
33. See Bamel, "Ptōchos, ktl," *Theological Dictionary of the New Testament*, 6:906.

to proclaim the good news to the poor, expanded into freedom to those in captivity, restoration of sight to the blind, sending the oppressed into freedom, and announcing the Lord's year of favor. In the neighboring v. 14 in the same chapter, Luke informs his readers that Jesus returned to Galilee in the power of the Spirit after the temptation by the devil. In the same way, the opening verse of the chapter documents that Jesus was full of the Holy Spirit (v. 1). These instances point to the fact that the third evangelist has the activities of the Spirit in the mission of Jesus in mind in this chapter. It is because God anointed him with the Holy Spirit that Jesus was able to exercise the ministry of healing those under the bondage of the evil one (cf. Acts 10:38).

However, these proclamations were not realized in Nazareth. Unlike Matthew and Mark that report few miracles that took place in Jesus' hometown, Luke is quiet on this. This is understandable because the Lukan report sees the people of Nazareth trying to throw Jesus out of the hill on which their town was built. In other words, they did not allow Jesus to demonstrate the power of the Spirit which he claims rests on him. Nonetheless, the proclamation in the synagogue of Nazareth was realized in the synagogue of Capernaum through the exorcism of the man who was held in captivity by the unclean spirit (4:31-37). The connection between these two episodes could be located in the fact that the demon categorized Jesus with his hometown: "Jesus of Nazareth" (4:34).

5. Missiology in Luke 4:16-21

I have already noted the intrinsic connection between pneumatology and Christology in our passage. I have also remarked on the connection between the Spirit and the mission of Jesus. It is striking that the mission of Jesus as the proclamation of the good news occurs in three places in this passage. The expression "to proclaim" (*euangelisasthai* and *kēryxai* [two times]) bears this out. On the other hand, the conceptual parallelism in v. 18a ("the spirit of the Lord is upon me") and v.18b ("for he has anointed me") show the role of the spirit of God in the mission of Jesus. In the same way as the subordinate clause in v. 18b announces the bringing of the good news to the afflicted, the subordinate clauses in v. 18c itemize those within this category (those in captivity, the blind, and the oppressed). These lines specify and intensify the recipients of the missionary work of Jesus.

I have also noted that Jesus was sent as God's ambassador. *Apostelō* ("to send") is a central factor in this passage. In the same way Jesus was sent by the Father, he is also to send forth into freedom those who are fettered in captivity. Those in captivity, the blind and the oppressed, are those classified as poor in our passage. These are the recipients of the mission of Jesus. Luke has introduced the theme of poverty in the infancy narrative. The raising high of the lowly, the filling of the starving with good things, and sending the rich away empty are central features in the song of Mary (1:52f). In addressing the host on the proper invitation to feasts, the poor and the blind are to be the chief recipients (14:13). This same group of people were those invited in the Lukan version of the parable of the feast as substitute guests (14:21). This notion of blessing for the poor and exclusion of the rich from the feast reaches its climax in the peculiar Lukan parable of the rich man and Lazarus (16:19-31). Here, it is the poor man that is given blessings while the rich man suffers alienation from God. In a similar fashion, the rich man who gave half of his riches to the poor is promised the gift of salvation (19:8).[34] If these references point to the eschatological banquet, it means that "only the marginal phenomena of human society . . . will partake of this feast."[35]

Since the Lukan presentation of the text of Scriptures in the synagogue of Nazareth is an adaptation of the LXX version of Isaiah 61:1-2,[36] the omission of the phrase "the day of vengeance of our God" and the addition of an element from Isaiah 58:6 "to send forth the oppressed into freedom"[37] has led to a Lukan "suppression of a potential focus on the theme of judgment or retribution"[38] and an intensification of the theme of freedom to those in captivity. This is an important theme in Luke's theology.

In all these, the spirit of God is the overriding principle of Jesus' actions. In other words, everything in the passage seems to be geared toward stressing the meaning of the mission of Jesus and the means of realizing this mission. One could then agree with Green that from this Galilean segment of the ministry of Jesus, "We begin to discern not only the *what* but also the *how* of God's purpose . . . We see how Jesus, empowered by the Spirit understood his vocation and engaged in its performance by means of a prophetic, itinerant ministry."[39] This prophetic, itinerant ministry was geared toward those at the margins of the society. It is the mission of Jesus to preach or proclaim the good news to them because he was sent by God through the anointing of the Spirit. This is seen as the fulfillment of the prophecy of Isaiah.

6. POSTSCRIPT: THE MISSION OF JESUS AND HIS FOLLOWERS AS MISSION TO THE POOR

Perhaps it needs to be stated again that the Gospel of Luke is the Gospel of the poor. This fact is pretty evident from such peculiar Lukan pericopes as 1:50-53; 6:20-26; 14:7-24; and 16:19-31. Luke's sympathy for the rich seems to be only on the condition that they no longer focus on secular concerns (cf. 12:22-23; 14:18-20; 16:13; and 17:26-33). For Luke, following Jesus requires surrender of all material possessions

---

34. Other important passages include 6:20, 24; 8:14; 12:15, 21, 33; 18:25.

35. Bamel, "Ptōchos, ktl," 6:906.

36. The LXX form of the Isaianic quotation in Luke 4:18-19 is given extensive discussion by J. Nolland, *Luke*, 193. See also Sanders, "From Isaiah 61 to Luke 4," 80–82.

37. For a fuller discussion on the adaptations made by Luke, see Bock, *Proclamation from Prophecy and Pattern*, 105–11.

38. Green, *Luke*, 77.

39. Green, *Luke*, 61, emphasis original.

(14:33). In Luke, Simon and Andrew did not just leave their nets (as in Matt 4:20 and Mark 1:18). Rather, they left *everything* and followed Jesus (5:11). It is only the Gospel of Luke that showers blessings on the poor and proclaims them heirs of the kingdom of heaven (6:20).[40] These instances show the preferential love which the good news as proclaimed by Luke has for the poor.

This option for the poor is also at the center of the mission of the church. Jesus' proclivity to the poor challenges his church to spring into action for the aid of the materially disabled members of the society. The fathers of Vatican Council II made this clear in stating that just like Christ was sent by the Father to bring good news to the poor and to heal the contrite of heart (Luke 19:10), the church encompasses with love all those who are afflicted with human weakness. The church also recognizes in the poor and the suffering the likeness of her poor and suffering founder. Hence she does all she can to relieve their need and in them she strives to serve Christ.[41] Therefore, helping the poor and "willingly contributing part of what we possess . . . for the support of the poor whom we should always love with the deep yearning of Christ"[42] are an integral part of being Christians. This is a call for both the clergy and the laity of the church.[43]

In a country like Nigeria and other countries where structural ills hamper the welfare of the poor, Christian evangelism should include the dismantling of such dehumanizing structures. The church must proclaim the message of liberation to the poor, especially through her deeds.[44] A system whereby the church's ministers and the laity associate mainly with the rich in order to eat from the crumbs that fall from their table is not in keeping with the missionary mandate of proclaiming liberation to the poor. Luke 4:16-21 serves as a mirror for evaluating the missionary activities of the followers of Jesus.

BIBLIOGRAPHY

Aryeh, D. N. A., and E. N. B. Anum. "Christology and Soteriology in Luke: Inner Texture Analysis of Luke 4:16–30." *The American Journal of Biblical Theology* 22, no. 26 (2021).

Bal, M. *Narratology: Introduction to the Theory of Narrative.* Toronto: University of Toronto Press, 2002.

Bamel, E. "Ptōchos, ktl." In *Theological Dictionary of the New Testament* 6. Edited by G. Friedrich. Grand Rapids: Eerdmans, 1968.

Bock, D. L. *Proclamation from Prophecy and Pattern: Lucan Old Testament Christology.* JSSNTSS 12. Sheffield: JSOT, 1987.

Booth, W. C. *The Rhetoric of Fiction.* 2nd ed. Chicago: University of Chicago Press, 1983.

---

40. Matthew has a spiritualized form of poverty in 5:3.
41. Vatican Council II, *Lumen Gentium*, 8.
42. Vatican Council II, *Perfectae Caritatis*, 13.
43. Vatican Council II, *Apostolicam Actuositatem*, 7.
44. Umoren, "Liberating the Poor," 126.

Combrink, H. J. B. "The Structure and Significance of Luke 4:16–30." *Neot* 7 (1973) 27–47.

Crockett, L. C. "Luke 4:25-27 and Jewish-Gentile Relations in Luke-Acts." *JBL* 88 (1969) 117–83.

Evans, C. A. "The Recently Published Dead Sea Scrolls and the Historical Jesus." In *Studying the Historical Jesus*. Edited by B. Chilton and C. A. Evans. Leiden: Brill, 1994.

Ezeani, I. E. *The Apologetic Revisited: Exonerating Luke from an Ancestral Exegetical and Theological Burden*. Frankfurt am Main: Peterlang, 2014.

Fee, G. D. *New Testament Exegesis: A Handbook for Students and Pastors*. 3rd ed. Louisville: Westminster John Knox, 2002.

France, R. T. *The Gospel of Matthew*. TNICNT. Grand Rapids: Eerdmans, 2007.

Green, J. B. *The Theology of the Gospel of Luke*. Cambridge: Cambridge University Press, 1995.

Haenchen, E. "Historie und Verkündigung bei Markus und Lukas." In *Das Lukas-Evangelium: Die Redaktions—und Kompositionsgeschichtliche Forschung*. Edited by G. Braumann. Darmstadt: Wissenschaftliche Buchgesellschaft, 1974.

Holladay, C. R. *A Critical Introduction to the New Testament: Interpreting the Message and Meaning of Jesus Christ*. Nashville: Abingdon, 2005.

Kingsbury, J. D. *Matthew as Story*. 2nd ed. Philadelphia: Fortress, 1988.

Marshall, I. H. *The Gospel of Luke: A Commentary on the Greek Text*. NIGTC 85. Grand Rapids: Eerdmans, 1978.

Moore, S. D. *Literary Criticism and the Gospels: The Theoretical Challenge*. New Haven: Yale University Press, 1989.

Nolland, J. *Luke 1-9:20*. WBC 35a. Dallas: Word, 1989.

Obiora, M. J. "'The Spirit of the Lord God Is upon Me' (Isaiah 61:1): The Use of Isaiah 61:1-2 in Luke 4:18-19." In *The Acts of CABAN* 10:49-63. 2018.

O'Collins, G., SJ. *Christology: A Biblical, Historical, and Systematic Study of Jesus*. Oxford: Oxford University Press, 1995.

Okure, T. "'He Gave Them Power to Become Children of God' (John 1:12-14): Divinization as God's Foundational Gift to Believers; A Survey in John's Gospel," *Acts of the Catholic Biblical Association of Nigeria* 10 (2018) 118–35.

———. *Johannine Approach to Mission: A Contextual Study of John 4:1-42*. WUNT 2/31. Tübingen: Mohr, 1988.

Olmstead, W. G. *Matthew's Trilogy of Parables: The Nation, the Nations and the Reader in Matthew 21.28-22.14*. Cambridge: Cambridge University Press, 2007.

Painter, J. Review of "The Johannine Approach to Mission: A Contextual Study of John 4.1–42," *Pacifica* 3, no. 3(1990) 347–49.

Petersen, N. R. *Literary Criticism for New Testament Critics*. Philadelphia: Fortress, 1978.

Powell, M. A. *What Is Narrative Criticism?* Minneapolis: Fortress, 1990.

Rhoads, D., and D. Michie. *Mark as Story: An Introduction to the Narrative of a Gospel*. Philadelphia: Fortress, 1982.

Sanders, J. A. "From Isaiah 61 to Luke 4." In *Christianity, Judaism and Other Greco-Roman Cults*, 80–82. Edited by J. Neusner. Leiden: Brill, 1975.

Schreck, C. J. "The Nazareth Pericope: Luke 4:16-30 in Recent Studies." In *L'Evangile de Luc: Problémes littérares et théologiques*, 399–471. Edited by F. Neirynck. BETL 32. Leuven: Leuven University Press, 1989.

Schürman, H. "Zur Traditionsgeschichte der Nazareth-Perikope, Lk 4,16-30." In *Mélanges bibliques*. Gembloux: Duculot, 1970.

Stamps, D. L. "Rhetorical and Narratological Criticism." In *A Handbook to the Exegesis of the New Testament*. Edited by S. E. Porter. Boston: Brill, 2002.

Umoren, A. I. "Liberating the Poor as Jesus' Evangelization Approach in Luke 4:18-19: Lessons for the Church in Nigeria." In *Acts of the Catholic Biblical Association of Nigeria* 6. 2015.

Uzowulu, C. C. "The Spirit of the Lord in a Pentecostal Era: The Study of Luke 4:16-19." *The Acts of CABAN* 10 (2018) 94–104.

Vatican Council II. *Apostolicam Actuositatem*. Decree on the Apostolate of the Laity (November 18, 1965).

———. *Lumen Gentium*. Dogmatic Constitution of the Church (November 21, 1964).

———. *Perfectae Caritatis*. Decree on the Up-to-Date Renewal of Religious Life (October 28, 1965).

Weinrich, H., et al. *Textgrammatik der deutschen Sprache*. Hildesheim: Georg Olms, 2007.

CHAPTER 11

The Commisioning of the Apostles in John 20:19–23
and Its Relevance to Christians in Africa

PAUL DANBAKI JATAU

INTRODUCTION

The precise meaning, nature, and scope of mission in John's Gospel are subjects of perennial debate, but the mission itself as *leitmotif* or "foundation theme of the Gospel" is hardly a matter of dispute. Though the word "mission" is not actually used, a sense of it pervades the Gospel.[1] The ever-recurring statement *kathōs'apéstalkén me hò patēr, kágō pémpō hùmās* ("as the Father has sent me, so I send you") is seen as the key to Jesus' understanding of his mission. The expression reveals his self-consciousness as one sent. As a result of this consciousness, Jesus does not do his will but the Father's (5:30), seeks not his own glory but the Father's (7:18; 8:50, 54), and is so dependent on the Father that he can do nothing of himself (5:19, 30). His mission is to reveal the Father and thus bring life, light, and knowledge to those who believe in him.

Jesus' mission is seen as central and normative. All other missions derive from and are in function of his: John the Baptist prepares the way for him, and the disciples continue his mission in the world. The reality of Christ's presence to them in their mission is actualized through the gift of the Holy Spirit: "When he had said this, he breathed on them and said to them, 'Receive the Holy Spirit'" (v. 22). Hence, the disciples bear divine authorization as did Christ. This article interprets it from the point of mission and the Holy Spirit as the principal agent of evangelization. Therefore,

---

1. Okure, *Johannine Approach*, 1.

using the historical critical and contextual methods of biblical exegesis, this article undertakes to reexamine John 20:19–23 in order to draw out its implications for Christians in Africa in the work of the proclamation of the good news, especially in such a continent bedeviled by persecution, wars, terrorism, banditry, kidnapping, etc. This paper argues that after a detailed exegetical analysis of John 20:19–23 in the historical, literary, and theological contexts of John's Gospel, the success of every mission depends on the risen Jesus and the bestowal of the Holy Spirit as the principal agent of evangelization.

JOHN 20:19–23 WITHIN ITS IMMEDIATE LITERARY CONTEXTS

The pericope of John 20:19–23, is set within a post-resurrection scene. It has a literary affinity with the next passage, which speaks of Thomas not being with the other disciples when Jesus appeared. A week later the disciples are back in the house with the doors locked, but this time Thomas is also there, and again Jesus comes (20:26). This time Jesus specifically addresses Thomas' doubts by showing him his hands and side, and instructing him to believe (20:27).

As a self-contained unit, vv. 19–23 is delimited from vv. 24–31 because the event holds a distinct element of time. The first of the two time elements appears in John 20:1, which reads, "Early on the first day of the week." A more literal translation of the Greek, *tē de mia tōn sabbatōn*, would be, "But on the first of the Sabbaths." The second time marker appears in 20:19, *ousēs oun opsias tē hēmera ekeinē tē mia sabbatōn*, "When it was evening on the same day, the first of the Sabbaths." These events are established within the same day—the day of the resurrection—and they form the basis for a Johannine understanding of time.[2]

The setting for these events places the disciples gathered together in a house with the door closed and "locked for fear of the Jews" (20:19). What transpires is complex, with several potential themes emerging. First, in 20:19 the entrance of Jesus into the room and his greeting as he stood amongst them, "Peace be with you," may reflect a Jewish premise. E. Coye Still finds another possible key theme contained in v. 20 where Jesus presents his wounds for examination. Still views Jesus' presentation of his wounds as a way of demonstrating the nature of their mission: they are being sent "to suffer in their proclamation of him to the world."[3] Third, in v. 21, during the commissioning of the disciples as a continuation of his own ministry, Jesus repeats the "shalom" greeting and then says, "As the Father has sent me, so I send you." Marianne Thompson writes, "It focuses attention not only on what the disciples are to do but also on the one who empowers and charges them to do it."[4] These various themes

---

2. Schneiders, "The Raising of the New Temple," 345.
3. Still, "Sent to Be Scarred: John 20:19–23," 190–91.
4. Thompson, "The Breath of Life," 76.

lead toward a potential overall missiological theme for the context of 20:19–23, which is that Jesus commissioned his disciples to continue the ministry he began.

The unit vv. 1–18 narrates Mary Magdalene's eagerness to see and touch the risen Jesus and her preparedness to do something about it. When she eventually recognizes him, she receives her commission. What vv. 1–18 and vv. 24–31 which delimit vv. 19–23 make clear is the fact that the one whom the two characters long to meet again is the Jesus of their old experience. For both this is a visible and sensible presence of the earthly Jesus, indicated by Mary's initial failure to recognize him (vv. 14–15) and her physical clinging to him (v. 17), and by Thomas in his thinking that to see and touch Jesus will provide him with proof that this is the Jesus he has known (v. 25).[5]

THE TEXT OF JOHN 20:19–23

> 19 When it was evening on that day, the first day of the week, and the doors of the house where the disciples had met were locked for fear of the Jews, Jesus came and stood among them and said, "Peace be with you. 20After he said this, he showed them his hands and his side. Then the disciples rejoiced when they saw the Lord.21Jesus said to them again, "Peace be with you. As the Father has sent me, so I send you."22When he had said this, he breathed on them and said to them, "Receive the Holy Spirit.23If you forgive the sins of any, they are forgiven them; if you retain the sins of any, they are retained."

Analysis of John 20:19–23

Building on what has been discussed, we now turn to the exegetical analysis of the text verse by verse.

In verse 19, the post-positive *oun* connects the following pericope with the preceding one.[6] This connection is further highlighted by the author's statement that it was *opsias tē hēmera ekeinē*.[7] Most scholars agree that the demonstrative pronoun is referring back to Easter day, mentioned first in John 20:1. Raymond argues that *tē hēmera ekeinē* is actually a reference to the Old Testament concept of the Day of the Lord.[8] He further argues that in Jesus' farewell discourse (John 14–17), he uses this term in reference to his return in the near future (John 14:20).[9] However, this argument fails to take into consideration the broader context in which this pericope is located—namely, that this story is simply one of a number of consecutive

---

5. Schnackenburg, *John*, 341–44.
6. Köstenberger, et.al., *Going Deeper With New Testament Gree*, 337.
7. Brown, *John (xiii–xxi)*, 1091.
8. Raymond, *John*, 1019.
9. Rossum, "The "Johannine Pentecost," 151.

post-resurrection appearances. Furthermore, the author further clarifies the time this appearance took place by stating that it was on the first day of the week.[10] Therefore, this event took place on the evening of the first day of the week after Jesus' crucifixion, the same day Mary went to the tomb and found it empty (20:1).

The author's comment that the doors had been locked is unique to John. The participle *kekleismenōn* is perfect in aspect, which indicates the doors were closed or locked in the past and were still locked at the time of Jesus' appearance.[11] The plural *thurōn* points to the fact that there was more than one door on the house. Many scholars believe the author mentions the locked doors to highlight the nature of Jesus' resurrected body.[12] His body is corporeal enough to see, but non-corporeal enough to pass through a door.[13] Witherington III and Carson note that just as Jesus had passed through his grave clothes (20:5–7), he now passes through a locked door.[14] Schnackenburg believes the Evangelist added this material, as he is the one who brought the theme of fear into the Gospel (7:13; 9:22; 19:38).[15] However, Morris believes the unique qualities of this Johannine account are explained by positing John used different sources than the Synoptics.[16] Ultimately, the text seems to indicate the primary reason the author mentioned the locked door was to highlight the disciples fear of *tōn Ioudaiōn* (20:19). The reason for this fear is not given, but presumably they are fearful that if they are identified as companions of Jesus, they too will suffer the same fate as their leader. This fear is then contrasted with the joy of the disciples when they see Jesus in the next verse (20:20).[17] Thus, the mention of the locked doors seems to primarily highlight the fear of the disciples and the possibly unique nature of his resurrection body.

Jesus came and stood among his disciples. The preposition *eis* ("into") after *ēlthen* ("came," a verb of motion) implies direction toward a goal.[18] The vague reference to the way Jesus entered the house has left many assuming he appeared out of thin air or was able to move through the door. Although this is possible, the manner in which Jesus appeared is not particularly important. The simple fact that Jesus returned to the disciples, as promised in the farewell discourse, is what is being portrayed.[19] Jesus promised not to leave the disciples as *orphanous*, and here he is fulfilling his promise (14:18–22).[20]

10. George, *Reading the Tapestry*, 85.
11. Michaels and Fee, *John*, 1008.
12. Bultmann, *John*, 690–91.
13. Bultmann, *John*, 558.
14. Witherington III, *John's Wisdom*, 342.
15. Schnackenburg, *John*, 322.
16. Morris, *John*, 843.
17. Keener, *John: A Commentary*, 1201.
18. Harris, "John," 330.
19. Burge, *John*, 559.
20. Burge, *John*, 559.

The Hebrew greeting *eirēnē humin* was common and is still used today. However, given its repetition in 20:21 and 26 and Jesus' promise in 14:27, it is clear Jesus' words are meant to imply much more than a customary greeting.[21] His words speak to the reality that because of his work on the cross, indeed his glorification, he is now able to fulfill the promises he made in the farewell discourse.[22]

In verse 20, after he announced peace to the disciples, Jesus shows his wounds to the disciples to identify himself as the same Jesus who had been crucified. In the parallel account in Luke, Jesus shows his hands and feet; however, in this account he shows his hands and side.[23] Whereas in the Lucan account Jesus' wounds could have been displayed by anyone who was crucified, Jesus' wound on his side left no doubt about his identity (John 19:34). It is worth noting that *cheiras* can refer to the hands and forearms.[24] This is significant because the weight of the body could tear the nails through the hands unless ropes were also used; thus it is more likely the nails were placed in the forearms or wrists. Only the beloved disciple and some of the women saw Jesus' side pierced (19:26–27), so either the author or a witness is present to confirm the wound or it is assumed that the other disciples would have heard the report from those who were present.

Evidently the disciples recognized Jesus once he showed them his wounds, as they rejoiced (*chairō*) in 20:20. This account fulfills Jesus' promises to return to his disciples and that the disciples' grief would turn to joy (John 14:17–18; 16:20–22).[25] Specifically, Jesus' statement in 16:20 and 16:22 that "Very truly, I tell you, you will weep and mourn while the world rejoices. You will grieve, but your grief will turn to joy" and that "Now is your time of grief, but I will see you again and you will rejoice, and no one will take away your joy" are fulfilled here.[26] Thus, in this verse the disciples were convinced that the man standing before them was Jesus, and their fear and grief was turned to joy.

Furthermore, in verse 21, the form, *kathōs . . . kagō* ("as the Father has . . . so I") is an invitation to "active participation in the divine mission."[27] The double sending has been repeated several times in the Book of Glory. For example, "As the Father has loved me . . . so I love you" (John 15:9) indicates that what Jesus is in relation to the Father, so now the disciples will be in relation to Jesus (John 15:9; 17:18, 21; 20:21). The sending neither reduces the one who sends nor amplifies the sender. Here the disciples are commissioned, sent into the world as God has sent Jesus into the world (John 20:21; 17:18). Central to this Greek grammatical construction is a continuity of

---

21. Michaels, *The Gospel of John*, 1008.
22. Witherington III, *John's Wisdom*, 342.
23. Brown, *John (xiii–xxi)*, 1021.
24. Harris, *John*, 400.
25. Morris, *The Gospel according to John*, 845.
26. Michaels, *The Gospel of John*, 1009.
27. Brodie, *John,*, 568.

the relationship between the Father and Son, and Son and disciples.²⁸ This is also a continuity of mission. The grammatical construction stresses a continuity rather than transcendence or hierarchy. From the Father to the Son and on to the disciples, the mission is permanent or unchanged.²⁹ Although the Fourth Gospel uses two verbs, *apostellō* and *pempō*, they are synonymous.³⁰ In this pericope, the first verb *apostellō* is in the perfect tense (*apestalken*), which implies that the mission of Jesus is continuous and effective and continuous. This fact is justified by the second verb *pempō*, which is in the present tense.

Jesus' repetition of the phrase *eirēnē humin* emphasizes the joy and peace brought by the resurrection and might have helped the disciples reflect on the full meaning of those words.³¹ This account of the commissioning of the disciples is unique and distinct from the accounts found in the Synoptics (Matt 28:19–20; Mark 16:15; Luke 24:49).³² The unique emphasis in this commissioning is found in the words *kathōs* and *kagō*, which emphasize the similarity between the sending of Jesus and the disciples.³³ As Witherington III explains, the disciples are commissioned as Jesus' agents, his representatives, just as he was the Father's agent.³⁴ Although the verbs *apestalken* and *pempō* are used, there is no significance in the variation as they are both used by Jesus and the disciples elsewhere in the Gospel.³⁵ Michaels also argues that the sentence structure, which is a comparison as indicated by *kathōs*, indicates the two verbs can be used interchangeably. The fact that Jesus has just showed the disciples his wounds is significant too; the disciples are sent in a similar manner as Jesus was and need to be prepared to suffer and even give up their lives (16:2).³⁶ Jesus is further identified with his Father here since he too becomes one who sends.³⁷

The exact nature of the disciples' commission is not given here. The perfect tense of *apestalken* highlights the stative aspect of Jesus' sending; he was and still is sent by his Father.³⁸ Clearly, Jesus believed his specific mission of going to the cross was finished (19:30), but his broader mission is continued by the disciples (14:12) and the Paraclete (14:16; 16:7–15).³⁹ As such, Schnackenburg argues that Jesus is inviting the

---

28. Kittel, *Theological Dictionary of the New Testament*, 405.
29. Kittel, *Theological Dictionary of the New Testament*, 435.
30. Rengstorf, "ἀποστέλλω," TDNT 1. 404–6.
31. Carson, *John*, 649.
32. Schnackenburg, *John*, 324.
33. Köstenberger, *Missions of Jesus*, 191.
34. Witherington III, *John's Wisdom*, 342.
35. Barrett, *The Gospel According to St. John*, 569.
36. Witherington III, *John's Wisdom*, 342.
37. Köstenberger, *The Missions of Jesus and the Disciples*, 191.
38. Pretlove, "John 20:22: Help From Dry Bones?" 99.
39. Köstenberger, *The Missions of Jesus and the Disciples*, 190–92.

disciples into his mission, not giving them a new mission.[40] Morris and Schneiders, however, contend that Jesus' mission has been completed and Jesus was sending the disciples on a new mission.[41] Both interpretations have some validity because, in one sense, Jesus had accomplished his specific mission on earth, but in another sense, his broader mission would be continued through the Spirit-enabled disciples.

In the discussion on the Paraclete in the previous section, it was clear that the mission of the Paraclete and the disciples' future roles were seen as a continuation of Jesus' mission on earth (17:18–23).[42] Therefore, the agent sent from the Father is now sending out his own agents to continue his mission to glorify God and reveal him to the world. Now, just as the Son received the Holy Spirit at the beginning of his mission, the disciples too will receive the Holy Spirit at the beginning of theirs.[43]

In verse 22, we encoutere a lot of controversy and debate in the scholarly community.Since it appears that Jesus gives the disciples the Holy Spirit, many have questioned the relationship of this Johannine passage with the Lucan account of Pentecost. Here an argument will be made that in 20:22 the Evangelist intended to communicate Jesus' giving the disciples the Holy Spirit in its fullness as a new-creational act, and that this action was intended to empower them to fulfill their commission as the renewed Israel.

George Johnston argues that because *pneuma hagion* is anarthrous, Jesus did not breathe the Holy Spirit, but a holy spirit.[44] Rudolf Bultmann similarly believes Jesus gave his disciples the spirit, which was a vital life source.[45] At first glance, this view seems to deserve some attention, but the vast majority of scholars have rejected this interpretation because there are examples in John where *pneuma hagion* is anarthrous and clearly refers to the Holy Spirit (John 1:33; 7:39b).[46] The fact that this interpretation rests on the assertion that an anarthrous *pneuma hagion* cannot be a reference to the Holy Spirit ultimately makes it untenable for the majority of scholars.

One of the more striking features of v. 22 is the Evangelist's use of *emphusaō*, a *hapax legomenon* occurring only here in the New Testament. However, it does occur in the Septuagint (LXX) in Genesis 2:7 and Ezekiel 37:9.[47] In Genesis 2:7, God breathes life into Adam, and in Ezekiel 37:9 the divine breath gives life to dry bones.[48] The use of this very specific verb alone should not be taken as a direct allusion to these

---

40. Schnackenburg, *The Gospel According to St. John*, 324.
41. Morris, *The Gospel according to John*, 846.
42. Köstenberger, *The Missions of Jesus and the Disciples*, 196.
43. Tuppurainen, "Jesus, the Spirit, and the Church," 45.
44. Johnston, *Spirit-Paraclete*, 11.
45. Bultmann, *The Gospel of John*, 692.
46. Carson, *John*, 650. Harris also notes πνεῦμα ἅγιον can be conceived as a proper name, which does not need an article. Harris, *John*, 330.
47. Peterson, *John's Use of Ezekiel*, 172.
48. Schneiders, "The Raising of the New Temple," 351.

passages, but the additional presence of a similar motif suggests John was alluding to these passages.[49] As Martin Hengel explains, John's use of the Old Testament centers on allusions and collecting the sense of a passage, instead of merely citing a verse.[50] Similarly, G. K. Beale notes that "the telltale key to discerning an allusion is that of recognizing an incomparable or unique parallel with wording, syntax, concept, or cluster of motifs in the same order or structure."[51] Given the use of a very specific verb, and the common theme of breathing life through the Spirit in these passages, the conclusion that the Evangelist was intentionally alluding to the contexts of these passages is warranted. However, more than simply verbal agreement, the imagery is important for John. Richard B. Hays explains that John focuses less on direct quotation or even verbal allusions and instead focuses on evoking familiar images from Israel's Scriptures.[52] Since the Evangelist was drawing on these passages, it is appropriate to determine what was happening in each.

In Genesis 2:7, God breathes the "breath of life" into man and he becomes a living creature.[53] The larger context of this verse is the account of the Lord making the heavens and the earth (Ge 2:4). Directly after the creation of this living man he is placed into the garden of Eden so he could take care of it (Gen 2:15). Then the Lord warns the man that if he eats from the tree of the knowledge of good and evil, he will die (Gen 2:17). Presumably, this is because he would be cut off from the tree of life (Gen 2:8, 22–24) and would not be able to eat from it anymore.[54] This would result in him losing the "breath of life" that transformed his physical body into a living one. The emphasis is that God is the giver of life.

In Ezekiel 37, Ezekiel is brought to a valley of dry bones and asked if these dry dead bones could live again (Ezek 37:3).[55] Ezekiel is doubtful and is told to prophesy to the bones that the Lord says he will breathe into them, and they will live (Ezek 37:5). Ezekiel does as he is told, and miraculously the bones begin to come together as flesh, tendons, and skin appear on the bones, but there was no breath in them (Ezek 37:8). Again, Ezekiel prophesies to the breath, and it comes into the bodies and gives them life (Ezek 37:10). Finally, the bones are identified as the people of Israel (Ezek 37:11).[56] Importantly, in this passage, Ezekiel is using creation language to depict Israel's spiritual renewal and return from exile as a sort of re-creation.[57] This vision in Ezekiel 37 refers to and interprets the event that Ezekiel talks about in 36:24–37,

---

49. Manning Jr, "Echoes of a Prophet," 10–11.
50. Hengel, "The Old Testament in the Fourth Gospel," 31–32.
51. Beale, *Handbook on the New Testament Use of the Old Testament*, 32.
52. Hays, *Echoes of Scripture in the Gospels*, 336.
53. Wenham, *Genesis 1–15*, 59–60.
54. Wenham, 86.
55. Allen, *Ezekiel 20–48*, 184.
56. Beale, *Biblical Theology*, 561.
57. Stordalen, "Echoes of Eden," 327.

where he will cleanse them from all impurities, give them a new heart, and put his Spirit[58] in them so they will be able to follow his decrees.

Ezekiel's oracle in 36:24–28 echoes the unclean/clean language of 36:17–18, which suggests it is meant to give the solution to Israel's disobedience problem.[59] In this oracle of the future restored Israel, their land is compared to the garden of Eden (Ezekiel 36:35), which again highlights the fact that Ezekiel sees this restoration of Israel as a renewal of creation.[60] Thus, in Ezekiel 37 the restoration of Israel is depicted as a re-creational event in which the breath of life, or Spirit (Ezekiel 37:14), is given to a spiritually dead people so that they will have life again.[61] The importance of the contexts of these passages is strengthened by the fact that the Evangelist draws on creational imagery and imagery from Ezekiel elsewhere. From the start of John, Jesus is presented as one who was present and active in the beginning (John 1:1). N.T. Wright explains that creational themes such as light and darkness, day and night, and the seed that will be fruitful and multiply are evident throughout John.[62]

Jeannie Brown suggests the *logos* (word) language evokes the Genesis theme that God spoke. She also notes the prevalence of life throughout John.[63] Many of Jesus' "I am" statements revolve around him as the source or sustainer of life, and the Gospel's stated purpose is that people may have life (20:31).[64] Jesus' arrest, crucifixion, and resurrection take place in a garden (18:1, 26; 19:41). Mary also mistakes Jesus as a *kēpouros* ("garderner") when she is outside the tomb (20:15).Interestingly, in Genesis and almost every place in the LXX where the garden of Eden is referred to, "garden" is translated with *paradeisos*; however, in Ezekiel 36:35, "garden" is translated as *kēpos*.[65] Some argue that Pilate's statement in 19:5, "Here is the man," is meant to be read as comparing Christ to Adam.[66]

Wright hints at this connection as well, noting that Pilate brings Jesus out on the sixth day, the very day that God created mankind. The irony, according to Wright, is that the man who truly displayed the image of God is rejected by God's people.[67] Jesus' work is completed at the end of the sixth day (19:30) just as God finished his work on the sixth day of creation. Furthermore, the fact that the day of Jesus' resurrection

---

58. Block, "The Book of Ezekiel: Chapters 25–48," 356.
59. Stordalen, "Echoes of Eden: Genesis 2–3 and Symbolism of the Eden Garden," 327.
60. Burge, *Anointed Community*, 125.
61. Allen, *Ezekiel 20–48*, 187–88.
62. Wright, *The Scriptures, the Cross*, 54.
63. Brown, "Creation's Renewal in the Gospel of John," 277.
64. Moore, *Signs of Salvation*, 67–77.
65. Moore, *Signs of Salvation*, 12.
66. Litwa, "Behold Adam," 142.
67. Wright, *The Scriptures, the Cross, and the Power of God*, 54.

is referred to as the first day of the week (20:1, 19) can be understood as a reference to the beginning of a new week of creation, a re-creation.[68]

Thus, a faithful interpretation of 20:22 must take into consideration the fact that the Evangelist, by choosing to use the imagery of *emphusaō* ("breathe") here, probably alludes to the LXX of Genesis 2:7 and Ezekiel 37:9.[69] In both of these texts, God is portrayed as the agent who breathes life, which enables people to serve and obey God, into humanity. Now, Jesus is portrayed as the agent who breathes the breath of life into his disciples (1:3).[70] The use of *lambanō* ("take" or "receive") with the *pneuma hagion* ("Holy Spirit") also became an early Christian formula for the reception of the Spirit.[71] This re-creational act accomplishes a few things. First, given the larger context of this as a resurrection appearance, Jesus' act further identifies him as not only human, but a divine being who has life in himself, just like the Father (5:26).[72] Second, this statement should be seen as the fulfillment of the eschatological promises of the giving of the Spirit, especially in light of the reference to Ezekiel 37:9.[73] Here the disciples are cleansed from impurity, given a new heart that enables them to obey Jesus' commandment of love, and fulfill their mission as the renewed Israel. The expectation that Jesus would give the Spirit is evident throughout the whole Gospel. The result of the giving of the Spirit is eternal life, which makes complete sense in light of the Evangelist's portrayal of this event as an eschatological act of re-creation.[74]

In the light of these various interpretations and arguments, and the context of John 20:19–23, it appears this verse is meant to depict the full gift of the Spirit to the disciples. The use of *enephusēsen* ("he breathed") is unique and brings re-creational imagery into the passage. It also serves to further identify Jesus, not only as a human as evidenced by his hands and side, but as the divine son of God.[75] The fulfillment language of the disciples' *phobos* ("fear") being turned into *chara* ("joy"), the context of the sending of the disciples and continuation of Jesus' mission through the Holy Spirit, and the author's presentation of Jesus' glorification as a single event all point to the fact that the author intended to communicate the giving of the Spirit in full in this passage.

In verse the construction *an tinōn* with the subjunctive *aphēte* could be an indefinite relative and be translated: "The sins of anyone you forgive, they are forgiven to

---

68. Brown, "*Creation's renewal in the Gospel of John*," 283.

69. The LXX of Ezek 37:9 reads: ἐμφύσησον εἰς τοὺς νεκροὺς τούτους καὶ ζησάτωσαν. The LXX of Gen 2:7 reads: καὶ ἐνεφύσησεν εἰς τὸ πρόσωπον αὐτοῦ πνοὴν ζωῆς, καὶ ἐγένετο ὁ ἄνθρωπος εἰς ψυχὴν ζῶσαν.

70. Burge, *The Anointed Community*, 125.

71. Bultmann, *The Gospel of John*, 616.

72. Thompson, "The Breath of Life," 69–48.

73. Burge, *The Anointed Community*, 125–26.

74. Manning Jr., *Echoes of a Prophet*, 167.

75. Thompson, "The Breath of Life: John 20:22–23 Once More," 69–78.

them."⁷⁶ However, the more likely translation is a third-class conditional clause: If you forgive anyone's sins, they are forgiven.⁷⁷ The aorist tense of *aphēte* highlights the perfective aspect of the forgiveness,⁷⁸ while the present *kratēte* points to the imperfective, or ongoing, aspect of the retaining of sin.⁷⁹ Others have noted that the passive tense of *apheōntai* and *kekratēntai* are divine passives. God is still the one who ultimately forgives and retains sin, the disciples are merely given authority to proclaim a person's reception or rejection of the gospel.⁸⁰

Given the context of the sending of the disciples, and them receiving the Holy Spirit, this statement fits well.⁸¹ The Spirit would enable the disciples to continue carrying out Jesus' mission and to announce forgiveness or judgment based on people's response to Jesus and his message (14:6).⁸² However, the disciples are not given the authority to "take away" sin, that task is reserved for Jesus alone (1:29).⁸³ Given the close parallels between Matthew 16:19 and 18:18, some have argued Jesus is simply giving the disciples authority to forgive sins in the context of the Johannine community. However, this view fails to interpret these verses in their Johannine context, where it is clear the coming of the Paraclete will enable the disciples for mission to the world (15:26-26; 16:8-11).⁸⁴ There is nothing in this passage to suggest this authority was limited to these disciples, since the Spirit is portrayed as the one who enables them for their mission.⁸⁵ Thus, in this verse, Jesus tells the disciples they have the power, through the Holy Spirit, to pronounce forgiveness or judgment on others.

After reviewing several important Johannine concepts and performing an exegesis of John 20:19–23, several conclusions can be made. First, based on the language the Evangelist uses throughout the Gospel to talk about Jesus' death, crucifixion, resurrection, and ascension, it is evident he viewed them as a unified series of events. He knows there is a difference between resurrection and ascension but prefers a language that stresses the unity of these events. The result or goal of these unified series of events, which is anticipated throughout the Gospel, is the arrival of the Holy Spirit. The exegesis of 20:19–23 revealed that the Evangelist was probably trying to communicate the moment when Jesus gave the Holy Spirit, the Paraclete, to the disciples. The allusions to Genesis 2 and Ezekiel 37 depict this as a new-creational and eschatological

---

76. ἀφέωνται is functioning as an intensive perfect, emphasizing the present state of the forgiveness. Köstenberger et. al., *Going Deeper With New Testament Greek*, 298.

77. Harris, John, 400.

78. Köstenberger et. al., *Going Deeper With New Testament Greek,*, 230.

79. Harris, John, 400.

80. Keener, *Gospel of John*, 1206.

81. Köstenberger, *Missions of Jesus and the Disciples*, 192.

82. Keener, *Gospel of John*, 1206.

83. Köstenberger, *Missions of Jesus and the Disciples*, 193.

84. Köstenberger, *Missions of Jesus and the Disciples*, 194.

85. Keener, *Gospel of John*, 1206.

significant event, and the fulfillment of many of Jesus' promises from the farewell discourse suggest the Paraclete also arrived here. The disciples are empowered to be Jesus' agents in the world, to live as the revivified Israel.

SUMMARY

The exegesis of 20:19- 23 revealed that the bestowal of the Holy Spirit and commissioning of the disciples is remarkably differentiated from the manner in which the Evangelist had spoken of the charge given to the disciples in 15:18–16:11. In John 20:19–23, it is not a matter of their *marturein* ("to witness"), but in a terminology otherwise foreign to that of the Gospel, their task is described in terms of the *aphienai* ("to forgive") and *kratein* ("to retain") of *hamartias* ("sins").

John 20:19–23 and Its Relevance to Christians in Africa

In John 20:19-23, Jesus kept his promise to the disciples that a little while after his departure they would see him and their hearts would rejoice (v. 20; see also 16:16). He gives them his "peace," freedom from fear and total well-being in body and mind, which the world cannot give (see 14:27). In this bestowal of peace, Jesus does not raise a word about their having to abandon him in his hour of trial, as human beings would have done. He shows them his wounded hands by which he will hold them fast and keep them from perishing (see 10:28; 17:12), and his side from which flowed and will continue to flow for them rivers of new life, which is the Spirit (7:37–39).

Jesus also breathes on them the Spirit he earlier promised them as the necessary gift to them in his temporary departure. Filled and strengthened by the Holy Spirit, they are effectively sent into the world as God had sent Jesus into the world (20:21; 17:18). As Jesus was sent into the world to take away sin and bring into communion, so are the disciples. The statement *an tinōn aphēte tas hamartias apheōntai autois, an tinōn kratēte kekratēntai* in (v. 23) is at times interpreted as scriptural basis for the current form of the sacrament of reconciliation in the Catholic Church, traditionally called "confession." The Johannine interpretation of the verse differs. It is more descriptive than prescriptive. The Lord's prayer in the verse invites Christians to forgive one another and remain in communion, even as Jesus forgives us and brings us into communion with the Father and the Spirit (see 14:23).One of the works of the Spirit is to make us one in Christ (1 Cor 12:13). To retain the sins of others is to exclude them from communion.

As disciples of Jesus, Christians in Africa are called to bear witness to the resurrection of Jesus by breaking the barriers of sin and division in their hearts and communities. Indeed, the real resurrection power often extolled in Pentecostal and charismatic circles lies here, not merely in the working of spectacular miracles, often without love in the heart (1 Cor 13: Rom 6:1–11).

CONCLUSION

The church's mission is grounded upon, and modeled after, Jesus' mission. Because Jesus did what only he could do because of his unique identity as the God-man, we are able to join God in his mission to bring him glory. As the Father sent the Son, so now the Son sends his disciples into the world, not to do what only the Son could do, but to carry forth the message of what the Son did. We are able to do this by the Spirit, whom the Son promised to send. Jesus was going back "to him who sent me," he said, but he would now "send" the Helper to us (16:5–11). The Spirit will continue the work of glorifying the Son and will help the church carry out the mission of God, grounded upon the Son's finished work (16:14–15). "As the Father has sent me, even so I am sending you.' And when he had said this, he breathed on them and said to them, 'Receive the Holy Spirit'" (20:21–22). The Gospel of John itself assists in this, as its purpose is that the readers, by believing, "may have life in his name" (20:31).

BIBLIOGRAPHY

Allen, Leslie C. *Ezekiel 20–48*. WBC 29. Dallas, TX: Word Books, 1990.
Beale, G. K. *A New Testament Biblical Theology*. Grand Rapids: Baker Academic, 2011.
———. *Handbook on the New Testament Use of the Old Testament: Exegesis and Interpretation*. Grand Rapids: Baker Academic, 2012.
Block, Daniel I. "The Book of Ezekiel." Chapters 25–48 in *NICOT*. Grand Rapids: Eerdmans, 1998.
Brodie, Thomas L. *The Gospel According to John: A Literary and Theological Commentary*. New York: Oxford University Press, 1993.
Brown, Jeannine K. "Creation's Renewal in the Gospel of John." *CBQ* 72, no. 2 (2010).
Brown, Raymond E. *The Gospel According to John (xiii–xxi): Introduction, Translation and Note*. Garden City: Doubleday & Company, 1970.
Bultmann, Rudolf, *The Gospel of John: A Commentary*. Philadelphia: Westminster, 1971.
Burge, Gary M. *The Anointed Community: The Holy Spirit in the Johannine Tradition*. Grand Rapids: Eerdmans, 1987.
———. *The NIV Application Commentary: John*. Grand Rapids: Zonderzan, 2000.
Carson, D. A. *The Gospel According to John*. Grand Rapids: Apollos, 1991.
Wallace, Daniel B. *Greek Grammar Beyond the Basics*. Grand Rapids: Zondervan, 1996.
George, Larry Darnell. *Reading the Tapestry: A Literary-Rhetorical Analysis of the Johannine Resurrection Narrative (John 20–21)*. New York: Peter Lang Publishing, 2000.
Harris, Murray J. "John." In *Exegetical Guide to the Greek New Testament*. Nashville: B&H, 2015.
Hays, Richard B. *Echoes of Scripture in the Gospels*. Waco, TX: Baylor University Press, 2016.
Hengel, Martin. "The Old Testament in the Fourth Gospel." *HBT* 12, no. 1 (1990).
Johnston, George. *The Spirit-Paraclete in the Gospel of John*. Cambridge: Cambridge University Press, 2005.
Keener, Craig S. *The Gospel of John: A Commentary*. Peabody, MA: Hendrickson, 2003.
Kittel, G. *Theological Dictionary of the New Testament*. Vol. 1. Translated by G. W. Bromiley. Grand Rapids: Eerdmans, 1964.

Köstenberger, Andreas J. *The Missions of Jesus and the Disciples according to the Fourth Gospel: With Implications for the Fourth Gospel's Purpose and the Mission of the Contemporary Church*. Grands Rapids: Eerdmans, 1998.

Köstenberger, Andreas J., et.al. *Going Deeper With New Testament Greek: An Intermediate Study of the Grammar and Syntax of the New Testament*. Tennessee: B&H Academic, 2016.

Litwa, David M. "Behold Adam: A Reading of John 19:5." *HBT* 32 (2010).

Manning, Gary T., Jr. "Echoes of a Prophet: The Use of Ezekiel in the Gospel of John and in Literature of the Second Temple Period." *JSNTSup270*. New York: T&T Clark, 2004.

Michaels, Ramsey J., and Gordon Fee, eds. *The Gospel of John*. NICNT 4. Grand Rapids: Eerdmans, 2010.

Morris, Leon. *The Gospel according to John: the English Text with Introduction, Exposition and Notes*. London: Eerdmans, 1971.

Moore, Anthony. *Signs of Salvation: The Theme of Creation in John's Gospel*. Cambridge: Jane Clarke & Co, 2013.

Okure, Teresa. *Johannine Approach to Mission: Contextual Study of John 4:1–42*. WUNT 2, Reihe 31. Tubingen: J.C.B Mohr and Paul Siebeck, 1984.

Peterson, Brian Neil. *John's Use of Ezekiel: Understanding the Unique Perspective of the Fourth Gospel*. Minneapolis: Fortress Press, 2015.

Rengstorf, Karl Heinrich. "ἀποστέλλω." *TDNT 1*.

Rossum, Joost Van. "The 'Johannine Pentecost': John 20:22 in Modern Exegesis and in Orthodox Theology." *STVTQ* 35, no. 2 (1991).

Schneiders, Sandra M. "The Raising of the New Temple: John 20.19–23 and Johannine Ecclesiology." *New Testament Studies* 52, no. 3 (2006).

Schnackenburg, Rudolf. *The Gospel According to St. John*. Vol. 3. NY: Crossroad, 1982.

Still, E. Coye, III. "Sent to Be Scarred: John 20:19–23." *Expository Times* 113, no. 6. (March 2002).

Stordalen, Terje. "Echoes of Eden: Genesis 2–3 and Symbolism of the Eden Garden." In *Biblical Hebrew Literature*. Leuven: Peters, 2000.

Thompson, Marianne Meye. "The Breath of Life: John 20:22–23 Once More." In *Holy Spirit and Christian Origins*. Grand Rapids: Eerdmans, 2004.

Tuppurainen, RikuPekka. "Jesus, the Spirit, and the Church: Succession in the Fourth Gospel." *JEPTA* 36, no. 1 (2016).

Wenham, Gordon J. *Genesis 1–15*. WBC 1. Waco, TX: Word Books, 1987.

Witherington, Ben, III. *John's Wisdom: A Commentary on the Fourth Gospel*, Louisville: Westminster John Knox, 1995.

Wright, N. T. *The Scriptures, the Cross, and the Power of God*. Great Britain: Society for Promoting Christian Knowledge, 2005.

Chapter 12

Identity and Mission in John 6

Mary Sylvia Nwachukwu, DLL

INTRODUCTION

This essay is dedicated to Sr. Prof. Teresa Okure, SHCJ, to the celebration of her academic maturity and remarkable contribution to the interpretation and propagation of the biblical message, especially the Gospel of Saint John. The choice of John 6 for this essay is inspired by the responsible devotion and attention which Sr. Teresa gave to the apostolate of the word of God. Her attraction to John's proclamation of the Word Incarnate that is seen, heard, felt, and touched reverberates in her writings and in her approach to scriptural interpretation. According to her, the interpretation of the Bible must not become an end in itself, it must become alive and active in the life of the Christian, in imitation of Jesus, the Word Incarnate.[1]

This interpretation of John 6 begins with a reference to the beautiful Hymn of the Pearl, which is a passage in the Apocryphal Acts of Thomas.[2] The hymn describes the exploits of a prince on a mission, having been sent by his father, the king, to Egypt to retrieve a pearl from an aquatic serpent. The prince embarked on the journey with full consciousness of his mission. The hymn further describes the distractions of the new environment in Egypt to which the prince succumbed. The text says,

---

1. Okure, "Alive and Active," 1–26.

2. The author of the hymn is unknown, but it was believed to have been composed by the first or second century Syriac gnostic Bardaisan from Edessa due to some parallels between his life and the content of the hymn.

> But in some way or another, they perceived that I was not of their country.
> So they mingled their deceit with me, and they made me eat their food.
> I forgot that I was a son of kings, and I served their king.
> And I forgot the pearl, on account of which my parents had sent me.
> Because of the burden of their exhortations, I fell into a deep sleep.

The "burden of their exhortations" made the prince forget his origin, his family, and his mission. However, upon reading a letter from his father, the prince recovered. He shook off his slumber; he woke from his sleep, and he remembered his mission.

> I remembered that I was a son of kings, I remembered the pearl,
> on account of which I was sent to Egypt.
> Then I began charming it, the formidable and hissing serpent.
> I caused it to slumber and to fall asleep,
> for my father's name I named over it . . . Then I snatched away the pearl,
> and I turned to go back to my father's house.
> And their filthy and unclean clothing, I stripped off and left it in their country.

Using an apocryphal text of Thomas to interpret John 6 might seem out of place. The decision to begin this interpretation in this way is defensible upon the intention to interpret John's text within the context of a shared perspective in a teaching of the early church. A very abridged version of this Hymn of the Pearl is found in Matthew 13:45–46 as the parable of the pearl of great price. It follows immediately after the parable of the hidden treasure, which has a similar theme. The parable does not appear in other Synoptic Gospels, even though it has close similarity with the story of the prodigal son in the Gospel of Luke. John, on the other hand, did not use parables to convey the good news of Jesus Christ, but the subject matter of the parable of the pearl is not lacking in his Gospel.[3] Certain aspects of this hymn are similar to the stories in John 6. Thematically, both John 6 and the Hymn of the Pearl have their stories arranged around three themes, which are: (1) the protagonist's relationship with his father, (2) his being sent on a mission, and (3) the burden of distracting exhortations experienced from those around him. With regard to the burden of exhortations, Jesus, more than the prince, remained focused in his mission. After the miracle of the loaves, the crowd wanted to make Jesus king, but he avoided them (John 6:14–15). He was also unrelenting when the crowd abandoned him because of his sayings that he came down from heaven (John 6:41) and that his flesh is real food (John 6:52). Nevertheless, in both texts of John 6 and the Hymn of the Pearl, the identity of the protagonists and the achievement of their mission are "my father" oriented, as the following texts show:

> For my father's name I named over it . . . Then I snatched away the pearl, and
> I turned to go back to my father's house. (Hymn of the Pearl)

---

3. The connection between identity and mission. The burdens of this world can so deeply affect identity or might even lead to the forgetfulness of the person's true origin that the achievement of mission becomes all the more impossible.

> Everything that the Father gives me will come to me, and anyone who comes to me I will never drive away; for I have come down from heaven, not to do my own will, but the will of him who sent me. And this is the will of him who sent me; that I should lose nothing of all that he has given me, but raise it up on the last day. This is indeed the will of my Father; that all who see the Son and believe in him may have eternal life; and I will raise them up on the last day." (John 6:37-40)

AIMS AND OBJECTIVES OF THE ESSAY

This study of John 6 has the aim of exposing the important connection between identity and mission. It addresses features of polarization in the lives of preachers of the Gospel, leaders of religious groups, and those dedicated to different kinds of ministries and apostolates, especially those which build the faith of the people. Identity is the distinguishing character or personality of an individual; it plays an important role in empowering individuals to realize their defined mission or calling in a commensurate manner.

Ministers and leaders of faith-based groups are respected as a people with strong spiritual connection to God; they are those trusted with the task of nurturing faith in the people and ensuring that their members live good Christian life in the society. Many parishes, churches, religious, and faith-based institutions have been driven through history on the wheels of the faith of their founders or leaders. The spiritual foundations of some institutions have also survived the test of time through a focus on the vision and mission that refused to yield to the temptations to compromise their values.

John 6 shows why it is important for ministers to understand themselves as Christians who are in close union with God. Our primary identity is a life and a worldview shaped by Jesus Christ, which in turn shapes the way we approach and exercise our professions as ministers, pastors, teachers, doctors, plumbers, or politicians. The text presents the figure of Jesus as a minister who experienced a growing pressure raised by the crowd who wanted to distract him from the objectives of his ministry, but Jesus exhibited a faithful devotion to service which is nurtured by his consciousness of his unity with the Father.

The Exposition and Interpretation of John 6

John 6 narrates one of the busiest events in the ministry of Jesus: a day packed with activities and long dialogues. The chapter encloses four large sections: Jesus feeds the five thousand (1-14); Jesus walks on the sea (15-21); Jesus gives the discourse of the Bread of Life (22-59); Jesus is rejected by the people, and his disciples abandon him, but Peter confesses belief in him (60-71). The interpretation of the sections will be limited to pointing out how the entire mission of Jesus is determined by his relationship with the Father and his identity as coming from the Father. It will therefore expose (a) the identity of Jesus, which grew out of his relationship with his Father, (b) the mission of Jesus, which derives from his Father's will, and (c) "the Burden of Exhortations" from the crowd.

The Identity of Jesus: Jesus and His Father

This section of the work discusses the identity, the understanding of the self, with which Jesus embraced his ministry. The interpretation hangs on the idea that identity determines a person's lifestyle and approach to ministry.

My attention is drawn to the two miraculous events in John 6:1–15 and 6:16–21, which precede the great discourse of the Bread of Life in 6:22–59. In fact, these two great signs[4] of the feeding of the five thousand in the desert and the walk on the sea function as narrative introduction to the identity of Jesus, which is expressed full-blown in the discourse in 6:22–59. The meaning of these two signs is appreciated in the context of the function of signs in the Gospel of John.

John does not have as many miracles as there are in the other Gospels, but the few that are recorded in this Fourth Gospel are interpreted by the author of the Gospel as signs that point directly to the divine identity of Jesus.[5] In order to make this association, John invokes Old Testament symbols and events that reveal God's extraordinary activity for Israel. For instance, the seven miracle stories recorded in John are given as signs not of the imminence of the coming of God's kingdom as the Synoptic Gospels present them, but signs of the presence of the power of God in Jesus. These are: the turning of water into wine at a marriage feast in Cana (John 3); the healing of the official's son who was at the point of death (John 4); the healing of a man at the sheep-gate pool (John 5); the feeding of the five thousand in the wilderness (John 6); the walking on water (John 6); the healing of the man born blind (John 9); and, finally, the raising of Lazarus (John 11). Each of these stories is used as an introduction to a discourse concerning the significance of Jesus as God who displays divine power in people's lives. In fact, the connection of the two events of the feeding of Israel in the desert and Jesus' feeding of the five thousand is underscored in different part of the discourse in John 6:

> "Our ancestors ate the manna in the wilderness; as it is written, 'He gave them bread from heaven to eat.'" Then Jesus said to them, "Very truly, I tell you, it was not Moses who gave you the bread from heaven, but it is my Father who gives you the true bread from heaven." (vv. 31–32)

---

4. Signs (sēmeiōn) in the Gospel of John are acts through which the glory (doxa) of Jesus was revealed and which inspired belief. Cf. Moloney, *The Gospel of John*, 69, 198–199.

5. Cf. Culpepper, *The Gospel and Letters of John*, 21.

Again, we hear:

> I am the bread of life. Your ancestors ate the manna in the wilderness, and they died. This is the bread that comes down from heaven, so that one may eat of it and not die. I am the living bread that came down from heaven. Whoever eats of this bread will live forever; and the bread that I will give for the life of the world is my flesh. (vv. 48–51)

The goal of this connection is to set Jesus in the context of salvation history and to highlight the supernatural aspect of the event, which is that in accomplishing this divine action, Jesus gives himself as real food for eternal life.[6] In fact, an outstanding theological basis of John's Gospel is its correspondence with the Old Testament conceptual world and that Jesus' activities matched the fabric of Old Testament information regarding the coming Messiah.[7]

The entire purpose of the Gospel of John is more christological than theological; it is to prove that Jesus is the Son of God and that he came from the Father.[8] The Jews already believed in God and in his mighty acts in history. The issue was whether they would believe that Jesus was the Messiah and Son of God. When the crowd asked him what they must do to do the works of God (John 6:28), Jesus did not direct their attention to the commandments and the law; he told them that the work of God is to believe in the one God had sent (John 6:29). The Evangelist himself says that the Gospel was written to encourage the reader to encounter Jesus, and from that encounter make a personal decision about Jesus' identity as Messiah and Son of God (John 20:30–31).[9] The discussion of the relationship of Jesus to the Father takes center stage in the Gospel.[10] God is described as the Father of the Son (John 5:17–23) and as the one who sent Jesus into the world (John 5:37).

In John 6, therefore, Jesus makes constant appeal to his heavenly origin, to his identity as coming from the Father; he makes appeal to the Father's will and to his God-given mission. In a particular way, he addresses God as Father.[11] His overarching appeal to God as Father,[12] together with the emphasis that he comes from the

---

6. A connection with the early church's celebration of the Eucharist is made here. Cf. Moloney, *Signs and Shadows*, 35.

7. Cf. Köstenberger, *Encountering John*, 39.

8. Köstenberger, *Encountering John*, 39.

9. Cf. Okure, "For Their Sake ," 244; Okure, *Johannine Approach to Mission*, 39–40.

10. Köstenberger, *Encountering John*, 39.

11. Among the Gospels, John stands out more than the Synoptic Gospels in portraying the identity of Jesus in majestic terms. In contrast to those in other early Christian writings. John says that Jesus is the Word of God; He is God and the creator of the universe. In a very unique and singular manner, John often speaks of Jesus' divine origin, while the Synoptic Gospels associate him with God through personages from Israel's past history.

12. Found 51x in John: 2:16; 5:17, 19, 43; 6:32, 40; 8:19, 38, 49, 54; 10:17, 18, 25, 29, 37; 11:41; 12:26, 27, 50; 13:1; 14:2, 7, 15, 20, 21, 23, 24, 31; 15:1, 8, 10, 15, 16, 23, 24, 26; 16:3, 10, 15, 17, 23, 25, 26, 27, 28, 32; 17:1, 5, 11, 21, 24, 25; 18:11; 20:17, 21. The expression is also found 33x in the Synoptic Gospels,

Father (his divine origin) and his insistence that his mission derives from the Father all give a picture of his ministry as "Father and heaven" centered. It is to these aspects of his connection to the Father that one must relate his ultimate claim that he is the "I Am." The phrase "I am" is the covenant name of Israel's God, which was revealed to Moses at the burning bush (Exod 3:14). This is Jesus' decisive claim to oneness or unity with God.

The statement in John 6:35 "*I am* the bread of life" is the first of the "I am" statements in John's Gospel. The statement is repeated in John 6:41 and 48, and even made more emphatic in v. 51: "*I am* the living bread." This must be understood in the context of similar statements in the Gospel of John. In other parts of the Gospel of John, Jesus continued to make a similar claim: "*I am* the light of the world" (8:12; 9:5); "*I am* the gate for the sheep" (10:7, 9); "*I am* the good shepherd who lays down his life for his sheep" (10:11, 14); "*I am* the resurrection and the life" (11:25); "*I am* the way, the truth, and the life" (14:6); "*I am* the true vine" (15:1, 5). The ultimate expression of the "I am" sayings is found at the beginning of the passion narrative in John 18. When the soldiers came to arrest him at the Kidron Valley, Jesus said, "*I am* he" (18:5). All these "I am" statements are expressions of Jesus' claim to oneness with God.

THE MISSION OF JESUS: JESUS AND HIS FATHER'S WILL

In the sixth chapter of the Gospel, Jesus defends his unity with the Father through saying that he came not to do his own will. He affirms by means of different expressions that his identity, his teaching, and the works that he did derive from the Father. These expressions point to his harmony of will with the Father in perfect obedience. They include statements about his being sent by the Father or coming from the Father,[13] or about the tasks from the Father,[14] his teaching from the Father,[15] and his intent to do not his will but the will of the Father who sent him.[16] It is the Father's will that Jesus does not lose any one whom the Father had given him (John 6:39). In fact, at the end of his ministry, Jesus rejoiced that he protected those whom the Father had given him; he guarded them and not one of them was lost (John 17:12; 18:9).

Moreover, Jesus' unity with the Father is further described in his and the Father's analogous live-giving activities. For this reason, Jesus' feeding of the five thousand corresponds to the biblical image of God feeding his hungry and needy people with bread, and Jesus is the bread of life which has come down from heaven.[17] In John 5:17–27 also, the activities of God the Father have analogy in the activities of the Son.

Acts of the Apostles, and the book of Revelation (Matthew 19x; Mark 2x; Luke 8x; Acts 1x; Rev 3x).

13. Cf. John 5:43; 6:44; 7:16, 28–29; 8:16, 18, 42; 14:24.
14. John 5:36–37; 17:4.
15. John 7:16; 8:28; 12:50.
16. John 5:30, 38–40; 6:37.
17. John 6:32, 51, 57–58.

When Jesus claimed that he is working just as his Father is working (5:17), the Jews accused him of making himself equal to God (5:18). His ultimate proof of his unity with the Father is argued out in John 10:37–38:

> If I am not doing the works of my Father, then do not believe me. But if I do them, even though you do not believe me, believe the works, so that you may know and understand that he Father is in me and I am in the Father.

Jesus fed the crowd that followed him, just as his Father fed his people in the desert. He loves them (13:1) just as the Father loves them (15:9) and shows special concern to preserve those his Father has given him (6:37, 44). In John 6, especially, the mission of Jesus is the same with the works of his Father.

The Burden of Their Exhortations

In the Hymn of the Pearl, the prince succumbed to "the burden of their exhortations," and this refers to how the natives coerced him into rejecting his identity. They convinced him to live like them in total forgetfulness of his mission. It also speaks of the pressure which people in his new environment exerted on him in regard to the kind of lifestyle they projected he should adopt and how they expected him to behave. Like the prince also, Jesus experienced the "burden of their exhortations" from the crowd. However, Jesus did not give in to their pressure. His response to "the burden of their exhortations" is presented here as proof that mission is sustained by a conscious and responsible focus on identity.

Beginning in John 6:22, the crowd that witnessed the multiplied loaves followed Jesus to Capernaum because they wanted more bread. While the disciples depict lack of understanding, the crowd is shown to always misunderstand the spiritual meaning of events. By searching for Jesus all night, they seemed to have an impressive interest in Jesus, but it was only for the food he had given them. Their response to the multiplied loaves is inspired by the text of Deuteronomy 18:15–18, which is a prophecy about a future Mosaic figure whose witness Jesus had affirmed in John 5:45. "This is indeed the prophet who is to come into the world" (John 6:14). Deuteronomy 18:15–18 is also associated with the Jewish hope expressed in 2 Baruch 29:9 about a second gift of manna that would mark the beginning of the messianic era.[18] Given this understanding from 2 Baruch 29:9, the crowd interpreted the multiplication of the loaves politically and wanted to impose this wrong interpretation of ministry on Jesus. The weight of the pressure of their expectation is indicated by the verb *harpazein* ("to take by force"), which shows that they were about to force their will on Jesus. However, unlike the prince of the Hymn of the Pearl, Jesus was not seduced by the pressure of the crowd. He did not concede to their request for a miraculous sign, but he pointed

---

18. Moloney notes that the link made between the gift of the manna and the messianic era in 2 Baruch is roughly contemporaneous with the Fourth Gospel. Cf. *The Gospel of John*, 99–200.

to the significance of the works he had already done.[19] When he realized the distraction this meant from the goal of his mission, he withdrew from them. Withdrawal is a very important reaction to persons or situations that pose a great threat to the goal of ministry. In fact, the text shows that Jesus exhibited a totally converged loyalty to his Father and focus on his mission.

Jesus is further confronted with another pressure from the Jews and some of his disciples who showed an attitude of distrust to Jesus. They complained about certain theological statements by which Jesus described himself. They had asked Jesus for a sign that he was sent from God and that his work is from God (John 6:30). In answer to this request, Jesus identified himself as the sign from God. He claimed to be the true bread which came them from heaven and which gives life to the world (John 6:33), and that his flesh is real food (John 6:55). The Jews distrusted him. John 6:43 gives the verb that expressed their disapproval (*engoguzeiv*, "to murmur"). This verb is used in the LXX for the murmuring of Israel when they lacked bread in the desert. This verb gives theological weight to the Jews' and disciples' complaint about Jesus' claims. His claim about coming down from heaven was dismissed on the basis of their local knowledge of his parentage (John 6:42), but the claim that his flesh is real food was understood literally, and this stimulated their rejection and withdrawal. Jesus was faced with the danger of losing his followers (John 6:60–66), but he was not deterred by it. So he asked "the Twelve" whether they would also walk away (John 6:67).[20]

CONCLUSION

The activities of Jesus, as John 6 describes them, have shown that ministers, even the most successful and faithful ones, could suffer the "burden of their exhortations." Twice, in John 6:15 and 6:61, Jesus withstood the pressures that would have distracted him from the will of his father. Jesus offers an example to the ideal of faithfulness which every minister must exhibit for identity to correspond with mission.

In the life of a minister, pressures might come from at least five sources. The first source is the admirers, close friends, and associates of the minister who might lead the minister to adopt an interpretation of his mission that deviates from what it is. The second source of pressure might come from fear in the minister of being rejected by an audience that would not be comfortable with a sincere preaching of the gospel that questions the way of life of the audience. The fear of losing the affection or trust of the audience for any reason might cause the minister to compromise the integrity of the gospel in favor of popular theology and expectations. An instance in the life of Saint Paul is recorded in 2 Timothy 4:9, where he mentions the betrayal and abandonment of a trusted co-worker, Demas, as one of the great burdens he bore.

---

19. Köstenberger, *Encountering John*, 101.

20. At this point, the mention of the Twelve for the first time in the chapter seems to be a guise to dissociate them from the crowd and the disciples.

Usually, ministers grieve over the loss of a close co-worker as one grieves for the dead, and some would compromise in order not to suffer such a loss. A third very common pressure for ministers comes from finances: "Where can we find the money to feed all these people?" In our own context, it is money to build structures instead of the faith of the people. It is unfortunate that sometimes the pressure of money is necessitated by reasons outside of the demands of the ministry. A fourth form of pressure comes from the lifestyle of the minister. Some ministers commit the heresy of work to the extent that they work at superhuman speed. They want to impress and meet the needs of everyone; they attend every event without rest and without prayer. John 6 records one of Jesus' busiest days. In spite of the thousands of people whom he fed and spoke to, he also withdrew to have a quiet moment with God in prayer. The final type of burden for a minister is the pressure to be like another successful minister. This problem might appear small but it is the gravest of all pressures. To want to be like another person is an obvious sign of the loss of one's identity. There cannot be mission where there is no identity. Jesus is the one who has given proof of what ministry is. He is the model every minister should try to emulate.

Ministers who have succumbed to any of or some of the above-mentioned pressures have turned their ministries into businesses. Some have become political figures, and others have yielded to pressure to accommodate the gospel to popular expectations. Ministers with polarized interests are those who seem to be very popular and well-established in their ministry, but who are evidently pursuing goals that contradict their defined mission. The image of Jesus which the sixth chapter of John presents is invoked in this interpretation as a strong recommendation for overcoming polarization in ministry. The minster might not realize the instance of the pressure or even the danger it represents if the minister is not in constant communion with God as Jesus was.

BIBLIOGRAPHY

Culpepper, R. A. *The Gospel and Letters of John*. Nashville: Abingdon Press, 1998.
Köstenberger, Andreas J. *Encountering John*. Grand Rapids: Baker Books, 1999.
Moloney, Francis J. *The Gospel of John*. Sacra Pagina Series 4. Collegeville, MN: The Liturgical Press, 1998.
Moloney, Francis J. *Signs and Shadows: Reading John 5–12*. Minneapolis: Fortress Press, 1998.
Okure, Teresa. *The Johannine Approach to Mission: A Contextual Study of John 4:1–42*. WUNT 2/31. Tübingen: Mohr, 1988.
———. "Alive and Active: God's Word in the Nigerian Context." In *Alive and Active: Images of the Word of God in the Bible*, 1–26. Edited by Teresa Okure et al. Port Harcourt: CABAN Publication, 2012.
———. "'For Their Sake I Consecrate Myself' (John 17:19): John 17 as Index to the Consecrated Life." In *Consecration and Vows in the Bible*. Edited by Bernard Ukwuegbu et al. Port Harcourt: CABAN Publication, 2016.

Chapter 13

Women and Religious Tolerance in Children in Nigeria in Light of John 13:33–35

OYERONKE OLADEMO

INTRODUCTION

Nigeria is a multireligious society marked with multilayered dimensions of cultural differences, including religious diversity. Nigeria's 1999 constitution (amended) prohibits the federal and state governments from adopting a state religion, bars religious discrimination, and provides individual citizens freedom to choose, practice, propagate, or change their religion.[1] However, the reality concerning interreligious relations in contemporary Nigeria is fraught with crises and tension. Consequently, by December 2, 2020, in accordance with the International Religious Freedom Act of 1998, as amended, the American secretary of state designated Nigeria a "country of particular concern" for having engaged in or tolerated particularly severe violations of religious freedom.[2] Nigeria has experienced religious crises of diverse dimensions and category, mainly between adherents of Christianity and Islam. The challenge of religious crises in Nigeria has been severally investigated over the years by scholars who proffered different explanations for it. These include the desire for self-preservation, mistrust, misinterpretation of scriptures, and the exclusiveness claim of each Abrahamic religion (Christianity, Islam, and Judaism) as the sole source of salvation.[3]

---

1. Article 38 of the 1999 Nigerian Constitution.
2. US Department of State 2020 Report on International Religious Freedom: Nigeria (Office of International Religious Freedom, May 12, 2021).
3. Akin-Otiko, "An Afrocentric Theory of Ethno-Religious Crisis," 52–60.

Yet religion is one of the most important agents of socialization and social control, especially religious socialization at childhood. Indeed, it has been submitted that parental religious participation is the most influential part of religious socialization.[4] Religious socialization has been defined as the process through which individuals learn and internalize religious beliefs, attitudes, values, and behaviors.[5] The foundation for a sound religious socialization is located at the level of primary socialization in the first five years of life, and the earliest primary caretaker of a child is more likely than not to be the mother. Thus, this paper proposes that women's role in children's socialization from the Christian perspective is a dependable avenue to foster religious tolerance premised on love and religious understanding. The teachings of Jesus as recorded by the Gospel of John 13: 33–35 will be examined to explicate the Christian teaching on love. Further, the theories of active tolerance and Schaffer's theory of early socialization will be utilized to examine issues in this paper. Also, the hermeneutic and feminist methods will guide the discourse in the paper. It is a qualitative design work, hence, key informant interviews (KII) and a Focused Group Discussion (FGD) will be conducted with a purposely sampled population in the Roman Catholic Church. Data will be analyzed descriptively and discussed along with the theories identified above.

Theoretical Framework

Active Tolerance

Tolerance is a crucial ingredient for understanding, especially in pluralistic societies. Tolerance could be passive, which involves suppression of interference with the disapproved conduct of others. Conversely, active tolerance manifests as giving approval to the capacity of others to engage in disapproved practices; an example is: "I disapprove of what you say, but I will defend to the death your right to say it."[6] Again, tolerance could refer to the "willingness to put up with those things one rejects."[7] It is a twofold concept in which there is an initial position of dislike/disapproval which makes tolerance different from ignorance, indifference, and apathy[8]. Tolerance involves intentional self-restraint which is not based on fear or compulsion.[9] Psychologically, passivity is less demanding and risky than active tolerance, while philosophically, taking no action against what one disapproves of is easier than a positive defense of it.[10] Tolerance

---

4. Schaffer, *Early Socialization*, 22.
5. Bengtson et al., "How Families Still Matter," 6.
6. Hall, *The Friends of Voltaire*, 2011.
7. Sullivan, Piereson, and Marcus, "An Alternative Conceptualization," 781–94.
8. Cohen, "What Toleration," 115.
9. Verkuyten and Yogeeswaran, "The Social Psychology of Intergroup Toleration," 72–96.
10. *Tolerance in Conflict*, 2013.

implies not a lack of commitment to one's own beliefs and way of life but requires one to put up with the religious, cultural, and ideological beliefs and practices of others.[11]

Early Socialization

Schaffers shows that social interaction in the earliest days and years of life is of central importance to human development.[12] He examined parental control techniques that are implemented in a non-imposing manner but which involve mutual influence. In this regard, parents are sensitive to their child's varying moods and state of being.[13] The child is by no means passive during the process of socialization; thus, both parent and child play active roles in determining the nature and course of their interaction, leading to a bidirectional influence. Children learn from birth in the context of loving and secure relationships and develop in individual ways at varying rates. They learn through active, purposive play with people, objects, ideas, and events that engage and involve them, sometimes for sustained periods.[14]

These two theories will be utilized in this paper to explicate how women serve as agents of socialization of children, thereby entrenching the teachings of Jesus Christ as recorded in John 13: 33–35 to guarantee love and understanding in Nigeria.

JOHN 13:33–35 — A HERMENEUTIC APPRAISAL (RSV VERSION)

The Gospel of John lays emphasis on a theological interpretation of Jesus' life and ministry toward the ultimate goal of human salvation.[15] The Gospel presents the divinity of Jesus in simple language. Some distinguishing features between the Gospel of John and the Synoptic Gospels include the fact that John locates much of Jesus' ministry in Judea and shows Jesus discussing at length theological matters. Scholars submit that John the Apostle wrote the Gospel, though debates on authorship continue inconclusively.[16] The Gospel is dated between 80 and 110 CE. The Gospel of John is divided into four sections:

a. The Prologue (1:1–18)

b. Book of Signs (1:19–12:50)

c. Book of glory (13:1–20–31)

d. Conclusion (20:30–21:25)

11. King, *Toleration*, 2012.
12. Schaffer, *Early Socialization*, 1995.
13. Handel, *Social Problems and Childhood Socialization*, 2006.
14. Wheeler and Connor, *Parents, Early Years and Learning*, 2009.
15. Lindars, Edwards, and Court, *Johannine Literature*, 80.
16. Oladotun, "The Authorship of John's Gospel."

John 13:33–35 is located within Jesus' farewell discourse, which is elaborated further in John 15:12–17.[17] Verse 33 says "Little children, I am with you only a little longer. You will look for me; and as I said to the Jews so now I say to you, 'Where I am going, you cannot come.'"

In this verse, and in form of an appraisal, "little children" connotes tenderness, compassion, and loving care, just as a parent would address his/her child. Jesus' earlier pronouncement to the Jews to which he referred in this verse was marked by condemnation for the Jews as opposed to encouragement for the disciples here.[18] Verse 34 says, "I give you a new commandment, that you love one another. Just as I have loved you, you also should love one another." This commandment is really not new as it already appears in Leviticus 19:18 and 34. However, "new" (*kainos*) here refers to the new order by Jesus' redemptive provisions.[19] As rightly noted, the newness of this command springs from the eschatological reality of Christ's redemption, which is an eternal reality and holds its people in the eternal order. Thus, this is a new command because this command is premised on Jesus Christ as the model of this love. Also, it focuses on the Christian community as a testimony to a larger world, inaugurates a new covenant which is openended, and a loving action rather than a feeling, because this action-love is a gift from Christ. This love will be a convincing demonstration that the disciples had partaken of Jesus' spirit and purpose by loving as Jesus did with no reservation or limit.

In addition verse 35 says, "By this everyone will know that you are my disciples, if you have love for one another." Love (*agape*) in this verse is a testimony to the Christian testimony in the world. Consequently, Christian service in any form or intensity always involves sacrificial love (1 Cor 13). However, to operate in *agape* love, Christians need to rely on God's grace and act lovingly toward all around them. Borchert argues that this command to love is not to be interpreted "exclusively as my little group, as it was by many Jews, but to be understood as breathtakingly explosive of old relationships and old patterns."[20] The goal is to proclaim Jesus to the world through apparent love with action.

Religious Tolerance in the Roman Catholic Church

The Roman Catholic Church has a rich heritage in the area of ecumenism and interreligious understanding. This church recognizes that all of humanity is equal and created in the image and likeness of God. Further, this church asserts that there is good in other religious traditions and believes that the Roman Catholic Church has been entrusted with the fullness of faith and represents in the closest manner the authentic

---

17. Beasley and Murray, *Word Biblical Commentary—John*, 247.
18. Burge, *Commentary*, 376.
19. Lincoln, *Black's Commentary*, 2005.
20. Borchet, *Commentary—John 12–21*, 99.

teaching of Jesus Christ as handed down from the apostles. Relevant church documents, including *Dei Verbum*, the 1993 PBC document *The Interpretation of the Bible in the Church*, and the 2010 *Verbum Domini* of Pope Benedict XVI, expound different dimensions of how the word of God remains central to Christian relationship with God and testimony to the world.

Of specific relevance to the focus of this paper is chapter six of *Dei Verbum*, which discusses the sacred Scripture in the life of the church and asserts that God's love must be shared with all. Also relevant is *Verbum Domini*, which consist of three parts: *Verbum Dei* (the word of God), *Verbum in Ecclesia* (the word in the church), and *Verbum Mundo* (the word to the world). The third part, *Verbum Mundo*, focuses on mission and evangelism and submits that the word of God which Christians receive is meant to be shared with everyone. It stated further that religious education is an essential part of the proclamation of the church, which consist of dialogue and cooperation with followers of other religious traditions but should follow lines established in the second Vatican Council's declaration *Nostra Aetate* and the subsequent *Magisterium*.

Women as Agents of Socialization-Religious Tolerance

Interreligious or interfaith relations have been and continue to be a viable option that Nigeria has keyed into with efforts across religious bodies, interfaith groups, and government establishments; examples include Nigerian Interreligious Council (NIREC), KAICIID Dialogue Centre, Interfaith Mediation Centre, Women's Interfaith Council, and Muslim-Christian Dialogue Forum. Primarily, interreligious ventures target adults and are not aimed at proselytization, apologetics, or conversion; rather, they focus on promoting understanding and respect among different religious groups. However, the focus in this paper is on women in the upbringing of children, proposing the position that religious tolerance and understanding would be easier and more effective as an integral aspect of the process of socialization of children by mothers. Women's role as mothers is thus central to the possibility of consciously instilling love for others in the socialization process.

Friedan[21] identifies three manifestations of feminism: (1) as an academic method, feminism signifies a definite transition from androcentric to androgynous models of humanity; (2) as a value system and a social vision, feminism views sexism and patriarchy as immoral, hence the need to foster alternative social arrangements that ensure equity; and (3) as an insider's discourse, feminism is an attempt to move from the prescriptive to the descriptive, so that women's lives become the textbook for the roles expected of them in society. This paper countenances the third manifestation of feminism as listed above by prioritizing the descriptive aspect of women's roles in children's socialization toward religious tolerance through Christian love. This stance

---

21. Friedan, *Feminine Mystique*, 87.

is premised on: (1) the need to pursue effective interfaith relationships toward mutual coexistence to lay strong emphasis on interpersonal relations, as well as to put in place programs that will positively promote such relationships; (2) in all religions, there are shared aims and common concerns such as fighting injustice, oppression, and poverty, and the early socialization of children to appreciate these common grounds will foster religious understanding in children as they grow. As mothers, women are agents of socialization, and they establish foundational values in children's early years, especially ages one through five, which is the basis of personality development in subsequent years of adulthood. The way a child develops can be largely attributed to the role that the parents and caregivers play in their lives. Children thrive when they have a secure and friendly relationship with people around them. Studies confirm that early childhood, when the synaptic brain functions are still developing, is the period in which, developmentally, a child learns a lot from his/her surroundings, and this significantly impacts their growing years.[22] The mother plays multiple roles in a child's development as the teacher in many aspects, including social, emotional, cognitive, and physical. Mothers teach by instruction and behavior; hence, it is important for mothers to have the knowledge of religious understanding in the parlance of active tolerance. Illustratively, the action of each mother at work, in the market, or in church should reflect the love of Christ, which is non-discriminatory. Consequently, though Christian women do not subscribe to the tenets of other religions, in love, they are expected to respect the right of others to hold different religious convictions from theirs. Once this is well appreciated by mothers, the transmission of the same to the children through word of instruction and conduct becomes easy.

Women in the Catholic Church and Children Socialization

I interviewed fifteen women from two parishes of the Roman Catholic Church in Ilorin, Kwara State, Nigeria, on their roles in bringing up children as mothers and members of the church. It came to the fore during the sessions that non-discrimination is a value inherent in the women's perception as Roman Catholics. Each of the women gave me examples to buttress this. For instance, Mrs. Sarah Ajiboye explained that the Roman Catholic Church employs teachers, workers, and contractors in their schools and church based on merit and integrity rather than insisting that such workers be members of the Roman Catholic Church, as is true of some Christian denominations. She explained further that students admitted into private schools established by the Roman Catholic Church also cut across religious affiliations. In addition, Mrs. Victoria Amodu explained that since mothers were socialized to love and not discriminate against people of other religions in the Roman Catholic Church, they pass this same on to the children. Mrs. Veronica Olori submitted that mothers teach their children

---

22. Britto, "How Children's Brain Develop-New Insight."

both by words and action, hence children observe their mother's conduct and emulate it. The women agreed that Jesus' instruction to all Christians to love themselves and use this as a testimony to the world is the premise for religious understanding across the board among Christian mothers. My respondents of eight women of the Fate Parish, Ilorin, at the Focused Group Discussion (FGD) agreed that the mother's role in early socialization of the children is crucial. Consciously teaching religious tolerance as a value during childhood was agreed upon as a pointer toward Christian love. Mrs. Elizabeth Adeyeye averred that if this component is taught to children between the ages of one to five years, it will significantly ameliorate religious crises in adulthood, as is the case in contemporary Nigeria.

CONCLUSION

An attempt has been made to explicate the role of mothers as crucial agents of socialization for religious tolerance by focusing on Christian love, using John 13:33–35 as a case study. The need for religious tolerance in Nigeria was justified by evidence of religious crises and the international label of Nigeria as a "country of concern." The paper employed two theories to examine the emanating issues: active tolerance and early socialization theories. A hermeneutic appraisal of John 13:33–35 was done to highlight key words in the passage for understanding. The paper noted that the Catholic Church has a rich heritage in matters of ecumenism and interreligious dialogue and understanding. Discussions of relevant sections of church documents were undertaken, especially the *Verbum Mundo*. The paper emphasized the crucial role of mothers in child socialization through their conduct and word of instruction. The paper also advocated for the integration of topics on religious tolerance and understanding into the Sunday School Manual of the Catholic Church, as well as the incorporation of fun-filled ventures such as role play, sketching, and other activities.

BIBLIOGRAPHY

Adelman, Levi Maykel Verkuyten, and Kumar Yogeeswaran. "Distinguishing Active and Passive Outgroup Tolerance: Understanding Its Prevalence and the Role of Moral Concern." *Political Psychology* 43, no. 4 (2022) 731–50. Available at https://doi.org/10.1111/pops.12790.

Akin-Otiko, Akinmayowa. "An Afrocentric Theory of Ethno-Religious Crisis: Way to National Unity in Nigeria." In *Readings in Peace & Conflict*. Edited by Elias Suleiman Bogoro, Matt Meyer, and Nathaniel D. Danjibo. Ibadan, Nigeria: Society for Peace Studies and Practice, 2019.

Beasley-Murray, R. George. *Word Biblical Commentary-John*. Vol. 36. WACO, TX: Word Books, 1987.

Bengtson, Vern, et al. "How Families Still Matter: A Longitudinal Study of Youth in Two Generations." *Contemporary Sociology* 32, no. 6 (2003) 695–96.

Bevans, B. Stephen. *Models of Contextual Theology: Faith and Cultures*. New York: Orbis Books, 2012.

Borchet, L. Gerald. *The New American Commentary—John 12–21*. Vol. 25B. Nashville: Broadman & Holman, 2002.

Britto, Pia. "How Children's Brains Develop—New Insights." Unicef Connect. May 14, 2014. https://blogs.unicef.org/blog/how-childrens-brains-develop-new-insights/.

Burge, M. Gary. *The NIV Application Commentary: From Biblical Text To Contemporary Life*. Grand Rapids: Zondervan, 2000.

Cohen, A. "What Toleration Is." *Ethics* 115, no. 1 (2004) 68–95.

Catholic Diocese of Ilorin. *Growing in Faith: Liturgical Manual for Children-Guide for Parents and Teachers*. 2020.

———. *Growing in Faith: A Catechetical Bulletin for Children*. 2020.

———. *Growing in Faith: A Catechetical Bulletin for Children*. 2021.

Cheetham, David, Douglas Pratt, and David Thomas, eds. *Understanding Interreligious Relations*. Oxford: Oxford University Press, 2013.

Fabella, Virginia, and Mercy A. Oduyoye, eds. *With Passion and Compassion: Third World Women Doing Theology*. Eugene, OR: Wipf & Stock, 2006.

Fredrikson, L. Roger. *The Preacher's Commentary—John*. Nashville: Thomas Nelson, 1985.

Friedan, B. *Feminine Mystique*. New York: Dell Publishers, 1983.

Frost, R. *Toleration in Conflict: Past and Present*. Cambridge: Cambridge University Press, 2013.

Gnanadason, Aruna. *With Courage and Compassion: Women and the Ecumeniccal Movement*. Minneapolis: Fortress, 2020.

Hall, Evelyn Beatrice. *The Friends of Voltaire*. France: Smith Elder & Company, 1906.

Handel, Gerald, ed. *Social Problems and Childhood Socialization: Social Issues*. Piscataway, NJ: Transaction Publishers, 2006.

Kalu, Hyacinth. *Principles and Practicalities of Interfaith Relationships in Nigeria*. Bloomington: iUniverse, 2011.

King, P. *Toleration*. London: Routledge, 2012.

Knitter, Paul. "Is the Pluralistic Model a Western Imposition? A Response to Five Voices." In *The Myth of Religious Superiority: A Multi-Faith Exploration*. Edited by Paul Knitter. Maryknoll, NY: Orbis Books, 2005.

Lincoln, T. Andrew. *Black's New Testament Commentary: The Gospel According to John*. London: Continuum, 2005.

Lindars, Barnabas, Ruth Edwards, and John M. Court. *The Johannine Literature*. Sheffield: Academic Press LTD, 2000.

Madges, William, and Michael J. Daley, eds. *Vatican II: 50 Personal Stories*. New York: Orbis Books, 2003.

Mann, Rafi, and Oleksandr Khyzhniak. "Active Tolerance as a Collective Project: Global and Local Dimensions." *IOSR Journal of Humanities and Social Science* 22, no. (2017) 13–25.

Nyiam, Tony. *Inter-religious Understanding as Meaningful Basis for Religious Tolerance*. Lagos, Nigeria: Pumark Nigeria Ltd., 2002.

Ryle, J. C. *The Duties of Parents: The Perfect Guide to Raising Children*. CreateSpace, 2014.

Schaffer, Rudolph. *Early Socialization*. Leicester: British Psychological Society, 1995.

Schreiter, J. Robert. *Constructing Local Theologies*. New York: Orbis Books, 1985.

Sheffer, E. D. "Summary of *Dei Verbum*—Dogmatic Constitution on Divine Revelation." 2018. www.d2y1pz2y630308.cloudfront.net/21056/documents/2018/9/LT%20Times%20-%20Summary%20of%20Dei%20Verbum%20_%20Divine%20Revelation.pdf.

Sullivan, J. L., J. Piereson, and G. E. Marcus. "An Alternative Conceptualization of Political Tolerance: Illusory Increase, 1950s–1970s." *American Political Science Review* 73, no. 3 (1979) 781–94.

"Summary of the Post-Synodal Apostolic Exhortation Verbum Domini by the Commission for Doctrine, Canadian Conference of Catholic Bishops." Canadian Conference of Catholic Bishops. November 17, 2010. www.cccb.ca/document/summary-of-the-post-synodal-apostolic-exhortation-verbum-domini-by-the-commission-for-doctrine-canadian-conference-of-catholic-bishops/.

Verkuyten, M., and K. Yogeeswaran. "The Social Psychology of Intergroup Toleration: A Roadmap for Theory and Research." *Personality and Social Psychology Review* 21, no. 1 (2017) 72–96.

CHAPTER 14

Receiving and Sharing Johannine Jesus' Abundant Life in the African Context

(John 10:10)

AGNES SOLOMON, SHCJ

INTRODUCTION

It is generally agreed by scholars that the Gospel according to John could be divided into three parts:

> A clearly designed theological prologue (1:1–18), followed by two long sections. The first (1:19–12:50) is devoted to the public life of Jesus until he withdraws from the crowds (12:36b)—a section John closes solemnly with concluding reflections (12:37–50). The second (13:1–20:31) is devoted entirely to Jesus' presence with his 'own' disciples, leading up to his glorification through the hour of the cross, resurrection and return to the Father. The final chapter (21) is seemingly an addendum.[1]

This paper is in honor of Rev. Sr. Prof. Teresa Okure, SHCJ, a renowned biblical scholar and a New Testament professor. She has lived her life, while giving life to others, referring to this passage (10:10) in what she does, writes, and speaks. She wrote her doctoral dissertation on John and titled it "The Johannine Approach to Mission: A Contextual Study of John 4:1–42." In the work, Teresa exposed the Jesus who gives life to the full. She says that "John 4:1–42 holds the key for understanding John's theology of and

---

1. In "Johannine Theology," Moloney shows how John situates its tenth chapter as part of the overall structure in the public life of Jesus. See Brown et al., *The New Jerome Biblical Commentary*, 1417–1426.

method in mission."² She goes further to emphasize that Jesus' respect for the woman of Samaria and the other Samaritans is seen as a challenge to all missionaries (the church) to respect people's realities, cultures, and empower them to become evangelizers/missionaries in turn. Teresa refers to her commentary on John as that which makes one feel at home in the Gospel and helps one appropriate "its life-giving message."³

John portrays Jesus as the realization of Old Testament hopes. He is the Good Shepherd (10:1–16) as opposed to the bad ones God would replace (Ezek 34). John makes Jesus the feast celebrated by the Jews in the Old Testament (Tabernacle/Booths, John 7:1–10:21). John 10:10 is also a powerful image of the church as the body of Christ, who is the head. This analogy extends to v. 17. The aim of the Gospel "is to evoke a lifegiving faith in the audience."⁴ Therefore, "One begins to experience concretely that fullness of life" which Jesus promises in 10:10. This verse is like a link between John 1:1 and 20:30–31. In 10:1–19 Jesus claims to be the Good Shepherd and to give his life for his sheep. Reinhartz says Jesus "is the gateway between the bondage of the fold and the freedom of the pasture."⁵ After Mary Magdalene has cried very seriously in 20:16, Jesus calls her, and she recognizes him. This response marks her as Jesus' sheep, who hears his voice and follows him (10:1–5), and as a believer like Lazarus, who hears his voice and is resurrected from the dead (11:44).⁶

The Gospel of John is filled with signs and symbols. The author speaks on two levels: the ideas in the Gospel quite often have two meanings. John 10:10 is a poetic language, symbolic with double meanings. Here there is a coherence of Jesus' words and deeds: physically he died to bring life and "to gather into one the dispersed children of God" (John 11:52). Symbolically Jesus spends his energy and life's blood in teaching in order that those who believe in him may learn the way to the Father, thus having life to the full.

LITERARY CONTEXT OF JOHN 10:10

This chapter opens with a solemn declaration: Ἀμὴν ἀμὴν λέγω ὑμῖν *(amen amen lego humin)*— divine pronouncement. Jesus says this twice before he speaks about giving life in verse 10. This sentence and pronouncement carry the emphatic ἐγώ *(ego)*, "I," before ἦλθον *(elthon)*, "came." The passage comes in contrast to and immediately after the healing of the man born blind (John 9:1–34). Jesus declares that he came into the "world for judgment so that those who are blind may see and the sighted become blind" (9:39). The passage under study is similar to the episode before it, yet different. The similarity with the healed man is the sheep that hears the shepherd's voice, comes,

---

2. Okure, *Johannine Approach,*, as quoted in Farmer et al., *The International Bible Commentary*, 1576.
3. Teresa, "John," 1512.
4. Teresa, "John," 1531.
5. Reinhartz, "The Gospel of John," 580.
6. Adele, "The Gospel of John," 592.

and gets healed and receives life. This life is full and eternal. Unlike the man's experience of being driven out by the Pharisees in 9:34, the Good Shepherd Jesus gives life and gives it abundantly.

Martyn presents "vividly and persuasively how on one level John reflects the trial and defenses of a community being expelled from the synagogue because of the divine claims they made about Jesus."[7] This refers to John 9–10. John 10:10 may also be used as "an inspiration for women who are struggling for liberation, upheld by their belief in the God of creation and salvation."[8] The passage emphasizes the God of abundance, making one feel at ease and eat to one's satisfaction. In presenting this passage immediately after the story of the man born blind, John invites the reader to see the contrasts and similarities and to decide with which character to identify. Just like the man who was born blind and later responded to Jesus' invitation to be healed and got healed, the sheep that listen, hear the voice of the Good Shepherd, also follow him, thus finding pasture and getting nourished. This stands in contrast to the Jews who accuse the healed blind man of being a sinner, who are likened to the sheep led by the bad shepherd.

Text and Interpretation

Two familiar ways of structuring the Gospel according to John are: (1) "Book of Signs" (1:19–12:50) and "Book of Glory" (13:1–20:31); or (2) "Revelation of Glory to the World" (chs.1–12) and "Revelation of Glory to the Disciples" (chs. 13–20). Whichever division one chooses, the giving of life in the first section permeates the whole Gospel and culminates in the resurrection (ch. 20), after the life-giving teaching on the Eucharist (ch. 6). This passage falls among the passages that deal "mostly with the question of the divine messianic identity of Jesus."[9] John 10:10 is also seen by Teresa as "the heart of the mission" of Jesus, which "is to give life to believers and gather together the scattered children of God (10:10; 11:52)."[10] That one kind of shepherd does one thing and the other kind does another means that there are two different kinds of shepherds: good and bad. Jesus compares the "bad shepherd" to the "good shepherd," the destroyer to the giver of life. John 10:10a is in direct contrast to 10:10b. Verse 10a talks about the thief, who comes *only* to "steal, kill and destroy." He scares the sheep and they run away from him. When this happens, because it happens, verse 10b takes over, talking about the good shepherd who came that the sheep "may have life, and have it abundantly." The presence of the good shepherd gives the sheep the freedom of coming in and out, finding pasture, food, and life. Hearing the shepherd's

---

7. John and Ronald, "Modern New Testament Criticism," 1144.
8. Raymond and Sandra, "Hermeneutics," 1162.
9. Teresa, "John," 1517.
10. Teresa, "John," 1519.

voice who calls them and leads them out, the sheep respond accordingly because the good shepherd goes ahead of and protects them.

Looking globally at John 10:1–15, there is a clear play on the two kinds of shepherds. The bad shepherd is a "thief" and "bandit"; he climbs in by another way (verse 1); this is repeated in verse 8. His chief aim is "only to steal, kill and destroy." He is a hired hand who scares the sheep, scatters them, and makes them run away because he does not care for the sheep. The good shepherd comes with a great contrast: he enters by the gate and calls each sheep by name because he knows them and he is interested in them. They also know him, are familiar with his voice, and are sure of the pasture and abundant life. Among the Jews, the shepherd would normally call the sheep by name and lead them out to pasture. This shepherd goes ahead of the sheep as he leads them out, protecting them in case dangers come. He himself is also the gate for the sheep, a safe passage and entrance through which the sheep move freely to find pasture. This shepherd came that the sheep may have life and have it abundantly. The fact that this life-giving shepherd is the good one is mentioned twice, in verses 11 and 14. There is a mutual knowledge between the shepherd and the sheep: "I know my own and my own know me, just as the Father knows me and I know the Father. And I lay down my life for my sheep." This life the good shepherd lays down for the sheep is the one that overflows and fills the sheep to an abundance. The Father is the ultimate source of this life.

Looking at the tenses used in verse 10a and 10b, it could be seen that there is a remarkable difference. Verse 10a says the thief *comes* (ἔρχεται, *erchetai*): he appears now—but from where? This happens in the now. Does he come now to try to confuse the sheep that hear the voice of the good shepherd and follow? Was he hiding to come in through another passage but the door/gate? The good shepherd, on the other hand, *came* ("I came," ἦλθον, *elthon*): in the past. When did this good shepherd come? John 1:1 is recalled here: "in the beginning"; he came since the beginning. In him was and is life (1:4); he it is who gives one the power to become a child of God (v. 12), and this Good Shepherd, the Word, dwells among us, lives with us, and so the sheep who hear him have life abundantly. ("To those who receive him he gives power to become the children of God"; cf. John 1:12). "That they may have life" indicates that the life is already given. This is the same life who was referred to in John 1:3–5; as the one who came into being, overcomes darkness, and is Jesus, the *Logos* and eternal life. This is Jesus, the *Logos*, eternal life who overcomes darkness. If John 10:1, therefore, is read in the backdrop of 20:30–31, it brings out the deep and full meaning of the Gospel. The signs in John's Gospel point to the reality of Jesus' claims: the raising of Lazarus (11:43–44) connects to his coming that people may have life to the full (10:10). In addition to giving life abundantly (10:10), John also presents to the reader of this Gospel the triple life-giving passages: "When I am lifted up I will draw all people to myself" (12:32); "feed my lambs" (21:15), "tend my sheep" (21:16), "feed my sheep" (21:17); and "have life in his name" (20:31).

Talking generally about the Gospel of John in its "First Reading," Teresa says: "All the events narrated in the Gospel have this one purpose, to persuade the reader to believe and confess along with others that Jesus is God's Son and Christ, sent by God out of love for the world, to give enduring life to those who believe in him. Every episode in the Gospel is an attempt to elaborate this thesis."[11] Following Teresa's idea, "For John, Jesus is the Good News because he liberates people from all death-dealing forces that oppress humanity and constitute the real threat to true (eternal) life. The heart of this good news is found in such passages as 3:16; 10:10; and 11:52. Believers today are to make this gospel their own good news by identifying the death-dealing forces and their concrete manifestations in their own social location by applying their faith in Jesus to eradicate them (cf. 20:21),"[12] and as such have life to the full. John 10:10 could be seen to be a parallel to 1:3–4, 18; 20:28; and 1 John 5:20. They all refer to the fact that "all things came into being through him." Perkins analyzes it that Jesus is the good, ideal, model shepherd who gives life to the sheep. "John insists that Jesus is the only source of salvation. Those who came before him, probably a reference to the Jewish teachers and the tradition to which they appealed, are rejected as thieves (v. 8). The contrast with thieves who will not bring salvation recalls Ezek 34. John has the saying in his own language: Jesus has come that they might have life (cf. 14:6 Jesus is 'the way, truth, and life')."[13]

Ezekiel 34:1–8 condemns bad leaders/shepherds. These bad shepherds are equally described as unpleasant in Jeremiah (cf. Jer 13:17; 23:1–3; 31:10;), and Ezekiel, Zephaniah, and Zechariah also express their disgust for these bad, unfaithful shepherds who lead the sheep astray or neglect them (Ezek 22:27; Zeph 3:3; Zech 10:2–3); their ultimate punishment is recorded in Zechariah 11:4–17. False leaders (shepherds) are those who abandon their duty, run away from the sheep ,and expose them as easy prey to wolves. This is due to their poor relationship with the sheep (the people they should lead).

In John 10:2 the image of the shepherd refers to the king and to the people entrusted with the task of leadership. Verses 11–16 refer to the good shepherd/leader. God will claim the sheep from the bad shepherds because they have neglected their duty of pasturing the sheep. The good shepherd prophesied in Ezekiel 34:23, David, will pasture the flock of the Lord, and God will direct David. The sheep will eat in abundance and there shall be peace. This is a state of well-being between God and the people. The offspring of David in John 10:11 is Jesus the Good Shepherd, who will fulfill God's promise in Jeremiah 23:4b–8; 31:10b. John 10:10a uses "they"; this refers to the ones who are humble and realize they need Jesus, the ones who cannot see, who admit their "blindness"—unlike those who claim to see (cf. John 9:40). John 10:1–14

---

11. Teresa, "John," 1513.
12. Teresa, "John," 1514.
13. Perkins, "John," 968.

explains John 9:39–40 better and further: the blind, needy, and poor need not worry, for Jesus the Good Shepherd has come to give them life to the full.

A few characters and images lead to this abundant life-giving shepherd. These are: (1) one who enters the sheepfold through the gate in order to shepherd the sheep (*poimen estin ton probation,* v. 2); (2) another enters through a secret, cunning way (a robber and thief) in order to harm the sheep (*cleptes estin kai lestes,* v. 1); (3) and yet another is the gatekeeper—useful for free movement in and out (*ho thyroros,* v. 3).

According to Moloney, "The thief comes only to steal, kill, and destroy. There is nothing lifegiving about those who have come before Jesus claiming to be shepherds but who are, in fact, thieves and robbers. Jesus has come that the sheep may have pasture (cf. Ezek 34:14), thus have life and have it more abundantly (cf. Ezek 34:25–31)."[14] In addition, and to enrich this image of the life-giving shepherd further, Moloney develops more:

> Jesus is the "door" *through whom* access to good pasture is made available and by means of which a sheepfold is protected. Those who enter (v. 9: *eiselthe*) are saved; those who go out (v. 9: *exeleusetai*) find pasture. Jesus, the door (v. 7), offers both salvation and provides the sheep with abundant life (v. 10). It is through him (v. 9: *di'emou*) that others have life (cf. 1:3–4, 17). In this polemic with the Pharisees "the door" of v. 2 has been rendered Christological in vv.7–10.[15]

This abundant life is given to the full because it is Jesus' life, given by him freely (v. 17). He does this because he has the authority (*exousia,* v. 18), which he exercises freely. Jesus is determined to save, to give life, and to direct the sheep to himself, and so he emphasizes, insists, repeats the fact that "I am the good shepherd" (v. 14a). He explains the source of this goodness: his oneness with the Father and the mutual knowledge he has with the Father and his flock (vv. 14b–16, 17–18). This reiteration is to convince the sheep to turn to him for good pasturing and for life.

Application

According to Irenaeus of Lyons, "the 'life' or 'eternal life' which presupposes faith in Jesus is not biological life . . . but communion with God the Father, through Christ, in the Holy Spirit."[16] Giving abundant life reminds one of the Word becoming flesh and living among us (cf. John 1:14). Jesus shares the life he has with humans (who hear his voice and respond; John 10: 16b). Jesus is the way, and the truth, and the life—he

---

14. Moloney, "Johannine Theology," 303.

15. Moloney gives a detailed analysis of the contrast between the Good Shepherd and others. See Harrington,"The Gospel of John," 303.

16. Quoted in Balas and Bingham, "John" in Farmer, William. *The International Bible Commentary,* 121

gives life in abundance, and this leads the believer to follow the way and the truth. It is all-encompassing—abundant life stirs up a clear vision of the way and the truth (*hodos kai aleites*).

What did Jesus mean by giving and having life in abundance? One way of having this life is using one's gifts, talents, and strengths to serve others. "Each day of our lives needs to be lived to the fullest ... along the spiritual road."[17] Jesus discusses his role as the Good Shepherd, and in verse 10 he states his purpose on earth: "I came that they may have life, and have it abundantly." How can one attain this abundant life? This could be attained through the imitation of Jesus, being close to him, learning from him, listening to, hearing, and recognizing his voice (vv. 3–5). It is knowing, responding to, and following Jesus (v. 9). This abundant life is God's free and unconditional gift to all. Abundant life is Christian teachings on fullness of life. "True, abundant life consists of love, joy, peace and the rest of the fruits of the Spirit (Gal 5:22–23)."[18] John 17:3 talks about eternal/abundant life; this is knowledge of God, which is the key to a truly abundant life. It is spiritual abundance, a God-centered life. One grows in the grace and knowledge of Jesus. Therefore, the abundant life is "a continual process of learning, practicing and maturing, as well as failing, recovering, adjusting, enduring and overcoming, because, in our present state, 'we see but a poor reflection as in a mirror' (1 Cor 13:12)."[19]

Abundant, *perisson,* exceedingly, very highly, beyond measure, more, superfluous, much more than what one would expect or anticipate (cf. Eph 3:20). John 1:12; 14:6; 19:30; Galatians 2:20—this is the ultimate giving of the abundant life. This abundant life has been expressed in the Gospel according to John in varied ways, beginning with "I am" (*ego eimi*). They are all declared by Jesus and have to do with life and are as follows: "I am he" (the Messiah/the Christ; 4:26; 18:5); and "I am the bread of life" (6:35, 48, 51 [living bread]). The rest are: "I am the gate for the sheep" (10:7); "I am the Good Shepherd" (10:11–14); "I am the resurrection and the life" (11:25); "I am the way, and the truth, and the life" (14:6); "I am the true vine" (15:1, 5 [vine]).

CONCLUSION

The study of John 10:10 has been used as a guide in appreciation of a life-giving woman who has given so much of herself that she has been nicknamed by some of her congregation sisters "John 10:10." Rev. Sr. Prof. Teresa Okure—a member of the Society of the Holy Child Jesus (SHCJ), a biblical exegete who specializes in the New Testament—quotes this text in practically every speech she makes. She lives it, refers to it, and encourages other people to live it too. She is so fondly loved by her sisters due to her ways of taking care of people that they call her "Aunty." This title was initiated

17. McConnell in gotquestions.org. accessed 21/3/22.
18. McConnell, accessed 21/3/22.
19. https://www.citizen-times.com>life, accessed 21/3/22.

by the first set of the SHCJ novices in Jos when the novitiate was begun in 1973. This first group of novices explained that since Teresa is "their elder sister" in the culture of some of them, it was a mark of respect and a suitable title for someone whose life is a model. This mark of showing honor "to whom honor is due" has been handed down to subsequent members of the Society of the Holy Child Jesus. Some sisters in recent times simply address her as "Aunty welcome, goodbye," for she would be in part of the globe one day giving talks and sharing her life and the very next day she has crossed over to another continent. Others still call her "Sister Prof. Aunty." This sign of love is because Teresa preaches with her life. On a relaxed, calm, jovial, and discussive mood and in spite of all the "titles" she has acquired from her life of example, she would explain: "The only title that really matters and which one should strive to attain is 'child of God.'" Teresa is cherished for who she is and loved for practically pouring her lifeblood for the church in Nigeria and beyond. This is obvious in her facilitation of Assemblies and Chapters, which are moments of renewal, for different religious congregations. In her own congregation, the SHCJ, she is very often assigned the duty of consultant, think tank, or moderator. On the occasion of her jubilee, one could only thank God for and with her over the "cancellation of her debts" in enjoying life in the Lord abundantly. Teresa has lived a life of faithful service to God; there is holiness of life in her; one can see humility and self-sacrifice for others.

She literally pours out her life for the students at the Catholic Institute of West Africa (CIWA), Port Harcourt. There she breaks down her teaching in detail and repeats so often (sometimes too often for students who cannot bear it repeated) in order to ascertain that all the students in the lecture hall at any given time have "at least heard," she would say. She is a real mentor and teacher; these have endeared her to her students who see her as their role model and call her "Aunty," "Mama," and "Prof." She is a teacher, mentor, and practical exegete of the Holy Scriptures; some of her students, in spite of their training in homiletics and long hours of preparation of homilies, would still expect her to make a comment or two after Mass to them, by way of analyzing the homily. Some of such priests would hurry off to the hostel at CIWA immediately after Mass to evade her. This is mainly because Teresa would tell them: "The homily should be based on the readings just heard and should nourish the congregation." She believes and teaches that every homily should be food/life-giving. It is for the same reason she would say to the students whose theses she moderates, "Read the text many times until you get the message it contains before you can make your analysis." At Bishops' Conferences, provincial and national, Teresa would very often be invited to share her rich and wide, life-giving experiences. Sometimes she would be given specific topics to expound to the bishops. Those who ever heard her are the best witnesses to testify.

This section of the Gospel (John 10:10) is very relevant to the life of Sr. Teresa Okure, SHCJ. She is the first African Sister in the Society of the Holy Child Jesus (SHCJ). She has made efforts to live like the first, setting an example for posterity.

With the efforts she makes to be more like Jesus, looking at the different ways she encourages people to imitate Christ, leading and guiding like the Good Shepherd, one could comfortably say that Rev. Sr. Prof. Teresa Okure was directed by the Spirit to the Society of the Holy Child Jesus, as their first African member to show the way and in order that other people may have life in abundance.

BIBLIOGRAPHY

Aland, et al., eds. *Novum Testamentum Graece*. Deutsche Bibelgesellschaft: Nestle-Aland, 2006.

Balas, David, and Jeffrey Bingham. "Patristic Exegesis of the Books of the Bible." In *The International Bible Commentary: An Ecumenical Commentary for the Twenty-First Century*, 84–135. Edited by WIlliam Farmer et al. Bangalore: Theological Publications in India, 2013.

Brown, Raymond, et al., eds. *The New Jerome Biblical Commentary*. Bangalore: Theological Publications in India, 2011.

Farmer, William, et al., eds. *The International Bible Commentary*. Bangalore: Theological Publications in India, 2013.

Fiorenza, Elizabeth, ed. *Searching the Scriptures: A Feminist Commentary*. Vol 2. London: SCM Press Ltd., 1995.

Harrington, Daniel, ed. *The Gospel of John*. Collegeville, MN: The Liturgical Press, 1998.

Hyacinth, Ichoku, and Martin Ibeh, eds. *Expanding the Frontiers of Pastoral Leadership in a Changing Society: Festschrift for Peter Damian Akpunonu on the Occasion of His Priestly Golden Jubilee*. Oxford: Peter Lang, 2016.

Kselman, John, and Ronal Witherup. "Modern New Testament Criticism." In *The New Jerome Biblical Commentary*, 1130–1135. Bangalore: Theological Publications in India, 2011.

Moloney, Francis. "Johannine Theology." In *The New Jerome Biblical Commentary*, 1146–1165. Edited by Raymond Brown and Sandra Schneiders. Bangalore: Theological Publications in India, 2011.

Okure, Teresa. *The Johannine Approach to Mission: A Contextual Study of John 4:1–42*. Tübingen: Mohr Siebeck, 1988.

Perkins, Pheme. "The Gospel According to John." In *The New Jerome Biblical Commentary*, 942–985. Bangalore: Theological Publications in India, 2011.

CHAPTER 15

Exploring the Scope of Jesus' Mission in Matthew 10:5–8
in the Context of the Nigerian Church

PETER C. ONWUKA

INTRODUCTION

Matthew 10:5–8 is the core section of the mission instruction of Jesus to his chosen twelve disciples. It includes the official commissioning of the Twelve to participate in his mission and stipulates where they should go and what they should say and do. The pericope has been of exegetical interest to scholars in trying to understand the scope and mission of Jesus Christ on account of some knotty issues therein. One of the areas that has attracted much interest is the restriction of the mission to the lost sheep of the house of Israel. The addition of Samaria to the exclusion list further compounds the problem bearing in mind that it was formerly part of Israel. This seems to go contrary to the universal outlook of the Gospel of Matthew, which at its beginning in the infancy narrative related how the Gentile world, represented by the wise men from the East, paid homage to the infant king. Again, how can this exclusive and particularistic mission of the apostles be reconciled with the universal mission of Matthew 28:18–20?

In contemporary Nigeria, the missionary mandate, especially as it concerns what to say and what to do, has remained a guide for Christians both as a body and as an individual in their mission. However, diverse interpretation of this mandate among different Christian groups and denominations has led to undue emphasis on one aspect or the other. Healing and exorcism have received undue attention, and this has resulted in an upsurge in healing ministries and centers, sometimes with some unwholesome practices that ridicule rather than promote the mission of Christ.

All this necessitated an exegetical study of this text to examine the nature and scope of the mission of Jesus and its implications for the Nigerian church. The work is divided into three parts. The first part examines the historical and literary context of Matthew 10:5-8. The second part, which is the exegesis of Matthew 10:5-8, begins by establishing the text, then its analysis and theological synthesis. The third part deals with the implication of the text to the Nigerian church.

HISTORICAL AND LITERARY CONTEXT OF MATTHEW 10:5-8

There is to a large extent greater agreement among scholars on the situation that shaped the Gospel of Matthew than of any other Gospel.[1] The Evangelist seems to have composed his Gospel in response to the situation following the Jewish revolt of 66-69 CE that led to the destruction of Jerusalem and the temple in 70 CE. The shattering experience of Jewish war with the Romans brought about a radical reorganisation of Judaism. With the unexpected disappearance of the Temple, the centre of Jewish religious practice with its attendant cessation of sacrifices and other religious activities, the petering out of the temple-based Sadducees and the decimation of such radical groups as Zealots and Essenes, it behoves on the Pharisees to chart a way for the survival of Judaism. Under their leadership, Judaism was reorganised on the basis of strict fidelity to the law, a situation that gave little or no tolerance to such peripheral groups like Christianity seen as diluting the orthodoxy of Judaism.

Therefore, the Gospel of Matthew is a Christian response to the situation created by the destruction of Jerusalem and the temple and its aftermath. Matthew, very likely a Jewish Christian, had to give some sense of direction to his predominantly Jewish Christian community who hitherto the Pharisaic reorganisation of Judaism had seen themselves as a sect within Judaism. His approach is two dimensional: first, to convince his fellow Christians whose expulsion from Judaism might have created some emptiness that Jesus is the fulfillment of all divine promises to their ancestors and that they are the true inheritors of those blessings; and second, to convince their Jewish critics who see Christianity as diluting and destroying Judaism and the law that Jesus, rather than destroying the law, brings about its fulfillment through a better understanding and interpretation of it. On account of this, Matthew argues that the mission of Jesus Christ is mission directed first and foremost to the Jews, to gather the scattered and lost sheep. It is for the same mission and purpose that he sent out his closest associates, the Twelve.

The Gospel of Matthew is structured differently by different scholars, ranging from two to seven sections.[2] However, one form of structuring that has received

1. Senior, and Stuhlmueller, . *The Biblical Foundations for Mission*,233.
2. McKenzie structures it into three: 1:1-4:16; 4:17-16:20 and 16:21-28:20 while W.G. Kummel,

favorable response from a number of scholars is that initiated by B. W. Bacon that Matthew arranged his work into five discourses with a prologue and epilogue. This structure has been modified by J. P. Meier, who argued that the Passion Narrative cannot be taken as an epilogue but as the climax of the book, and W. Harrington, who rather proposes seven sections or what he calls "a drama of seven acts on the coming of the kingdom of heaven," with the infancy narrative and passion taken as sections rather than prologue and epilogue.[3] In this arrangement, Matthew 10:5–8 falls within the third section, Matthew 8:1–10:42, which is made up of two parts: the narrative on the healing ministry of Jesus Christ (Matt 8:1–9:34) and the missionary discourse (Matt 9:35–11:1). The latter is further divided as follows:

- (Matt 9:35–38)—The setting for the apostolic mission discourse, which provides the circumstance the led to the mission of the Twelve

- (Matt 10:1–15)—The primary mission discourse, which dwells on the instruction given to the Twelve on the mission; this section is still further divided into three subsections:

    - (Matt 10:1–4)—The introductory part
    - (Matt 10:5–8)—The heart of the mission discourse
    - (Matt 10:9–15)—Instructions on the execution of the mission

- (Matt 10:16–42): The secondary mission discourse, which is believed to be later instructions for mission in general and not specifically for the Twelve on the mission during the ministry of Jesus Christ

Exegesis of Matthew 10:5–8

Establishment of the Text of Matthew 10:5–8

The twenty-seventh edition of Nestle-Aland's *Novum Testamentum Greece* of the text of Matthew 10:5–8 has few textual issues. In verse 5, the textual problem has to do with λεγων, which D it vg$^{s.st.ww}$ substitutes with *kai legōn* while 1424 *ℵ and Origen omitted it. The text is left as it is for the variants have few manuscripts that support them. In verse 6, the phrase πορευεσθε δε is substituted with υπαγετε by D. The variation has only one witness. In verse 7, the variation has to do with οτι, which 251 pc and sa^{mss} replace with μετανοειτε οτι while B and sys omit it. The replacement with

---

into two: 1–12 and 13–28. See McKenzie, *Dictionary of the Bible*, 554; Kummel, *Introduction to the New Testament*, 103–105.

3. Harrington structures Matthew into seven sections as follows: 1–2: Introduction; 3–7: Promulgation of the Gospel of the Kingdom; 8–10: Preaching of the Kingdom of heaven; 11–13:34: Mystery of the kingdom of heaven; 13:35–18:35: church the first fruit of the Kingdom; 19–25: Near Advent of the Kingdom; and 26–28: Passion and Resurrection. See his *Record of Fulfilment*, 143–44.

μετανοειτε οτι is likely influenced by Matthew 4:17. The omission of *hoti* may also be due to the influence of Matthew 4:17, where it is also omitted. The text should be left as it is. The textual issue in verse 8 has to do with the order of three instructions coming after healing the sick. While P W Δ pc sy[h] have 3–6 12; 348 al have 341256, 28 has 5634, 1324 has 56, C3 KLΓΘ 700 M f (syp) sa mae and Eusebius have 3–6 while the text is supported by ℵ B C among others. Though there is nothing to guarantee the order in which this was said, some omitted the instruction on raising the dead perhaps because the apostles did not perform such during their ministry at time of Jesus. However, Matthew seems to have mirrored these instructions based on the ministry of Jesus outlined in Matthew 8–9 to show that the ministry of the apostles follows the pattern of that of Jesus. On the basis of this, it is better to leave the text as it is.

The Text

> These twelve Jesus sent out after instructing (them) saying: "Do not go along the way leading to the Gentiles, and nor enter the town of the Samaritans, 6 but proceed rather to the lost sheep of the house of Israel. 7 As you go, proclaim the good news saying, 'The kingdom of heaven has come near.' 8 Cure the sick, raise the dead, cleanse the lepers, cast out demons. You received without payment; give without payment."

Analysis of Matthew 10:5–8

Matthew 10:5–8 may be structured into three parts as follows:

- v. 5a: Introduction
- vv. 5b–6: Where to go
- vv. 7–8: What to say and do

Verse 5a: Introduction and Commission

Verse 5a, which serves as the introduction to this periscope, deals with the commissioning for mission, indicating the person behind the mission and those being sent. The author of the mission is Jesus Christ, whose name "Jesus," Matthew explains, is to save his people from their sins (1:21) and whose mission, so far, is clearly shown in Matthew 4:17–7:23 and 8:1–9:38, and who has chosen his twelve disciples for the same mission (Matt 10:1–4). Matthew indicated in Matthew 10:1 that Jesus called to himself (*proskalesamenos*) twelve disciples—namely, Simon, also called Peter, Andrew his brother, James and John, sons of Zebedee, Philip, Bartholomew, Thomas, James son of Alphaeus, Thaddeus, Simon the Cananite, and Judas Iscariot, who later became the traitor.[4] Having mentioned their names in verses 2–4, here the Evangelist simply refers to them as these Twelve (*toutous tous dōkeka*). Though the choice of the twelve disciples is not limited to the Gospel of Matthew, the evangelist must have seen in the choice a connection between the chosen twelve and the twelve tribes of Israel. As the old Israel was built on the twelve sons of Jacob, so is the new Israel built on the twelve disciples chosen by Jesus. However, the chosen twelve enjoy a higher status than the twelve sons of Jacob because they will sit with Christ judging the twelve tribes of Israel (Matt 19:28).

Having chosen these twelve and given them authority over unclean spirits to cast them out and to heal all forms of diseases (Matt 10:1), Jesus officially sent them out. The verb *apesteilen* (aorist indicative of *apostellō* and compound of *stellō*, "to send") has the basic meaning "to send forth." This verb occurs about 135 times in the New Testament and over 20 times in Matthew. Though sometimes it is used to indicate nothing but the act of sending, either of a person or a thing, in other instances it carries the nuance of sending with authorization or in representative capacity. The second sense is the one used here. Jesus sent the Twelve having given them authority to do what he is doing. They are to act as his envoys and emissaries. The Twelve were sent out with instructions (*parangeilas*, from *parrangellō*) on what to do. Verse 5a therefore deals with the commissioning of the Twelve, which entails their being sent out with specific instructions. Verses 5b–8 deal with various sets of mission instructions.

Verses 5b–6: Where to Go

The first two instructions have to do with where to go and where not to go in reverse order. The first instruction, made up of two parts arranged in parallel indicates, where the Twelve should not go:

> *Eis hodon ethnōn mē apelthēte*
> *eis polin samaritōn mē eiselthēte*

Hodon is in parallel with *polin*, *ethnōn* with *samaritōn*, and *apelthēte* with *eiselthēte*. The first part of this command or prohibition, *eis hodon ethnōn*, here means "unto the path, way or road leading to the (territory of the) Gentiles." *Mē apelthēte* is a specific prohibition made up of the negative particle *me* and aorist subjunctive of *aperchomai*, which means "to go out or away." This means that this command is specific to this particular mission of the Twelve and may not be taken as a general instruction for all missions. The Twelve should not go out or away on the way or path

---

4. The names and their order are slightly different in Mark and Luke. In Mark, James and John come before Andrew, and Thomas is named before Matthew, while Luke and Matthew follow the same order in naming the first six apostles, Matthew is named before Thomas while Thaddeus is replaced with Simon the Zealot.

leading to the Gentiles. The prohibition concerns going to the cities or territories of the Gentiles rather than encountering Gentiles on the way.[5] In other words, they should not leave the territory marked out for them to go to that of the Gentiles. The command is geographical rather than ethnic as it does not prevent them from ministering to Gentiles that lived within the specified territory.

The second command, which is more precise, forbids them from entering (*eiselthēte*) the city or territory (*polin*) of the Samaritans. This is also a specific command meant for this particular mission. According to France, for Matthew, the Samaritans together with the Gentiles represent the wider world outside "the house of Israel which is the jurisdiction of the apostles." Based on this instruction, R. T. France and Gundry say that their mission is restricted to Galilee, while W. F. Albright and C. S. Mann suggest three possible ways the apostles could travel to Israel without entering the territory of the Gentiles or entering city of the Samaritans: along the coastal plain, along the Jordan valley, and along the watershed ridge.[6]

Verse 6 indicates where they should go. The particle *de* is disjunctive in function and contrastive in meaning and it is intensified with adverb *māllon*, to show a contrast between what follows and what has been said in verse 5. Unlike verse 5, which deals with prohibitions, verse 6 deals with positive command. The present imperative *poreuesthe* from the verb *poreueomai* means to go or proceed and here has the nuance of going straight. Instead of lingering on the way that leads to the Gentiles or entering the city of the Samaritans, they should rather go straight to the lost sheep of the house of Israel. The expression "lost sheep of the house of Israel" re-echoes the complaint of Jesus in Matthew 9:36 that the people were like sheep without a shepherd as well as the complaints of the prophets against the leaders of the people of Israel who, due to their neglect and high-handedness, had allowed the sheep to scatter (Jer 50:6; Ezek 34:5). The prophets equally looked forward to a time when God would either gather his flock himself or do so through his anointed one. Matthew considers this an essential aspect of the mission of Jesus Christ which he has already started through his mission and which he extends through that of his chosen twelve. Most scholars agree that "lost sheep of the house of Israel" refers not just to a section or even a remnant but the entire people of Israel.[7] The mission of Jesus and that of his chosen twelve is a mission directed primarily to the house of Israel.

These three instructions raise some questions: Why are the Twelve prohibited from going toward the Gentiles or entering the city of the Samaritan? Why is their mission restricted to the people of Israel? Are these commands to be taken as temporary or permanent commands? In the first place, a comparison with parallel passages

---

5. See also France, *Matthew*, 382.

6. France, *Matthew*, 382; Gundry, 185; Albright and Mann, *Matthew*, 119.

7. See Harrington, *Matthew*, 140; Leske, "Matthew," 1288. According to Viviano, the expression refers first and foremost to Israel as a whole and secondly to the people of the land, those who are marginalized and alienated from the main circle of religious leaders. See Viviano, "Matthew," 651.

in Mark and Luke shows that this instruction is only found in Matthew, and this shows that Matthew has serious reason for inserting it. It must therefore have something to do with Matthew's understanding of the mission of Jesus Christ. The claim for a restricted mission to the lost sheep of the house of Israel is also made during Jesus' encounter with a Canaanite woman in Matthew 15:24. While some scholars are of the view that the prohibitions may not have come from Jesus himself but from his followers, others believe that it comes from Jesus. On this, Barclay maintains that the command is so uncharacteristic of Jesus that no other person would have invented it if not Jesus himself.[8] According to France, Matthew sees Jesus as the Messiah of God's people, Israel, whose mission is the salvation of his people from sin; therefore, it is not surprising that the mission is restricted then. However, he pointed out that the restriction is limited to the initial period of proclamation until the undeniable primacy of Jesus' mission as the mission of Israel had been established.[9] This is also the view of C. S. Keener, who maintains that the limitation of mission to Israel fits the historic priority of Israel in salvation history.[10] For Leske, Israel is first to be gathered so that it can fulfill its purpose of being the light of the nations.[11] Most scholars are of the view that this instruction or prohibition is only limited to the mission of the apostles during the ministry of Jesus Christ, as Matthew 28:19–20 indicates that Gentile mission had to wait until after his resurrection. Matthew anticipates such mission even in the mission discourse, especially in Matthew 10:17, where reference is made that the disciples' persecution will serve as testimony both to their persecutors and to the Gentiles. Barclay and France are also of the view that the reason Jesus restricted his mission is because his disciples were not yet ready to cross ethnic barriers. Matthew therefore sees the mission of Jesus as one directed first and foremost to the lost sheep of the house of Israel. This, however, does not foreclose mission to the Gentiles, only that mission to Israel takes priority. Matthew, a Jewish Christian writing to a predominantly Jewish Christian community, addresses one of the key messianic expectations of the Jewish people, which is the gathering the dispersed people of Israel into one fold (see Isa 35; 49:8–13; 60:1–7).

Verses 7–8: What They Are to Say and Do

Verses 7 and 8 constitute the heart of the mission discourse. Here Jesus specifies what the apostles are to say and do. Verse 7 indicates what they are to say, specifying the manner and content. Their activities center on the kingdom: they are to go announcing and demonstrating the kingdom.[12] The present participle *poreuomenoi* links

8. Barclay, *Matthew*, 303.
9. France, *Matthew*, 382.
10. Keener, *Matthew*.
11. Leske, "Matthew," 1288.
12. Leske, 1288.

verses 7–8 with verse 6 and shows that mission is a course or process that embraces other activities. In the course of their mission, they are to make proclamation. The present imperative *kērussete* from *kērussō* is linked to *kērux*, which means a herald. The manner of their proclamation depicts how a herald or messenger of a king delivers the king's message to the people.

The content of the message is: *ēngiken hē basileia tōn ouranōn* ("The kingdom of heaven has drawn near"). The expression *basileia tōn ouranōm* is specific to Matthew, where it occurs thirty-two times, though in a few occasions he uses *basileia tou theou* (Matt 6:33; 12:28; 19:24; 21:31; 21:43), unlike Mark and Luke, who use consistently *basileia tou theou* ("kingdom of God") fourteen and thirty-two times, respectively. Today, a majority of scholars are of the view that "kingdom of heaven" in Matthew is equivalent to "kingdom of God" in Mark and Luke and that heaven is used as circumlocution to avoid mentioning God.[13] However, a few scholars, like Pennington, are of the view that "kingdom of heaven" in Matthew has a different meaning from "kingdom of God."[14] The expression *basileia tōn ouranōn* in Matthew and *basileia tou theou* in Mark and Luke is central in the Synoptic Gospels and therefore needs some elaboration.

The term *basileia* in Greek means "kingdom" or "territory ruled by a king or queen."[15] However, the expression *basileia tōn ouranōn* or *basileia tou theou* draws its meaning from the Hebrew expression *malkût šāmayîm* or Aramaic expression *malkûtā' dišmayā'*, which rather means "kingship," "sovereignty," or "reign of God." Though the expression is not found in the Old Testament, the idea is very common in it. In the Old Testament, the people of Israel, in different ways, expressed their belief in the kingship of God not only of the people of Israel but of the entire universe (1 Sam 8:7; Pss 47:8; 93:1; 97:1; 99:1; 103:19; Dan 4:34–35). The Intertestamental and Second Temple literature bears witness to this belief in the kingship of God (see Jub 1:28; 1 Enoch 9:4; 25:7; Pss of Sol 2:20; 17:1). However, the Israelites were aware that the reign of God had not been as expected and that other nations had not recognized the kingship of God and they looked forward to when the kingship of God would be witnessed not only by the Israelites but by the whole world and when the Israelites' enemies would be vanquished and Israel would take its position as the privileged people of God. They looked forward to when "God of Heaven will set up a kingdom that shall never be destroyed and which shall stand forever" (Dan 2:44), and when "the holy ones of their Most High shall receive the kingdom and possess it forever" (Dan 7:18). Both in Qumran and Rabbinic literature, there is an understanding that God is the

---

13. See Meier, *Mentor*, 239.

14. Pennington argues that "kingdom of heaven" is not exactly the same as "kingdom of God." According to him, "kingdom of heaven" is used in contradistinction to the kingdoms of earth. It is a kingdom that is not earthly but from above. See Pennington, *Heaven and Earth*, 67–76; Schreiner, *New Testament Theology*, 46–47.

15. See *A Greek-English Lexicon of the New Testament and Other Early Christian Literature* (BDAG), 169.

king of the universe and also that God's kingdom is yet to be realized in its fullness (see 4QFlor 1:3; 1QM 12:8; Tg. Zech 14:9).[16]

Therefore, when Jesus, at the beginning of his ministry, stated that the kingdom of God/heaven has drawn near and commanded his apostles to do the same, it does not sound totally strange to his audience. The question rather is, What does Jesus mean by the expression *ēngiken basileia tōn ouranōn*? *Ēngiken* is perfect indicative of *engizō*, which means to draw near or to draw close. Perfect tense indicates an action already completed but whose effect continues in the present. It literally means that the action of drawn near has already taken place but its effect continues. Matthew used this verb in this tense five times (Matt 3:2; 4:17; 10:7; 26:45; 26:46), and while Matthew 3:2 and 4:17 repeat the same phrase in Matthew 10:7, its use in Matthew 26:45 and 26:46 is different and may throw some light on its meaning. In Matthew 26:45, Jesus told his disciples to arise because the hour of his betrayal has drawn near (*ēngiken*). In Matthew 26:46, he says: "Behold the one who is to betray me has drawn close (*ēngiken*)," and in verse 47, while he was still saying it, Judas came in with a large crowd to arrest him. It shows that Matthew uses the expression to show something that is almost or practically there. Dunn is of the view that what is meant is imminence rather than presence.[17] However, from the way the expression is used, it is better to say that it is imminence that includes presence to some extent. It is said to be drawn near because it is both yet and not-yet. It has been inaugurated but not yet consummated. Its impacts are being felt but its fullness still remains in the future.

As Dunn asked: What is this kingdom of God that has drawn near and why is it that it is said to have drawn near and not that it has come? The kingdom of God in the Synoptic Gospels represents the mission of Jesus Christ. He comes to bring about the realization of the kingdom of God. By this is not meant to bring to reality that God is king because that has always been, but to bring about the full implication of the kingship of God, to lead people to proper submission to the kingship of God, and to defeat forces that are opposed to such kingship. According to T. R. Schreiner, the kingdom of God entails a time when God's enemies are demonstrably defeated and the righteous are visibly blessed, and in the ministry of Jesus this new era has dawned and the saving promises of old are being fulfilled.[18] What is meant by the expression "the kingdom of heaven has drawn near" is that through the person and ministry of Jesus Christ, this new era of the kingship of God has been inaugurated. It means that a new era has dawned in the salvation history, an era when divine promises of old are being fulfilled and saving deeds of God are experienced not only by the people of Israel but also by

---

16. In his commentary in Exod 17:14, Rabbi Eleazar was quoted as saying: "At that time when idolatry will be eradicated together with its worshippers, and God will be recognized throughout the world as One and His kingdom will be established for all eternity"; cited in Duling, "Kingdom of God, Kingdom of Heaven," 53.

17. Dunn, *Christianity in Making*, 408.

18. Schreiner, *New Testament Theology*, 54.

other nations. The apostles are therefore called to share with Jesus in this mission of bringing about the full realization of the kingdom of heaven.

The proclamation and other activities of the apostles are geared toward the full realization of the kingdom of God. Apart from the proclamation, Jesus also gave his disciples specific instructions on what they are to do. Matthew indicated four instructions, all in the present imperative, indicating their continuity within a specific period. The first is *asthenountes therapeute*. The sick are literally referred to as those who are not strong (*a-stenous*). They are those incapacitated by ailment and disease. The work of the disciples is to heal them and restore them to strength. Healing the sick is part of the nearness of the kingdom. Jesus, in the course of his ministry, healed many who were sick, and the healing of Peter's mother-in-law showed how healing restores a person to health and strength. Jesus also, through his preaching and teaching, restored hope and strength to those who were spiritually and morally weak. Healing here should not be limited to physical, as Jesus has indicated that his healing goes beyond physical even to the salvation of the person.

The second is *nekrous egeireter* ("raise the dead"). Scholars have observed that this instruction is not found in Mark or Luke and even in some manuscripts of Matthew's Gospel. On account of this, some have doubted if it was originally in the instructions that Jesus gave to his disciples. Although it was not among the deeds recorded as accomplished by the disciples of Jesus during his public ministry, it was included in Matthew's version of the mission of the Twelve to show that the mission entrusted to the apostles is exactly the mission being carried out by Jesus. Since the mission of Jesus as recorded in Matthew 8–9 included the raising of the dead (see the raising of Jairus' daughter in Matt 9:23–26), it is not surprising that Matthew, who sees the mission of the apostles as a replica and extension of that of Jesus, includes it among the mission of the apostles during the ministry of Jesus. Jesus, during his ministry, not only raised the dead but also resuscitated those who had died spiritually. Raising the dead is not limited to resuscitating the physically dead, but also includes bringing back to life spiritually those who through their actions or way of life have become dead in their relationship with God.

The third is *leprous katherizete* ("cleanse the leper"). Leprosy or what has come to be referred to as various forms of skin infections was a form of disease highly dreaded at the time of Jesus and in the Old Testament. The dread comes more from the religious and social implications of the disease than its health implication. The lepers are made both religious and social outcasts. According to Leviticus 13:3, 45–46, any person verified by the priest as having leprosy or skin disease is declared unclean and should be isolated from the people, wear torn cloth and disordered hair, cover their upper lips, and shout "Unclean, unclean." As leprosy renders its victim religiously and socially dead, its cleansing restores the person to his or her social and religious life. Matthew records that Jesus cleanses a number of lepers during his ministry and therefore sees Jesus as entrusting the same mission to the apostles.

The fourth is *daimonia ekballete* ("cast out the demons"). Matthew indicated a number of times that Jesus in the course of his ministry cast out demons (see Matt 4:24; 8:28–34; 9:32–34). Conquering the kingdom of Satan is one of the primary missions of Jesus Christ and the sign of the nearness of the kingdom. For this, Matthew's Jesus considers it a serious sin against the Holy Spirit to attribute his divinely saving powers to Satan. Since pulling down the kingdom of Satan, entering the strong man's house, and tying him up in order to plunder his house is key to the mission of Jesus, it is not surprising that he entrusted the same mission to his chosen twelve. Casting out demons is not new among the people of Israel; what is new is the way Jesus does it which is by words of mouth. For this, his followers marveled that he gave an order to the unclean spirits and they obeyed him.

The final instruction is the need to give freely since they received what they have freely. The apostles were not chosen because they are more talented or more intelligent or holier than others. Their call and choice came graciously. Consequently, they are required to carry out their work without asking for gratification.

Theological Synthesis

Matthew 10:5–8 is the heart of the mission discourse, which can be seen as the mission theology of Matthew. It deals with the mission of the Twelve, which is an extension of the mission of Jesus Christ. The mission of Jesus Christ is a saving mission, which is already contained in the name the angel gave him before his birth: "Jesus because he will save his people from their sins" (Matt 1:21). Jesus is the Messiah promised in the Old Testament and whose arrival was awaited by his people. Matthew made this clear with the series of Old Testament citations which are fulfilled in him. His mission is to gather the dispersed sheep of the house of Israel into the kingdom of God (Matt 15:24). The theme of gathering the lost and scattered sheep of the house of Israel has been a very common and popular one among the prophets.[19] Matthew therefore sees these messianic promises as being fulfilled in Jesus Christ. Matthew maintains that for Jesus to do this, he has to become that Israel which Israel could not be, that obedient son which God always wanted Israel to be.[20] Jesus gathers Israel by becoming true Israel and that son with whom God is well pleased (Matt 3:17; 17:5). For Matthew, the

---

19. Isaiah looked forward to a time when the scattered children of Jerusalem will not only be gathered but gloriously carried home like princes and princesses (Isa 60:1–7). Jeremiah also looked forward to a time when the dispersed people of Israel will return home with joy (Jer 31: 1–14). He says: "He who scattered Israel will gather him and keep him as a shepherd a flock" (Jer 31:10). Ezekiel equally talked of a time when the dispersed people of Israel will be restored to their land and to their glory (Ezek 39:25–29)

20. He is that son whom he called out of Egypt (Hos 11:1; Matt 2:15), who received the gifts from Midian, Sheba, and Epha (Isa 60:6), realized in the gifts of the wise men from the East (Matt 2:11), and who did not succumb to the temptation to disobey or murmur against God on account of lack of food (Deut 8:3; Matt 4:4).

primary destination of the mission of Jesus Christ as well of that of his chosen twelve is Israel. It is a mission that gives priority to Israel because of her privileged position and role in salvation but is also open to humanity in its entirety. Saint Paul shares the same view in Romans 9:4–6 on the priority of Israel.

The mission of Jesus is equally that of proclaiming the nearness of the kingdom of God. He not only gathers the dispersed Israel, but he gathers them into God's kingdom. By "kingdom of heaven" (or God), Matthew means the reign of God, which is different from the earthly and human reign. Although God has always reigned, the coming of Jesus marked a new phase in the reign of God. It marks a period when the saving promises of God made in the past come to fulfillment. In reply to the question posed by John the Baptist through his messengers, Jesus said: "Go and tell John what you hear and see: the blind receive their sight, the lame walk, the lepers are cleansed , the deaf hear, the dead are raised and the poor have good news brought to them" (Matt 11:4–5). The proclamation of the nearness of the kingdom is therefore not limited to verbal proclamation but is accompanied with saving works of God. As Matthew puts it: "Jesus went throughout Galilee teaching in their synagogue and proclaiming the good news of the kingdom and curing every disease and every sickness among the people" (Matt 4:23).

Jesus came to bring about the kingdom of God, to make it possible that God reigns truly in every heart. In his ministry, the kingdom is inaugurated, and it tends toward its full realization. With him, the kingdom has dawn near, but its fullness still lies in the future. He engages the services of his chosen companions, the apostles, who will help in driving the mission forward. He vested them with his authority and commissioned them to do the same work he is doing: to proclaim the nearness of the kingdom and to heal, raise the dead, cleanse the leper, and cast out demons.

Implication for the Nigerian Church

The text and message of Matthew 10:5–8 has a number of implications for the Nigerian church, which is "a people brought into unity of the Father, the Son and the Holy Spirit" within Nigerian context (L.G. 4).[21] The context of Matthew 10:5–8, which is clearly spelled out in Matthew 9:36, is similar to the Nigerian context. Matthew's community was depressed and distressed because of the situation following the fall of Jerusalem and the destruction of the temple as well as due to Jewish hostile attitudes toward them. The church and indeed the entire Nigerian populace are going through a lot of distressing situations occasioned by sociopolitical and economic problems. On account of poor political leadership, there is an upsurge in criminal activities like banditry, kidnapping, armed robbery, religious and tribal or ethnic extremism like Boko Haram terrorism and Fulani herdsmen attacks, and economic problems like

---

21. For a comprehensive exposition and understanding of the nature and meaning of Church, see *Lumen Gentium*, nos 1–8.

poverty, lack of employment, and very high inflation rate. All these have made the mission mandate more relevant to the Nigerian situation.

Our Lord Jesus Christ inaugurated the kingdom of heaven first through his person and his saving works and second through the church, represented in the choice of the Twelve to whom, even during his earthly ministry, he entrusted the work of sharing in his mission. The church in Nigeria, as a visible manifestation of the same church of Christ in our time, continues the mission of Christ in our time. It proclaims the good news to people distressed by sociopolitical and economic situations in Nigeria and brings about the saving works of Christ to bear in the life of the people. The church in Nigeria no doubt, to a reasonable extent, has remained committed to her mission of proclaiming the good news of Jesus Christ and bringing the effects of the saving mission of Christ to the lives of the people. The Catholic Bishops Conference of Nigeria (CBCN) both collectively and individually has consistently, through their communiqué, pastoral letters, and homilies, given hope to the distressed people of Nigeria and condemned various forms of criminalities and injustices. The clergy, through their homilies and ministries, have continued to proclaim the good news of the kingdom to the Nigerian people and to bring healing to the sick, to restore the outcasts, to give life to the dead, and to liberate those under the clutches of the evil one. The religious and the laity have also contributed in various ways in the mission of Christ in Nigeria.

However, the church in Nigeria has its challenges. First, the existence of denominations within Christianity in Nigeria with often conflicting teachings and ideologies has continued to affect the effectiveness of the proclamation of the good news. Sometimes Christians and non-Christians are confused on what to believe. Second, undue emphasis on healing and exorcism by some ministers and some denominations has given the wrong impression that the mission of Christ is nothing but healing and exorcism and that an ideal Christian life is that characterized by material prosperity and the absence of suffering. This understanding has given rise to an upsurge in healing ministries and centers, false prophecy, and deception and exploitation of people by unscrupulous and self-acclaimed pastors and "men and women of God."

The church in Nigeria needs to rise up to these challenges. Though the CBCN has a number of times given directives on various aspects of the life of Christians, especially as it concerns proclamation of the gospel and ministries, it needs from time to time to reexamine to what extent these directives are carried out. They need to call to order, and when necessary sanction, priests, religious, and lay faithful whose methods of proclamation of the good news and exercise of ministries are contrary to the mind and teachings of Christ. In the training of the future ministers, efforts should be made to help them to cultivate proper attitudes toward the mission of Christ and to shun materialism and preaching of themselves. The laity should be helped to understand what Christian life entails and that the cross is part and parcel of Christian life.

CONCLUSION

The mission of Jesus Christ as enunciated in the apostolic discourse in Matthew 10:5–8 is that of gathering the dispersed people of God into God's kingdom. It is a mission that gives priority to the people of Israel because of their divine election and in fulfillment to the promises God made to their ancestors. Its limitation to Israel is only temporary as it is meant for the humanity in its entirety (Matt 28:18–20). It is a mission of proclaiming the nearness of the kingdom of heaven. The kingdom of heaven, which is the reign of God, has drawn near with the ministry of Jesus Christ because, through him, God's saving promises of the past are being fulfilled. Through him, humanity is liberated from the clutches and dominion of the evil one. In the ministries of Jesus, the kingdom of God is inaugurated but not consummated or exhausted, and this is why Jesus commissioned his chosen twelve and later all his disciples to share and carry his mission to the ends of the earth. The church in Nigeria both collectively and individually continues the mission of Christ in our time. Although remarkable success has been made, there is need to check abuses that have continued to slow down the pace and effectiveness of the mission. Nigeria, with its present socio-economic situation and myriad of problems, needs it now more than ever.

BIBLIOGRAPHY

Albright, W. F., and C. S. Mann. *Matthew: Introduction, Translation and Notes*. AB 26. New York: Doubleday, 1971.

Barclay, W. *The Gospel of Matthew, Vol. 1: Chapters 1–10*. The Daily Study Bible. Bangalore: Theological Publications, 1975.

Brown, R. E. *An Introduction to the New Testament*. New York: Doubleday, 1997.

Brown, R. E., J.A. Fitzmyer, and R. E. Murphy, eds. *The New Jerome Biblical Commentary*. London: Geoffrey Chapman, 1989.

Carson, D. A., J. Douglas, and Leon Morris. *An Introduction to the New Testament*. Grand Rapids: Zondervan, 1992.

Denker, Frederick W., et al., eds. *Greek-English Lexicon of the New Testament and Other Early Christian Literature (BDAG)*. 3rd edition. Chicago: University of Chicago, 2000.

Duling, I. D. C. "Kingdom of God, Kingdom of Heaven." In *Anchor Bible Dictionary* 4. Edited by D. N. Freedman. New York: Doubleday, 1992.

Dunn, James D. G. *Christianity in Making, Vol. 1: Jesus Remembered*. Grand Rapids: Eerdmans, 2003.

France, R. T. *The Gospel of Matthew*. Grand Rapids: Eerdmans, 2007.

Gundry, Robert H. *Matthew: A Commentary on His Literary and Theological Art*. Grand Rapids: Eerdmans, 1982.

Harrington, D. J. *The Gospel of Matthew*. Sacra Pagina 1. Collegeville, MN: Liturgical Press, 2007.

Harrington, W. *Record of Fulfilment*. Chicago: Priory Press, 1965.

Keener, Craig S. *A Commentary on the Gospel of Matthew*. Grand Rapids: Eerdmans, 1999.

Kuasiewicz, J. *The Synoptic Gospels Today*. Translated by Sergius Wroblewski. New York: Alba House, 1996.

Kummel, W. G. *Introduction to the New Testament*. London: SCM, 1979.

Leske, Adrian. "Matthew." In *The International Bible Commentary*, 1253–1330. Collegeville, MN: Liturgical Press, 1998.

McKenzie, J. L. *Dictionary of the Bible*. Bangalore: Asian Trading Cooperation, 1998.

Meier, J. P. *Mentor, Message and Miracles: vol 2 of A Marginal Jew: Rethinking of the Historical Jesus*. New York: Doubleday, 1994.

Pennington, J. *Heaven and Earth in the Gospel of Matthew*. Novum Testamentum Suplement 126. Leiden: Brill, 2007.

Pope Paul VI. *Lumen Gentium: Dogmatic Constitution on the Church*. 1964.

Schreiner, T. R. *New Testament Theology. Magnifying God in Christ*. Grand Rapids: Baker Academic, 2008.

Senior, D., and C. P. Stuhlmueller. *The Biblical Foundations for Mission*. New York: Orbis Books, 1983.

Viviano, B. T. "The Gospel According to Matthew." In *The New Jerome Biblical Commentary*, 630–74. London: Geoffrey Chapman, 1993.

CHAPTER 16

Human Import as Instrument of Divine Mission
in the Prophecy of Ezekiel 36:22–23

GERALD EMEM UMOREN

INTRODUCTION

It is possible to imagine that every divine action in the Old Testament would benefit the overall plan of creation and election. One aspect of the divine plan that needs to be addressed is how much and in what way human involvement in any divine mission is desired and allowed. The Old Testament is basically a history of salvation typified in God's relationship with Israel. At a point, God allowed Israel to be taken into exile. Though this was traumatic, it paradoxically ignited the flame of hope. The renewal of Israel, for example, is a major article of hope in the life of Israel as they struggled with the demands of the postexilic rehabilitation. The place of human involvement in divine mission calls for an objective study because of how much it can shape the attitude, mentality, and disposition to divine mission.

The renewal of Israel is presented, in most cases, as a divine project in the Scriptures. It becomes a viable situation to determine the extent, level, and nature of human involvement in it. Of course, the general tendency is to expect some human involvement in this type of divine action. But how? Especially in a divine mission for his benefit, would man be indifferent or would he have anything to do in collaboration? If yes, what and to what extent?

In order to better understand the focus here, there is need to clarify the usage of a few terms within this context. These terms would include "mission," "divine mission," "renewal of Israel," and "human instrumentality."

Ordinarily, the word "mission" connotes the entire idea of reaching out to spread the faith. It is both the vocation to, and the pursuit of, the mandate to propagate faith in God, especially among outsiders (like non-Israelites in the Old Testament and non-believers today). But to understand the missionary dimension of this, it is important to explore the precise meaning, nature, and scope of mission from the passage.[1]

It is not enough to have the need to reach out, but one must also have the mandate (whether explicit or implicit) with which to motivate and activate that need. But this essay would consider mission in a broad and inclusive way. It will include any and every task, religious and secular, which one sets out to achieve and accomplish. When it is a task that God sets out to do, it is referred to as "divine mission," and when it is a task that man sets out to do, it is called a "human mission." "Mission" captures also the aspect of evangelization and other man-related tasks of life. The defining attitude here is that God or man—as the case may be—sets out to do something or act in some way for the enlightenment or benefit of a situation or people.

Again, the reference to "renewal of Israel" in this work also needs to be clarified. One defining point in the life of Israel was the exile. With the Babylonian exile, Israel lost three important things in one day. They lost their king, their land, and their temple. In the exile, Israel lost her identity as a sovereign polity. In this context, a reference to postexilic restoration is understood and captured as "renewal." Renewal, here, therefore means a return of the people and nation to preexilic dignity. But Israel did not return herself. That was caused to happen. The understanding is that God caused it to happen. God himself declared that the return of Israel was a task for him to effect and accomplish. It qualifies, in this context, to be called "divine mission." This mission is termed that of renewal because it renewed the hopes and aspirations of Israel, which, at a point, were almost lost.

Another term used here is "human instrumentality." This is looking at the possibility and extent that human involvement in divine mission can take. The decision to refer to it as being instrumental is because all divine missions have God as a primary facilitator of the task while human collaboration can only best be described as instrumental. The big question that this work hopes to answer is: What, then, would be the nature and extent of this human collaboration or instrumentality, and how far/much can this benefit future divine-human collaboration? There is the hope that lessons and conclusions would be drawn from this to benefit future divine-human collaboration in mission.

Exegesis of the Text

Even though the focus of our essay would be on Ezekiel 36:22–23, the entirety of Ezekiel 36 (especially vv. 16–31) would provide the working environment of this research. For brevity, this work would primarily present Ezekiel 36:22–23 for analysis.

---

1. On the meaning, nature, and scope of mission in the Bible, a useful reading would be the very detailed presentation by Okure in her book. See Okure, *Johannine Approach*, 1ff.

A Biblical Approach to Mission in Context

Text in Transliterated Hebrew

22 lākēn ʾĕmōr ləbêt-yiśrāʾēl kōh ʾāmar ʾădōnāi ʾădōnāi lōʾ ləmaʿankem ʾănî ʿōśeh bêt yiśrāʾēl kî ʾim-ləšēm-qādəšî ʾăšer ḥillaltem baggôyim ʾăšer-bāʾtem šām. 23 wəqiddaštî ʾet-šəmî haggādôl hamməḥullāl baggôyim ʾăšer ḥillaltem bətôkām wəyādəʿû haggôyim kî-ʾănî ʾădōnāi nəʾum ʾădōnāi ʾădōnāi bəhiqqādəšî bākem ləʿênêhem.

Text in English (NRSV)

22 Therefore say to the house of Israel, Thus says the Lord God: It is not for your sake, O house of Israel, that I am about to act, but for the sake of my holy name, which you have profaned among the nations to which you came. 23 I will sanctify my great name, which has been profaned among the nations, and which you have profaned among them; and the nations shall know that I am the Lord, says the Lord God, when through you I display my holiness before their eyes.

Analysis of the Text

As has already been noted above, the meaningful overview of this text will have to accommodate the entire narrative from verses 16 to 31. It is within this larger environment that the shorter, verses 22 and 23, will make meaning—as part of the whole. The entire passage is an explanation of Israel's plight. It reveals the sins of Israel (infidelity); the consequences of their sins (exile); and the reversal of those consequences (renewal). Taking the passage the way it is presented to us,[2] it is generally seen to focus on a divine task that plays out in the renewal and rehabilitation of Israel as a people and as a nation. For a systematic appreciation, together with its literary criticism, this exegesis will attempt a structural, historical, formal, and detailed analysis of the text.

It is important to appreciate the structural pattern of this passage. Generally, many scholars agree that the book of Ezekiel could be divided into three parts:[3] (1) the divine punishment of Israel (Ezek 1–24); (2) prelude to the restoration and punishment of the foreign powers that oppress Israel (Ezek 25–32); and (3) the promise of the restoration of Israel as a new people to a new Jerusalem (Ezek 33–48).[4] Our passage of concentration, study, and focus falls within this third section—the oracle of

---

2. There are no major textual issues in this passage. Even with a few possible editings, it is safe to accept the final text, as we have it, as authentic. For the purpose of this essay, we work with the passage in its final form.

3. The scholars who share this thought include Carvalho, "Ezekiel," 731–72; Davis, *Swallowing the Scroll*, 7ff: 55; Lyons, *An Introduction to the Study of Ezekiel*, 49ff; and Odell, Ezekiel, Smith, and Helwys, *Bible Commentary*, 33ff.

4. See Udoette, *Messengers of God*, 191; and also see Udoette, "Prophecy," 2001.

the restoration/renewal of Israel as presented in Ezekiel 36:16–32.[5] Within this circle, too, this research sets out to study verses 22–23.

Though different scholars may have reasons for different explanations of the pattern of this passage,[6] this essay reads into this work a tripartite progressive pattern that is typically didactic. First of all, it is good to take the entire stretch of verses 16 to 31 as seen in three parts: The first part (vv. 16–21) is the statement of case. It captures the initial default in Jerusalem (vv. 16–17); the initial divine judgment (vv. 18–19); further default outside Jerusalem (vv. 20–21); and God's concern (v. 21). Part two has to do with divine restoration (vv. 22–27). This captures divine declaration in v. 22 and details of divine intervention in vv. 23–27. Part three (vv. 28–31) talks about the missionary effects of divine intervention.

The structure of the main text of Ezekiel 36:22–23 is to be understood from the structure of the wider passage as shown above. Ezekiel 36:22–23 is very clear and sequential. Verse 22 is a declaration of divine mission, and verse 23 captures the way the mission will be carried out. Taken together, they are also very instructive of the way this divine task (mission) was to ensue and the nature, if any, that the human instrumentality is to be understood.

The structure attests to some imminent plan of sure action for this divine mission. The structure is somewhat that of parallelism. The evident repetition of the resolve to act, the way to act, and the reason to act confirm the intent of emphasis. The parallelism also reflects in the presentation of the key players in the intended divine mission: God, Israel, and the nations.

> It is not for your **sake**, O house of Israel, that I am about to **act**,
> but for the **sake** of my holy **name**, which you have **profaned** among the nations to which you came.
> I will sanctify my great **name,** which has been **profaned** among the **nations**, and which you have profaned among them;
> and the **nations** shall **know** that I am the LORD, says the Lord GOD, when
> **through you** I display my holiness before their eyes.

Gathering all the pieces of this structural analysis, it is clear that God is about to perform a "task" for a "reason" and in a "manner" that will yield the desired "result."

The historical background of this text will also help in its appreciation. The remote background of this passage is the return from exile and the eventual restoration of Israel. At the exile, the loss of the land, temple, and king meant a lot to Israel and

---

5. Read also Allen, "Ezekiel 20–48," 1990; Biggs, *The Book of Ezekiel*, 1996; and Feinberg, *The Prophecy of Ezekiel*, 1969.

6. Paul M. Joyce tends to agree with Michael Lyons and Daniel I. Block that the book of Ezekiel has a substantial coherent core and an overt structure that combines different literary presentations which make it difficult to narrow its structure to a particular one. Each passage needs a contextual determination of its peculiar structure depending on the perspective of study. Cf. Joyce, *Ezekiel*, 37.

their belief in Yahweh. Ezekiel 36:16–32 reflects the reason, consequences, and reversal of the unfortunate consequences of Israel's conduct. But there is also the proximate background of this text. The attack of Israel by the Edomites[7] and all the challenges of the postexilic restoration constitute the proximate milieu of this passage. God allowed Israel into the hands of its enemies as judgment for their infidelity, but the effect of this divine judgment must have become more injurious to the religious integrity of the people. The God of Israel may have been seen by the nations as a God who was not capable of saving his people. This background may have called for the proposed "quick action" by God. The situation truly called for intervention,n and this passage, Ezekiel 36:22–23, reflects this historical background.

Even from the larger unit of this passage referencing the renewal of Israel as a divine mission, one can appreciate the historical background mentioned above. Ezeliel 36:16–31 presents a unit of divine pronouncement beginning with the typical prophetic formula of Ezekiel: "The word of the Lord came to me" (v. 16), and ending with a confirmatory divine sign-off: "says the Lord God" (v. 32). There is a progression from the *statement of Israel's default*, to the *declaration of divine intervention to renew the people*, and to the *nature and effects* of such renewal. It is an address that touches the *past*, the *present*, and the *future* of Israel. Yahweh redeems Israel for the sake of his name. It is within the understanding of this divine mission that one can see the place of human instrumentality.

Apart from the historical analysis above, a detailed analysis of the text, which would capture the literary and, possibly, the text-critical overview, would help not only to uncover the true nature, reason, and manner of the divine mission but also shed light on the human instrumentality here. This text could thus be paraphrased:

> Thus says the Lord to Israel. For the sake of my name which you profaned, I am about to act, through you, to sanctify that Name so that the Nations would know that I am God.[8]

This paraphrase helps to bring out the *nature, reason,* and *manner* of this divine task.

God is about to act (*'āšāḥ*) for the sake of his name (*šēm*), which was profaned (*ḥālal*) by Israel among the nations. The desired resultant effect is for the nations to know (*Yāḏaʿ*) God. The two verses (vv. 22–23) answer the *why* and *how* of this divine mission. In both verses, man (Israel) is involved. In the first, he is accused of being part of the problem. He profaned God's name, and in verse 23, he is reminded to be part of the solution.

The study text of Ezekiel 36:22–23, therefore, is God's resolve to correct the wrong impression by the nations. God resolved to act (v. 22). He was not acting for

---

7. In the time of Nebuchadnezzar II, the Edomites may have come against the inhabitants of Jerusalem and Judea in 587 or 586 BC. See Ps 137:7 and Obad 1:11–14.

8. This paraphrase does capture the main points in the text: The mission of God, the reason for the mission, and the manner it is to be carried out.

the sake of Israel. But he declared his intent to act "through" the Israelites. This has opened up the debate on human involvement in divine mission. By bringing Israel back, in verses 22–23, God concretized his mission to restore the honor of his name. In verses 25–27, God would not only renew them physically and spiritually, he would, in verses 28–30, also renew the land to which they would return. All those, as seen in verses 31–32, were primarily to restore the honor of his name among the nations who used to mock him. But God needed to restore and preserve the integrity, honor, and holiness of his name. He needed the nations to "know" him and realize his sovereignty. This was to be better done "through" the Israelites themselves. The entire text of Ezekiel 36:22–23 projects a thesis that most divine mission is for man's good and would need human cooperation and involvement for it to meaningfully achieve the intended divine purpose. This human cooperation and involvement can better be defined in terms of instrumentality. In Ezekiel 36:22–23, the intended goal of the divine mission was to be reached through the human instrumentality of Israel. This analysis result opens up the import of human instrumentality in divine mission.

RENEWAL OF ISRAEL IN EZEKIEL AS A DIVINE MISSION

The fact of renewal is clear in the passage. God moves to restore his people. But there are some aspects of this renewal that are important for our discussion on human instrumentality. In determining the place of human instrumentality, there is need for better appreciation of the motivation and effect of divine mission.[9]

Nature of Divine Mission

As found out from the analysis above, Israel was obviously in exile. The divine mission has unfolded itself in God's resolve to facilitate the return from exile. It was God, moved by the profanation of his name, who intervened to bring Israel back to space. The divine mission, by nature, was to be an action that would prove a point about the might of God and his ability to restore his chosen people and the integrity of his name. The use of the verb "act" (ʽāśāḥ) is very significant. This verb connotes doing something practical and tangible. The nature of the divine mission here would have entailed a physical action to restore the integrity of His name.

Motivation for the Divine Mission of Renewal

God was motivated to act. The situation that gave the motivation is very instructive of the relevance of human instrumentality in this divine mission. God was about to do

---

9. For more reading on this, see Ganzel, "Restoration of Israel in Ezekiel," 197–211; Greenberg, *Ezekiel 21–37*, 32ff; Smith, *Interpreting the Prophetic Books*,.1ff; Tuell, *Ezekiel*, 47ff; Gemeren, "The Spirit of Restoration," 81–102; Crane, "Israel's Restoration," 2008.

something. In the past, God took responsibility for the judgment of his people. In the context of the judgment, the passage introduces a negative conjunction in verse 20: Israel rather profaned (*ḥalal*) the name of the Lord, and that became a real concern for the Lord. The use of the verb *ḥamal* is significant. The wide connotation of meaning of *ḥamal* reveals much about the attitude of God here. The verb *ḥamal* connotes "feeling compassion," "pity for," "sparing," "keeping back." All these suggest an attitude of "concern" on God's part. He was concerned about his holy name. *wā' eḥmōl ' al-šēm qādəšî ' ăšer ḥilləlûhû bêt yiśrā' ēl baggôyim ' ăšer-bā' û šammāh* ("But I had pity for my holy name which the house of Israel had profaned").[10] A God who has concern about his name would not lack concern about the plight of his suffering people.

> Therefore say to the house of Israel, Thus says the Lord God: It is not for your sake, O house of Israel, that I am about to act, but for the sake of my holy name, which you have profaned among the nations to which you came.[11]

God's motivation for the renewal of Israel is the concern he has for his divine reputation.[12] But would this mean that God would not have intervened in the judgment of Israel if the reputation of his name were not threatened? When God judged Israel in verses 16–20, it was as a result of their misconduct. God was indirectly protecting his integrity. Now again, in verses 21–22, He is intervening directly to protect His integrity. But one can ask: Why did God's restoration and renewal not wait for human initiative? Given that the profanation of God's name was caused by Israel, one would wonder why repentance was not a prerequisite for God's redemptive act.[13] God had concern. God was mindful. God was anxious, and God needed to be careful. God will both cleanse them of their past impurity and ensure their future compliance.[14] In mission, as demonstrated by this passage of Ezekiel, it is God who takes the initiative to send, and most often, as in this case, for the sake of his name.

Again, one could still ask: Where is the concern for the people? The answer to this puzzle is contained in verse 23. God sets out to restore, renew, and reposition Israel in order to achieve, through her, his mission of getting the people to know him. The primary motivation may have been a mission for the restoration of his name, but the implied motivation, even if secondary, was the reestablishment of his covenanted people.[15] Even though God may have said in verse 22 that he was not acting for the

---

10. Ezek 36:21 shows the divine quality of concern, compassion, and pity.

11. Ezek 36:22 follows immediately from verse 21, which could connect that quality of concern for his name to concern for his people.

12. Dar, *The Book of Ezekiel*, 1491.

13. For more on this debate, see Dar, *Ezekiel*, 1491; also cf. Block, *Ezekiel: Chapters 25–48*, 107ff.

14. Dar, *Ezekiel*, 1491.

15. The text is very clear on the reason for the renewal. This is captured well in v. 22. God started by correcting some impression. The reason for renewal was not for the sake of Israel (*lō' ləma' ankem ' ă[set caron over a]nî ' ōśeh*). It was for the sake of God's name (*šēm*). Does it mean that Israel was not important in the sight of God? No it only means that there was something much more at stake. The

sake of Israel, consistency in biblical theology of salvation cannot exclude the fact that God was also motivated to act out of concern for his people Israel. With this attitude, God set out to act, and he spells out his divine mission in verses 22–23. Yes, the name had to be redeemed; the nations would have to come to the knowledge of God—but all this would happen "through" the instrumentality of Israel. This is confirmed in the eventual renewal of Israel which gives meaning to the terms of the covenant: "You shall be my people and I will be your God."[16]

THE NATURE AND DEMANDS OF HUMAN INSTRUMENTALITY IN DIVINE MISSION

Ezekiel 36:23 captures vividly the manner of the intended renewal of Israel.

> I will sanctify my great name, which has been profaned among the nations, and which you have profaned among them; and the nations shall know that I am the Lord, says the Lord God, when through you I display my holiness before their eyes.[17]

Here God is saying one thing in two ways. He is saying that he would rehabilitate Israel. The passage talks about sanctifying God's great name (*wəqiddaštî' et-šəmî haggāḏôl*),= and also displaying God's holiness before the eyes of the nation (*bəhiqqāḏəšî bākem lə' ênêhem*). These are not entirely two separate actions. It is one action with multiple effects. The fact is that the conduct of Israel had brought reproach to God's name. Now, even though God is resolved to embark on this divine mission, just as Israel was part of the default, she is being invited to be part of the repair also. It is from this point of view that this passage reflects well desired information about human instrumentality in divine mission. What, then, are the demands of this human instrumentality?

It is here that this research must project the import of the preposition "in" or "through." The Hebrew preposition *bə* is what defines the nature of the human instrumentality. This preposition can be expressed in many ways depending on the content and context. It is "in." But it can be "through." It can be "to." The display of holiness has to be in Israel, by Israel, through Israel, etc. Israel now becomes not just a channel of the display of God's holiness; Israel becomes an instrument through which God's holiness would be displayed and enforced. From the analysis of the text, the nature of human instrumentality here is that of active involvement in promoting the design of God's action. The action is God's, the design is God's, but man is accommodated as a facilitating agent especially because the actor, God, wants him to benefit maximally from the divine mission.

---

profaned name of God had to be sanctified first before the restoration of Israel would make meaning. But there is another dimension to this in v. 23 that the sanctification of God's name would entail the physical rehabilitation of Israel to their land.

16. See Ezekiel, 17ff.
17. Ezek 36:23. Emphasis mine.

It is also to explore the demands of this human instrumentality. Since the goal of this divine mission is to bring the nations to know God, Israel can also be seen as a teacher and model of such holiness. Given the background of Israel—their recurrent infidelity to the covenant term in the past—this responsibility is more or less a call to holiness. Israel cannot be passive in divine mission. Human instrumentality in divine mission demands, first of all, fidelity to the terms of the covenant. It demands holiness and responsibility. It demands good discipleship and faithful projection and representation of divine commands. As verse 23 captures, the human agent needs to be disposed to "display" the holiness of God among the nations. The Hebrew word used here is *N' um*, which connotes declaration as when a prophet makes an utterance. In divine mission, human instrumentality would demand that the agent act like a prophetic messenger, declaring the greatness and holiness of God by word and action.

The Effect of the Divine Mission of Renewal

This divine mission has both short-term and long-term effects. The short-term effect, as implied in the passage, is the return and restoration of Israel to their land and heritage. This will lead to the sanctification of God's name. But the long-term effect is to get the nations not only to know (*Yāda‘*) the Lord, but to learn divine holiness displayed by the rehabilitated Israelites. The nations have to come to realize the way of God and the mission of God. They will come to this knowledge and realization through Israel.[18]

From a broader perspective, going further, one sees other effects of renewal in verses 28–32. Not just that the people will be restored but the land would also be renewed. The people would be "purified, transformed and totally obedient."[19] The entire passage has a covenantal outlook.[20] But the most significant effect of God's intervention in the plight of Israel is the renewal of the covenant relationship.[21] This is why the human instrumentality is very relevant. Part of the announcement of Israel's restoration explicitly reminded them of, and recalled them to, covenant relationship.[22]

Human Instrumentality as Mandate to Make God's Name Known

The renewal of Israel is truly a mission to make God's name known. God is the ultimate determinant of the course of mission.[23] Mission cannot exclude mandate. Mandate has to be given by an authority for a good reason. Depending on the object of

---

18. The effect of this divine mission would really be seen in the nations when they come, through the instrumentality of Israel, to the knowledge of holiness and good conduct.
19. Dar, *Ezekiel*, 1492.
20. See Boadt, "Ezekiel," 325.
21. See Raitt, *A Theology of Exile*, 78ff.
22. See Eissfeldt, *The Old Testament*, 380–81.
23. See Eichrodt, *Ezekiel*, 74ff.

mission, it is important that the subject determine the course. From the analysis of our text above, human instrumentality in divine mission constitutes a mandate to make God's name known to the nations.

God explicitly declared: "I will sanctify my great name, which has been profaned among the nations, and which you have profaned among them; and the nations shall know that I am the Lord, says the Lord God, when through you I display my holiness before their eyes" (Ezek 36:24). The two important component words in this missionary mandate are "name" (šēm) and the verb "know" (Yāda'). The verb Yāda' connotes more than ordinary cognitive ability. In addition to gaining knowledge, this verb calls for the appreciation of what is known and the rightful declaration by word and action of the true value and worth of God's name. It shares the connotation of "acknowledging" or "acceptance." The name referred to here is God's name. It is not merely the name as an appellation or a title, it is also the significance of that appellation. God's name is YHWH, and by it God reveals himself. It is by YHWH that God can be known and is actually known. This name is sacred, distinctive, and incommunicable. God is known by this name and his major attributes are discerned by it. This is the mandate that the human agent by instrumentality is given to exercise. In Ezekel 36: 23ff., God is concerned about the profanation of that name. Not the profanation of the appellation alone but, more still, the profanation of the import of that name, the profanation of the divine being. It was the deprivation of its value of holiness and fidelity by the Israelites and eventually by the pagan nations that caused a serious concern for God. He had to quickly intervene to redeem his image and integrity. God quickly, even if implicitly, gave a mandate to Israel to make the import of that name known, respected, hallowed, and appreciated. The same Israel that was the cause of the profanation of this name is called to be the agent of its restoration. God says in verse 23 that it would be done "through" Israel: " the nations shall know that I am the Lord, says the Lord God, when through you I display my holiness before their eyes."[24] In this mission, the mandate of Israel, by human instrumentality, was to make God's name known. Israel was to spearhead the restoration of the sanctity and the holiness associated with the name of God as a faithful God.[25]

Human Instrumentality as a Call to Witness in Divine Mission

It is interesting to see that the same Israel that caused the profanation of God's name is the same Israel that is projected in Ezekiel as the vessel of the restoration of the integrity of God's name. But what did Israel do to profane God's name? Verse 16 records that, first of all, they defiled their land and displayed bad conduct before God: "When the house of Israel lived on their own soil, they defiled it with their ways and their deeds; their conduct in my sight was like the uncleanness of a woman in her

---

24. Ezekiel 36:23b is presented here to demonstrate the emphasis, which is mine.
25. For more on the subject of mission, see Carley, "The Book of the Prophet Ezekiel," 137ff.

menstrual period." Again, after God had judged them and punished them with exile, it was Israel again who formed the object of the profanation of God's name "in that it was said of them, 'these are the people of the Lord, and yet they had to go out of his land'" (Ezek 36: 20b).

What happened to Israel sent a wrong signal to the pagan nations who felt the Israelite God was not as faithful as claimed. By implication, it means that Israel did not show proper witness to the worth of their God. This idea of witnessing, as an important aspect of mission, is seen in verse 23 when the prophecy of Ezekiel explicitly holds that the pagan nations would come to the full knowledge of God "through" Israel. Israel has to witness in order to restore the reputation of their God among the pagan nations.[26] Human instrumentality in divine mission is fulfilled in witness.

Human Instrumentality in Mission: A Divine Call to Holiness

The passage under review, Ezekiel 36: 16–32, shows that mission is a divine call to holiness. Israel, by virtue of her calling, has always been on mission—a mission to witness to her privileged election by the God of the covenant. Ezekiel 36: 17 captures the uncleanliness of the Israelites as the cause of their profanation of God's name. God's name was desecrated by the attitude of the Israelites.[27] The choice of the verb *tm'*, connoting defilement, pollution, and even idolatory, and the comparison with a situation of a woman's menstrual flow, with all the "cultic uncleanliness" associated with it, reveals how unholy Israel had become in their ways and deeds: "their conduct in my sight was like the uncleanness of a woman in her menstrual period."[28] God had expected Israel to witness to his holiness by also remaining holy, undefiled, and uncontaminated in and outside their land, but here, they failed and were not spared of God's judgment. This missionary dimension of a divine call to holiness cannot be overlooked in the context of the renewal of Israel in Ezekiel.

Evaluation

Most of what could be called divine mission, as understood in this context, is for the benefit of man. But when God sets out to accomplish a task, especially those that are not only related to man but also beneficial to him, it is necessary to determine if and what the nature, level, and extent of the expected human involvement in such divine mission could be. Ezekiel 36:22–23 has provided a relevant study text for the appreciation of such human involvement in divine mission. From the analysis of that text, this research has found out that even though God set out to act for the sake of his name and not for the sake of Israel, he still left room for the involvement and

26. For more on this idea of witnessing, see Derek, *Ezekiel 36:16-32*.
27. Cf. Coogan et al., "Commentary on Ezekiel 36:15-32," 1989.
28. Dar, *Ezekiel*, 1488.

collaboration of Israel in the eventual restoration of the land and the people. This research confirmed not only the "room" for human involvement in divine mission, but also the nature, demands, and extent of such involvement. The involvement of man is confirmed to be a type of instrumental involvement. This research, therefore, has not only established the existence of instrumentality in divine mission, but also has explored the extent of such instrumentality. Man is not only called to be a receptacle of divine holiness, he is to display such holiness before the nations in order to lead them to the full knowledge of God. Drawing inspiration from this, human instrumentality has become a very relevant dimension of divine mission. The results of the enquiry into the import of this human instrumentality in divine mission have turned out to be so relevant that this research is projecting human instrumentality as a paradigm for divine-human collaboration. After a detailed examination of the import of this human instrumentality in divine mission, both in the Old Testament times and as it would apply today, it is only right that useful recommendations also be made before the final conclusion is given.

Projecting Divine-Human Collaboration in Mission

Even though God does not necessarily depend on man for the materialization and success of his plans, tasks, and mission, man depends on God for the maximal realization of the full potentials and benefits of divine mission. But, interestingly, God expects man to at least be a willing receptacle of his divine mission. All that this means is that some sort of divine-human collaboration is a meaningful requirement in divine mission.

The idea of instrumentality fits in here. Divine mission is God's task. But man could and should be a ready, willing, and useful instrument in God's hand for the eventual realization of the goal of such divine mission. This type of collaboration would then be projected as a paradigm and would need to be enforced. Human instrumentality entails that the human partner in a divine mission—whether it is a person or a group—should readily see himself or themselves as partners in mission.

Divine mission must eventually manifest God. The human instrumentality demands that such knowledge or manifestation of God be done through the instrumentality of the human agent. This human instrumentality becomes a witness to the divine design and an invitation to renewed responsibility and collaboration with the tasks of God. This would enhance meaningful results for mission, on the one hand, and also challenge the human partner unto renewed integrity and responsibility to make God known and sustain the holiness of his name, on the other. If this is adopted by all who participate in divine mission, the results would be awesome for mission, for missionaries, and for all concerned in pastoral ministry. It is from this point of view and emboldened by the findings of this research that it is safe to project the attitude and practice of human instrumentality as a paradigm in divine mission.

CONCLUSION

In the course of the submissions above, the analysis of the text has revealed that God needs man in order to save man. Divine human collaboration would always be desired, especially in mission. Among many ways that this can be done, the idea of instrumentality proves to be the most meaningful type of collaboration that man can have with God. By instrumentality, man is not expected to be just a passive receiver of divine favors. He is called to be an active participant in the divine mission. By instrumentality, man is called to be the face of God in the world. There is always a missionary dimension to one's faith journey. However this mission is lived out, it cannot be seen to be complete until man presents himself as a ready channel of divine communication. The world needs to know God. The world needs to understand God. Man, and only man, can be the agent of this mission. God needs human agents as instruments of his divine mission. It is not that God cannot do without human agents, but because he knows they cannot do without him. Just as the restoration of the reputation of God's name was to be done *through* (meaning: by the instrumentality of the words and deeds of) Israel in the text we studied, every divine mission can, could, and should definitely be pursued to its final goal through the instrumentality of a human agent. When and where this need for human instrumentality is projected and utilized in divine mission, gains for scholarship and benefits for pastoral care and missiology,would abound.

BIBLIOGRAPHY

Allen, L. C. "Ezekiel 20–48." In *Word Biblical Commentary 29*. Waco, TX: Word Books, 1990.

Biggs, C. R. *The Book of Ezekiel*. London: Epworth Press, 1996.

Blenkinsopp, J. *Ezekiel*. International Bible Commentary. Louisville: John Knox, 1990.

Block, D. I. *The Book of Ezekiel: Chapters 25–48*. New International Commentary of the Old Testament (NICOT). Grand Rapids: Eerdmans, 1998.

Boadt, Lawrence. "Ezekiel." In *The New Jerome Biblical Commentary*, 305–28. Edited by Raymond E. Brown et al. NJ: Prentice-Hall, 1990.

Carley, K. W. "The Book of the Prophet Ezekiel." In *The Cambridge Bible Commentary on the New English Bible*. Cambridge: Cambridge University Press, 1974.

Carvalho, Corrine. "Ezekiel." In *The Paulist Biblical Commentary*, 731–72. Edited by Jose Enrique Aguilar Chiu et al. Mahwah, NJ: Paulist Press, 2018.

Coogan, Michael D., et al., eds. "Commentary on Ezekiel 36:15–32." In *The New Oxford Annotated Bible*. 3rd edition. NY: Oxford University Press, 1989.

Cooke, G. A. *A Critical and Exegetical Commentary on the Book of Ezekiel*. The International Critical Commentary. London: T&T Clarke, 1936.

Crane, Ashley E. "Israel's Restoration: A Textual-Comparative Exploration of Ezekiel 36–39." SUPPLEMENTS TO *Vetus Testamentum 122*. Leiden: Brill, 2008.

Dar, K. P. *The Book of Ezekiel: Introduction, Commentary and Reflections*. The New Interpreter's Bible VI. Edited by Leander E. Keck et al. Nashville: Abingdon, 2001.

Davis, Ellen F. *Swallowing the Scroll: Textuality and the Dynamics of Discourse in Ezekiel's Prophecy*. JSOTSup 78. Sheffield: Sheffield Academic, 1989.

Eichrodt, W. *Ezekiel: A Commentary.* The Old Testament Library. London: SCM Press, 1970.

Eissfledt, Otto, *The Old Testament: An Introduction.* Edited by Peter R. Ackroyd. NY: Harper & Row, 1965.

Feinberg, C. L. *The Prophecy of Ezekiel.* Chicago: Moody Press, 1969.

Ganzel, Tova. "The Descriptions of the Restoration of Israel in Ezekiel." *Vetus Testamentum* 60, no. 2 (2010) 197–211.

Greenberg, Moshe. *Ezekiel 21–37: A New Translation with Introduction and Commentary.* Anchor Yale Bible 22A. New Haven: Yale University Press, 2008.

Joyce, Paul M. *Ezekiel: A Commentary.* Library of Hebrew Bible/Old Testament Studies 482. New York: T&T Clark, 2007.

Kutsko, John. *Between Heaven and Earth: Divine Presence and Absence in the Book of Ezekiel.* Winona Lake, IN: Eisenbrauns, 2000.

Lyons, Michael A. *An Introduction to the Study of Ezekiel.* T&T Clark Approaches to Biblical Studies. New York: Bloomsbury, 2015.

Nyoyoko, Vincent G. "The Structure of Old Testament Cosmic Covenant: Its Relevance in Contemporary Society." *The Oracle* 1, no. 6 (2003) 94–105.

Odell, Margaret S. *Ezekiel, Smith & Helwys Bible Commentary.* Macon, GA: Smith & Helwys, 2005.

Okure, T. *The Johannine Approach to Mission: A Contextual study of John 4: 1–42.* Tübingen: JCB Mohr, 1988.

Raitt, T. A. *A Theology of Exile.* Philadelphia: Fortress Press, 1977.

Smith, Gary V. *Interpreting the Prophetic Books: An Exegetical Handbook.* Grand Rapids: Kregel Academic, 2014.

Taylor, J. B. *Ezekiel: An Introduction and Commentary.* The Tyndale Old Testament Commentaries. Tyndale Press, 1969.

Tuell, Steven. *Ezekiel.* Edited by W. Ward Gasque et al. Understanding the Bible Commentary Series. Grand Rapids: Baker, 2009.

Udoette, D. "Prophecy in Israel and in the New Religious Movements in Nigeria." *The Oracle* 1, no. 2 (2001).

———. *Messengers of God.* Uyo: Bricks, 2008.

Van Gemeren, W. A. "The Spirit of Restoration." *Westminster Theological Journal* 50 (1988) 81–102.

Westermann, C. *Prophetic Oracles of Salvation in the Old Testament.* Louisville: Westminister John Knox, 1991.

Wilder, Derek. *Ezekiel 36: 16–32: A Crisis and Recovery of Honour.* N.p. N.d.

Chapter 17

Sr. Teresa Okure, SHCJ
A Narrative of Personal Encounter Rooted in John 10:10

Bernadette Eyewan Okure, SHCJ

BACKGROUND

Holy Child Sister Teresa Okure was born into the God-fearing and humble family of Chief Basil Udo and Madam Paulina Affiong Okure, both first-generation Christians in their families. Sister Teresa was raised with sound spiritual and moral values by her parents, who were staunch Catholics, teacher-catechists entrusted with many leadership roles. They were instrumental in opening new churches and schools, founded Legion of Mary groups, prepared people for the sacraments, and conducted morning prayers during weekdays and Sunday services when a priest was not available.

Besides the inspiration of her devout parents and immediate family, Sr. Teresa learned from other teachers and formators too many to count, from primary through high school to initial formation in religious life, undergraduate studies, ongoing formation, and post-graduate studies, all of which have positioned her to take initiative and responseability to make outstanding contributions to academia, ecclesial, and human transformation within Nigeria, Africa, Europe, Asia, and America.

This write-up is not a biography of Sr. Teresa Okure, a consummate biblical scholar, a woman passionate about life as God's profound gift, and who in her mentoring and accompaniment of others—young scholars, colleagues, graduate students, neophytes, associations, and academic bodies—empowers them to become their God-given best, not somebody else's second best. Rather, it is a reflection on an aspect of my experience with her as a mentor in my academic journey and how her rootedness in the Scriptures is brought to bear in that encounter.

INFLUENCE OF THE SCRIPTURE—JOHN 10:10

In the Gospel according to John, Jesus proclaims his mission thus: "The thief comes to steal and kill and destroy, but I have come that you may have life, life in all its fullness" (John 10:10). This Scripture passage has a profound impact on Sr. Teresa (a.k.a. Aunty) and has shaped her engagements in many ways. Her frequent reference to this passage has earned her the name "John 10:10," given to her by her religious sisters and younger siblings. This name, John 10:10, is not just a label but is an appreciation of her obviously deep love for and faith in Jesus, who has come that we may have life, life in all its fullness. The fruit of this faith in Jesus gives rise to her commitment to accompany others in their academic and spiritual life journey in such a way that enables them to discover for themselves this Jesus who has come that we may have life and consequently lead others to do the same with multiplying effects.

EXPERIENCE OF HER MENTORSHIP

In gratitude to God, I share this short narrative of one instance of my experience with and learning from Sr. Teresa. I have learned a lot from her, my big sister, as mentor, as role model in the religious life, and as a Christian who is grounded in the life of Jesus. The one experience I wish to share concerns her mentorship and accompaniment as my field academic supervisor. I give glory to God for the gift of her and for my benefiting firsthand from her expertise in my academic journey, particularly during the 2002–2007 intensive academic work. As a doctoral student researcher, I chose, with the approval of my faculty, to return to Nigeria for an extended human subject research. My school asked me to give three names of possible field supervisors in Nigeria. I submitted three names for vetting, and, to my delight, Sr. Teresa was their first choice to assist me as my external field supervisor and their representative.

I came home happy that she was the first choice for both me and my academic team but knowing that she would be critical and firm, not in any way lenient with me. I was challenged by and attracted to her outstanding academic discipline, honesty, integrity, excellence, and Christ-centered detachment. Listening to and watching her, I came to realize how important it was to dedicate the study to Jesus and therefore how necessary it was to sit before the Blessed Sacrament at least an hour daily to listen to God, and consequently to learn how to hear what the participants were sharing with me. This short story focuses on one encounter; there are others, but I have chosen this particular one as it demonstrates how God used Sr. Teresa to enable me and the multiplying effects of that enabling.

ENCOUNTERS AS FIELD SUPERVISOR

I conducted my field research for six months in three locations in Lagos based on the process approved by my school at the Graduate Theological Union, Berkeley. Her honest and positive regard empowered me to engage in own my fieldwork, further clarify my questions, and search for the answers by myself. In my research work, I engaged fifteen adults, five each from three locations. She encouraged me not to overlook my mistakes or to run away from them but rather to take a critical look at them as a constructive platform for learning toward growth and transformation. By interacting with her at this level, I was inspired to engage in the research not just as an academic exercise but also as a spiritual journey with the people I interviewed. I drew strength from this exercise and trusted what Venerable Cornelia Connelly said:

> It is most particularly before the Blessed Sacrament that our good thoughts present themselves and many a difficulty is there solved that our weakness could not have encountered alone."

Discovering Personal Values

At the initial stage of the process, she inspired me to make a list of what I would value in the course of the research. My list included: prayer, daily reading and listening to the Gospel, positive self-regard, discipline of the tongue, high regard for the selected participants of the research process, punctuality, truth (no exaggerations), seeing the participants not as objects of my study but rather as disciples of Jesus, and strict adherence to the approved human subject protocol policy and the approved research outline.

Need to Take Ownership of the Process

She encouraged me to so engage the participants in a way that they too would own the exercise and make themselves open to the transforming work of the Holy Spirit. That I:

- Observe strict accountability according to the process approved by the faculty, not deviating by thinking no one was looking at me
- Bear in mind that God was observing me
- See the fieldwork as vision-driven beyond the academic degree and as an instrument of the Spirit
- Listen deeply to the participants with ears to the ground because God was speaking through them; they were not just respondents but chosen disciples to collaborate in the transforming work of God—*Ad Majorem Dei Gloriam*
- Take ownership of the fieldwork and its connection with the whole academic process, the critical assessment by the faculty and its outcome—the dissertation

I noticed how Prof. Teresa observed her boundaries as field supervisor and external examiner rather than a sibling. She was accountable at different levels to me, the student, and to the faculty at the GTU Berkeley. She did not mix up her duty by interfering with the content of the study but ensured that I kept to the approved process. If I had a question to ask her, she would let me answer it first myself before she contributed her input. She believes that the questioner always knows something about the question she or he has raised. Rather than spoon-feed the learner, she will walk one through to discover the solution personally and thus build self-confidence.

Research Process: A Celebration of Life

Listening to her, I appreciated the need for balance in the realization of the project not as a rigid process of study toward a degree but as a celebration of life. According to her, human subject research should engage the participants' mind, body, and emotions in a spirit of duty for the common good. The researcher should appreciate the fact that the participants made a free decision to let go other important needs and responsibilities to give time to the numerous research meetings. This generosity should not be taken for granted. It is not enough to mention the participants in the acknowledgement of the dissertation. It should set a standard as a celebration of life, of people volunteering to collaborate for the greater good and transformation of the society.

There were some outstanding experiences for me in my encounter with the participants of the research, of which two stand out. The first very touching one was the observation made by the participants when they said they noticed that my process was inclusive, enlightening, and deepened their spiritual life and the bond among them. Secondly, by asking if I would be willing at the end of my study to return to Nigeria, to give them a further orientation so they can deepen their groups to go around the rest of the country and engage other women in the process, they asserted, "This is what women need." Since I worked with women in the research process, I had to have a neutral person, a man to serve as my secretary, recording the responses verbatim while I concentrated on the flow of the process. The reason was that a women would find it a challenge to sit though and not be allowed to contribute to the conversation. At the end of the research, he surprisingly made a passionate appeal that men should also be given an opportunity to engage in a similar process in my next project and to benefit from it. This was thanks to Sr. Teresa's guidance that I engage the participants as disciples of Jesus rather than as subjects for research. In today's Pope Francis' formulated concept, inspired by the Holy Spirit, it is clear that Sr. Teresa encouraged the use of "Synodal process" in human subject research. No wonder she is so enthusiastic and ignites others to participate actively together in the "synod on synodality."

Presence at the Defense

As my field supervisor and external examiner, she had to come to Berkeley for my defense. The hall was full not just because of me but because news had circulated that she was coming. At the defense, she made a clarification that though she was my blood and religious sibling, she took me as she would any other student whom she would have the privilege to accompany in their academic process. She noticed the fact that the school placed their confidence in her which she, a fellow scholar, would not betray. She said she needed to clear any doubt concerning the fact that she and Bernadette were siblings and reiterated the fact that she was the choice of the faculty from among three nominees.

Many who had studied her work, especially biblical and gender hermeneutic scholars, came to have a face-to-face encounter with her and to settle some questions they had nursed about her works.

Students' Interactive Session at Graduate Theological Union (GTU) Berkeley

Since the students did not have enough time to engage with her, they decided to organize an interactive seminar with her. There were so many questions of different kinds, and Sr. Teresa listened to all patiently, showing great positive regard for each. Rather than a question-and-answer session, she made it interactive and conversational—a celebration of academic exchange between younger scholars and a senior professor. She told the students, "I too want to learn from you, to understand those questions that are of great concern for you." At the end of the seminar, one of the students said, "You made me feel I matter," and this was echoed by many. One said:

> I made up my mind and I came to fight you, but I soon realized how stupid that was. Your presence does something words cannot explain. I would like to follow you home for a while and watch and listen to you more. You live what you write.

CONCLUSION

I have shared my experience of her mentorship while at the same time trying to avoid making it a tribute to Sr. Teresa Okure. It is the one thing she does not encourage: focusing on herself. If it came across as a tribute, I am rather giving a super tribute to God, who has brought her to this world and shaped her understanding of being a disciple of Jesus through her family and the Society of the Holy Child Jesus (SHCJ) and the church in general. There is no doubt that God has used her to journey with many young and even experienced scholars, empowering them to discover their own God-given talents and strength for the greater glory of God and the advancement of the academia. Her childlike simplicity is very inspiring and challenging. She asserted that encounter with Jesus makes one realize that one's entire life is purely a gift from God and our vocation is to make that life what God wants it to be. This emphasizes Cornelia Connelly's belief that "Doing the will of God is the only happiness and the only thing worth living for."

If I were to write everything about my experience journeying with Prof. Teresa (John 10:10), it would run beyond the scope of this work as it may form a book. The reflection of what I have learned from her as her biological and religious sibling and a junior scholar whose love for human progress and academic enthusiasm continues to inspire me. God has used her to build me up and empower me to do the same for others. Thanks be to God.

I wish to affirm the dynamic Fr. Prof. Michael Ufok Udoekpo, Dean, Faculty of Humanities, Veritas University Abuja, and the editor-in-chief of this project, for the invitation extended to me to share as Sr. Teresa's sibling. May he be richly blessed in all his responsibilities at Veritas University and beyond. May God's abundant blessings be upon all who have contributed to this Festschrift to the greater glory of God. May God grant Sr. Teresa many more years in her journey of loving and respectful mentorship accompaniment and empowerment of others to discover and be true disciple of Jesus who has come that we may have life in all its fullness. To God be the glory.

CHAPTER 18

Living the New Life in Christ (Col 3:1–4) and Its Implications for Nigerian Christians

VIRGINIA SHUAIBU

INTRODUCTION

In Nigeria, churches are springing up at an alarming rate; almost every street has at least two churches, not counting the rooms and parlors converted into churches. The Redeemed Christian Church of God, for example, has a five minutes' walking distance church-planting vision across the nation. But as the number of churches has increased, so has the crime rate in the nation. The proliferation of churches has yielded little or no positive impact; on the contrary, negative effects are witnessed in the nation.

The Christian life is one that calls its followers to a completely new orientation, new focus, and a new way of living. It behoves Christians to a new orientation in Christ, focusing on Christ, and living for Christ in this ungodly, wicked, and sinful world. This is in contrast to how the majority of Christians in Nigeria presently profess the Christian faith but their lifestyle is influenced by the allure of the world. They often defend their faith at the drop of a hat, but their personal lives deny the very doctrine they profess. It is detrimental if Christians declare and defend their faith verbally but fail to demonstrate it in their lives, as exemplified in the life of our honoree, Sr. Prof. Teresa Okure, SHCJ.

The pagan religions in Paul's time did not promote personal morality. They bowed to idols, sacrificed on the altars of the idols, and continued in their life of sin. Their belief had no connection to their behavior.[1] Some Nigerian Christians are no different from the pagans in Paul's days; they can be said to be living like those pagans.

1. Wiersbe, *Colossians*, 113.

But the Christian faith has a very definite connection with how they behave because faith in Christ means being united to him, and if they share his life, they must follow his example. Paul exhorts them to seek heavenly things and set their minds heavenward, a teaching very relevant and much needed by Christians in Nigeria.

PAULINE AUTHORSHIP AND DATE

Paul's authorship of the letter to the Colossians has undergone heated controversies, some in favor and others against. Those against Paul's authorship of the book base their arguments on "literary style, vocabulary, and doctrinal emphasis that suggest a different author, but others (in favour) point out that the letter addresses unique situation which accounts to Paul's speaking in a different way."[2] They further buttress their position by pointing out the similarities between Colossians and the Letter to Philemon, which is widely accepted as written by Paul. Both letters were sent by Paul and Timothy (Col 1:1; Phlm 1); both letters talk about Paul's imprisonment (Col 4:3; Phlm 1); both revealed that Paul is surrounded by the same friends (Col 4:10–14; Phlm 23–24); both named the runaway slave Onisimus (Col 4:9; Phlm 12).[3] Still others favoring the Pauline authorship attribute the theological shift to the natural development of his thinking over time. Furthermore, with the differences in style, it is posited "that Paul in preparing this letter gave rather free rein to the secretary."[4] These arguments affirm Pauline authorship of the Letter to the Colossians and strengthen its acceptability. The date of writing is placed "towards the end of his life (around) AD 56–60 when he was a prisoner in Rome or, less likely, at Caeserea."[5]

Structure of Colossians 3:1–4

Structurally, Colossians is a typical Pauline letter, with an introduction containing an address and thanksgiving, followed by the body of the letter, affirmations and exhortations closely linked, and concluding with various personal data, greetings, and benediction.[6] Colossians 3:1–4 belongs to the whole section of exhortations to lead a Christian life (Col 3:1–4:6). The text, titled "Fundamental Appeals," covers the whole of Colossians 3:1–17. Colossians 3:1–4 is titled "seek the things that are above," "position of the believer" and "Christ is our life," respectively.[7] For this study, Colossians 3:1–4 is outlined thus:

2. Hahn, *Colossians*, 158.
3. Hann, *Colossians,* 158.
4. Achtemeier, *Colossians*, 191.
5. Achtemeier, *Colossians*, 191.
6. Freedman, *Colossians*, 1090.
7. Freedman, *Colossians*, 1090.

- (Col 3:1)—Seek heavenly things where Christ is with God
- (Col 3:2)—Set your minds on heavenly things
- (Col 3:3)—Hidden life with Christ in God
- (Col 3:4)—Appear with Christ in glory

ANALYSIS OF THE TEXT

Colossians 3:1–4 is a continuation of the exhortation that started in Colossians 2:16–23, as signalled by the use of *oun* ("therefore"). The text under review belongs to the paragraph that has a generic exhortation to seek the things above (3:1–3), in 3:5ff Paul explains exactly how he expects the Colossians to seek the things above by putting to death the old self and its motivations.[8] The use of *oun* ("therefore") in 3:1 indicates a shift from Colossians 2:16–23. Considering the warning Paul gave in Colossians 2:16–23, the Colossians are exhorted to seek the things above. Paul uses two active imperative commands that should be read in parallel: (1) seek the things above, where Christ is seated at the right hand of God (3:1); and (2) set your minds on things above, not on earthly things (3:2).[9]

Paul uses four indicative verbs that function together as three separate grounds for this exhortation. The Colossians should seek/set their minds on the things above, first, because "you have been raised with Christ" (3:1; *synegerthete*),[10] second, because "you died" (3:3; *apethanete*)[11] and "your life is hidden [*kekruptai*[12]] with Christ in God"; and, third, because "when Christ who is your life appears, then you also will appear [*phanerothesesthe*[13]] in glory" (3:4). Put differently, Paul is appealing to what is true of the Colossians' past ("you have died and been raised with Christ"), what is true of their present ("your life is hidden with Christ"), and what will be true of their future ("you will appear in glory") as grounds or reasoning for his command for them to seek what is above.s[14]

Seek Heavenly Things Where Christ Is with God (Col 3:1)

In the first four verses of Colossians 3, Paul articulates the central part of his overall argument: for those in the community of faith, the starting and ending point of

---

8. Paz, *Colossians*, 1705.
9. Paz, *Colossians*, 1705.
10. This is an aorist passive indicative.
11. This is also an aorist passive indicative.
12. This is perfect passive indicative.
13. This is a future passive indicative.
14. Wiersbe, *Colossians*, 114–15.

existence is Christ. Christ brings death *and* life, and as they have died with Christ, they now live *in* and *with* Christ. This is the meaning of the Christian life. The clear imperatives in these verses are where the believers are to set their focus.

The first imperative instructs Christians to "seek the things that are above." What does it mean to seek, and what are the things that are above? The Greek verb *zēteō* is an equivalent for the Hebrew verb *bāqash*; both mean to "seek" or "search." *Bāqash* and *zēteō* are common verbs that are frequently used in the Bible; in the Old Testament, *bāqash* occurs 225 times, while *zēteō* occurs up to 120 times in the New Testament. Both verbs are predicated to God and human beings; God is said to seek those who will worship him (John 13:14); Jesus seeks to do the will of God (John 5:44). Human beings seek wisdom (1 Cor 1:22) and spiritual blessing (Matt 7:7; Luke 11:19); they search for rest (Matt 12:43) and for peace (1 Pet 3:11). They "seek after" the kingdom of God (Matt 6:33; Luke 12:31; 13:24).[15] The text under review exhorts the Colossians to seek heavenly things. Heaven is thought of figuratively as above, "it is not to be defined spatially, but in relation to the presence of Christ. Above means the sphere in which Christ lives and reigns."

Colossian 3:1–4 pulls back the curtain, as does all of Scripture, on the most fundamental reality of all: *God*. Colossians 3:1b: "Seek the things that are above, where *Christ is, seated at the right hand of God*." This is the eternal, loved Son referred to in Colossians 3:13. Once he was dead (1:18, 22; 2:12, 20), now he is alive, because God raised him from the dead (2:12). Three positional things are said in Colossians 3:1 about this eternal Son of God and Christ (Messiah) who entered history, died, and rose: (1) he is *above*; (2) he is *at the right hand of God*; and (3) he is *seated*.

1. He is *above*. Not just above the clouds. And not just above some space and some stars. But he is above all the stars and all the space. He is not just above this created world, he is absolutely above creation. He is at the right hand of God, and God is not a creation. This is a mystery—the mystery of the incarnation, the penetration of the divine into the realm of creation. So the mystery of the ascension is the penetration of the creation into the realm of the divine. As today, Christ is the God-man: true God and true man.

2. He is *at the right hand of God*, the place of highest honor, dignity, power, and authority, not below, not above God, but acting as God, and God acting through him, as Colossians 1:15–20 describes. Peter describes the power of this place, the right hand, as: "[He] is at the right hand of God, with angels, authorities, and powers having been subjected to him" (1 Pet 3:22). All the powers of the universe are under Christ. And Paul adds that this position authorizes Christ to intercede for all (Rom 8:34): "[He] is at the right hand of God, who indeed is interceding for us."

---

15 Renn, *Seek*, 870–71; Paz, *Colossians*, 1705.

3. He is *seated*, meaning his great, decisive, saving work is finished. Hebrews 1:3: "After making purification for sins, he sat down at the right hand of the Majesty on high." Christ is above, seated at the right hand of God.

Christians are to seek things above because, as one seated at God's right hand, Christ is enthroned as the universal king and has been given all powers in heaven and on earth. The Colossians are released from all lower allegiances so that they may acknowledge only him to rule their lives according to his will.[16]

Set Your Minds on Heavenly Things (Col 3:2)

"Set your minds." The imperatives *zētiete* and *phroneite* are in the present tense to indicate a continuing attitude, in contrast with the aorist *sunēgerthēte*, which refers to the accomplished experience of resurrection with Christ.[17] This second present active imperative, together with the one in verse 1, "seek the things that are above," should be read in the sense "to be constantly seeking the things above," that is, the mindset that Christians ought always to be pursuing—things associated with and where Christ is. This is in contrast to setting their minds on "earthly things," possibly a reference to the elements of the Colossian heresy that Paul mentioned in 2:16–23—human regulations, etc.[18] The Colossians were admonished to lift their eyes from the temptations of the heresy that threatens their spiritual health and focus their gaze on Christ. "Because he has been elevated to the position of highest sovereignty over the universe, he pervades the universe with his presence."[19] The thoughts of their minds, like the aspirations of their hearts, are to be focused on the heavenly realm into which their lives have been transferred.[20] The reference to Christ being seated at God's right hand in verse 1 is an illusion to Psalm 110, which describes the kingly authority of the Messiah. This is a strong motivation to set the mind on heavenly things. He rules above all earthly powers.

Therefore, the Colossians are asked to set their minds on what is above, and not on what is earthly. Paul reminds them of what Christ has done, what Christ is doing, and what Christ will do in them, as grounds for their continued faithfulness and pursuit of Christ.

First, Paul appeals to what has happened in their past. They have "died" (v. 2) and "been raised with Christ" (v. 1). They have died to who they once were, and Christ has raised them to a new life. What does it mean to be raised? To be raised by Christ means they now have no life of their own. "Their life is the life of Christ, maintained

---

16. Renn, *Seek*, 870–71.
17. Beare, *Colossians*, 210.
18. Beare, *Colossians*, 210.
19. Buttrick, Colossians, 210.
20. Buttrick, *Colossians*, 210.

in him at God's right hand and shared by him with all his people."[21] Therefore, they ought to set their minds on things above.

Secondly, Paul appeals to what is true of their present experience. They are "hidden with Christ in God" (v. 3). Paul uses the perfect tense, emphasizing the completion of an action in the present.[22] Though they died, the life they now live is hidden, or covered, by Christ. This is a reference to their union with Christ and the atoning (covering) work of Christ. They are hidden from the wrath of God because they are in Christ. This serves as a motivation for their thinking of the things above.

Thirdly, Paul appeals to what will be true of their future. When Christ, who is their life, appears, they will "appear with Him" (v. 4). The word for "appear," *phaneroo*, refers to the appearance of Christ in the second coming, a view strengthened by Paul's use of *en doxa* ("in glory"). The relationship between Paul's imperatives in verses 1–2 and his indicative statement in v. 3 is therefore seen as an ethical expectation on the basis of an eschatological reality. Because one day Christ will appear, and the Colossians will appear in glory with him, they should live ethically in the present as those who are pursuing Christ and the things associated with Christ. That is to emulate the characteristics of Christ in glory, which includes growth in holiness, depth in prayer, and advancement in spiritual power.

Hidden Life with Christ in God (Col 3:3)

Colossians 3:3a, "You have died," means that their death is behind them. In baptism, it has already happened. And their life is not what the world thinks. "It is a hidden life as far as the world is concerned, because the world does not know Christ."[23] The Christians' sphere of life is not this earth, but heaven; and the things that attractsand excite them belong to heaven not to earth. It does not mean that they are to neglect earthly responsibilities. It rather means that their motives and strength come from heaven and not the earth.[24] The implication is that the Colossians should not take their cue from the world but from Christ. Consequently, in chapter 1 of Colossians, Paul stresses the hidden secrets from which the Christian life begins. In chapter 2, he enumerates the hidden treasure it enjoys; and in chapter 3, the hidden control to which it bows.[25] Colossians 3: 3b states: "Your life is hidden with Christ in God." *Kekruptai* ("hidden") is the third person singular perfect passive indicative of *krupto* ("hid"). "Hid" here denotes two things. Firstly, the new life of the Colossians is a mystery; they cannot understand or explain how God creatively indwells them to transform and infuse them with cleansing and re-creating power, even though they can experience

21. Bruce, *Colossians*, 132–33.
22. Beare, *Colossians*, 210.
23. Bruce, *Colossians*, 134.
24. Bruce, *Colossians*, 134.
25. Carson, *Colossians and Philemon*, 80.

and know the fact of his indwelling. Secondly, the new life is secured; it is protected and guaranteed against the strains and stresses of secular life and against the moral corrosions of evil because their life does not depend on human defence, or personal resolution, but on God.[26] Their life is not only hidden "with Christ" but hidden "with Christ in God," a double divine fortification. The expression "in God" is not common in the Pauline corpus, compared to the expression "in Christ" or "in the Lord." The closest parallel is Ephesians 3:9, where the mystery received and proclaimed by Paul is said to be "hidden from all eternity in God."[27] The divine purpose preserved in that mystery is said to have been conceived, embodied in Christ from all eternity (cf. Eph 1:4; 9:10; Col 2:2). The life of the believer is hidden "with Christ" because they have died and have been raised with him. It is hidden "in God" because all created things have their being in God, Christ himself has his being in God (cf. John 1:18), and so those who belong to him have their being there too.[28]

Appear with Christ in Glory (Col 3:4)

Colossians 3:4 states, "When Christ who is your life appears . . ." Christ is present now; he is right now reigning over the world. They cannot lift their finger apart from Jesus Christ. Their most terrible experience of death is behind them, and their most glorious experience of life awaits them. Christ, who is now ignored and rejected by the world, will be revealed in his glory when the full splendor of his divine being will be seen.[29] Christ is the very life of the Colossians; he is not only the source of life, but he lives in them, so that their new life is really his life in them. Consequently, there is an organic spiritual unity between them and their Lord. Therefore, when Christ is revealed, the life of the Colossians, long despised or ignored by the world, will also be revealed as something that endures eternally, while the temporary things of this world will be doomed to destruction.[30] "Hidden life" refers to a state of mind wherein Christ is the inward measure of (their) projects and desires, and where everything is referred through him to its ultimate source.

THEOLOGICAL REFLECTION OF THE TEXT

In this chapter, Paul diverted from the negative to the positive side of the argument. Colossians 2:12 stated that the Colossian Christians have been buried with Christ in baptism, representing the "Participation . . . of the believer with Christ in death to this

---

26. Wersbe, *Colossians*, 114.
27. Wersbe, *Colossians*, 115.
28. White, *In Him the Fullness: A Study in Colossians*, 101.
29. Macloed, *Colossians*km, 211
30. Bruce, *Colossians*, 135.

world and resurrection to the life of the world to come, life eternal."[31] That verse parallels what Paul mentioned in Romans 6:3–5, where he portrayed baptism as a burial and resurrection with Christ; the burial of the old self, the before-Christ self, and the resurrection of the new self, the after-Christ self, to new life.[32] Being dead with Christ, "The Christian . . . is forever removed from the sphere of the elemental spirits, and the ascetic regulations which their service imposes and that have no further validity on them."[33] As per being risen with Christ to a new and heavenly life, Christians have to concentrate all their thoughts, attention, and desires heavenward, to the domain of their risen and exalted Lord. The entire life of the Christians is to be transformed into this new relationship. Thus, rather than seeking vainly to win their way to heaven through an earthly discipline, Christians must seek to give effect in all earthly relationships to the heavenly nature which they share with Christ. Paul emphasizes that the Christian life is not the means by which they seek to win salvation, but the necessary consequence of the new relationship to God in Christ, into which they enter by faith.[34]

Again, to be united with Christ in his death and resurrection means that, although Christians continue to live on earth in their mortal bodies, they have set out on a new way of life. The energy empowering and enabling them to go on with the new way of life is bestowed on them by Christ from the glory in which he now lives. Having partaken of his risen life, their interest now centers on him; his interests now become theirs. They are to "pursue the things which belong to the heavenly realm where he reigns; their mind, their attitude, their ambition, their whole outlook must be characterized by their living bond with the ascended Christ."[35] This new life calls them to shape their behavior in accordance to their new identity. It is not for more rules and regulations, "for asceticism or flights of mystical ecstasy. Their growth in God is one that comes through their way of living together in communities."[36] "Seek the things that are above, where Christ is, seated on the right hand of God" (v. 1b). Seeking here is continuing action. Thus, Paul is telling these Christians to seek and to keep on seeking the things that are above. It is a lifetime quest.[37] As a consequence of their new life in Christ, Christians need to lift their eyes from the mud at their feet to the stars above. They need to leave behind their concern with worldly things so that they will focus their concerns on "the things that are above." They are to focus their attention on heavenly realities rather than earthly temporalities, "where Paul has repeatedly located concerns and practices of the false teaching."[38] "Set your mind on

31. Bruce, *Colossians*, 135.
32. Carson, *Colossians and Philemon*, 80.
33. Carson, *Colossians and Philemon*, 80–81.
34. Buttrick, *Colossians*, 208.
35. Durken, *Colossians*, 643–44.
36. Buttrick, *Colossians*, 209.
37. Buttrick, *Colossians*, 209.
38. Bruce, *Colossians*, 131.

the things that are above, not on the things that are on the earth" (v. 2). Paul instructed them to aim heavenward, to set their minds above and let it give character to their outlook on everything. The gnostics of the Colossian community equally believed in pursuing what was above; they seriously aimed at living on a higher plain rather than the mundane one. But Paul has in mind a higher plain than theirs; higher than the principalities and powers which dominate the planetary sphere, for Christ has ascended far above these (Eph 1:20–21). Paul warned not to let their ambitions be earthbound, on transitory and inferior objects. He admonished them not to "look at life and the universe from the standpoint of these lower planes; look at them from Christ's exalted standpoint. Judge everything by the standards of that new creation to which they belong."[39]

Many people think of "heart-religion," or an emotionally based faith, as superior to "head-religion," or faith with less emotional content. While passionate faith can be a good thing, the Bible speaks much more frequently of what we might call "head-religion" than it does of "heart-religion." While "heart" is a literal translation of the Greek word *kardia*, biblical people thought of the heart as the center of the intellect and will rather than the emotions.[40]

The Bible continually calls on believers to believe, which is a head-based activity. The Bible places much emphasis on the mind, the intellect, and beliefs. This is because people act based on their beliefs; if they believe things that are not true, they will act on those false beliefs and will suffer the consequences. If they have been well taught, and believe what is true, they will benefit immeasurably by their teaching and by their true beliefs. Furthermore, faith is rooted in believing, and faith is key to discipleship and salvation (Rom 3:28, 30; 4:5, 11–16; 5:1–2; 9:30–32; 10:6; Gal 2:16; 3:8ff; 5:5). The Christian life of faith is above all that is transitory, sensual, and mundane. The heart and mind must be turned toward the Lord they believe in.[41]

Colossians 3:3a states: "For you have died." Death is a serious transition; it ends everything. In this case, the Colossian Christians died to the old order. Their old selves no longer existed. But, for them, death is not the end. They have been "raised together with Christ" (v. 1), raised to a new life. In v. 3b, Paul states, "Your life is hidden with Christ in God." There is a good deal of hidden mystery associated with God. After all, God says, "My thoughts are not your thoughts, neither are your ways my ways . . . For as the heavens are higher than the earth, so are my ways higher than your ways, and my thoughts than your thoughts" (Isa 55:8–9). This hidden secret, or mystery, is Christ in you the hope of glory, the central truth that all Christian insights, faith, and understanding spring from. Here, Paul diverts attention from slavish imitation of worldly thinking to the secrets only people of faith share, "from prevailing fashion of

---

39. Johnson, *Colossians*, 399.
40. Johnson, Colossians, 400.
41. Fowl, *Colossians*, 855.

thought to the 'open secret' of the gospel they have learnt in Christ. The indwelling teacher, the light within the soul of all who follow the light of the world."[42]

There is also the hidden treasure given by Christ, with all the treasures of wisdom and knowledge. Here, Paul implies the spiritual wisdom by which the Christian lives. The mind of the Christian "is full of the riches of the Christian life, the riches of the glory of mystery of Christ, the riches of the full assurance of understanding, the word that dwells within (them) richly, and the peace that rules (their) hearts most royally."[43] The hidden treasure concerns the fullness of life in Christ, the hidden treasure of a wealthy, rewarding life laid up for them in Christ. This is the inner enrichment that Jesus speaks about as the "the pearl of great price, that is worth selling all, to possess it, the treasure hidden in the fields of life to be discovered by those whose hearts are in the kingdom."[44]

Again, there is the hidden control of Christ, seated at the right hand of God. Paul says that the life of the Christian is hidden with Christ in God. This is not a life devoid of the world's hurt, nor is it a place where Christ is exalted for safety; it is hidden because it is "not easily understood by onlooker, not obvious or transparent in its direction or motives or resources, because it is directed and ruled from a hidden throne."[45] "When Christ who is our life appears, then you also will appear with him in glory" (v. 4a). The first thing noticeable here is that Christ is "our life." The life of the Christian is no longer simply "with" Christ, but actually identified with him. Affirming this, Paul states, "For to me to live is Christ" (Phil 1:21); "I have been crucified with Christ, and it is no longer I that live, but Christ living in me" (Gal 2:20). Now he suggests that what is true for him is true for every Christian. The return of Christ in glory points strongly to the basic Christian hope where Paul offers a perfect transition from fundamental principles to practical exhortation. Christians have something to look forward to, while undertaking the program of self-conquest listed in 3:5ff.[46] "The Christian's hopes are fastened on God's plans, Christ's appearing to rule the world, and (their) appearing with him in glory. Inevitably therefore, Christian life is strange, eccentric, hidden except to those who bow to the same inner sovereignty and acknowledge the same inner control."[47]

One of the practical implications of "Christ being our life" is the fact that Christ makes believers privy to eternal life, which involves the life they live here as well as the life they anticipate—eternal life. Eternal life has as much to do with the quality of life as with its quantity, although both quality and quantity are involved. Eternal life begins in the here and now and stretches beyond time.[48] A Christ-centered life for the

42. Bruce, *Colossians*, 134.
43. Renn, "Heart," 478.
44. Rogers, *Colossians*, 48.
45. White, *In Him the Fullness*, 101.
46. White, *In Him the Fullness*, 101.
47. White, *In Him the Fullness*, 102.
48. White, *In Him the Fullness*, 102.

Christian takes on a new character that is far more positive than the life they lived prior to knowing Christ. As navigators possess compasses that point to the true north, they can live with confidence that Christ is leading them aright. They might not be able to see around the next corner, and their lives will include hardships, but their goal and direction are certain. They live with the promise that "it is (their) Father's good pleasure to give (them) the Kingdom" (Luke 12:32).

Paul identifies "above" as "where Christ is seated at the right hand of God." By so doing, he draws attention to Christ's lordship. The one who reigns as Lord of the universe, the one at the center of life, is none other than the crucified Jesus, the image of God, who came to renew life.[49] The lordship of Christ is intrinsically connected to their being buried and raised with Christ. Drawing attention to Christ's lordship illuminates a different sort of "divine reality" for Paul's audience. While it is not certain what the other "philosophy" is that influenced those in Colossae, it might involve some sort of escapism or focus on some sort of communion with the heavenly realm. By drawing attention to Christ as the one "above" who should capture their attention and steer their lives, Paul draws attention not to escapism but to a heavenly reality that has made itself known in human form. *This is down-to-earth-ism.* Christ in this letter is not just another divine intermediary by which one can attain union with the divine. For so many people today, Jesus is a means to heaven. The manifestation of the mystery of God in Christ does not condone an escape from the earthly life; it is an embrace of this earthly life for the purpose of transformation and renewal. The hope of glory is not in heaven, it is in the body of Christ (Col 1:24–27).

Implication of Colossians 3:1–4 for Nigerian Christians

The implication of seeking heavenly things for Christians in Nigeria includes impressing Scripture upon their heart. It is through Scripture that Christians renew their minds and start to think on things that are noble, good, and righteous; and they start to think more like God. Deuteronomy 6:6–9 spells out to the Israelites how to impress God's commandments upon the heart: they are to teach it, to talk about it everywhere, to put on their foreheads, hands, doorframes, and gates of their houses.

Following Moses' instructions, Nigerian Christians are to teach the word of God to their children. To think of heavenly things, they must be teachers who teach the word of God to their friends, in small groups, and to strangers. They are to talk about the word of God everywhere: at home, when walking, when lying down, when getting up. They are to develop reminders to help them memorize it; they are to tie it on their hands, foreheads, doorframes, and gates. In other words, Nigerian Christians are to set up places and times in their daily life where they will always encounter the word of God. This includes things like daily meditation, small group sharing, or accountability meetings.

---

49. Rogers, *Colossians*, 49.

To seek heavenly things, Nigerian Christians are to reject everything that is not from God. Paul said they should not only seek things above but also turn away from earthly things such as lust, anger, envy, jealousy, and anything else that is not of God (cf. Col 3:5–9). Practically, this may mean not watching certain TV shows, reading certain magazines or books, listening to certain music, visiting certain sites, or hanging around certain people, especially when such contacts contribute to drawing them away from God and godly thoughts. Nigerian Christians must take captive every search/choice and bring it into submission to Christ.

To seek heavenly things, Christians in Nigeria are to develop a consistent life of prayer and foster healthy fellowship. It is through the discipline of prayer that they can seek heavenly things. They must learn how to pray at all times, bringing every thought before the Father. They must foster fellowship with wise, godly believers who help them seek spiritual things.

The implication of setting their minds on heavenly things is that Nigerian Christians are to free their minds from doubts, fears, anxieties, worries, worldly thoughts, and preoccupations. They are to focus on God and his kingdom. In the Lord's Prayer, Christians are taught to be consumed with God's name being hallowed, and his kingdom and his will being done on earth as it is in heaven (Matt 6:9–10). The believer's mind should be consumed with heavenly things. In Scripture, those who practice right thinking receive tremendous blessings. Isiah 26:3 says, "You will keep in perfect peace him whose mind is steadfast, because he trusts in you." The person whose thoughts are consumed with God and his kingdom will have perfect peace instead of anxiety and worry. When believers find themselves anxious or worried, they can be sure that they have lost a God-centered mindset.

The implication of our text of study for Christians in Nigeria is that they develop a "heavenly mindset" that is focusing on their resurrected position, rejecting everything that is not from God, and living a life of continual discipline, focusing on their crucified position by way of reckoning their death with Christ. With Christ they have died to sin, to self, to the world, and to the power of the devil. They are to focus on their hidden life in Christ, which is a reflection of protection—they are protected by Christ—and a reflection of their identification with Christ—the world does not recognize them.

CONCLUSION

In Colossians, Paul addresses a way of thinking and existing that runs counter to the thought of earthly affairs. He presents a life rooted in the good news and person of Jesus Christ, which is the Christian life, as demonstrated by Sister Okure, SHCJ. Many Nigerians profess the Christian faith, but their way of living does not correspond to the faith they profess. Nigerian Christians must rethink their new life in Christ. As the Colossians in Paul's time, they must be grounded in the basics of faith, and Christ must be at the center of that faith—not for personal benefit, personal enrichment, or popularity.

The mind, heart, and will of the Christian must be centered upon Christ; the inner life is oriented by reference to Jesus' ascendance, reigning, and coming. He is the center, the hidden secret from which they start, the hidden treasure they enjoy, the hidden control to which they bow; and from him as center, all the circumference of their life is drawn. Christians, in all their public concerns and social awareness, their evangelistic anxiety to explain themselves, they must remember the hiddenness of life in Christ. If they fail to do that, they will lose their security because the only answer to the outward pressure of the world is the inward constrain of life in Christ. They will lose their leadership because the world only follows those who at last overcome it. They will lose their testimony and have nothing fresh and authentic to say, descending to mere debate. They will lose their resilience because the only cure for the drain of life is inner vitality. They will lose their hope of revival because church renewal always comes from within the inner life of individuals open to the movement of the Holy Spirit. Finally, they will lose touch with Jesus, who tried very hard to teach them "the kingdom of God is within (them)."[50]

BIBLIOGRAPHY

Achtemeier, Paul, J. *Harper Collins Bible Dictionary*. Bangalore: Theological Publications in India, 1996.

Bruce, F. F., ed. *Colossians*. The New International Commentary on the New Testament. Grand Rapids: Eerdmans, 1984.

Buttrick, George A., ed. Colossians. *The Interpreter's Bible* XI. New York: Abingdon Press, 1955.

Carson, H. M. *Colossians and Philemon*. Tyndale New Testament Commentary. London: Inter-Varsity Press, 1978.

Durken, Daniel. ed., *Colossians*. New Collegeville Bible Commentary: New Testament. Collegeville, MN: Liturgical Press, 2008.

Fowl, Stephen. *Colossians*. The New Interpreter's Bible: One Volume Commentary. Nashville: Abingdon, 2010.

Freedman, N. *The Anchor Bible Dictionary 1*. New York: Yale University Press, 1992.

Hahn, Scott. *Catholic Bible Dictionary*. New York: Doubleday, 2009.

Johnson, Luke Timothy. *The Writings of the New Testament: An Interpretation*. Bangalore: Theological Publication in India, 2009.

Mora Paz, Cesar Alejandro. *Colossians*. The International Bible Commentary. Collegeville, MN: Liturgical Press, 1998.

Renn, Stephen D., ed. *Expository Dictionary of Bible Words*. Peabody, MA: Hendrickson, 2012.

Rogers, Patrick V. *Colossians*. New Testament Message. Wilmington, DE: M. Glazier, 1980.

Okure, T. "Holy Thursday Message to CABAN Members." CABAN WhatsApp Platform. 2022.

Wiersbe, Warren W. *Be Complete: Colossians*. BE Commentary. Colorado Springs, CO: David C. Cook, 2008.

White, R. E. O. *In Him the Fullness: A Study in Colossians*. London: Pickering & Inglis, 1973.

---

50. White, *In Him the Fullness*, 103.

CHAPTER 19

Mission on the Margins
Reading Matthew 10:5–7 in Contemporary Nigeria

CAROLINE N. MBONU, HHCJ

INTRODUCTION

The explosion of ministries in contemporary the Nigerian Christian landscape, with its attendant interpretations of the biblical text, continues to shape and reshape the religious practice of adherents of the biblical faith tradition in the country. Myriad of preachers produce a cacophony of "the Bible says" that hardly represents the good news. Sadly, most of the preaching represents an inversion of the gospel in favor of material well-being, thus substituting the good news to the poor, which is consistent with the seeking out of those at the margins, the *raison d'être* of the incarnation, and a central focus of Teresa Okure's theology. This exegetical and descriptive essay addresses the problematic situation with insights from Matthew10:5–7 and draws largely from the works of Teresa Okure as well as other theologians. The Matthean text chosen is a part of the larger mission discourse (9:35–11:1) and the immediate context of the first missionary journey of the twelve disciples, conveying the essence of Jesus' mission (Matt 10:7).

The New Testament attests to the good news of Jesus as consistent with seeking out those at the margins of society (Luke 4:18–19), a passion of Okure. But an understanding of the good news appears inverted in Nigeria as many self-proclaimed men and women of God appropriate the idea of good news to the poor, to self-aggrandizement, thus emptying the gospel of its redemptive meaning. Disproportionate emphasis on material well-being and the abhorrence of suffering or any form of discomfort interrogates the ethics of the emerging religiosity[1] in terms of the deeds with which it is associated. With little or no knowledge of Scripture, these so-called ministers of the gospel parade almost every nook and cranny of the country peddling the word of God for sordid gain (1 Tim 3:8) and at the same time distorting the good news. But this turn of events in the Christian scene is not peculiar to the New Religious Movements (NRMs). traditional mainline churches, Catholics, and traditional Protestant churches are not exempt; they appear to have fallen prey to the trendy brand of rendering the gospel of "prosperity," a current that bears all the characteristic of a movement driven by a primitive acquisition of money, wealth, and power at the expense of the poor, the subjects of the good news. In light of this, Okure contends that the so-called prosperity preachers tend to douse the fire the word cast upon the earth,[2] a fire of love deriving from Jesus breaking into human history. For Okure, therefore, for the word to be realized, it must be on fire, it must be alive, it must be actively burning "to help people to reverse their inability to read correctly their own signs of the times . . . in their concrete part of the earth."[3] Okure's theologizing, rooted in the aliveness of the word and its dynamism, vigor, and activism in the world, criticizes what today can be termed contaminated Christianity. It also questions its redemptive value, for it is no longer alive in the context in which it was handed down, the Bible. For Okure, therefore, redemption is realized when the word truly becomes alive and active.[4] The Letter to the Hebrews provides the term "alive and active" in giving flesh to the word of God, an expression which sums up the nature of the word in general.[5]

With narrative criticism and socio-cultural hermeneutics as methodological tools, including a contextual reading of the text, which reflects my social location as a Catholic Christian and a Nigerian woman who lives and works in a pluralistic environment, and a particular affiliation with the youth whom I teach at a tertiary institution, I explore the mission to those on the margins in present-day Nigeria. Suggesting ways of revitalizing, preaching of the gospel (Rom. 1:1–6), a message otherwise termed the "good news to the poor," for a more all-inclusive reception, is part of the present contribution. The rest of the essay is laid out in four sections. A brief background to the gospel according to Matthew is followed by an exegetical survey of Matthew 10:5–7; then follows a cursory review of the reception of the Word in modern Nigeria. Discussion and appropriation precede the conclusion.

---

1. Mbonu, "Money God-Talk," 18.
2. Okure, "Enkindling Fire in the Mission," 11.
3. Okure, "Enkindling Fire in Mission," 9.
4. Okure, "Alive and Active," 1–26.
5. Okure, "Alive and Active," 4.

BRIEF BACKGROUND TO THE GOSPEL ACCORDING TO MATTHEW[6]

Written about AD 80–90, in perhaps Antioch of Syria, the Gospel according to Matthew bears the social character of its original context, as internal evidence attests. The author cast his narrative in the form of a Jewish story that begins with a genealogy of its hero, Jesus of Nazareth, and continues with all the events that characterize his extraordinary life until his death and resurrection. A dynamic narrative, Matthew is the product of a church in transition and in the process of defining itself,[7] which is evident in its forceful emphasis on the quest for Christian identity and concern for those on the margins. The narrative is situated in a milieu characterized by intra-Jewish conflicts such as struggles between the Matthean Jewish-Christian community, the local Jewish communities, and the movement's principal opponents, the Pharisees. Signs of instability in first-century Palestine dot the gospel. Acrimonious rhetoric manifest in the story confirms the hostile relationship, hence, the caustic and exclusivist language as evidenced in a significant portion of the Gospel (e.g., 11:2–12:50; 13:24–30; 23). From the Matthean point of view, therefore, excluding non-Jews, those who come from outside, and Samaritans as well, are equally excluded from the first mission of the Twelve. All of these fit well into the challenges Matthew's audience faces with their co-religionist, non-Jews, Samaritans, and outsiders as well. But Matthew uses authoritative traditions to confront those within the accepted group, who have opted for the imperial project and have forgotten the most defenseless, those at the margins.[8]

Matthew 10:5–16 (parallel Mark 6:7–13; Luke 9:1–6), Delimit, Matthew 10:5–7

The chosen Matthean text (Matt 10:5–7) for the study comes from the immediate context of the mission of the Twelve (10: 1–16) and the much larger context of mission discourse (9:35–11:1); the author of Matthew draws some of the material in this discourse from Mark 13 and from Q. The transitional verses, 9:35–38, present the pastoral needs of the people, *a harvest* of leadership, spiritual and political for the people, *sheep without a shepherd* (9:36). Jesus turns the problem of leadership into an opportunity for those who have been under his tutelage, the Twelve: a prospect to serve as he himself serves. Hence, he asks them to pray to *the Lord of the harvest to send laborers into his harvest*. He would later enlarge the number of laborers to seventy, representing the nations (Luke 10:1; cf. Gen 10:2–31). Having completed the portrait of Jesus as teacher, preacher, and healer, the author moves quickly to the missioning of the Twelve. Matthew models the mission of the Twelve on Jesus' mission model, which is a mission to the lost in Israel, dejected and abandoned, those at the margin,

---

6. I owe insights in this section to the work of Donald Senior and Pheme Perkins, "The Gospels and Acts," 371–86; Also, "The Gospel according to Matthew," 630–74.
7. Duarte, "Matthew," 352.
8. Duarte, "Matthew," 351–60.

exemplified in the episodes of the previous two chapters (8 and 9), featuring a total of ten healing episodes; this setting informs the choice of the three verses, Matthew 5–7.

The English text of Matthew 10:5–7 says:

> The Twelve Jesus sent out with the following instructions: "Go nowhere among the Gentiles, and enter no town of the Samaritans, but go rather to the lost sheep of the house of Israel. As you go, proclaim the good news, 'The kingdom of heaven has come near.'" (Matt 10:5–7 NRSV).

The Greek text of Matthew 10:5–7 says:

> *Toútous toús doódeka apésteilen ho Ieesoús parangeílas autoís légoon Eis hodón ethnoón meé apéltheete kaí eis pólin Samaritoón meé eiséltheete 6 Poreúesthe dé mállon prós tá próbata tá apoloolóta oíkou Israeél 7 Poreuómenoi dé keerússete légontes hóti Eéngiken hee basileía toón ouranoón*

In verse 5, Jesus, having exposed the Twelve to his mission, which is consistent with unconditional love for the poor, weak, and the downtrodden through the varied healing episodes in the previous two chapters (8 and 9), sends them out with the same authority (10:1) with which he achieved his mission (7:28–29; 8:16; 9:8; compare 8:34), to heal, perform exorcisms, and even raise the dead (8:20; 10:10); these work of the kingdom would entail some level of difficulty, as is evident in Jesus' own mission. The Twelve, however, had a limited mission field, a reflection of the insider-outsider issues in the Matthean community, at least for the purpose of the maiden undertaking. He *parangeilas* them thus: "into the place of the Gentiles (non-Jews) not go" (*Eis hodón ethnoón meé apéltheete*); they must remain within the confines of Jewish territory. And that is not all: the Twelve must also *eis pólin Samaritoón meé eiséltheete*. Going solely after the lost sheep of the house of Israel and proclaiming the good news (4:17 and 10:7) is in line with Jesus' own practice. Recall his encounter with the Canaanite women: "I was sent only to the lost sheep of the house of Israel" (Matt 15:24). The contradiction between the good news of Jesus and the exclusion of non-Jews and Samaritans from the ingathering raises some questions at this point. Response to these inquiries can be found in the world behind the Matthean Gospel narrative as elucidated earlier. Moreover, scholars attribute the paradox to the Jewish consciousness of Matthew's own special tradition,[9] since neither of the parallels, Mark 6:7–9 and Luke 9:1–6, have such restrictions. There is also a suggestion here that since Matthew makes the land of Israel Jesus' mission field, the mission of the Twelve was bound to the same territory in keeping with the character of the text. But this restriction is only temporary for, after the resurrection, the disciple's mission will extend to the Gentiles (Matt 28:16–20).[10]

---

9. Viviano, "The Gospel according to Matthew," 651.
10. Carter, *Matthew and the Margins*, 234.

In verse. 6, *Poreúesthe dé mállon prós tá próbata tá apoolóta oíkou Israeél*, the lost sheep of the house of Israel, the covenanted people, comprise the immediate mission field to which the Twelve must go. They are to go seek out those who have not kept the faith, the lost, and bring them back to covenantal fidelity. In Mark and Luke, the mission of the Twelve was not restricted to *the lost sheep of the* covenanted people, *the house of Israel*, a peculiar Matthean concern, but to *oíkou*; the house can function for humanity. In Mark and Luke, the Twelve were instructed, "Wherever you enter a house" (Luke 9:4; Mark 6:10, "whatever house you enter"), suggesting a more cosmopolitan or universal character of the good news of the kingdom.

Furthermore, Israel's lost sheep signify persons, the ruined, perishing, ignorant, without hope, sick, possessed, on the margins of the Israelite society; these are persons who have neither voice nor agency, very little power, and no influence. Jesus' command, *proceed* and seek out these lost ones, hacks back to the prophecy of Ezekiel, on the mission of the shepherd (Ezek 34: 11–16). The duty of the shepherd is to rescue and care for the sheep that were lost from wherever they have been scattered during the confusion of life, the mist, and darkness (Ezek 34:5–6). They could also be those who have no access to Jesus as a result of their low position in society (margin) or as a result of the deliberate effort of the religious leaders to hide the truth from them. They are the victims of misrule both from the political and religious leaders, which the Ezekiel text amply supports.

In verse 7, *Poreuómenoi* as you go, movement forward, a disciple is not an armchair teacher or preacher; the one *sent* must be on the move, a movement outward toward an object, and *dé keerússete légontes*, that which Jesus did proclaim, *hóti Eéngiken hee basileía toón ouranoón*, the exact proclamation as he did (Matt 4:17) and also in the footsteps of John the Baptist (Matt 3:2). Mark's twelve were instructed to proclaim repentance "so they went out and proclaimed that all should repent" (Mark 6:13, 1:4); repentance is a condition of entering the kingdom of heaven. The nearness of the kingdom is presumed in the mission expressed in healing and exorcism. Luke's universalism comes through in the direction of his boundaryless mission field: "They went through the villages," with no restrictions, "bringing the good news and curing diseases everywhere" (Luke 9:6); "everywhere" is another indication of the unrestrained mission field. Although the Twelve are all successors in the new revelation,[11] the authority they received for their first missionary journey (Matt 10: 1) limits their mission to healing and preaching (Matt 10:8). Note that they were not commissioned to teach, only to preach and to heal; this will change when the revelation is complete (Matt 28:20).[12]

Matthew 28, which encompasses the Great Commission, allows us in Nigeria to be part of Jesus' mission and compels us to proper stewardship of the spiritual heritage received through Jesus, the Word of God. Furthermore, the post-Resurrection events

11. Duling, *New Testament*, 348.
12. Duling, *New Testament*, 348.

extend the notion of the lost sheep and the margins in Matthew 10:6 to include more than those of the house of Israel; it would comprise also those who are not faithful to the covenant that is fulfilled and personified in Jesus.[13] The challenge here then is to keep alive the fire cast on earth by interpreting the word for a more holistic reception among adherents of the biblical faith tradition in Nigeria.

INTERPRETING AND RECEPTION OF THE WORD IN THE CONTEMPORARY NIGERIAN CHRISTIAN SETTING

The way and manner of preaching the gospel in present-day Nigeria continue to raise critical concern for the body of Christ, the sheep of the Lord's pasture. Scripture presents corrective measures to false teaching and conducts therefrom. Okure contends that the motivating issue of the First Letter to Timothy appears to be connected with curbing the behavior of erring teachers who spread the wrong teaching in the Christian community of Ephesus (1 Tim 6–7).[14] Many of our so-called men and women of God spread teaching erroneously fraught with ignorance of Scripture. Doctor and Church Father Saint Jerome puts it, "Ignorance of Scripture is Ignorance of Christ." A lack of familiarity with the Scriptures translates to obtuseness in Christian life and of the law, for a sound knowledge of the Christian life is rooted in God's grace and mercy and not in manipulation of religious identity for personal and group self-interest.

Growth in the knowledge of the Christian faith evokes tangible deeds of love, a position Okure has persistently taught and written on. A myriad of so-called church preachers are stuttering discordant voices of the Bible, unmediated utterances that hardly represent the sense of mission in the New Testament, a church birth by the Holy Spirit at Pentecost, "a church on fire with God's love; it lives to celebrate this love and to proclaim it to the entire world."[15] The incongruity impinges on the reception of the word at the grassroots and stands in need of redemption. To this end, Okure forcefully asserts that ignorance of the gospel can be said to be the single most important factor in the problem of the church and society, globally.[16]

The problem of arising from ignorance of Scripture can be dangerous to the church and society as well. Given the symbolic power of Scripture, one must assume responsibility for the use of the sacred text.[17] It is not a coincidence that the rise in corruption in Nigeria, and other untoward activities, can be traced to the rise in the number of ill-educated Bible-carrying preachers across the land.

---

13. Carter, "Matthew and the Margins," 234.
14. Okure, "Paul's Mercy," 192.
15. Okure, "Enkindling Fire in the Mission," 6.
16. Okure, "Paul's Mercy," 206.
17. Duarte, "Matthew," 359.

Okure cites an example of false teaching within the church that takes the form of preaching and enforcing payment of tithes as the way to win God's favor.[18] Imposing payment of tithe is anchored on the maxim, "If you do not pay tithe, God will make things tight for you," she notes. Such utterance shows the level of exploitation of the adherents' God-sense and good disposition.[19] Teaching that pays less attention to faith in God's grace and mercy disenfranchises the word of God, leaving the adherents bereft of its saving mission. "The author of First Peter underscores faith and the reception of the good news by reminding his audience that though they had not seen Jesus, their faith, manifested in their love for Jesus, should sustain them through thick and thin"[20] and not the "tithe" they pay to the church. For some Catholic clergy involved in this form of extortion, Okure observes:

> Wrong use of Scripture for material gains, turning the Eucharistic celebration into a privileged moment for extorting money from the people (asking them to "donate to God" to show appreciation or win God's favour), replacing the church's sacred liturgical traditions with loud choruses that have little or no solid theological content ... emphasis on miracles and testimonies rather than on faith; excluding suffering from the life of the Christian in favour of the prosperity gospel; and preoccupation with building prestigious structures at the expense of building God's people.[21]

The biblical text scarcely supports touting things divine for pecuniary interest (Act 8:9–24). As such, one decries the not-so-uncommon *modus operandi* of some Catholic clergy, whose faith formation and elaborate theological formation prepare them to engage Scripture as alive and active, challenging them to become disciples of a church-in-mission but who rather participate in peddling religion, and especially the good news, at the altar of the self-serving prosperity gospel.

Much as religion pervades the life of Nigerians, the phenomenon of a ministry, a prayer house, or a church at every street corner of the country, the South, with its attendant prosperity bent is becoming problematic.[22] Rather than preach the Bible passage allotted to a particular worship section, prosperity preachers convert every

---

18. Tithe, a recent practice in the Catholic Church, is becoming a source of concern. While beneficiaries of the practice, the clergy, welcome the development, it appears as a vexing subject for some members of Christ's faithful because the funds realized are largely not accountable for. It seems to me that the Scripture readings for the Solemnity of Corpus Christi Year C put tithing in perspective: Abraham gave the priest Melchizedek a tithe of everything (Gen 14:20); in the Gospel, Jesus made the crowd welcome, talked to them about the kingdom, and then fed them (Luke 9:11–17). The proceeds from tithe, therefore, are for the priest to "give the people something to eat," particularly those on the margins. The Second Reading of the day, 1 Cor 11:23–26, caps the relationship of Christians to the active word of God in action.

19. Kowfie, "Pentecostal-Charismatic Evangelism in West Africa," 82.

20. Okure, "President's Welcome Address," xxi.

21. Okure, "Paul's Mercy," 206–7.

22. Okai, "The Proliferation of Churches."

opportunity to speak about getting rich and living big. Very little if any exhortation is heard from the pulpit on fundamental Christian values, such as mercy, love of neighbor, fidelity, humility, suffering, and lifting up the downtrodden, to mention a few, Even concerns on morality are hardly themes for a homily. It is noteworthy that wealth does not suggest depravity; indeed, the concept of wealth as a blessing from the Lord is replete in the Hebrew Scripture.[23] "Wealth is one of the clearest proofs that the just man is rewarded in this world."[24] Also, the Hebrew Scripture attests to the idea of poverty as a curse (Prov 30:8—9), which the sage Agur, in the book of Proverbs, prays against. The sage, however, pleads for moderation, neither poverty nor riches.[25] He is painfully aware of the dangers of both extremes; for the wise and prudent, therefore, virtue lies in the middle. Incessant propagandizing and praying for affluence, without a corresponding thought on some level of deprivation of suffering, suggest a form of idolatry.

Proponents of a gospel of material wealth reject suffering. "Suffering," they insist, "is not my portion." The saying, "Not my portion," has become a mantra among Nigerian prosperity seekers; they invoke the phrase as a form of prayer against any form of personal inconvenience or likely negative outcome. These opulence-seeking Christians remain oblivious of the fact that the Christian faith is born out of suffering—the suffering and ignominious death of Jesus on a cross (Phil. 2:8). God, however, raised him because he did the will of the Father, "not what I want, but what you want" (Mark 14:36; Luke 22:24); Jesus drank the cup of suffering. Because of this, God raised him up (Acts 2:24, Rom 8:11; 1 Cor 6:14; 15:14, etc.). To prepare his disciples for the mission, Jesus taught them the lesson of the cross in Mark 8:31–33: that he, the "Son of Man," must suffer greatly and be rejected. And not only must he suffer, but all who would follow him must also be willing to take the same path of suffering, "and whoever does not take up the cross and follow me is not worthy of me" (Matt 10:38 NRSV). That is to say, a Christian must be willing to make sacrifices. Okure notes that "through sacrifice, humans seek to encounter the divine"; through "sacrifice, they project themselves into the invisible world, penetrate into the divine presence and commune with the deity."[26] "Sacrifice," she further stated, "creates a bridge between humans and God and serves to sustain the established relationship."[27] Religiosity without sacrifice, therefore, questions the authenticity of one's Christian faith. Suffering, sacrifice, and the cross remain indelible the character of the "portion" of Christian authenticity. Moreover, Paul, the apostle of the Gentiles, "reminded us that there is no other gospel, prosperity included (Gal. 1:6–10). He declares as accursed any who preaches a gospel different from the one, we have received from Jesus."[28] A holistic approach to preaching the

23. Mbonu, "Discipleship," 1–2.
24. Mbonu, "Discipleship," 3.
25. Mbonu, "Money God-talk," 20.
26. Okure, "Hebrew's Sacrifice," 535.
27. Okure, "Hebrew's Sacrifice," 535.
28. Okure, "Thin sowing means thin reaping," 245.

gospel is indeed good news for those torn between the ever-pummeling sound of prosperity preaching and humble service of God.

Discussion and Appropriation

The mission of the Twelve is a continuation of the mission of the Jesus. Luke introduces his readers to this mission in a Nazareth gathering scene where Jesus declares to his hometown audience his mission (Luke 4:18–19; cf. Isa 52:7). From Jesus' proclamation of the text from the prophet Isaiah, the Evangelist makes us understand that the *raison d'être* of Jesus breaking into human history, the incarnation, is to proclaim the Lord's year of favor through the various good deeds to the poor. The poor include, in actuality and metaphorically, the captives, the blind, and the oppressed. His interpretation and announcement of himself as the fulfillment of the Isaiah prophecy draws him suffering from the hands of his own townsfolk, but he was not deterred,[29] as can be seen in the text under study; he sent out followers who continued in his footsteps. Fidelity to that mission means attention to those on the margins. If it were today, Jesus would give the Twelve a written constitution enshrining his manifesto; he would also have given them a directory to include the instruction on Matthew 10:9–42 and elsewhere. With these liberating witnesses (Matt 10:5–16; Mark 6:7–13; Luke 9:1–6), preachers of the gospel in contemporary Nigeria ought to seek no further template in formulating their mission statement and preaching of the word as well. Summarily, Matthew makes mission to those in the margins, service to the weakest, the criteria for hope for the kingdom of heaven (Matt 25:31–46).[30]

Hope for the kingdom of heaven appears elusive in the preaching of wealth-seeking pastors. One of the factors responsible may not be unconnected with a poor articulation of Jesus' mission statement in their program of "winning" souls. Another and more existential aspect is the economic downturns; the paucity of learning and a tendency to circumvent established rules of engagement with the biblical text contribute to the problem with religion on the ground. Sidestepping established guidelines continues to turn out uninformed preachers, who present an inversion of the gospel, constituting, essentially, self-serving and materialistic propensities. Such upturn tends to devalue the gospel message and consequently empty the good news of its redemptive power. Devaluation of the gospel equally beclouds a fuller appropriation of the Holy Spirit, that immutable force of renewal, depicted by fire.[31] One may ask whether the current practice of the Christian faith tradition reflects the thoughts raised in this essay. Is there clear-cut attention directed toward the mission mandate to those on the peripheries?

To confront the problem of the negligence of Jesus' mission mandate, particularly the consideration of those on the margin, requires a deeper analysis of the state of

29. Okure, "President's Welcome Address," xxiii–xxiv.
30. Mbonu, "Matthew 25:35—Crossroads Encounter," 88–90; See also Duarte, "Matthew," 354.
31. Okure, "Enkindled Fire on the Mission," 5–8.

the practice of Christianity on the ground. There is no gainsaying that we as a people of the biblical faith tradition need to pursue and look inward for some answers. The search for answers has begun. Within the last decade, scholars have produced volumes on the activities of New Religious Movements in West Africa and Nigeria in particular. These writings criticize the *modus operandi* of the leaders of the church groups, challenging them to good stewardship of the gospel. Although some scholars affirm the activities of these groups such as communality, others project more the negative impact, particularly from the point of view of prosperity preaching that devalues the ethics of hard work, lack of creative imagination, and over-dependency on the pastor in decision making, a loss of the indigenous religious sense. The result of this shortfall portends underdevelopment. Otherwise, how can we have super-rich mega general overseers whose adherents live in shanties and perpetually beg for crumbs? These followers are constantly being fed with false hope of "we are believing God." Most of those affected by the "get rich without hard work" are persons on the margins, those whom the powers that be and their unjust structures have scattered in the mist and darkness of life; these remain the primary beneficiaries of Jesus' mission, "good news to the poor."

Appropriation

The biblical text, the church's book from which adherents draw a manual of the Christian life, embodies motivating values to fully engage in life. In the Bible, we find life-giving values such as love, family, hope, forgiveness, service, truth, and justice. These ethics, when adopted, can expand the frontiers of relationships to include those excluded from the table where decisions are made and as such subjects of right. In this regard, Chinua Achebe's wisdom is apt: "While we do our good works let us not forget that the real solution lies in a world in which charity will have become unnecessary" (*Anthills of the Savannah*). Ritual agents, women, and men of God can explore ways to espouse biblical ethics while incorporating them into their teaching and preaching for the nourishment of adherents, spiritual and physical. Such an all-inclusive approach to the word of God would deemphasize prosperity preaching and encourage work ethics, communalism, personal responsibility, and bring about development. Culturally, the simplicity of ritual agents from African natural religion challenges modern Nigerian women and men of God. Hearers of the word presume the integrity of the preacher in furthering the kingdom of God, but when it becomes obvious that the preacher's motive is literally to gather in the harvest for themselves, their families, and cronies, it becomes problematic.

CONCLUSION

Jesus, the Word of God, an embodiment of good news, sends the Twelve and indeed all of his followers, to seek the lost in our respective enclaves. Empowered by the Holy Spirit and equipped with the pattern for the encounter, the mission is to bring persons to the kingdom through teaching and preaching the word of God. This sacred duty abhors self-serving attitudes. In the Synoptic Gospels, Jesus commissions us to expand the horizon, to fan into a bonfire the flame of the Spirit which the word heralds, expanding the margins to include the less fortunate, those on the fringes of the social order. Teresa Okure, in her teachings and numerous writings, followed this mandate as attested in some of the citations in this essay. The onus is on the younger generation of teachers, writers, and preachers—Catholics as well as Protestants of all denominations—to become more familiar with the word in its aliveness, for it is only when the word truly becomes alive and active in the lives of persons—teachers, preachers, and hearers alike—that we fully realize the Lord's year of favor.

BIBLIOGRAPHY

Carter, Warren. *Matthew and the Margins: Sociopolitical and Religious Reading*. Bangalore: Theological Publications in India, 2007.

Duarte, Alejandro. "Matthew." In *Global Bible Commentary*, 350–60. Edited by Daniel Patte. Nashville: Abingdon Press, 2004.

Duling, Dennis C. *The New Testament: History, Literature, and Social Context*. Forth edition. Toronto: Thomas Wadsworth, 2003.

Kowfie, John. "The Bible in contemporary Pentecostal-Charismatic Evangelism in West Africa." *Bulletin of Ecumenical Theology* 26 (2014) 82–108.

Mbonu, Caroline. "Money God-Talk: Reading Proverbs 30:7–9 in a Milieu of Opulence Religiosity." In *Culture, Precepts, and Social Change in Southeastern Nigeria: Understanding the Igbo*, 17–28. Edited by Apollos O. Nwauwa and Ogechi E. Anyanwu. New York: Lexington Books, 2019.

———. "Matthew 25:35—Crossroads Encounter of African Peoples on the Move." *Bulletin of Ecumenical Theology* 31 (2019) 85–99.

———. "Discipleship in Luke 9:23–24: A Critique of the Prosperity Gospel." *ASUU Journal of Humanities* 3, no. 2 (April 2016) 1–12.

Okai, Moses Onyendu. "The Proliferation of Churches in Modern Nigeria: A Socio-Political and Economic Reconsideration." *Research on Humanities and Social Sciences* 6, no. 18 (2016).

Okure, Teresa. "Paul's 'Mercy': A 'Pattern' of God's Inexhaustible Patience for Future Believers (1 Timothy 1:12–17)." *Acts of the Catholic Biblical Association of Nigeria* (CABAN) 9 (2017) 192–209.

———. "President's Welcome Address on Sixth Annual Convention of the Catholic Biblical Association of Nigeria with Theme: The Bible on Faith and Evangelization." *Acts of the Catholic Biblical Association of Nigeria* (CABAN) 6 (2015) xvii–xxviii.

———. "'Thin Sowing Means Thin Reaping' (2 Cor. 9:6): An Exploration of Paul's Meaning in Context." *Acts of the Catholic Biblical Association of Nigeria* (CABAN) 5 (2014) 217–45.

———. "Alive and Active: God's Word in the Nigerian Context" *Acts of the Catholic Biblical Association of Nigeria (CABAN)* Maiden Edition (2008) 1–26.

———. "Hebrew's Sacrifice in an African Perspective." *Global Bible Commentary*, 535–38. Edited by Daniel Patte. Nashville: Abingdon Press, 2004.

———. "Enkindling Fire in the Mission." In *To Cast Fire upon the Earth: Bible and Mission Collaborating in Today's Multicultural Global Context*, 2–31. Edited by Teresa Okure. Pietermaritzburg: Cluster Publications, 2000.

Senior, Donald, and Pheme Perkins. "The Gospels and Acts." *The Catholic Study Bible, Second Edition*. Oxford: Oxford University Press, 2006.

Viviano, Benedict T. "The Gospel according to Matthew." In *The New Jerome Biblical Commentary*, 630–74. Edited by Raymond E. Brown, Joseph A. Fitzmyer, and Roland E. Murphy. Bangalore: Theological Publications in India, 1995.

CHAPTER 20

The Mission of Jesus as Purposed by God in 1 Peter 1:18–20

and Its Resonance among African Christians

CHRISTOPHER NASERI

INTRODUCTION

A biblical approach to mission in the African context demands an interpretation of the missionary impetus and paradigms contained in the Bible for the eschatological and earthly benefits of the African readers. It implies reading and directing the principles for mission contained in the Bible toward a response to the missionary challenges within Africa. It is a reading and understanding of the Bible that is oriented to the missionary needs of the African readers in their quest for nourishment from the Scriptures for their faith and their life.[1] This work studies the text of 1 Peter 1:18–20 and highlights the Petrine view on the mission of Christ in relation to the Petrine Christians and to God. The study is undertaken for the purpose of identifying the text's possible theological contributions to the incarnation of the salvific mission of Christ within the African setting and among African Christians.

African Christians or readers refer particularly in this work to the Nigerian Christians or readers of the Bible. They are notably caught between the ways of their ancestors on which they have been brought up and the new way offered by Christianity, which they have publicly accepted and professed. This African way of life embraces the religion of their fathers, which evidently manifests itself in their thought pattern, speech, and approach to life. It includes the understanding of evil, and the sources of

---

1. Fitzmyer, *Biblical Commission's Document*, 93.

illness and misfortunes. Misfortunes are generally ascribed to fellow human beings who are believed to possess the spiritual powers that permit them to manipulate and destroy others.[2] Nothing is considered as a natural occurrence; evil forces believed to be deployed by humans are acknowledged to be behind accidents, death, childlessness, unemployment, joblessness, mental illnesses, and even the recklessness of an individual.[3] This approach to life and view of the world still remains an inalienable part of some African Christians. They carry with them these beliefs as Christians in their actions and their responses to the challenges of life. How can the profession of the Christian faith be reconciled with this disposition? How can this tension be addressed without offending the sensitivity of the African culture to which this religious tradition belongs? The text of 1 Peter 1:18–20 is most appropriate especially from the standpoint of its exhortation to the Petrine Christians against returning to the ways of their forebears. Peter reminds his audience of the cost of their newfound religious beliefs. This cost consisted in the shedding of the precious blood of the unblemished lamb, Jesus Christ. It was foreordained by God as Christ's mission for the redemption of the Petrine Christians. Through this very expensive and valuable redemption, the Petrine Christians were won over to God from the religious traditions of their fathers. They took a decision to profess this new faith and live it out as their new habit. African Christians have taken the decision to profess the Christian faith; they are equally to make it as their new custom.

The Mission of Christ in Relation to the Petrine Christians (vv. 18–19)

The text outlines the content of the mission of Christ as consisting in God's pricey and precious redemption of the readers from the way of life inherited from their ancestors (v. 18). This redemption is expressed in the present indicative passive *lutroomai*. The verb means "be purchased with a ransom," "to free by paying a ransom, to redeem." It also means to liberate or rescue from an oppressive situation. The term is often used to describe the manumission of slaves in the Greco-Roman world.[4] A third party purchases a slave and becomes the slave's new master or purchases the freedom of the slave and becomes the slave's patron. It is used to translate the Hebrew *gāʾal* and *pādâh* in terms of their specialized meaning of bringing persons to freedom.[5] It is in this context of freedom that the two terms are used to describe the liberation of the Israelites from slavery in Egypt (Exod 6:6; 15:13) and Babylon (Isa 44:22–23; 51:11; 52:3), "the reclaiming by Yahweh into his rightful ownership of 'the people of his possession.'"[6] It is used in the LXX as a verb and as a noun to describe

---

2. Amadasu, "Africaemanus and Syncretistic Movements," 13.
3. Omomia and Seriki-Sotayo, "Evil in African Cosmology," 30.
4. Bauer et al., "*lutroō*," 606.
5. Brown, "Redemption," 193.
6. Brown, "Redemption," 193.

the redemption of property (Lev 25:26–49), the retribution for faults committed (Exod 21:30), the ransom of the firstborn (Exod 13:12–13), and the atonement price expected of every Israelite (Exod 30:12–16).

The noun *lutrōn*, which derives from the verb, is a combination of *luō* ("loose") and *tron* ("means"). Together the noun implies the "means of release." It denotes what is exchanged in return for getting a release of what had been taken possession of or has been conscripted, ransom. In antiquity it was used predominantly in the plural in relation to prisoners of war, debtors, and slaves. "*Lutrōn* is thus the 'price of release' for the liberation of a prisoner or debtor, in which the extent of the price of redemption and the manner of its payment follows certain conventions, but is commonly determined by 'right of the sovereign.'"[7] In the cultic sense the acceptance of ransom is a mark of graciousness from the deity, which in some instances implies non-acceptance of any form of payment. Ransom thus functions as a moment in which law and grace meet. It arises when the law is not applied in its stringency.[8]

The Old Testament and some rabbinic texts associate ransom with atonement (Num 35:31; *b. B. Qum*, 40a, 41h; *b. Mak.* 2b). There is a transition within the Jewish thought from understanding ransom as payment, to the understanding of ransom as expiation; thus a "ransom is paid for the expiation of a life that has fallen into debt."[9] It is within this context that the idea of ransom emerges as expiation through the vicarious suffering of the righteous. This idea of ransom in the Jewish setting therefore underlines "the belief in the atoning power of righteous suffering."[10] Jewish beliefs emphasize the atoning value of suffering and martyrdom in the immediate pre-Christian period. It is this relationship (of atonement to ransom in the Old Testament and Jewish thoughts) that informs the New Testament use of *lutrōn* and its cognate terms especially of Jesus Christ.

The term is used in the New Testament to describe Jesus' redemption of humankind from its bondage to sin (Luke 24:21; Titus 2:14). Jesus personally offers to give himself as a ransom (Mark 10:45). Consequently, the New Testament especially considers Jesus as the ransom for the many who are saved. Jesus surrenders his life in return for the liberation of the people. Through the shedding of his blood and death, Jesus has purchased freedom for all from enslavement to sin. He has bought humanity over for God, who now becomes its owner.[11] But the author of 1 Peter specifies God as the one who pays the ransom using the theological passive aorist verb *elutrōthēte*, which implies God as its subject (see v. 21). In other words God is the architect of the redemption, he pays the purchase price with the blood of Jesus. The blood of Jesus has

---

7. Kertelge, "*lutrōn*," 365.
8. Büchsel, "*lutrōn*," 341.
9. Karl Kertelge, "*lutrōn*," 365.
10. Büchsel, "*Lutrōn*," 341.
11. Watson and Callan, *First and Second Peter*, 34–35.

been used to purchase freedom for the people so that they in turn may become clients of the God who facilitated their freedom from the old ways.

REDEMPTION FROM THE FUTILE WAYS OF YOUR FATHERS

The use of *lutrōmai* here does not necessarily refer to the material price paid; it refers instead to the redeeming activity of God. It is the thought of the deliverance that is primary.[12] It refers to God reclaiming the people from their former ways into his rightful ownership as his possession. The liberation entails not just the means by which the readers are ransomed, but equally and importantly, that from which they are ransomed.

The liberation is from the futile or useless or foolish way of life *tēs mataios* of their fathers that characterized the neighboring culture to which the readers belonged. Essentially from the elements of their fathers, which are not in consonance with God's ways. These include the religious beliefs and ethical values and actions of their fathers. They are here described as futile to indicate that they are worthless and "empty of hope, and value when viewed in the light of the gospel (1 Cor 3:20; Eph 4:7; cf. Rom 1:21; 8:20; Jer 1:26).[13] Apart from implying futile and vain, *mataios* is used to describe the gods of the Gentiles or the idolatrous life of pre-Christian converts (Lev 17:7 LXX; Jer 8:19: 10:15; Acts 14:15; cf. Rom 1:21). This would refer to life without God understood generally as futility, emptiness, and meaninglessness.[14] Living in abominable idolatry (1 Pet 4:3–4); people who were without the mercy of God (1 Pet 2:9–10); people who lived by their concupiscence and ignorance; "passion of their former ignorance" (1 Pet 1:14) because they lacked the knowledge of God.

They have been living in the bondage of this ignorance passed on from their ancestors, *patroparadotos*. Peter intends here the living and valuable tradition passed down from the ancestral era. During those times this tradition was upheld as sacrosanct; deviation from it meant jeopardizing the stability or risking the extinction of the society. The author's juxtaposition of *patroparadotos and mataios* is deliberate and purposeful. It denotes that, in comparison with the new way of life initiated by Christ, these inherited traditional practices once appreciated by the people, as bases for the health and stability of their society, appear hopeless and meaningless.[15]

Prior to the reception of the gospel of Christ, the Petrine Christians appreciated their own culture with its values and religion and had profound regard for it as the highest norm *mos maiorum*. With their experience of Christ, their sincerity and allegiance to the importance and beauty of this ancestrally received culture not

---

12. Brown, "Redemption," 193.
13. Davids, *First Epistle of Peter*, 72.
14. Brown, "Redemption," 200.
15. Davids, *First Epistle of Peter*, 72n4.

withstanding, they can now see that this their former way of life was a futile existence.[16] "Ordinarily in this culture, living according to the ways of the ancestors would be wise counsel, but here this way of living is empty because it does not know God (1:14) and is guided by the desires of flesh (2:11; 4:2–4)."[17] One must, however, acknowledge the challenges the Petrine Christians face in having to make social adjustment and religious change because of their new religion. They are constrained to make painful acculturation and cope with the risk of being socially excluded.[18] This risk is capable of forcing a change of mind or a relapse. But, mindful of the preciousness of what it took to cause them to make the change, and what they have experienced from making the change, reversion, according to the author, is unnecessary and unthinkable. It is an explanation of the Christian life as an invitation to nonconformity and holiness in relation to the world.

Ransom is primarily based on the loss of freedom; the recipients were separated. The text conjectures an imagery that recalls the acquisition of slaves by a new master. Consequently, the slaves so bought are expected to become subjects to the ownership of their new master *theou doulou* (2:16) in his household *tou oikou* (4:17).[19] They have been bought out of their former servitude *ek tēs mataios* (1:18) to a new reality that demands allegiance to the one who has acquired them (2:16); reverence toward God (1:17), they now become slaves to their new master. The one who redeems is God, the redemption is from the futile ways of their forebears, the means of redemption is the precious blood of Christ rather than silver or gold, the implication of the redemption consists in submission to God. According to Fika, the *terminus a quo and the terminus ad quem* of the thesis can be outlined thus:

> They were the property of some other powerful person, not specified in the metaphor, sold into slavery. God has redeemed them, and now they are free! They were slaves to an empty way of life handed down to them from their forefathers, but now they are slaves to God, having been redeemed by God![20]

The text connotes freedom from dependence, and from being lost.

The Precious Blood of Christ as the Means for the Ransom

This ransom is not paid with silver and gold, a price that could purchase the freedom of slaves. These two items are considered the most valuable and indestructible assets (Prov 8:18) available in the world, for which every human craves. They engineer an avaricious, idolatrous, and consumerist society and are the expressions of human

---

16. Davids, *First Epistle of Peter*, 72.
17. Watson and Callan, *First and Second Peter*, 35.
18. Horrell, "*Christianos*," 376; see also Chester and Martins, *Theology*, 89.
19. Van Rensburg, "Salvific Metaphors of 1 Peter," 388–89.
20. Van Rensburg, "Salvific Metaphors of 1 Peter," 389.

fixation on the transient. They would normally be used for sacral manumission, and anyone who possesses them is in a position to acquire virtually anything in the world.[21] The author's negation of these as the worth for the redemption implies the incomparable worth of God's redeeming activity for the Petrine Christians. This goes to reinforce the contrast between the life of reverence toward God achieved for the Petrine Christians and their former futile ways of idolatry. The LXX often associates silver and gold with idolatry (Deut 29:17; Dan 5:23; Wis 13:10; cf. also 9:20). It is "a contrast between two ways of life and their opposite theological valuation," for while gold and silver are procured at the exploitation of the life of others (Jas 5:1–6; cf. Rev 17:4), redemption takes place through the offering of life.[22] Just as the old life is futile and incomparably less in worth and non-preferable, in relation to the new life, the means by which the old ways of the fathers are shaped and promoted and their essential components of silver and gold are incomparable in worth in relation to the means by which the redemption is achieved: the precious blood of Christ. They are incapable of freeing one from the ephemeralness of human existence and cannot even save on the day of the Lord's wrath (Zeph 1:18; Ezek 7:19). They are of a lesser value, corruptible, and perishable (1 Cor 9:25) compared to the timeless and imperishable value (precious) of the blood of Christ. Over and above the ransom price of 1 Corinthians 6:20, the Petrine message here is that the redemption has no correlation with things associated with the Petrine Christian's former idolatrous way of life; rather, it takes place by means of God's own act in Christ (vv. 20–21).[23]

The blood of Christ is represented as what is offered in exchange for the Petrine audience (v. 19). The author is aware of Isaiah 52:3: "You were sold for nothing, and you will be redeemed without money." Interestingly, the LXX for this text has *apguriou* ("silver") translated as "money." It is a redemption won without a cost on the recipients, "silver and gold," but with a cost on God, who offers to pay on their behalf with the blood Christ, a vicarious act. This highlights the freely offered redeeming act of God. Blood here implies Christ's suffering and death. The sacrificial blood of Christ is proposed by the author to be viewed in the context of *hōs*, the unblemished lamb of sacrifice. As a sacrificial lamb, Christ does not live on others but for others. He is the unblemished (*amōmos*) and spotless (*aspilos*) lamb (1:19b) appreciated as the worthy and acceptable sacrifice.

The term *aspilos*, "spotless" or "without defect," denotes lack of moral corruption in the New Testament (1 Tim 6:14: Jas 1:27), and in 2 Peter 3:14 it is also paired with *amōmos*. The author of 1 Peter 1:19 employs the terms here to emphasize the absolute perfection and effectiveness of Christ as the means used by God for the redemption (cf. Heb 9:14). The terms recall the Israelite cultic notion of unblemished animals for true sacrifice (Exod 29:1; Lev 22:17–25) and the Passover Lamb of Exodus 12:5.

21. Feldmeier, *First Letter of Peter*, 115.
22. Feldmeier, *First Letter of Peter*, 118.
23. Achtemeier, *1 Peter*, 128.

In other words, the unblemished status of the sacrificial animals was a condition for their acceptability and the effectiveness of the sacrifice. John 1:29, 36; and 19:36 ties this Passover to Jesus and his redemptive death on the cross (see also 1 Cor 5:7). The author of 1 Peter underscores this Passover as God's redemption of the Petrine Christians from their futile ways. While the Passover in Egypt was accomplished with the blood of unblemished animals, the redemption of the Petrine Christians is unique and more precious because it is by the blood of the spotless Son of God the Christ. While the spotlessness demanded of the offered lamb was physical, that of Jesus is total integrity, ethical, cultural, and spiritual and even ontological.[24] The redeeming act is thus unquantifiable and incomparably valuable, perfect, and effective in enhancing salvation. By his vicarious service of suffering and death for the salvation of Christians, the Petrine Jesus "brings to bear the 'free-of-charge character of the redemption by God in history.'"[25] This text is expressive of the author's knowledge and conviction of the early Christian tradition of the atoning and vicarious death of Jesus Christ spelled out in Mark 10:45 and reminiscent of Isaiah 53:10-12. Here Jesus' sacrificial suffering and death is understood as a vicarious deed "for many." His imperishable blood is the material cause of the redemption.[26] There are, however, objections regarding the allusion to Isaiah 53. These are based on the absence of *lutron* in Isaiah 53 LXX.[27]

Imprisoned in their futile ways without God, the Petrine Christians stood in need of an initiative from outside of them to set them free. So, in relation to them and their futile ways, Jesus through his blood stands as the ransom. The source of their redemption is Jesus Christ whose blood has set them free. The blood of Jesus is a means of redemption, and through it God has changed the ways of the Petrine Christians from those of their fathers by giving them new life in the new community that is God's. The mission of Jesus consists in this solidarity with the Petrine Christians who were formally in the state of imprisonment to idolatry.

THE MISSION OF CHRIST AS THE PLAN OF GOD (V. 20)

The verb *proginōskō* means "foreknowledge" or "choose beforehand" and it implies that God planned and executed it, predicted and predestined it (see Isa 37:26). In the New Testament it refers to God whose foreknowledge "is an election or foreordination of his people (Rom 8:29; 11:2) or Christ (1 Peter 1:20)."[28] It is the overarching, as against passive, presence of God in the story and mission of Christ both from the point of view of his creative and salvific will. Jesus was foreknown and chosen by God before the foundation of the world for his redemptive mission at the end of time. This

---

24. Mazzeo, *Lettere di Pietro, Lettera di Giuda* , 78.
25. Kertelge, "*lutron*," 366.
26. Martin, "Tasting the Eucharistic," 519.
27. Cf. Brown, "Redemption," 196; Kertelge, "*lutron*," 365.
28. Bultmann, "*proginōskō*," 715.

is a familiar understanding for the Jews in 4 Esdras 6:1–6 and is carried over by the Christians in the understanding of salvation as foreknown by God and executed in time (Rom 16:25; Acts 2:23; 1 Cor 2: 6–10; Titus 1: 2–3).

The foreknowing election of Christ by God is a "fixed plan" traced to eternity, but in relation to the people it is set within a historical framework of the redeemed people. That historical framework is for the author "now" as witnessed by the prophets (1:10–12). It is viewed in the context of the Jewish Passover of Exodus 12, in which the Passover Lamb is selected prior (tenth Nisan) to the day of the sacrifice (fourteenth Nisan).[29] It implies the preexistence of Christ before his revelation in time (Heb 9:26; 1 Tim 3:16); he is also preexisting as his final appearance is being awaited (1 Pet 5:4). The "end of times" thus refers to the period between the first appearance of Christ and his expected final appearance (1 Cor 10:11). It is the Christian period or Christ-time, identified by the author as "time of your exile" (1 Pet 1:17), given to the Petrine Christians to live out the holiness of their redemption (1 Pet 1:13–17).

Just as the election of Christ is foreknown by God, so is the election of the Petrine Christians (1 Pet 1:2). God elects Christ for the purpose of electing the Petrine Christians through Christ. The use of *proginōskō* and its implied cognates *pronoein* or *prognosis* is not to be understood purely from its originally Stoic Hellenistic notion of divine predestination or divine steering of the world by providence. The author here expresses the Christian appropriation of the concept as a theological conviction that God's election of Christ for the redemption of the Petrine Christians is consistent with God's eternal design and desire for the salvation of his people. The divine plan of driving world events was established before creation by God. This divine willing of salvation is a mystery that was already determinative in the announced Old Testament prophecies (1 Pet 1:10f) and already established before the creation. This divine plan is now manifested in time in Christ (Eph 3:3–11; 2 *Clem* 14:2), who himself was chosen before time. The mission of Christ for the salvation of the people was purposed by God and is therefore the work of God. Though recently manifested in the event that has taken place in Jesus Christ in time, it was pre-planned, designed, and executed by God himself in his dealing with creation and history; it is ascribed to "a divine self-determination before all time that precedes all created being."[30]

The text recalls the early Christian juxtaposition of the pre-temporal divine plan and its historical actualization in time (see Rom 16:25–26; John 17:24); it is done in view of channelling all things and especially in the Petrine time of exile, out beyond it, back to its source, God, at the final revelation of Christ. The redemption marks in God's plan the change of age in the succession of definite ages; the last of ages inaugurated by the life and ministry of Jesus (Acts 2:16–21) as the Petrine Christians await the final appearance of Christ (1 Pet 1:17).[31] Between these pre-temporal and

29. Chester and Martins, *Theology*, 109.
30. Feldmeier, *First Letter of Peter*, 57, 119.
31. Watson and Callan, *First and Second Peter*, 36.

the expected final revelation is the "end of times," time of your exile, within which the Petrine Christians stand on the brink or at the margin of the world because they belong to the center of salvation history. So, in relation to God, the mission of Christ is the eternal plan and work of God. God is the one who supervises the events of Christ and of his people; the saving mission of Christ was in the eternal plan of God. While it is God that plans before time and executes the mission of Christ as revealed in time, the phrase is also an assurance to the readers that their story is tied to God and under God's direction, and therefore their redemption is reliable. So even in the challenge of having to avoid conformity to the world around them in their quest for reverence toward God, they should not be afraid of being defeated. They must stand firm in their hope and put up a firm but polite resistance (1 Pet 1:13; 5:9, 12).[32] "They are not at the mercy of feckless chance or historical accidents (a point explicitly made in 1:4)."[33] The author sees Christ as God's novel and ultimate act that attracts Christian conformity even at the expense of abandoning former cultural allegiances. "All of this is set within a cosmic frame of reference, both in terms of God's decisions prior to the creation of the world and in terms of the impending conclusion of that creation (v. 20)."[34]

READING 1 PETER 1:18-20 AS AN AFRICAN CHRISTIAN

Readers of 1 Peter in Africa are required to appropriate the redemption made possible by the shedding of the precious blood of Christ. God chose Jesus his Son in advance before the foundation of the world for the purpose of redeeming the Africans. As African Christians read this text in this present age, Christ is revealed to them for their sake as their redeemer. They, by their encounter with Christ "now," are set within the historical framework of the redeemed people. They are understood to have been part of the plan of God in choosing Christ in eternity for the redemption of his people. This redemption is equally now being manifested in their own times. God purposed their encounter with Christ just as he purposed the mission of Christ; their election was foreknown by God just as the election of Christ was foreknown by God. They were God's people who, for a period, lacked the knowledge of God and were under the influence of superstitious practices and beliefs handed down by their fathers. Their encounter with Christ's gospel locates them within their own "end of times," Christ-time. In this Christ-time God has reclaimed them from their former ways into his rightful ownership as his possessions. Like the Petrine Christians, this "the end of times" or "Christ-time" is given to the African readers too to live out the holiness of their own freedom from superstitious beliefs and practices (1 Pet 1:1-2).[35] They

---

32. Horrell, Arnold, and Williams, "Visuality, Vivid Description," 716.
33. Chester and Martins, *Theology*, 108.
34. Achtemeier, *1 Peter*, 124.
35. Naseri, "Petrine Christians," 91.

have taken the decision to profess the Christian faith as their new way of life; they are equally to wear it as their new habit.

They are to consider the gains that come with the acceptance of Christ in relation to their former existence; they are to be ready to relentlessly make the sacrifices of abandoning these old ways, make social adjustments, religious changes, and painful acculturation that may even risk their being socially excluded from their communities. The church through its agents must make provision, in the various communities where this Christ-encounter generates tensions, to care for the Christian victims of social exclusions and segregations. The ecclesial agents must build the bridge between the traditionalists and the pro-Christian members of the traditional societies where the gospel is propagated. African Christians are reminded that being elected in eternity implies that God is in charge of their history; their encounter with Christ, which has occurred, is not a historical accident. Therefore the challenges of social exclusion and segregation that arise from their consequent nonconformity and holiness in relation to the superstitious practices of their traditional societies cannot overrun or overpower them. Even the anxieties over illness and death which sometimes encourage the resort to or a revisiting of superstitious beliefs and practices become exaggerated when the African Christian loses sight of the overarching presence of the God of the Christian faith in history. They are to also make a distinction between their choice of abandoning the old ways of their forebears as a fundamental option, and the temptation to show disrespect for those practices and their adherents. While acknowledging the "slippery nature of culture,"[36] they are to bear in mind that those practices still fall within the cultural heritage of their traditional societies and attract respect. It is on the basis of this promotion of respect and appreciation that a favorable context for a meaningful dialogue can emerge.

BIBLIOGRAPHY

Achtemeier, Paul. *1 Peter*. Minneapolis: Fortress Press, 1996.

Amadasu, Idahosa. "Africaemanus and Syncretistic Movements in Africa: A Challenge for Inculturation." *The Oracle* 3, no. 5 (Dec 2017) 1–25.

Brown, Colin. "Redemption." In *The New International Dictionary of New Testament Theology*, 3:190–200. Edited by Colin Brown. Grand Rapids: Zondervan, 1978.

Bultmann, Rudolf. "Proginōskō." In *Theological Dictionary of the New Testament*, 1:715–16. Edited by Gerhard Kittel. Translated by Geoffrey W. Bromiley. Grand Rapids: Eerdmans, 1964.

Büchsel, F. "lutrōn." In *Theological Dictionary of the New Testament*, 4:340–49. Edited by Gerhard Kittel. Translated by Geoffrey W. Bromiley. Grand Rapids: Eerdmans, 1967.

Chester, Andrew, and Ralph P. Martins. *The Theology of the Letters of James, Peter, and Jude*. Cambridge: Cambridge University Press, 1994.

Davids, Peter H. *The First Epistle of Peter*. NICNT. Grand Rapids: William B. Eerdmans, 1990.

---

36. Manus, "Jesus' Consecration," 192.

Feldmeier, Reinhard. *The First Letter of Peter*. Waco, TX: Baylor University Press, 2008.

Fitzmyer, Joseph A. *The Biblical Commission's Document "The Interpretation of the Bible in the Church" Text and Commentary*. Roma: Editrice Pontificio Istituto Biblico, 1995.

Horrell, David G. "The Label *Christianos*: I Peter 4:16 and the Formation of Christian Identity." *Journal of Biblical Literature* 126, no. 2 (Summer 2007) 361–81.

Horrell, David G., Bradley Arnold, and Travis B. Williams. "Visuality, Vivid Description, and the Message of 1 Peter: The Significance of the Roaring Lion (1 Peter 5:8)." *Journal of Biblical Literature* 132, no. 3 (Winter 2013) 697–716.

Kertelge, Karl. "*lutrōn*." In *Exegetical Dictionary of the New Testament*, 2:364–66. Edited by Horst Balz and Gerhard Schneider. Grand Rapids: Eerdmans, 1991.

Manus, Chris Ukachukwu. "A Study of Jesus' Consecration in the Temple (Luke 2:21–38) in the Light of an Igbo Traditional Consecration Rite in Nigeria: Implications for Inculturation of Consecrated Life in the African Church." In *Consecration and Vows in the Bible, Acts of the Catholic Biblical Association of Nigeria (CABAN)*, 8:174–195. Edited by B. Ukwuegbu, M.J Obiorah, A. Ewherido, V. Nyoyoko, and C. Gotan. Port Harcourt: CABAN Publications, 2016.

Martin, Troy W. "Tasting the Eucharistic Lord as Usable (1 Peter 2:3)." *Catholic Biblical Quarterly* 78, no. 3 (July 2016) 515–25.

Mazzeo, Michele. *Lettere di Pietro, Lettera di Giuda*. Milano: Figlie di San Paolo, 2002.

Naseri, Christopher. "Petrine Christians as Strangers and the Globalization of Christianity: A Study of 1 Peter 1:1; 1:17; 2:9 and 2:11." *The Nigerian Journal of Theology* 31 (June 2017) 77–95.

Omomia, Austin, and Seriki-Sotayo. "Evil in African Cosmology and Pentecostal Christianity: A Comparative Approach." *Veritas Journal of Religious Studies* 1, no. 1 (Dec 2018) 21–37.

Van Rensburg, Fika J. "The Old Testament in the Salvific Metaphors of 1 Peter." In *The Catholic Epistles and the Tradition*, 381–86. Edited by J. Schlosser. Leuven: Leuven University Press, 2004.

Watson, Duane F., and Terrance Callan. *First and Second Peter*. Grand Rapids: Baker Academic, 2012.

CHAPTER 21

Knowing the True God in the Liberation Account of Exodus 1–14
and Its Missionary Significance

Luke Emehiele Ijezie

INTRODUCTION

God's dealings with Israel are mostly geared toward making them know who he is. This is brought to a climax in the revealing of the name to Moses and the liberation of the people from bondage in Egypt. The name revealed to Moses sums up the nature and modus operandi of Israel's God. The whole liberation efforts in Egypt were aimed at demonstrating the meaning of the name YHWH. The people would know at the end that God's name is really YHWH and that it was this YHWH-God that sent Moses into their midst. More importantly, the Egyptians will come to know YHWH through the mighty acts he will do in their midst. This motif of making Pharaoh and the Egyptians know occurs many times within the corpus of Exodus 1–14 (7:5, 17; 8:6, 18; 9:14, 29; 10:2; 11:7; 14:4, 18), all showing that it is properly worked into the plot of the narrative.[1] The present essay examines the motif of knowing in the narrative and how it relates to the whole exodus event and the meaning of God's name. The analysis follows both synchronic and diachronic approaches because of the complex nature of the narrative.

---

1. See various identifications of this motif i: Greenberg, *Understanding Exodus*, 164–67; Ska, *La passage de la mer*, 57–60, 75; Tucker, *You Shall Know that I am YHWH*.

DELIMITATION OF THE TEXT

The present study is a thematic investigation within the text range of Exodus 1–14, which narrates the story of Israel's experience of persecution in Egypt and experience of deliverance. The text begins with the experience of persecution when the people groaned and cried for divine intervention. The last point of the text relates how the people rejoiced at the divine intervention and acknowledged the identity of the Deliverer God. Although the text is a very long one, the discussion will focus on the salient areas that help to understand the significance of the theme of knowing YHWH in the story.

STRUCTURE OF THE TEXT: THE PERSPECTIVE OF THE KNOWING MOTIF

The text of Exodus 1–14 shows a preponderance of the motif of knowing or not knowing. From this perspective, one can structure the argument. The story begins with the information regarding the Pharaoh who did not know Joseph, one of the great ancestors of the Israelites in Egypt. This lack of knowledge brings about persecution. Then the people cry out to God, and God hears and shows that he knows the people and their grief. To demonstrate his knowing of the situation, God reveals himself to Moses and tells him that he knows the people and their grief. Then he makes himself known to Moses by the new name YHWH. The narrative program now is to make the people of Israel and the Egyptians know this name, and this will be done through the events of the deliverance from Egypt. The structure runs as follows:

- (Exod 1–2)—Pharaoh's Lack of Knowledge of Israel's Past versus Divine Knowledge
- (Exod 3–5)—God's Self-disclosure
- (Exod 6–14)—Program to make YHWH known

ANALYSIS OF THE TEXT

Pharaoh's Lack of Knowledge of Israel's Past versus Divine Knowledge (Exod 1–2)

The text of Exodus 1, after introducing the presence of the Israelites in Egypt (Exod 1:1–7), anchors the rest of the information on the notice that a new pharaoh is in town and he does not know (*lōʾ-yādaʿ*) Joseph, the great ancestor of the Israelites in Egypt (1:8). The consequence of this lack of knowing is seen in the subsequent events. The hostile pharaoh initiates a regime of aggression and persecution against the Israelites. Then the Israelites in their anguish cry out, and their outcry reaches the God of their fathers, who now pays attention. Consequently, the pharaoh's lack of knowing is counterbalanced by the announcement of God's knowing (*yādaʿ*) in Exodus 2:25.[2]

---

2. The text of Exod 2:23–25 is interpreted by Coats, "A Structural Transition in Exodus," 29–142 as

God responds to the cry of the people in four ways: (1) he heard (*wayyishma'*) their groaning; (2) he remembered (*wayyizcōr*) the covenant with Abraham, Isaac, and Jacob; (3) he saw/recognized (*wayyar'*) the children of Israel; and (4) he knew (*wayyēda'*). God intervenes because he hears the groaning of the oppressed. He feels committed to his covenant with the patriarchs. He remembers. In moments of crisis, Israel will always ask God to remember his covenant. By remembering he takes notice of the people's suffering. This leads to the fourth response: God's knowledge. But an important question is: What really is meant by the statement that God knows? It is not directly stated what he knows. The Hebrew verb *yāda'* basically expresses experiential acquaintance with reality.[3] According to Terence Fretheim, God's knowing here refers to his awareness or experience of Israel's suffering.[4] If the effect of Pharaoh's lack of knowing is persecution and bondage for the Israelites, the effect of God's knowing would be liberation for the Israelite people. This liberation would be brought to completion with Israel's own knowing of the liberator God. This means that God must make himself known to the people.

God's Self-Disclosure in the Call and Mission of Moses (Exod 3–5)

In this section, God reveals Himself to Moses in the form of a burning bush and sends him on a mission to liberate Israel from Egypt. The point of emphasis is that God lets Moses know that he knows (*yāda'*) about all that the Israelites are suffering in Egypt and has decided and even come down to deliver them. But, then, the people need to know who this Deliverer-God is. Two particular moments in this encounter with Moses are God's declaration of his knowledge of Israel's suffering in Exodus 3:7 and the revelation of the divine name in Exodus 3:13–15.

God's Knowing of Israel (Exod 3:7)

The text of Exodus 3:7 runs as follows: "YHWH then said, 'I have indeed seen the affliction (*'ŏnî*) of my people in Egypt. I have heard them crying for help on account of their taskmasters. Yes, I know their sufferings.'"

God's response to Israel's state of oppression is expressed with three significant verbs:

1. seeing (*rā'îtî*)—"I have seen"
2. hearing (*shāma'tî*)—"I have heard"
3. knowing (*yāda'tî*)—"I have known, I know"

---

a transition text functioning to anticipate the speech of 3:7–8. See also Coats, "Moses in Midian," 3–10.

3. Cf. Lewis, "*yāda'*," 366–67.
4. Fretheim, "yd'," 412.

These three verbs refer to the three categories of suffering of the people in Egypt which God has come to address:

1. affliction (ʿŏnî)—"I have seen the affliction of my people"
2. cry for help (tseʿāqāh)—"I have heard their crying for help"
3. sufferings (makʾôb)—"I have known/know their suffering"

The divine action, which is of particular significance in this essay, is the act of knowing—yādaʿtî ("I have known, I know"). But what does God know in this context? In the use of the verb "to know," God shows how he is intimately involved with the sufferings or pain (makʾôb) of his people. The Hebrew noun makʾôb is derived from the verb kāʾab, meaning "to have pain, be sorrowful."[5] This divine knowing of the pain can be understood as both divine compassion and divine empathy. God feels for His people and identifies with their suffering. One can notice the gradation in the expression of the divine action: he sees; he hears, and he knows. These are indicative of God's deep involvement in the situation. He knows his people and their plight. This was his modus operandi with the ancestors, and he is replicating same with this generation in Egypt.

Revelation of the Divine Name (Exod 3:13–15)

The Deity speaking to Moses first reveals his identity in Exodus 3:6 as the God worshiped by the three patriarchs: Abraham, Isaac, and Jacob. Now he gives a fuller revelation of himself in verses 13–15. The question of the divine name is raised by Moses himself in verse 13 as he requests God to reveal his real name. For Moses, the idea of the God of the fathers is too vague for the suffering Israelites. They would like to know the specific name of the God coming to save them. They will ask, "What is his name?" (mah-šᵉmô). Moses is aware of the existence of many gods in Egypt. Is this ancestral Deity more powerful than all of them? According to John I. Durham, "What Moses asks, then, has to do with whether God can accomplish what he is promising."[6] This may not be an expression of doubt on God's credibility but a search for something in God's reputation that will convince the people. As Durham interprets, "How, suddenly, can he be expected to deal with a host of powerful Egyptian deities against whom, across so many years, he has apparently won no victory for his people?"[7] The question is based on what this ancestral God can do that he has not yet done. Is he capable? The ancients believed in the power of the name. The Egyptians had the common belief that the knowledge of the name of a god gave one the power over that god. From this perspective, Moses could be understood as seeking to appropriate this power through

---

5. Oswalt, "kāʾab," 425.
6. Durham, *Exodus*, 38.
7. Durham, *Exodus*, 38.

knowing the name. According to André LaCocque, there is some ambiguity or hidden agenda in the desire of Moses to know the divine name, as he is actually looking for a name of power which he can use to protect himself from adversity in Egypt.[8]

At this point God answers Moses regarding his name in verse 14. The text reads:

> God replied: "I am who I am" (*'Ehye 'ašer 'Ehye*). He further says, "Thus you shall say to the Israelites, 'I am (*'Ehye*) has sent me to you.'" (3:14)

The name is so strange that interpreters usually argue whether originally it was intended to be a name.[9] According to Durham, the answer is not really a name but "an assertion of authority, a confession of an essential reality."[10] The nature of the question posed by Moses in verse 13 needed such an answer. The name is not explained directly but indirectly. The insistence on the present, "I am," points to the fact that this Deity is always in the present. As Durham puts it: "YHWH Is, and his Is-ness means Presence."[11] The name, thus, refers to YHWH's active presence in the situation. He comes as a liberator God and reveals his name as YHWH, which actually means one who is present.[12] This name expresses his identity and role in the people's life and history, and this is the significance of a name in the ancient Near East.

Joseph Blenkisopp follows the same line of interpretation, pointing out that it is not a name but a phrase which echoes the assurance already given to Moses in Exodus 3:12 that "I will be with you" (*'ehye 'immāk*).[13] According to him, it is "meant to convey something about presence and assistance in the uncertain events about to unfold."[14] This active presence will be so demonstrated that the people will come to know that he is really what he confesses to be. The whole text can be read from this point of view—namely, God's demonstration that he is YHWH, that he is actively present, and the people's realization that he is YHWH, that he is actively present.

Moses is made to understand that he is being sent on mission in the name of this active and present deity, and this is the way he will speak of God to the Israelites. This is further stressed in Exodus 3:15: "Thus you shall say to the Israelites, 'YHWH, the God of your ancestors, the God of Abraham, the God of Isaac, and the God of Jacob, has sent me to you': This is my name forever, and this my title for all generations." The text of Exodus 3:15, which seems to repeat what is already said earlier,[15] stresses the point that all generations must identify Israel's God, who is the same God that

---

8. LaCocque and Ricoeur, *Thinking Biblically*, 309–311.

9. See discussion in Hertog, "The Prophetic Dimension," 213–28.

10. Durham, *Exodus*, 38.

11. Durham, *Exodus*, 39.

12. See McCarthy, "Exod 3:14," 23.

13. Blenkinsopp, *Pentateuch*, 149.

14. Blenkinsopp, *Pentateuch*, 149.

15. Some interpreters regard Exod 3:15 as a later redactional addition. For this view, see Ska, *Introduzione alla lettura del Pentateuco*, 99.

Abraham, Isaac, and Jacob worshiped, with this new name. All that YHWH now does for Israel centers on making this name permanent in the consciousness of the people. It is a missionary responsibility on the part of Moses to make the name known. Every generation must know that God is YHWH.

Mission of Moses and Pharaoh's Lack of Knowledge of YHWH (Exod 3:16–5:23)

The divine name revealed to Moses is at the very center of his mission. One can hardly speak of this mission without the role of the name in it. With the power of the divine name and the authority behind it (3:16–4:17), Moses initiates his mission, which experiences temporary setbacks in the episodes narrated in Exodus 4:18–5:23. The greatest factor in these setbacks is the stubbornness of Pharaoh linked to his avowed lack of knowledge of who YHWH is.

In Exodus 5:1, Moses and Aaron meet Pharaoh and ask him in YHWH's name to let Israel go, but Pharaoh refuses and dares YHWH: "Who is YHWH that I should obey His voice to let Israel go? I do not know YHWH, and besides, I will not let Israel go" (Exod 5:2). What Pharaoh is saying in effect is that Israel's Deity has no power to command him. For him, YHWH is not only of no relevance in this matter but is of no relevance at all. That he does not know YHWH means also that he does not recognize him as a divine authority. This is, no doubt, a great challenge to the power of YHWH.

The gravity of the matter is better felt when one recalls that the demand to let Israel go is presented as a direct speech from YHWH. He is the one who commands Pharaoh to release his people: "Let my people go!" This phrase occurs several times (Exod 5:1; 7:16; 8:1, 8, 20–21; 9:1, 13; 10:3, 4), and functions almost as a refrain in the whole drama. It is worded in the first person. So, it is not Moses or Aaron or the elders of Israel demanding that their people be released. YHWH, the God of Israel, is the one giving the command to Pharaoh to release his people. YHWH is not just helping Moses to liberate Israel. He is, rather, fully involved in this matter. By refusing to heed to this demand, Pharaoh is putting himself at loggerheads with YHWH. So the battle in Exodus is actually between YHWH and Pharaoh. Since Pharaoh is challenging the authority of YHWH and saying he does not know YHWH, he must be thoroughly defeated to prove to both the characters and actors in the field that YHWH has no rival and by this he will know who YHWH is.

With this new challenge, it becomes necessary to revitalize the mission of Moses. Within the narrative context, the mission gets reinvigorated with another divine revelation of the name and renewal of the program of liberation, all of which gravitate toward making YHWH's identity and power better known.

Program to Make YHWH Known (Exod 6–14)

This large section of Exodus (6–14) narrates all the practical efforts to get Israel out of Egypt. It is a section full of dramatic events. The chief protagonist in the whole drama is YHWH, while Moses and Aaron are his agents. The game plan is that the Israelite people should come to know this Deity, called YHWH, understand his modus operandi and adopt him as their national Deity. The people would need many signs and wonders to be able to come to this level of knowledge and understanding. Linked to this program is the plan to make Pharaoh and the Egyptians to know who YHWH really is. All the events and actions narrated in Exodus 6–14 are geared toward realizing this knowledge. The text begins with what appears as a second revelation of the divine name in Exodus 6:2–7:7 and ends in Exodus 14:31 with Israel's confession of faith in YHWH.

Second Account of the Name-Revelation and Mission of Moses (Exod 6:2–7:7)

This section of the Exodus account has long been a subject of great discussion by interpreters. The perplexity is the repetition of the revelation of the divine name and the mission of Moses. The tension is, however, resolved from the point of view of source criticism. It is presently widely agreed that the account in Exodus 6:2–7:7 is the Priestly writer's own version of the call and mission of Moses.[16] While it resembles the first version, both differ on essential points.

The text of the divine speech in Exodus 6:2–8 reads:

> 2 God spoke to Moses and said to him, "I am YHWH. 3 I appeared to Abraham, Isaac and Jacob as El Shaddai, but my name YHWH I did not make known to them. 4 I established my covenant with them to give them the land of Canaan, the land in which they were living as aliens. 5 Now, I have heard the groaning of the Israelites, whom the Egyptians have enslaved, and I have remembered my covenant. 6 Therefore, say to the Israelites, "I am YHWH. I shall bring you out from the forced labour of the Egyptians; I shall rescue you from their slavery and I shall redeem you with outstretched arm and mighty acts of judgment. 7 I shall take you as my people and I shall be your God. And you will know that I am YHWH your God, who is bringing you out from the forced labour of the Egyptians. 8 Then I shall lead you into the country which I swore I would give to Abraham, Isaac and Jacob, and shall give it to you as your heritage, I am YHWH."

This long text establishes a coherent program of the liberation from Egypt. Five elements can be identified in this program:

1. the revelation of the name YHWH (vv. 2–3)
2. the remembrance of the covenant with the patriarchs (vv. 4–5)

---

16. See Blenkinsopp, *The Pentateuch*, 153.

3. the divine decision and plan to liberate Israel (v. 6)

4. the plan to make Israel become God's people and know that God is YHWH (v. 7)

5. the plan to lead Israel into the land promised the patriarchs (v. 8)

The first element as seen in verses 2–3 establishes the identity of the liberator God. This identity is expressed in the self-declaratory formula "I am YHWH" (*'anî YHWH*), and it occurs four times within verses 2–8 (vv. 2, 6, 7, 8). The formula is an assertion of divine authority and active presence in the situation.[17] Here in verses 2–3, YHWH declares that he is coming to liberate the people with his identity as YHWH. This name was not revealed to the patriarchal generation, but it is now being revealed for a purpose.

The second element as seen in verses 4–5 presents the liberation as a fulfillment of the covenant with the patriarchs. The remembrance of this covenant is a recurring theme in the YHWH-Israel relationship. The third element, which is seen in verse 6, enumerates three things involved in the liberation: freeing from forced labor, rescuing from slavery, and redeeming through mighty acts. All these are the things YHWH will now accomplish to bring Israel out of Egypt. They encompass all that will happen in Exodus 7–14.

The whole objective of these liberating acts is summed up in two moments. The first is presented in the fourth element in verse 7, which is to make Israel a people belonging to YHWH and knowing YHWH as their God, and the second is in the fifth element in verse 8, which is the leading of the Israelites into the land promised the patriarchs, Abraham, Isaac, and Jacob. The idea is that Israel will enter the land as the people of YHWH and as people who already know YHWH. The text of verse 7 is presented in form of a covenant formula. This covenant formula expresses the idea that YHWH liberates Israel in order that the suffering Israelites in Egypt may become his people (*'am*) and know him as YHWH, their liberator God.

The proposal in Exodus 6:7 of making Israel YHWH's people in the future may seem to conflict with the fact that Israel is already identified by YHWH himself as his people in Exodus 3:7 and 10. The question is: If Israel is already the people of YHWH, why does Exodus 6:7 again say they will become the people of YHWH with the liberation from Egypt? In the first place, if Exodus 6:7 is read in harmony with the statement in Exodus 6:4,5, the liberation from bondage emerges as a result of YHWH's remembrance of the patriarchal covenant, a covenant that also contains the promise of entering into a God-people communion with the descendants of the patriarchs (see Gen 17:7–8). From this point of view, the proposal of Exodus 6:7 becomes a way of fulfilling the covenantal promise of Genesis 17:7–8. Secondly, apart from the fact that Exodus 3:7, 10 and 6:7 belong to two different literary sources, one can still harmonize them within the narrative context.[18] The idea of becoming the people of YHWH is a

---

17. See Durham, *Exodus*, 76.

18. Rendtorff, "Some Reflections," 15 notes that the Priestly texts related to their non-priestly

process that needs to be completed, and it is actually tied to knowing and accepting YHWH as the national Deity. According to Rolf Rendtorff, "God began to be the god of Israel through Abraham, he continued by taking Israel as his people through Moses."[19] The point is that being YHWH's people and knowing YHWH constitute the main reason for the whole liberation from Egypt.

Another significant moment in the text of Exodus 6:2–7:7 is in 7:3–5, where God outlines his plan of action to Moses. He will harden the heart of Pharaoh so that he will not let the people go until YHWH does mighty works of judgment in Egypt. God tells Moses,

> But I will harden Pharaoh's heart, and I will multiply my signs (*'ôtôt*) and wonders (*mōphetîm*) in the land of Egypt. When Pharaoh does not listen to you, then I will lay My hand on Egypt and bring out My hosts, My people the Israelites, from the land of Egypt by great judgments. The Egyptians shall know (*yāde 'û*) that I am Yahweh, when I stretch out My hand on Egypt and bring out the Israelites from their midst.(Exod 7:3–5)

This text makes it clear that God's foremost intent is to make the Egyptians know (*yāde 'û*) who YHWH is, that is, to acknowledge his identity and authority. It is only then that they would let Israel go. This idea of making the Egyptians know YHWH is repeated a number of times in Exodus 7–14 (7:5, 17; 8:6, 18; 9:14, 29; 10:2; 11:7; 14:4, 18). The mighty acts of judgment already mentioned in Exodus 6:6 are the very things that will make Pharaoh and the Egyptians free Israel and to know the true God YHWH.

What one gathers from Exodus 6:2–7:7 is that Moses is the bearer of the direct revelation of the divine name YHWH. Others will come to know it through the divine acts. The Israelites will come to know this YHWH through their experience of his saving acts of liberation, and the Egyptians will know him through the mighty acts that he will do against them as means to the liberation.

The Mighty Acts of Judgment—The Plagues of Egypt (Exod 7:14–12:36)

The actions regarded as the mighty acts are described in Exodus 7:14–12:36 as the ten plagues of Egypt. In the accounts, one encounters three important terms that qualify the plagues. The general term is *magēphôt* ("plagues"), while the other two are *'ôtôt* ("signs") and *mōphetîm* ("wonders"). In the Exodus account, these *magēphôt* are also regarded as "signs and wonders" and are so described in ancient Hebrew hymns (Pss 78; 105; 135; 136).[20] The ten plagues are presented as the divine punitive instruments aimed at letting Pharaoh release the people of Israel. However, many theories and

---

contexts, and this is the case with the text of Exod 6:2–8.

19. Rendtorff, "Some Reflections," 19.
20. See Hoffmeier, "Plagues of Egypt," 1056.

hypotheses abound on the reality and meaning of the plagues. Some have tried to explain them historically by linking them to ecological phenomena that happened in various epochs of Egyptian history. Some others are more alarmed at the idea of God procuring such ecological disasters. Scholars have continued to exercise their fertile imagination on what actually happened. However, most biblical scholars do not dabble into such supposed scientific and historical explanations. They, rather, take the data of the text seriously. Within the text itself, one finds the religious meaning and purpose of the plagues. An important point in the divine speech to Moses in Exodus 7:4–5 is that the plagues are designed as divine judgments (*mishpatîm*) on the land of Egypt.

The common denominator in all the plagues is that each is a corruption of the created order and a source of disharmony within the society. This disorder is found in all the ten plagues: the blood, the frogs, the gnats, the insects, the livestock disease, the boils, the hail, the locusts, the darkness, and, finally, the death of the firstborn. These are all natural phenomena. What makes them instruments of disharmony and death is that they are located in the wrong places. They all disrupt and pollute the environment. At the end, it became abundantly clear to Pharaoh and his people that they were dealing with a superior force. Pharaoh finally came to his senses and sent Israel packing: "Pharaoh arose in the night, he and all his servants and all the Egyptians, and there was a great cry in Egypt, for there was no home where there was not someone dead. Then he called for Moses and Aaron at night and said, 'Rise up, get out from among my people, both you and the sons of Israel; and go, worship the Lord, as you have said. Take both your flocks and your herds, as you have said, and go, and bless me also'" (Exod 12:30–32).

In all these plagues, YHWH allowed Pharaoh to live so that he might witness all the signs and wonders and truly know that YHWH was incomparable. This was made clear to Pharaoh in the seventh plague in Exodus 9:16: "But this is why I have let you live: to show you my power, and to make my name resound through all the earth."

KNOWING OF YHWH BY THE EGYPTIANS AND THE ISRAELITES (EXOD 14)

The text of Exodus 14 marks the final exit of the Israelites from Egypt. The exit is recounted in a dramatic way as a crossing through the Red Sea or the Sea of Reeds, as some call it. It marks the climax moment in the book of Exodus. It can be called the real exodus from Egypt. It is an experience in freedom and new life. The text is evidently composite,[21] but it makes a coherent reading in its present form. The biblical author narrates what follows with a lot of drama and *pathos*. The master planner is YHWH himself. He makes Israel to take the way of the sea so that Pharaoh and his

---

21. See Ska, *Introduzione*, 83–92.

army will pursue them to bring them back to bondage. In this way, YHWH wants a final battle against Pharaoh and also to let Pharaoh know definitively who YHWH is, as he tells Moses in 14:4: "I shall then make Pharaoh stubborn and he will set out in pursuit of them; and I shall win glory for myself at the expense of Pharaoh and his whole army, and then the Egyptians will know that I am YHWH."

Israel marches with boldness thinking that all is well, but Pharaoh marches with greater boldness hoping to arrest the fugitives. The Israelites look back and see the intimidating army of the Egyptians on their heels. Their hearts melt within them. Their boldness evaporates instantly. They cry to YHWH for help. But that is not enough. They transfer their aggression to poor Moses, blaming him for bringing them out of Egypt (see Exod 14:11–12). Fear has the power of destroying everything. Israel now is a victim of fear, a terrible sense of hopelessness. What does a leader do in such a situation? It is a terrible moment for any leader. But great leaders prove their mettle in such situations of near despondency. Moses, the great leader, animates his people with these immortal words that continue to be quoted in every age: "Do not fear! Stand by and see the salvation of YHWH which He will accomplish for you today; for the Egyptians whom you have seen today, you will never see them again forever" (Exod 14:13).

The summary of Moses' speech is that the Lord will fight for his people. The battle is between YHWH and Pharaoh and not between Israel and Pharaoh. Life is full of terrifying moments as this one, but fear evaporates once one gets convinced that invisible divine forces are on the rescue. Moses the leader has the burden to carry the traumatized people along on this blind faith. YHWH encourages him to ride on, repeating his game plan: "And I will harden the hearts of the Egyptians so that they shall go in after them, and I will get glory over Pharaoh and all his army, his chariots, and his horsemen. And the Egyptians shall know that I am YHWH, when I have gotten glory over Pharaoh, his chariots, and his horsemen" (Exod 14:17–18). It happens as instructed, and all took place in two significant moments. First, Moses strikes the sea, as God commanded him. The dry land appears, and Israel marches on. Then the Egyptians also enter in to swallow them up. Second, Moses strikes the sea again, the great waters return, and the Egyptian army is gone with its pharaoh, fruit of stubbornness. Pharaoh, who defied God, is now gone with the sea wind and rough waters.

Then comes the triumphant note: "When Israel saw the great power which YHWH had used against the Egyptians, the people feared YHWH, and they believed in YHWH and in His servant Moses" (14:31). Here the story achieves its aim. Israel has finally come to know and acknowledge YHWH as the liberator God.

It is significant how the final redaction of Exodus 1–14 has unified the different sources and harmonized the motif of knowing YHWH to run through the whole narrative. The theme is very common to the Priestly source, but other non-Priestly sources also attest to the popularity of the theme. One can therefore conclude that it is a central motif in the redaction of the text. It is significant that Pharaoh and his army do not live to testify to the greatness of YHWH, but the narrative takes it for granted that the surviving Egyptians and nations around have learned a great lesson.

MISSIONARY SIGNIFICANCE OF THE KNOWING MOTIF IN THE TEXT

The theme of knowing YHWH has been seen as a guiding motif in the account of Exodus 1–14. The fact that the text ends on a note of confession of belief in YHWH and his servant Moses means that all the elements within the narrative are geared toward this end. From a unified narrative perspective, the whole text is about God making himself known as YHWH and letting his actions contribute to the knowledge of this identity by all characters in the story. It can be said that YHWH is on a mission to let his identity be known. The principal agent of this mission is Moses, assisted by Aaron.

The first part of the mission is making himself known to the principal agent of the mission. This is accomplished in the revelation of the name in Exodus 3:13–15 and 6:2–8. These revelatory encounters equip Moses with the requisite knowledge to speak with authority about YHWH and also to act in his name. The signs and wonders in Egypt help to make the name known and feared not only among Pharaoh and his Egyptian folk but beyond the borders of Egypt. According to the text of Exodus 9:16, these mighty acts make the name of YHWH to resound all through the earth.

It is clear then that an essential aspect of the mission of Moses in Exodus 1–14 is to make the name of YHWH be known. By extension, it becomes the missionary responsibility of all Israel to make the name known among the nations. But they did not fare so well in this. Because of this, YHWH laments in Ezekiel 36:20: "They have profaned my holy name among the nations where they have gone, so that people say of them, 'These are the people of YHWH; they have been exiled from his land.'"

One finds this mission better fulfilled in the role of Jesus and his disciples in the New Testament. In the prologue of John's Gospel, Jesus is presented as the only one who makes God known. He is the unique exegete or interpreter of God: "No one has ever seen God; it is the only Son, who is close to the Father's heart, who has made him known" (John 1:18). In John's Gospel, to see Jesus is to see God because Jesus is the very reflection and presence of God. Teresa Okure puts it thus: "In Jesus, God's glory abides permanently with human beings, in human form. To know God fully one needs to study, know, and imitate Jesus and savor the joy of communion fellowship with him."[22] It is significant that in this very context of the prologue of John, Jesus is bought into comparison with Moses: "For the Law was given through Moses, grace and truth have come through Jesus Christ" (John 1:17).

This knowing motif comes to a climax in the farewell discourse of Jesus in John, specifically in the final prayer for his disciples: "And this is eternal life, that they may know you, the only true God, and Jesus Christ whom you have sent" (John 17:3). In

---

22. Okure, "John," 1461.

this text, Jesus gives account of his mission to the Father. The basis of that mission is to make God known or, as Okure puts it, "to reveal God's name to the world and thereby impart life-giving knowledge of God."[23]

CONCLUSION

The idea of knowing God is a powerful guide in understanding the biblical text. The exodus narrative, particularly, was written to advance this knowledge. The type of knowledge that the text espouses is the knowledge of the name YHWH in its modus operandi. Later Israel needed this knowledge in moments of suffering and near hopelessness to understand that God was always in their midst. Knowing the true God is itself therapeutic as the knowledge helps the knower to readjust in every adverse situation, conscious of the fact that the God in question is a promise-keeping God, a God who is ever-present and ever-active. Knowing the true God is a taste of eternal life, and Jesus came to enhance that knowledge and make it a living reality. Today, one comes to know God better by identifying with the person of Jesus and his message. Thus, the mission given to Moses in Exodus 1–14 continues to be relevant in the contemporary Christian context.

BIBLIOGRAPHY

Binz, S. J. *The God of Freedom and Life. A Commentary on the Book of Exodus.* Collegeville, MN: Liturgical Press, 1993.
Blenkinsopp, J. *The Pentateuch. An Introduction to the First Five Books of the Bible.* ABRL. New York: Doubleday, 1992.
Coats, G. W. "A Structural Transition in Exodus." *VT* 22 (1972) 129–42.
Coats, G. W. "Moses in Midian." *JBL* 92 (1973) 3–10.
Durham, J. I. *Exodus.* WBC 3. Waco, TX: Word Biblical Commentary, 1987.
Fretheim, T. E. "yd'." *NIDOTTE* 2:409–14.
Greenberg, M. *Understanding Exodus.* New York: Behrman House, 1969.
Hertog, C. D. "The Prophetic Dimension of the Divine Name: On Exodus 3:14a and Its Context." *CBQ* 64, no.2 (2002) 213–28.
Hoffmeier, J. K. "Plagues of Egypt." *NIDOTTE* 4:1056–59.
LaCocque, A., and P. Ricoeur. *Thinking Biblically: Exegetical and Hermeneutical Studies* Chicago: University of Chicago Press, 1998.
Lewis, J. P. "yāda'." *TWOT* 1:366–67.
McCarthy, D. J. "Exod 3:14: 'History, Philology and Theology.'" *CBQ* 40 (1978) 311–22.
Okure, T. "John." In *International Bible Commentary,* 1461. Edited by William R. Farmer. Collegeville, MN: Liturgical Press, 1998.
Oswalt, J. N. "kā'ab." *TWOT* 1:425.

---

23. Okure, "John," 1493.

Rendtorff, R. "Some Reflections on the Canonical Moses: Moses and Abraham." In *A Biblical Itinerary: In Search of Method, Form and Content; Essays in Honor of George W. Coats*, 11–19. Edited by E. E. Carpenter. JSOTS 240. Sheffield: Sheffield Academic Press, 1997.

Ska, J. L. *Introduzione alla lettura del Pentateuco: Chiavi per l'interpretazione dei primi cinque libri della Bibbia*. Roma: Edizione Dehoniane, 1998.

———. *La passage de la mer, Etude de la construction, du style e de la symbolique d'Ex 14:1–31*. AnBib 109. Rome: 1986.

Tucker, P. *You Shall Know that I am YHWH: The Holiness composition in the Book of Exodus*. n.p. 2016.

CHAPTER 22

The Bible, Migration, and Mission

GRANT LeMARQUAND

INTRODUCTION

The global problem of refugees and migrants is a vast and multidimensional issue. As of the date of this writing there are approximately one hundred million refugees in the world, a third of whom are children.[1] I do not have satisfying political solutions to the problems raised by this crisis. On the other hand, I have spent a lot of my life reading and teaching the Bible, and part of my life as a bishop in a part of Africa deeply affected by war which has led to significant displacement.

In this contribution I intend to do only two things: first, advance the claim that, among many other things, the Bible is a book about migrants and refugees[2] and, second, outline a bit of the refugee experience in the place where I was formerly the Anglican bishop—in western Ethiopia near the border with South Sudan. In juxtaposing these two realities—the biblical story and a contemporary African story—I simply urge that those who are followers of Jesus and therefore claim to be shaped by the biblical narrative cannot ignore the sufferings of those experiencing displacement. I offer this essay in thanksgiving for the work of Professor Teresa Okure who has spent so much of her academic career reminding us that the Bible is not a dead letter dealing

---

1. "In the first months of 2022, more than 100 million individuals were displaced worldwide as a result of persecution, conflict, violence or human rights violations. This accounts for an increase of 10.7 million people displaced from the end of the previous year. In a matter of a few months, the world's forcibly displaced population reached the highest ever on record." "Global Trends at a Glance," UNHCR, accessed September 16, 2022, https://www.unrefugees.org/refugee-facts/statistics/.

2. As will be evident, I take here a diachronic approach to the biblical text.

only with people of the past. Rather the Bible is a living text which moves those who read it to be concerned about every aspect of life.

THE BIBLE AS A BOOK ABOUT MIGRATION

Migration is multifaceted. Some, not the majority, migrate because they are able to choose what they hope will be a better place to live. Such people have the resources to relocate in order to pursue a career or a lifestyle that they find more attractive or more lucrative. Not surprisingly, few characters in the Bible had such upwardly mobile opportunities. Of course some biblical texts recount the lives of migrants who are simply nomadic—their culture is to follow the needs of their cattle, constantly seeking water and fresh grass. There are numerous biblical characters in this category: the so-called patriarchs and matriarchs Abraham and Sarah, Isaac and Rebekah, Jacob and Rachel, and their extended families. We will see, however, that even the lives of those who are normally nomadic can be disrupted. Food insecurity, which may have multiple causes, will often interrupt the normal patterns of finding water gazing land. Some migrants are those who are sent, people who are on a mission. Such "missionaries" fall into at least two categories: those who go voluntarily and those who flee some danger, but nevertheless bring God's good news with them.

On the other hand, most migrants relocate not because they want to move, but because they are forced. They travel because famine or war have driven them from the place they have considered home. Most migrants are escaping. Some migrants are captives. Not able to escape violence, they are taken from their homes, often as slaves, or perhaps rounded up and moved to isolated areas where they can be executed out of sight. Many of the stories about migration in the Bible fall into this category of forced migration. The Bible is filled with accounts of entrapment, of exodus and exile, of capture, of enforced removal, and sometimes of escape.

THE FIRST COMMISSION: "FILL THE EARTH"

Although the Bible appears to begin in a "home," even in that idyllic setting of the garden of Eden, God gives Adam and Eve a commission which will involve travel: "Be fruitful and multiply"[3]—perhaps the only commandment that human beings have been inclined to obey! This command is followed by a corollary: "Fill the earth and subdue it" (Gen 1:28). The family of Adam and Eve are not to stay put in one place, but to fill the earth. This command is reiterated to Noah after the flood ("be fruitful and multiply and fill the earth," Gen 9:1). In this story, travel is no evil thing. Human beings are commissioned to make all of God's good creation a part of the

---

3. All biblical references are from the NRSV.

temple-garden.[4] As humans "tend and keep" the garden (Gen 2:15), more and more of the creation is to be a place of flourishing.

Expulsion from Eden

But the biblical story of Eden, as foundational as it is, takes up remarkably little space in the pages of Scripture. It is "a love story gone awry."[5] By the end of the third chapter of the Bible, we have the first forced migration. Adam and Eve are banned from the garden.

> Then the Lord God said, "See, the man has become like one of us, knowing good and evil; and now, he might reach out his hand and take also from the tree of life, and eat, and live for ever"—therefore the Lord God sent him forth from the garden of Eden, to till the ground from which he was taken. He drove out the man; and at the east of the garden of Eden he placed the cherubim, and a sword flaming and turning to guard the way to the tree of life. (Gen 3:22–24)

The expulsion from Eden is a fascinating because it is both a punishment (Adam and Eve are removed from the Edenic home), and it is filled with unexpected grace: in distancing humanity from the tree of life, God protects them from remaining forever in a fallen state. In spite of the element of grace in the story, banishment is still a form of forced migration. The theme of removal continues in the story of Cain and Abel in Genesis 4 in which Cain is banished after he murders his brother. But even in that story, God is gracious. God still protects even the guilty Cain (Gen 4:15). The rest of the Bible is, in a sense, a story of the quest (God's quest) to regain a place of home for his people. Throughout the biblical narrative God seeks out his people and finds ways to meet with them, ways to be with them.

BABEL: THE EMPIRE TRIES TO CONTAIN THE SPREAD OF GOD'S RULE

Moving through Genesis we come to the story of the tower of Babel. The usual reading of this narrative in Genesis 11 is that it is an etiological legend, an origin story in which the beginning of the multiplicity of languages is explained. In this usual reading, God judges the people of Babel for their hubris by confusing their speech. A few details of story should lead us to re-think this common interpretation.

First, it is not always noticed that the judgement on Babel results in a form of migration. The people are dispersed. This is not necessarily a negative thing. After all, the earliest chapters of Genesis, as we have seen, command human beings to spread over the face of the earth. Second, Genesis 11 follows Genesis 10—a chapter in which

---

4. See Beale, *Temple and the Church's Mission*, 2004.
5. The phrase is from Trible, *God and the Rhetoric of Sexuality*, 1986.

there are already seventy nations (seventy probably being a number of completeness) "in their lands, with their own language, by their families, in their nations" (Gen 10:5; cf. vv. 20, 31). At least in the narrative of Genesis, a diversity of language precedes the building of Babel. Third, the Babel story tells us that God "came down" (Gen 10:7). Usually in the Bible, when God comes down, he comes both to judge and to save. I conclude that the judgement on Babel is a judgement on imperial aspirations, the desire of powerful nations (like Babylon?) to subjugate other nations and homogenize their cultures and languages. The judgement on Babel is simultaneously an act of salvation for oppressed nations who are now freed to express their culture in their own mother tongues as they spread over the face of the earth.[6]

Israel's Patriarchs as Nomadic

After the fall of Babel, the book of Genesis turns our attention to the story of a nomadic family. The story of Abraham is a key turning point in the biblical narrative. The rabbinic midrash on Abraham's story sums up his significance by having God say, "I will make Adam first and if he goes astray I will send Abraham to sort it all out."[7] God's plan is to save the world through one family, the family of Abraham. God begins by calling Abram to leave his ancestral home and become a nomadic migrant.

> Now the Lord said to Abram, "Go from your country and your kindred and your father's house to the land that I will show you. I will make of you a great nation, and I will bless you, and make your name great, so that you will be a blessing. I will bless those who bless you, and the one who curses you I will curse; and in you all the families of the earth shall be blessed" (Gen 12:1–3)

As the eucharistic canon from the Anglican Church of Kenya states, "From a wandering nomad you created a family." Abraham, Isaac, Jacob, and their families were migratory people, nomadic people. They lived with their cattle and sheep and goats, dependent on the land and on God, who gives land and water and vegetation.

At times these families are also refugees—Abraham and Sarah had to flee to Egypt because of a famine (Gen 12:10–20), Jacob ran from his brother Esau (Gen 28), and the whole family of Jacob (Israel) found refuge, again in Egypt, when there was a famine in Canaan (Gen 46).[8]

---

6. For a similar reading see José Míguez-Bonino, "Genesis 11:1–9: A Latin American Perspective," 13–16.

7. Wright's paraphrase of *Genesis Rabbah*, 251.

8. For a discussion of the positive significance of Egypt in the biblical narratives, especially as a place of refuge, see LeMarquand, "'Blessed Be My People Egypt,'" forthcoming.

Slavery and Exodus

Of course Egypt the place of refuge also became Egypt the place of slavery and suffering. Years after Jacob's family found safety and food in Egypt, the political situation in Egypt changed: "Now a new king arose over Egypt, who did not know Joseph" (Exod 1:8). The people of Israel were subjected to forced labor and violence. But God hears the cry of his people and delivers them (Exod 3). The story of the Exodus, the "going out," becomes the Bible's paradigm for all other stories of rescue and redemption and liberation. This experience of slavery and exodus forms the basis of much of the legislation of the Torah, including the Torah's attitude to strangers, sojourners. In the process of this deliverance from slavery, God teaches his Israel something of what he is like. He is the delivering-from-slavery God. God is the one who hears the cries of the poor and the victims of violence. God cares for the most vulnerable. God comes down to deliver. This experience of deliverance shapes the Torah legislation of God's people:

> For the Lord your God is God of gods and Lord of lords, the great God, mighty and awesome, who is not partial and takes no bribe, who executes justice for the orphan and the widow, and who loves the strangers, providing them with food and clothing. You shall also love the stranger, for you were strangers in the land of Egypt." (Deut 10:17–18)

And why does God command his people to care for strangers, for foreigners? "You shall also love the stranger, for you were strangers in the land of Egypt" (Deut 10:19).

But the exodus event is not simply about deliverance from slavery in Egypt. The book of Exodus does not quickly move from Egypt into the promised land—the exodus is also a story of wandering as Israel spends a generation in the desert before entering the promised land. The wilderness wanderings are a both a punishment and a test, a time of preparation for God's people before entering the promised land. Deuteronomy tells us that God through Moses presents Israel with a choice: obey God and have life, or disobey and go into exile, be scattered among the nations (Deut 30).

Between the Exodus and the Exile

It may appear at first glance that the period between the exodus and the exile is a time in which the people of Israel are "at home." Certainly they are in their land and enjoy a certain amount of security—but only limited security. In fact, they live in a continual tension with other nations in the land. This insecurity extends beyond the time of the conquest and the judges into the period of the monarchy.

For our purposes, a key illustrative text is the story of a foreigner. This story is consequential since Jesus himself uses it as an illustration of God's concern for all peoples (Luke 4:27). The story is the story of Naaman in 2 Kings 5. Naaman was a non-Israelite soldier, a commander who used to carry out raids in Israel. In one such raid Naaman captures and enslaves an Israelite girl. She remains nameless in the story, but clearly she is a believer in the God of Israel. When Naaman contracts leprosy and is unable to find healing in his home country, the slave girl tells her "owner" that there is healing in Israel, that if Naaman would go to see the prophet Elijah, he would be healed. Certainly the story is about God's care for a non-Israelite. But the story also tells us of a victim of human trafficking who still bore witness that the God of Israel was a healing God. The slave becomes an accidental "missionary" bringing the good news of God to a foreign nation.

Forced Migration: The Exile

The exile promised to Israel if they were disobedient (Deut 30) indeed happens. If the exodus is the Bible's paradigmatic story of God's rescue, the exile is the Bible's paradigmatic story of judgement. The latter part of the Old Testament is the story of the exilic and post-exilic life of Israel. But the exile is not a complete abandonment. Even in Babylon God is with his people. Even though the temple, the place of meeting, is destroyed, God is still present with his people. Psalm 139 promises this universal presence of God:

> Where can I go from your spirit?
> Or where can I flee from your presence?
> If I ascend to heaven, you are there;
> if I make my bed in Sheol, you are there.
> If I take the wings of the morning
> and settle at the farthest limits of the sea,
> even there your hand shall lead me,
> and your right hand shall hold me fast. (Ps 139:8–10)

The vision in Ezekiel 1 illustrates God's continuing presence with his people when the prophet sees God's throne. Surprisingly, the throne has wheels; the throne is a chariot. There is a double significance to this vision. First, in spite of the exile, God still reigns; he is on the throne. And second, although the people are removed from the land and taken by force into exile, God does not abandon them. God is a God who moves with his people. God is not a God like the divinities of the nations who are limited to one place. God is the God of all creation, not restricted to the land of Israel.

Jesus the Refugee and the Vagabond

The New Testament begins with a story which recapitulates the story of Israel. In Matthew 2:13–18 the holy family flees from tyranny, and like Abraham and the family of Jacob before them, they find refuge in Africa, in Egypt. And so Jesus and his family become refugees. This one simple fact—that Jesus was a refugee—should be enough for Christians to look with sympathy on all those who flee tyranny, hunger, and deprivation in our own time. If Jesus was a refugee, we ought to care for those in a similar situation.

Jesus' experience as a wanderer does not end after his family returns home after the death of Herod the Great. Jesus continues to roam. At the beginning of his ministry, Jesus spends forty days in the desert. According to Tom Wright, this time in the wilderness has great symbolic significance. "Jesus is acting the great drama of Israel's exodus from Egypt, Israel's journey through the wilderness into the promised land."[9] Jesus reenacts the story of Israel as God's wandering people.

Indeed, throughout the course of his ministry, Jesus and his disciples are on the move. In scholarship on the historical Jesus it has usually been assumed that the itineracy of Jesus, his ministry of teaching and healing in the context of traveling from place to place, was a mode of life which Jesus took on himself, much as holy men and women in India have often chosen a peripatetic life. There is evidence in the Gospels, however, that challenges this assumption. Luke's Gospel, for example, programmatically portrays the opening of Jesus' ministry with a story of Jesus preaching in his hometown (Luke 4:16–29), an event which has as its climx the attempt by the people of Nazareth to put Jesus to death by throwing him off a cliff. (v. 29) Due to this negative response, Jesus must escape. The theme of Jesus needing to escape is repeated throughout the Gospel accounts. Interestingly, this may explain a strange silence in the Gospels: although Tiberias and Sepphoris were perhaps the most important cities in Galilee in the time of Jesus, there is no account of Jesus ever ministering in either of these places. In fact, Sepphoris is not even mentioned by name in the Gospels, even though it was only a few miles from Nazareth itself. Could it be that Jesus avoided these places because they were centers of political and economic power in Galilee, and because a preacher with a message like that of Jesus would have been unwelcome, perhaps even endangered by going to these places? Capernaum, a small fishing village, does seem to be a kind of base of operations for Jesus for a time, but still Jesus must say, "The Son of Man has no place to lay his head" (Matt 8:20).

The homelessness of Jesus, in other words, is a kind of forced exile—just as Israel was displaced by sin, so is Jesus forced into a lifestyle of homelessness in identification with God's people. Perhaps John's Gospel explains this. The homelessness of Jesus is a narrative way of saying that "He came to what was his own, and his own people did not accept him" (John 1:11). Once again, the simple fact that Jesus experiences a degree of homelessness should be enough for followers of Jesus to have a burning within them to help all who have become homeless.

---

9. Wright, *Mark for Everyone*, 6.

THE EARLY CHURCH AS AN EXILIC COMMUNITY

The early church, likewise, is frequently spoken of in the New Testament as aliens, exiles, the dispersion. The first letter of Peter addresses his letter to "the exiles of the dispersion" (1 Pet 1:1) and then later says, "Beloved, I urge you as aliens and exiles to abstain from the desires of the flesh that wage war against the soul" (1 Pet 2:11). Similarly, James addresses his epistle "to the twelve tribes in the Dispersion" (Jas 1:1). Paul argues that the Christian's first allegiance is not to any earthly place because "our citizenship is in heaven" (Phil 3:20). No doubt these expressions of the homelessness of the church of earth are related to the reality of earthly suffering, and especially of persecution.

Migration and Mission

Of course, not all movement of people is forced exile. The New Testament also calls the church to mobilize for mission. In a recapitulation of the call in Genesis to spread over the earth, the so-called Great Commission of Matthew 28:16–20 sends the church to the world. We must spend a few moments looking at this passage because it is often misunderstood. The usual English rendering of Matthew 28:19a is "Go therefore and make disciples of all nations." There is a problem with this translation, however, since the word usually translated "go" is not an imperative (a command) in the Greek. It is a participle. The imperative in the sentence is the verb "to disciple." I urge that the clause would be better translated, "As you are going, make disciples."[10] Of course the early church is certainly commanded to go into all the world: Christians are commanded to be witnesses of Christ "in Jerusalem, Judea, Samaria and the ends of the earth" (Acts 1:8); as the Father sent the Son, so those who believe in Jesus are sent by Jesus in the power of the Spirit (John 20:21). The churches should be intentional about sending, about going into the world in mission. But not all who go realize they are sent. Not all missionaries who go realize they are missionaries. Remember Namaan's slave girl: she did not intend to go to a foreign nation to preach the good news of the God of Israel. She was an accidental missionary. Likewise, not all the early Christians who scattered over the earth were intentional missionaries. The message of the gospel did not leave Jerusalem because the early church devised a strategic plan to reach the world. The church was scattered because of Stephen's martyrdom.

> Then they dragged him out of the city and began to stone him; and the witnesses laid their coats at the feet of a young man named Saul. While they were stoning Stephen, he prayed, "Lord Jesus, receive my spirit." Then he knelt down and cried out in a loud voice, "Lord, do not hold this sin against them." When he had said this, he died. And Saul approved of their killing him. That day a severe persecution began against the church in Jerusalem, and all except

---

10. I have argued this more fully in "'As you are going' (Mt 28:19): Some Reflections on "Unintentional Mission," 40–50.

the apostles were scattered throughout the countryside of Judea and Samaria. (Acts 7:58—8:1)

The story in Acts bears a striking similarity to the story of the martyrdom of young Christian converts in Uganda, Catholic and Anglican alike. Threatened with death, the Christian survivors of martyrdom dispersed around the kingdom of Uganda and beyond. And as they fled, they brought the message of Jesus with them.

SUMMARY

This review of biblical evidence concerning migration has only skimmed the surface of the canonical narrative. Space prevents us from examining a myriad of other passages that deal with the reality of people movements. What we have seen, however, is sufficient to make the point that migration is a major biblical theme, and that the Bible speaks of population movements in several ways. Some migrations are benign, nomads moving with their cattle as a way of life. Some migrate to find a better life in a new place. Some relocations are in response to God's call to preach the gospel to those who do not know the story of God's love for the world. But not all missionary movements are intentional. Some people find themselves in a missionary situation because their circumstances have brought them to a new place—sometimes violently. And, most importantly, especially in our day, many people migrate because they are forced out of their homes, or even captured and taken from their homes by force. The Bible not only speaks of refugees and of enslavement, but it continually reminds God's people that they must care for refugees, for strangers, for foreigners—because Israel herself was enslaved and delivered from oppression by God, because God is the kind of God who loves and cares for the widow and the orphan—and the refugee.

Living among Refugees in Gambella, Ethiopia

For six years I was the Anglican bishop of the Horn of Africa, an area which included Djibouti, Somalia, Eritrea, and Ethiopia. Most of our churches were in Ethiopia. That country has never had a large Anglican presence—partly because it was not colonized by the British (or anyone). And so for many years Ethiopia had only one Anglican parish, an English chaplaincy church in Addis Ababa.[11] But in the 1980s during the horrific civil war between north and south in the Sudan, Sudanese refugees came across the border into Ethiopia, and in their refugee camps many Anglicans Christians built makeshift churches out of sticks and mud and thatch. They began to preach to those around them, both in the camps and in the local villages. Now, after forty years, there are well over a hundred Anglican churches in the Gambella region of western Ethiopia—some inside refugee camps and some in local villages. The first Anglicans in this

11. See LeMarquand, "Anglicans in the Horn of Africa," 196–210.

area were Jieng-speaking (Dinka) people, but they reached across ethnic boundaries and so now there are also Nuer, Anuak, Po, Mabaan, Mezhenger, Jum-Jum, and Murle churches in the Gambella region. The refugees fleeing war in the Sudan were unintentional missionaries.

Of course they are not just missionaries—they are human beings who have suffered and who still suffer because of displacement. A few years ago I sat with a group of newly arrived refugees. They had fled the new civil war in South Sudan which had begun in December 2013. The Gambella region where my wife and I lived had three hundred thousand residents when we arrived there in 2012. Within a couple of years there were at least six hundred thousand people living in Gambella—three hundred thousand being newly arrived refugees. At one point in our discussion with this group of newly arrived refugees, I asked them what they were able to carry when they ran from South Sudan on foot. Their response was, "Mostly what we could carry was our children." And what did they leave behind? They did not mention homes or property. Mostly what was left behind was their elders, those who were too old and too weak to run from the bullets. They lost those who knew their traditional wisdom.

And why were they running? In my context at least, refugees were running because of ethnic violence. We have discovered that among some people groups in our area, baby boys, especially the firstborn, are often dedicated—sometimes by blood sacrifice—to the revenge of their fathers' enemies. To be a man, therefore, means that you must fight and kill the perceived enemies of your people. It is simply a part of your identity, a part of who you are. In the church, therefore, we have begun promoting a different kind of blood relationship. Hebrews 12:24 states that the blood of Jesus "speaks a better word than the blood of Abel." The story of Cain and Abel, as we have seen, tells us that Cain killed his brother out of jealousy. But Cain is not the only "bad guy" in the story. Abel cries for vengeance against his brother (Gen 4:10). Jesus' blood, on the other hand, cries for forgiveness and reconciliation: "Father forgive them" (Luke 23:34), he says from the cross. And so in the churches in Gambella we say: "There is one God, the Father; there is one blood, the blood of Jesus, not the blood of vengeance; and there is one family, created by the blood of Jesus and brought together by the Holy Spirit."

One of our refugee churches is in a camp near the town of Dimma. These believers decided that although they were from different ethnic groups and speak different languages, they wanted to worship together, to demonstrate to their people that it is possible to live together. And so we called their church "Holy Family," not only because they, like Jesus, Mary, and Joseph, are refugees, but also because in deciding to worship together across ethnic and linguistic differences, they have exhibited true holiness.

I do not have answers to the refugee crises of today. I do not know whether some refugees will become a danger to the people in their new homes, as some people sometimes fear. Perhaps some will (some have become dangerous in Gambella where we lived). I do not know what kind of legislation Christians should encourage, lobby for, or vote for in their respective contexts. I do know that Christians are commanded to care for the strangers in their midst. I know that our spiritual ancestors, from Abraham and Jacob to Jeremiah and Ezekiel, were refugees and exiles. I know that Mary, Joseph, and Jesus were refugees in Egypt. I know that Jesus spent most of his ministry without a place to call home. I know that followers of Jesus are called into the world in mission. And I know that a significant aspect of that mission today involves loving the stranger, the refugee, and the homeless.

BIBLIOGRAPHY

Beale, G. K. *The Temple and the Church's Mission: A Biblical Theology of the Dwelling Place of God*. New Studies in Biblical Theology 17. Downers Grove: IVP Academic, 2004.

Beck, B. E. *Christian Character in the Gospel of Luke*. London: Epworth, 1989.

Carroll, M. D. "Biblical Perspectives on Migration and Mission: Contributions from the Old Testament." *Mission Studies*, 30, no. 1 (2013) 9–26.

De Ligt, L., and L. Tacoma, eds. *Migration and Mobility in the Early Roman Empire*. Leiden: Brill, 2016.

Fitzmyer, J. A. *The Gospel According to Luke (I–IX): Introduction, Translation, and Notes*. 2nd edition. Garden City, NY: Doubleday, 1986.

Hanciles, J. J. "Migration and Mission: Some Implications for the Twenty-First Century Church." *International Bulletin of Missionary Research* 27 (2003).

———. "Migration." In *Dictionary of Mission Theology: Evangelical Foundations*. Edited by J. Corrie. Downers Grove: IVP, 2007.

———. *Beyond Christendom: Globalization, African Migration, and the Transformation of the West*. Maryknoll: Orbis, 2009.

———. "Migration." In *Global Dictionary of Theology: A Resource for the Worldwide Church*. Edited by W. A. Dyrness and V.- M. Kärkkäinen. Grand Rapids: IVP Academic, 2008.

Käsemann, E. *The Wandering People of God: An Investigation of the Letter to the Hebrews*. Minneapolis: Augsburg, 1984.

Kugel, J. L. "The Beginnings of Biblical Interpretation." In *A Companion to Biblical Interpretation in Early Judaism*. Edited by M. Henze. Grand Rapids: Eerdmans, 2012.

LeMarquand, Grant. "'As You Are Going' (Mt 28:19): Some Reflections on 'Unintentional Mission.'" *Trinity Journal for Theology & Ministry* 2, no.1 (2008).

———. "'Blessed Be My People Egypt': Isaiah 19–20 with Special Reference to Reception by the Coptic Church in Egypt." Forthcoming.

———. "Anglicans in the Horn of Africa: From Missionaries and Chaplains to a Missionary Church." In *The Oxford History of Anglicanism, V: Global Anglicanism, c. 1910–2000*. Edited by Williams Sachs. New York: Oxford University Press, 2017.

———. "The Anglican Church of Kenya." In *The Oxford Guide to the Book of Common Prayer: A Worldwide Survey*. Edited by Charles Hefling and Cynthia Shattuck. New York: Oxford, 2006.

Little, C. R. *Mission in the Way of Paul: Biblical Mission for the Church in the Twenty-First Century*. New York: Peter Lang, 2005.

Longenecker, R. N. *Introducing Romans: Critical Issues in Paul's Most Famous Letter*. Grand Rapids: Eerdmans, 2011.

Míguez-Bonino, José. "Genesis 11:1–9: A Latin American Perspective." In *Return to Babel: Global Perspectives on the Bible*. Edited by John R. Levison and Priscilla Pope-Levison. Louisville: Westminster John Knox, 1999.

Okure, Teresa. "First Was the Life, Not the Book." In *To Cast Fire Upon the Earth: Bible and Mission Collaborating in Today's Multicultural Global Context*, 194–214. Edited by Teresa Okure. Pietermaritzburg: Cluster, 2000.

Ott, C. "Diaspora and Relocation as Divine Impetus for Witness in the Early Church." In *Diaspora Missiology: Theory, Methodology, and Practice*. Edited by Enoch Wan. 2nd edition. Portland: Institute of Diaspora Studies, 2012.

Pervo, R. I. *Acts: A Commentary*. Minneapolis: Fortress, 2009.

Riesner, R. "Pauline Chronology." In *The Blackwell Companion to Paul*. Edited by S. Westerholm. Oxford: Wiley Blackwell, 2011.

Ruiz, J. -P. *Reading from the Edges: The Bible and People on the Move*. Maryknoll: Orbis, 2011.

Rutgers, L. V. "Roman Policy toward the Jews: Expulsions from the City of Rome during the First Century CE." In *Judaism and Christianity in First-Century Rome*. Edited by K. P. Donfried and P. Richardson. Grand Rapids: Eerdmans, 1998.

Santos, N.F. "Exploring the Major Dispersion Terms and Realities in the Bible." In *Diaspora Missiology: Theory, Methodology, and Practice*. Edited by E. Wan. 2nd edition. Portland: Institute of Diaspora Studies, 2012.

Schnabel, E. J. *Paul the Missionary: Realities, Strategies and Methods*. Nottingham: IVP/Apollos, 2008.

Stenschke, C. "The Status and Calling of Strangers and Exiles: Mission According to First Peter." In *Bible and Mission: A Conversation Between Biblical Studies and Missiology*. Edited by R. G. Grams et al. Schwarzenfeld: Neufeld, 2008.

———. "Married Women and the Spread of Early Christianity." *Neotestamentica* 43, no. 1 (2009) 145–94.

Trebilco, P. *Self-Designations and Group Identity in the New Testament*. Cambridge: Cambridge University Press, 2012.

Trible, Phyllis. *God and the Rhetoric of Sexuality*. Overtures to Biblical Theology 2. Philadelphia: Fortress, 1986.

Walls. A .F. The *Missionary Movement in Christian History: Studies in the Transmission of Faith*. Maryknoll: Orbis, 1996.

Wan, E., ed. *Diaspora Missiology: Theory, Methodology and Practice*. 2nd edition. Portland: Institute of Diaspora Studies, 2011.

Wright, N. T. *Mark for Everyone*. London: SPCK, 2001.

———. "Genesis *Rabbah* 14.6." In *The New Testament and the People of God*. Minneapolis, MN: Fortress, 1992.

Epilogue I

A Well-Deserved Honor

Bishop Martin D. A. Olorunmolu

As the popular saying goes: "It is good to give honor to whom honor is due." In the above twenty-two well-written essays, I believe that a well-deserved honor has been given to a well-known and truly erudite biblical scholar in the person of Sr. Prof. Teresa Okure, SHCJ, whom I fondly call: "My Teacher."

Truly, Sr. Prof. T. Okure remains my teacher because I did New Testament studies under her in the Catholic Institute of West Africa (CIWA), Port Harcourt, from 1986 to 1988 and got a licentiate degree in the discipline. She was my main teacher in the two-year study program and supervised my thesis project at the end. Later, when I went back to the same CIWA for my PhD program in the same discipline, I still met her in the institute, and she still took me in a number of courses for the program.

I am not the only student of Sr. Prof. T. Okure who has become, by the grace of God, a Catholic bishop today; I can count up to four others. We thank God who has used her very much to touch academically the lives of some of us bishops and many of our priests who have studied in CIWA.

Her pioneering work and many years (since 1985) of meritorious services in CIWA deserve mentioning and special commendation. Her indomitable spirit and total commitment/dedication to duty, even in difficult situations, were very much displayed during the many years of her service in CIWA. A person of great courage, she stood her ground firmly and expressed her views boldly and emphatically in matters that were considered controversial. She did so with much clarity, manifesting her very high level of thinking and personal conviction.

Sr. Prof. T. Okure's profound scholarship in biblical studies, especially in the New Testament, cannot be overrated. She is a "guru" in the discipline. In fact ,for me, she is a "New Testament genius." Much of this fact has been well reflected in some of the essays presented above. Her understanding of the mission of Christ (which is the same as the mission of the church, i.e., our Christian mission), from the biblical perspective, is obviously very deep and profound. Her works and writings clearly show this. Therefore, it is very appropriate that she is being honored with this publication that focuses sharply on mission. This is a befitting homage to her who is certainly an Academic of no mean repute.

From the presentations in the above essays, it is clear that the concept and understanding of mission, from the biblical perspective, can be expressed variously. Kudos should be given to all the writers of the essays for doing so much to help one learn more about the subject, "mission," which for us Christians, especially leaders, constitutes the main object of our calling.

Some of the presenters of the twenty-two essays above are well-known members of the Catholic Biblical Association of Nigeria (CABAN), and other famous biblical organizations. They have jointly carried out this work in the name of CABAN to make the association give due honor to its founding leader and president for many years now, in the person of Sr. Prof. T. Okure, SHCJ.

It is hoped that the great inspirations that the association has drawn over the years from the dynamic leadership of this dedicated leader will help it, for a long time to come, to remain strong, focused, and effective in the church's evangelizing mission in our country, Nigeria, especially from the biblical perspective.

Bishop Martin Bishop Martin D. A. Olorunmolu
Catholic Bishop of Lokoja Diocese

Epilogue II

Sister Teresa Okure, SHCJ
A Great and Unassuming Leader from Behind at the Service of the Church

Aniedi Okure, OP

RESPONDER TO THE NEEDS

About five years ago, while living in Washington, DC, I visited Nigeria for a workshop with Women Religious on advocacy as an integral part of our Christian calling, organized by the Africa Faith & Justice Network (AFJN) and the Nigerian Conference of Women Religious (NCWR). As I was about to return, Sr. Teresa gave me copies of the proceedings of the Catholic Biblical Association of Nigeria (CABAN), of whom she is the founding president, to mail them from Washington to her colleagues in the United States and Europe. It was faster that way. I obliged. When I mailed them, I included a brief note and my contact information to the recipients to let them know who I was and on whose behalf I sent the CABAN proceedings.

Her colleagues sent me acknowledgements, grateful to have received the proceedings. One acknowledgment stands out vividly—one that keeps me thinking even as I write. The recipient was grateful to receive the book, praised the content of the proceedings, and commended the leadership of Sr. Teresa, then added: "It is good to see how the research are focused on the context and wrestling with the questions people are asking. Some of us in the West are busy providing answers to questions that no one is asking." I had a good chuckle for myself, albeit alone.

This colleague of hers, whom I have not met, has endeared himself to me, not just for his praise of my sister's leadership, but for that "contextual" insight. As one whose engagement is about human beings, the context they live in, and how that context impacts their lives, his remarks took on an added flavor for me. Her colleague described in that one sentence what is clearly the guiding principle of Sr. Teresa's scholarship in Scripture, theology, pastoral care, and the entire spectrum of her engagements in the service of the church and her people.

THE WORD AMONG US

To render appropriate service to the church and God's people, one must understand that the "Word" which became incarnate in a human context (John 1:14) is "alive and active" (Heb 4:12) and ever calling us to listen and respond to what is happening in our present context and to bring the Living Word to bear on what is happening. True Christian scholarship and our ministry must be a service to the Word incarnate: "The Word became flesh and dwelt among uss" (John 1:14). Failure to understand the implications of the Word that is alive and active, the Word that dwells among us, and the bearing of the Word on the people, the local ecclesial community, and the society, is failure to be grounded in the Christian faith itself. It is tantamount to living an alienated Christian life, looking for God atop Mount Kilimanjaro while God is there right beside us. Our theologizing must be related to real-life situations.

THE POPE AND THE CONTEXT OF EVANGELIZATION

In his homily on July 13, 1969, during the eucharistic celebration for the conclusion of the symposium organized by the Bishops of Africa in Kampala Uganda, Pope Paul VI declared,

> And in this sense, **you may**, and **you must**, **have** an **African Christianity**. Indeed, you possess human values and characteristic forms of culture which can rise up to perfection such as to find in **Christianity**, and for **Christianity**, a true superior fulness, and prove to be capable of a richness of expression all its own, and genuinely **African**.[1]

The pope was not advocating for a schism, the invention of new doctrines, or the abrogation of the cherished faith tradition handed down to us over the millennia. Rather, the pope was encouraging contextual pastoral care and evangelization. He was clear in pointing out that "the need for adaptation of the Christian life in the fields of pastoral, ritual, didactic and spiritual activities is not only possible, it is even favoured by the Church."[2]

---

1. "Eucharistic Celebration," 1969.
2. "Eucharistic Celebration," 1969.

ADVANCING POPE PAUL VI'S ENCOURAGEMENT

Sr. Teresa put on a sustained effort to make people understand the relevance of the context in which a theological enterprise is carried out. Some African scholars think that they must quote someone from abroad, more specifically the Western world, to validate their scholarship, forgetting that those they are quoting are or were striving to respond to things in their own context. This becomes more intriguing when it concerns things African, when it concerns things in the locality of the context of the African scholar. The scholar feels a need to justify the research by referencing a Western scholar, even if tangentially. It becomes even comical when there is an African colleague that has treated the subject before with original research, focused on the context and with clear insights, but ignored in favor of referencing a Western scholar to validate one's scholarship.

This is not an advocacy for provincialism. We must learn from the research of others. However, it is a form of inferiority complex to think that even one's original research that is grounded in one's context must be validated by an "outsider" from the Western world. Perhaps those who adhere to such a practice are trying to ensure that the saying "A prophet is honored everywhere except in his own home and among his people" (cf. Luke 4:24) is not forgotten. Sister Teresa in many ways worked persistently to let her African colleagues focus on original research, to value it, and to understand and value their originality, that they must not feel the need to quote "external" people to valid who they are, and their research, as long as the work is original. To put it more directly, she is committed to decolonize the minds of her African colleagues.

Mental Decolonization

Decolonization of the mind is a big task for the entire spectrum of African academic, political, social, economic, and religious enterprise. I dare say it is the most important undertaking in the effort to free Africans from enslavement. Unfortunately, a considerable number of those who would have formed the mental liberation army have not only succumbed to the "theirs is better syndrome," but they are also determinedly promoting and enforcing that dependency mindset. Sister Teresa has in many ways been the quiet and unassuming leader from behind, helping people be actors rather than subjects needing to be helped, assisting people to claim their dignity as children of God, helping people to have a paradigm and mental shift that they can.

Scholarship When Needed

What is interesting about this eminent scholar who is much sought after by the outside world, and an aspect of her unassuming attitude, is that you will not find dozens of "books" bearing her unique name, but you will find dozens of works that she has contributed to producing. This includes works intended for the academia, pastoral care, applied theology, book chapters, articles, and contributions to encyclopedias. She writes generally when she is asked to. She responds to *needs*, not just writing for the sake of writing or to get a name. She writes to give answers to questions people are asking. She does so by examining the context of the people, and she brings Scripture to bear on the context to empower the people and to let the people realize that they have the means to tackle the challenges they face.

At the Service of the Church

Sister Teresa is deeply concerned about the church and her mission to the universal church in general and the church in Africa in particular. Over the years, she has received offers by some Ivy League academic institutions in the United States, but she declined and opted to serve the church in Nigeria, and in a special way the formation of clergy, working tirelessly for people who for the most part take her for granted. But she forged on as a true humble servant of the Word, at the service of the Lord, rather than seeking the praise of people.

One of her concerns is the plight of the rich, the powerful, and those in authority who misuse their privileged position. Many suffer from self-inflicted wounds. I recall when she was invited to give a faculty lecture at the University of Notre Dame some years ago, she was sent a topic that focused on preferential options for the poor, but Sister Teresa decided to focus this lecture on the salvific option for the rich, emphasizing that the rich need to be liberated from themselves, to be enlightened to see how their lifestyle is actually detrimental to their future, like the parable of the rich man and Lazarus (Luke 16:19–31). Such enlightenment would enable them to work toward achieving salvation.

Formators of Church Leaders

Sister Teresa, along with her siblings Sr. Mary Liguori, a canonist, and Sr. Bernadette, an educator and counselor—all engaged in the formation of church leaders. They learned from their parents Basil and Paulina Okure that service of the church is service of God, so whether they are affirmed by people or not is irrelevant. I am proud to have them as my siblings. They represent millions of women worldwide who quietly work behind the scenes to keep the faith alive, who sustain the church in so many ways, who bear testimony to the ministry of service and who do so without touting their accomplishments.

GRATITUDE

I am grateful to the contributors, especially Fr. (Prof.) Michael Ufok Udoekpo for organizing this forum to honor a Holy Child, Sister Teresa Okure, SHCJ, Professor of New Testament and Gender Hermeneutics, whose scholarship is grounded in context, and at the service of the church, a contextual educator, a cheerleader for her students, and a great leader from behind.

Glory to God for the women dedicated to the service of the church.

Aniedi Okure, OP
General Promoter of Justice and Peace
Permanent Delegate to the United Nations
Order of Preachers

www.ingramcontent.com/pod-product-compliance
Lightning Source LLC
Chambersburg PA
CBHW080729300426
44114CB00019B/2524